D1686307

# EFFECTIVE ENGLISH

### SERIES AUTHORS

**PHILIP L. GERBER**
Brockport, New York

**NORMAN L. HAIDER**
Pennsbury, Pennsylvania

**VIOLET NEUSCHULZ**
Montclair, New Jersey

**TERRY C. LEY**
Auburn, Alabama

**BARBARA PANNWITT**
Evanston, Illinois

**HOWARD K. BATTLES**
Branford, Connecticut

**VERNON H. SMITH**
Bloomington, Indiana

**SILVER BURDETT COMPANY**
Morristown, New Jersey • Glenview, Ill. • Palo Alto • Atlanta • Dallas

# EFFECTIVE ENGLISH

NORMAN L. HAIDER

BARBARA PANNWITT

TERRY C. LEY
with
VERNON H. SMITH

VIOLET NEUSCHULZ

| CONSULTANTS | CRITIC READERS |
|---|---|
| Barbara Mathis<br>State Department of Education<br>Atlanta, Georgia | Hugh B. Cassell<br>Jefferson County Public Schools<br>Louisville, Kentucky |
| | Helen Sprouse<br>Goodlettsville High School<br>Goodlettsville, Tennessee |
| Charles H. Coburn<br>Spaulding High School<br>Barre, Vermont | |
| | Marya Rubio Alderte<br>Calhoun High School<br>Port Lavaca, Texas |
| Jeanne-Marie A. Miller<br>Howard University<br>Washington, D.C. | Brother Regis Moccia, S.C.<br>St. Joseph High School<br>Metuchen, New Jersey |

©1979 SILVER BURDETT COMPANY.
All Rights Reserved • Printed in the United States of America • Published simultaneously in Canada. This publication, or parts thereof, may not be reproduced in any form by photographic, electrostatic, mechanical, or any other method, for any use, including information storage and retrieval, without written permission from the publisher. ISBN 0-382-03303-5

**ACKNOWLEDGMENTS** We wish to thank the following authors, publishers, agents, corporations, and individuals for their permission to reprint copyrighted materials. Pages 71 and 75: "Conjunctions" and "Interjections" from *Words Words Words* by Mary O'Neill. Copyright © 1966 by Mary O'Neill. Reprinted by permission of Doubleday & Company, Inc. and World's Work Ltd. Pages 117-118: Excerpt from *A Day No Pigs Would Die* by Robert Newton Peck. Copyright © 1972 by Robert Newton Peck. Reprinted by permission of Alfred A. Knopf, Inc. Page 128: Poem "Motto" from *The Panther and the Lash: Poems of Our Times* by Langston Hughes. Copyright 1951 by Langston Hughes. Reprinted by permission of Alfred A. Knopf, Inc. and Harold Ober Associates. Page 215: The Viking Press, Inc. for excerpt from *The Gift of Tongues* by Margaret Schlauch. Copyright 1942, renewed © 1970 by Margaret Schlauch. Page 217: Excerpt from *How Things Work in Your Home (and what to do when they don't)*, p. 278. © 1975 Time Inc. Reprinted by permission of Time-Life Books Inc. Popular Science Pub. Co., Inc. for excerpt from "Small Buses—the Most Versatile Wagons" by Jan P. Norbye and Jim Dunne from *Popular Science Monthly*, July 1971, p. 20. © 1971 Popular Science Pub. Co., Inc. Page 218: Arizona Highway Department for excerpt from "Praise . . . For Our Sister the Water" from *Arizona Highways*, December 1971, Vol. XLVII, No, 12, p. 3. © 1971 Arizona Highway Department. Excerpt from *Let Freedom Ring*, Silver Burdett Social Science. © 1977 Silver Burdett Company. Excerpt from *Tough, Sweet & Stuffy* by Walker Gibson. Copyright © 1966 by Indiana University Press. Pages 218-219: Excerpt adapted from "The Suburban Mind" by Carl von Rhode from *Modern Composition, Book 4* by Wallace Stegner, Edwin H. Sauer, and Clarence H. Hach, p. 26. Copyright © 1969, 1964 by Holt, Rinehart, and Winston, Inc. Page 221: Excerpt from *Flowering House Plants* by James Underwood Crockett and the Editors of Time-Life Books, p. 73. © 1971 Time Inc. Reprinted by permission of Time-Life Books Inc. Page 222: Excerpt from *Musical Structure and Style*. © 1975 Silver Burdett Company. Page 223: Excerpt from *Science: Understanding Your Environment*. © 1975 General Learning Corporation. Page 224: The Viking Press, Inc. and McIntosh and Otis, Inc. for excerpt from *Travels with Charley in Search of America* by John Steinbeck, p. 41. Copyright © 1961, 1962 by The Curtis Publishing Co., © 1962 by John Steinbeck. Pages 224-225: Excerpt from *The Face of North America: The Natural History of a Continent* by Peter Farb and John Hay. Reprinted by permission of Harper & Row Publishers Inc. Page 225: Excerpt from *The Other America* by Michael Harrington. (Copyright © Michael Harrington 1962, 1969.) Reprinted by permission of Macmillan Publishing Co., Inc. Pages 225-226: Excerpt from *Young Readers Edition of the Primates* by Sarel Eimerl and Irven DeVore, p. 42. © 1968 by Time Inc. Reprinted by permission of Time-Life Books Inc. Page 228: Excerpt from "Let It Ring, Let It Ring" reprinted from her volume, *I Try to Behave Myself* by Peg Bracken. © 1963, 1964 by Peg Bracken. Reprinted by permission of Harcourt Brace Jovanovich, Inc. and Arlington Books (Publishers) Limited, London. Pages 228-229: Excerpt from "Jenner Defeats Smallpox" (Jenner: The First Vaccine) from *Pioneer Germ Fighters* by Navin Sullivan. Copyright © 1962 by Navin Sullivan. Reprinted by permission of Atheneum Publishers and George G. Harrap & Company Ltd. Page 229: Excerpt from *The Art of Composition Module, Teacher's Edition*. © 1975 General Learning Corporation. Page 230: Excerpt from *Music of North American Indians*, Silver Burdett Music. © 1975 Silver Burdett Company. Excerpt from "Fred Truslow's favorite pictures" from *Audubon*, copyright © 1976, The National Audubon Society. Pages 230-231: *Science American* for excerpt from "Life and Light" by George Wald, October 1959, pp. 40-42. Page 231: Excerpt from *Let Freedom Ring*, Silver Burdett Social Science. © 1977 Silver Burdett Company. Sigma Delta Chi, Professional Journalistic Society, for excerpt from "Keys to D-Day?" by Gordon T. Morris, Jr., in *The Quill*, July 1971, p. 16. © 1971 Sigma Delta Chi. Excerpt reprinted from "Humming a Rhapsody in Blue" by Roy Blount, in *Sports Illustrated*, July 12, 1971, p. 22. © 1971 Time Inc. Page 232: "Some Great Mountain Ranges of Today" from *The First Book of Mountains* by Francis Smith. Copyright © 1964 by Franklin Watts Inc. Reprinted by permission. Page 235: Excerpt adapted from *Student Themes* by Percival Hunt by permission of the University of Pittsburgh Press. © 1939 by the University of Pittsburgh Press. Page 237: Excerpt reprinted by permission of Lothrop, Lee and Shepard Company from *How to Get in Shape for Sports* by Stanley L. Englebardt. Copyright © 1976 by Stanley L. Englebardt. Pages 237-238: Random House, Inc. for excerpt from *I Know Why the Caged Bird Sings* by Maya Angelou, p. 179. Copyright © 1969 by Maya Angelou. Page 238: *Diet for a Small Planet* by Frances Moore Lappé, p. 35, Ballantine Books, Inc. Copyright © 1971 by Frances Moore Lappé. *Inaugural Addresses of the Presidents of the United States from George Washington 1789 to Lyndon Baines Johnson 1965*, pp. 269-270, United States Government Printing Office, Washington, D.C. 1965. Excerpt from *Silent Spring* by Rachel Carson, p. 9. Copyright © 1962 by Rachel L. Carson. Reprinted by permission of the Estate of the Author and Houghton Mifflin Company. Pages 241-242: Excerpts from *Small Voices* by Josef and Dorothy Berger. Copyright © 1966 by Josef and Dorothy Berger. Reprinted by permission of Paul S. Eriksson, Inc. Pages 245-246: Excerpt from "My Favorite Failure" by Jim Bishop. © King Features Syndicate Inc. 1976. Page 247: Excerpt, adapted, from "Famous Tears." © 1977 by The New York Times Company. Reprinted by permission. Page 249: Doubleday & Company, Inc., Vallentine, Mitchell & Co. Ltd., and Otto H. Frank for excerpt from *Anne Frank: The Diary of a Young Girl* by Anne Frank, p. 237. Copyright © 1952 by Otto H. Frank. Page 250: Excerpt from "Retirees' Guide to Public Speaking" by Ken and Pat Kraft. Reprinted by permission from *Modern Maturity*. Copyright 1977 by the American Association of Retired Persons. Pages 250-251: Excerpt from *Biology* by William L. Smallwood and Edna R. Green. © 1977 Silver Burdett Company. Page 251: Excerpt from *Adventures in American History*, Silver Burdett Social Science. © 1976 Silver Burdett Company. Pages 254-255: Excerpt from "The Rocking-Horse Winner" from *The Complete Short Stories of D. H. Lawrence, III*. Copyright 1933 by the Estate of D. H. Lawrence, © 1961 by Angelo Ravagli and C. M. Weekley, Executors of the Estate of Frieda Lawrence Ravagli. Reprinted by permission of The Viking Press, Inc. Pages 256-257: Excerpt from *The Ballad of the Sad Cafe* by Carson McCullers. Reprinted by permission of Houghton Mifflin Company. Page 257: Excerpt from "Joy in Self-Forgetting" from *The Story of My Life* by Helen Keller. Reprinted by permission of Doubleday & Company, Inc. Page 259: Excerpt from "The Louvre" by Hereward Lester Cooke, Jr. from *National Geographic*, June 1971, Vol. 139, No. 6. © 1971 National Geographic Society. Pages 259-260: Paul Gitlin, Administrator C.T.A., Estate of Thomas Wolfe, for excerpt from *You Can't Go Home Again*. Copyright 1940 Maxwell Perkins, Executor; copyright renewed 1968 Paul Gitlin, Administrator, C.T.A. Pages 262-263: Excerpt from *Notes of a Native Son* by James Baldwin, pp. 5-6. Copyright © 1955 by James Baldwin. Reprinted by permission of Beacon Press and Michael Joseph Ltd. Page 263: Excerpt from "See How They Run" by Mary Elizabeth Vroman. Copyright © 1951 by The Curtis Publishing Company, Inc. Reprinted by permission of Paul R. Reynolds, Inc. Excerpt from the story "At the Landing" from *The Wide Net and Other Stories* by Eudora Welty. Reprinted by permission of Harcourt Brace Jovanovich, Inc. and Russell & Volkening, Inc. Page 265: Excerpt from "The Interlopers," from *The Complete Short Stories of Saki* (H. H. Munro). Reprinted by permission of The Viking Press Inc. Page 339: Excerpt from "The Black Rhinoceros" by John Goddard reprinted with permission from *Natural History* magazine, April 1973. Copyright © The American Museum of Natural History, 1973. Page 340: Excerpt from "Health: Insomnia" by Arthur Frank, M.D. and Stuart Frank, M.D. from *Mademoiselle*, July 1976 issue. Reprinted by permission of authors. Page 341: "Median Age" Bar Graph from *Newsweek*, February 28, 1977. Reprinted by permission of Fenga & Freyer, Inc. Pages 353–354: Excerpt from "The Bison is Beleagured Again" by Henry G. DeYoung reprinted with permission from *Natural History* magazine, May 1973. Copyright © The American Museum of Natural History, 1973. Page 368: Poem "Barter" from *Collected Poems* by Sara Teasdale. Copyright 1917 by Macmillan Publishing Co., Inc., renewed 1945 by Mamie T. Wheless. Reprinted by permission of Macmillan Publishing Co., Inc. Page 408: Excerpt from *Readers' Guide to Periodical Literature*. Copyright © 1976, 1977 by The H. W. Wilson Company. Material reproduced by permission of the publisher.

**ART & PICTURE CREDITS** Cover: Silver Burdett Photo. 3, 4, 7, 8 Don Silverstein for Silver Burdett Company. 16 New York State Department of Commerce. 20 Everett C: Johnson, Leo de Wys, Inc. 31, 36 Don Silverstein for Silver Burdett Company. 38 Culver Pictures 51 Martin W. Vanderwall, Leo de Wys, Inc. 92, 96 Don Silverstein for Silver Burdett Company. 99 Photo Trends. 115 Ray Burns for Silver Burdett Company. 122 Courtesy, Americana Review. 129 Courtesy, Rols Royce, Inc. 133 Pleiades Records. 144, 156, 177 Don Silverstein for Silver Burdett Company. 214 John D. Firestone & Associates, Inc. 216 Howard Brainen. 219 Amy Stromsten, Photo Trends. 220 Reprinted by permission of William Morrow and Company, Inc. © 1973 Florence Adams. 226 Don Silverstein for Silver Burdett Company. 234 The Bettman Archive. 242 Solomon D. Butcher Collection, Nebraska Historical Society. 243 Alain Dagbert/Viva, Woodfin Camp & Associates, Inc. 247 Edward Clark, Life Magazine, Time, Inc. 248 The Bettman Archive. 251 James Harvin. 252 Prepared for the Asphalt Institute by Van Sant Dugdale and Company. 255 Ginger Chih. 257 Werner Wolff, Black Star. 260 top left Howard Brainen; top right Peter Karas; bottom left Owen Franken, Stock, Boston; bottom right Erika, Peter Arnold, Inc. 266 Culver Pictures. 269 Ray Burns for Silver Burdett Company. 273 Plasencia Design Associates. 280 Ebony Magazine, Johnson Publishing Company. 281 & 282 Courtesy of the United States Department of Interior. 283 Eva Cellini. 284 Courtesy of the United States Department of Interior. 285 Ellen Pines, Woodfin Camp & Associates, Inc. 288 John D. Firestone & Associates, Inc. 305, 309, & 313 The Bettman Archive. 321 Owen Franken, Stock, Boston. 341 Courtesy, Fenga & Freyer. 342–345 John D. Firestone & Associates, Inc. 415 Silver Burdett Photo.

# CONTENTS

## GRAMMAR

**DEFINING A SENTENCE**
1. Subjects and Predicates — 2
2. A Closer Look at Subjects and Predicates — 6
3. Word Order, Fragments, and Run-on Sentences — 11
   Review — 14

**NOUNS AND PRONOUNS**
4. Kinds of Nouns — 16
5. Kinds of Pronouns — 21
6. Functions of Nouns and Pronouns — 26
7. The Personal Pronoun — 29
   Review — 33

**VERBS AND THEIR HELPERS**
8. Verbs and Verb Phrases — 35
9. Tense — 39
10. Voice — 43
    Review — 46

**A LOOK AT ADJECTIVES**
11. Characteristics of Adjectives — 48
12. More About Adjectives — 52

**ADVERBS IN ACTION**
13. Characteristics of Adverbs — 56
14. More About Adverbs — 59
    Review — 62

**PREPOSITIONS**
15. Prepositions and Prepositional Phrases — 65
16. Adverb, Preposition, or Verb? — 68

## OTHER PARTS OF SPEECH

17 Conjunctions 71
18 Interjections 75
   Review 77

## KINDS OF PHRASES

19 More About Prepositional Phrases 79
20 Infinitives and Infinitive Phrases 82
21 Participles and Participial Phrases 85
22 Gerunds and Gerund Phrases 88
   Review 91

## MORE ABOUT SENTENCES

23 Basic Sentence Patterns 93
24 Kinds of Clauses 100
25 Four Kinds of Sentences 103
   Review 107

Reviewing Grammar 109

# USAGE

## DIALECTS IN AMERICA

26 Regional Dialects 114
27 Social Dialects 119
28 Special Vocabularies 125
   Review 128

## SENTENCE SENSE

29 Sentence Fragments 130
30 Run-on Sentences 135
   Review 139

## CHOOSING THE RIGHT WORDS

31 Subject-Verb Agreement 141
32 Pronoun Reference 148
33 Case of Pronouns 153
34 Irregular Verbs 160
35 Troublesome Verb Pairs 165
   Review 170

**LANGUAGE POLLUTION**

36 Redundancy and Verbosity — 172
37 Cliches and Pet Phrases — 176
   Glossary of Usage — 180
   Review of Usage — 206

# COMPOSITION

**THE ART OF EXPLANATION**

38 Getting Started — 212
39 The Structure of an Expository Paragraph — 214
40 Using a Topic Sentence — 217
41 Explaining a Process — 220
42 Developing a Paragraph Through Examples — 222
43 Using Cause-and-Effect Relationships — 224

**THE WHOLE COMPOSITION**

44 Developing a Good Composition — 227
45 The Introductory Paragraph — 230
46 Developmental Paragraphs — 233
47 The Concluding Paragraph — 237
48 Choosing an Effective Title — 239

**DEVELOPING YOUR WRITING**

49 Starting a Journal — 241
50 Telling What Happened — 244
51 Writing About Your Private World — 248
52 Audience and Purpose — 250
53 Point of View — 254
54 Tone in Writing — 256
55 Using Figurative Language — 258
56 Other Writers' Styles — 261
57 Writing Dialogue — 264

# VOCABULARY

## WHAT IS LANGUAGE?

58 Language Beginnings 268
59 Language Family Trees 271
60 Characteristics of Language 275
61 Nonverbal Communication 279

## FROM LATIN AND GREEK

62 Latin Roots 286
63 Greek Roots 290
64 Latin and Greek Prefixes 293
65 Latin and Greek Suffixes 297
66 Words as Puzzles 301

## WORDS FROM MANY SOURCES

67 Words from Mythology 304
68 Words from Literature 308
69 Words from History 312

## BUILDING YOUR VOCABULARY

70 Synonyms for Exact Meaning 316
71 Everyday Abbreviations 320
72 Testing Your Vocabulary 325

Reviewing Vocabulary 330

# SKILLS HANDBOOK

## READING AND STUDY SKILLS

1 Developing Your Reading Skills 334
2 Taking Notes on What You Read 338

|  |  |  |
|---|---|---|
|  | 3 Reading Graphs | 341 |
|  | 4 Reading Newspapers | 346 |
|  | 5 Learning Words by Reading | 350 |
| **WRITING REPORTS AND ESSAYS** | 6 Writing Reports | 355 |
|  | 7 Writing Essays | 359 |
|  | 8 Writing Reviews | 361 |
|  | 9 Writing Essay Tests | 366 |
|  | 10 Manuscript Form | 369 |
| **MECHANICS OF WRITING** | 11 Punctuation | 375 |
|  | 12 Capitalization | 388 |
|  | 13 A Plan for Spelling Success | 393 |
| **USING YOUR LIBRARY** | 14 The Classification and Arrangement of Books | 399 |
|  | 15 The Card Catalog | 401 |
|  | 16 The Reference Section | 405 |
| **EFFECTIVE SPEAKING** | 17 Giving a Talk or Oral Report | 411 |
|  | 18 Group Discussions | 418 |
| **ENGLISH FOR BUSINESS** | 19 Business Letters | 423 |
|  | 20 Getting a Part-time Job | 430 |

# GRAMMAR

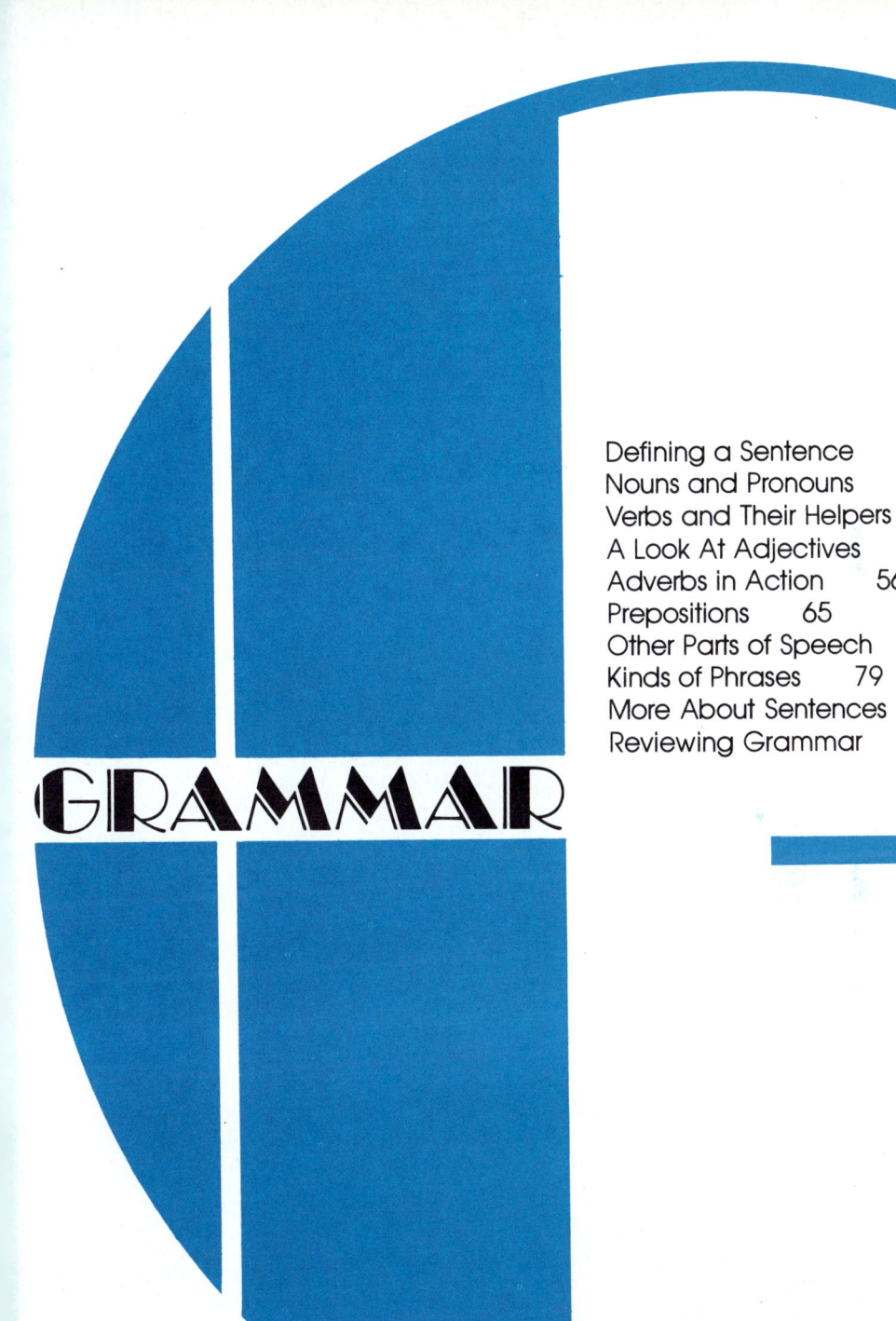

Defining a Sentence 2
Nouns and Pronouns 16
Verbs and Their Helpers 35
A Look At Adjectives 48
Adverbs in Action 56
Prepositions 65
Other Parts of Speech 71
Kinds of Phrases 79
More About Sentences 93
Reviewing Grammar 109

# DEFINING A SENTENCE

## 1

## Subjects and Predicates

If you have ever played a game—and who hasn't—you know that rules are important. In chess, for instance, the rules require that pawns make certain kinds of moves, rooks make other kinds, and knights still other kinds. All players must follow these rules or the game will turn into chaos.

So it is with grammar. **Grammar**—although it is not a game—is a system with definite rules involving the structure and functions of words and the arrangement of words into sentences.

In building sentences, you make instant, automatic decisions about words and word order. You don't often stop to think about the rules of grammar. But those rules exist—just as surely as the rule on how to move a rook exists in chess. You follow them, and you should know about them.

Grammar, then, is a system of rules. These rules need terms and definitions. One of the most difficult terms to define is *sentence*. Let's try to define it.

Study the cartoons on the next page. Which ones contain sentences? This may be a difficult question to answer, for the answer depends on your definition of a sentence. There is no single foolproof definition. Yet if we are going to talk about sentences, we have to agree on what a sentence is.

If we define a sentence as a word or group of words used to express an idea, all the cartoons contain sentences. Even the single word "Yes!" in the first cartoon expresses a complete thought. When "Yes!" is taken out of context, we don't know what it means. But in the context of a cartoon or a conversation, the word "Yes!" can carry a complete meaning.

"They ate the tacos!"

"Of all the silly things!"

"This hill looks steep!"

**Subjects and predicates** Grammarians define a **sentence** as a group of words that contains a **subject** (the person or thing about which something is being said) and a **predicate** (the part of the sentence which tells what is happening or what something is).

If we accept the definition that a sentence is a group of words containing two major parts, a subject and a predicate, it should be possible to (1) tell whether or not a group of words is a sentence and (2) divide every sentence into its two major parts.

Look at the cartoons again. Do any of them have both a subject and a predicate? It is usually easier to find the predicate first because it tells what is happening.

In the second cartoon, *ate the tacos* tells what is happening, so it is the predicate. In the fourth cartoon, *looks steep* is the predicate because it tells what something is.

Once you know the predicate, ask *who* or *what* before it in order to find the subject. In the second cartoon, if you ask Who *ate the tacos?* you find that the subject is *They*. Using the same method, you find that the subject of the fourth cartoon is *This hill*.

On the other hand, we can see right away that the caption in the third cartoon is not a sentence. It has neither a subject nor a predicate. Our understanding of what is happening in the third cartoon relies on the picture.

Inverted order   Sometimes a sentence is inverted; that is, the predicate comes before the subject. To find the subject and predicate of such a sentence, you must first put the sentence into its natural order. For example, the order of the caption under the following cartoon is inverted because it is a question.

"*Do you have any lighter reading?*"

By changing the question into a statement you get: "You do have any lighter reading." Now you can see that *do have any lighter reading* is the predicate, and *You* is the subject.

## EXERCISES

**A.** Identifying sentences   Write the numbers 1–10 on your paper. Read the following groups of words. Write *sentence* if the words form a grammatically complete sentence. Write *expression* if the group of words is a conversational expression that is *not* a grammatically complete sentence.

1. The idea was entirely his own.
2. She said it again.
3. To have your parent's permission.
4. I doubt it.
5. Why me!
6. Not once all day.
7. Somebody cares.
8. Right next door.
9. After dinner.
10. Making plans early.

**B.** Identifying subjects and predicates   Write the numbers 1–10 on your paper. Copy the following sentences and draw a vertical line between the subject and the predicate.

EXAMPLE:   The dogs in the vacant lot | were barking all night.

1. My friends joined a roller-skating club.
2. The younger of the twins resembles his father.
3. The weatherperson forecast snow.
4. We flew to Europe on a 747.
5. I put your coat in the closet.
6. All the hanging plants will be on sale tomorrow.
7. I can usually find the mistake.
8. All the houses on that street were in real danger.
9. She loves blueberry yogurt.
10. My friend's parents have invited me to dinner.

**C.** Forming sentences   Write the numbers 1–10 on your paper. Each of the following groups of words is an acceptable conversational expression but is not a complete sentence. Add whatever you think is necessary to make each expression a grammatical statement or question.

1. Sometime next week
2. Maybe
3. Because I said so
4. Whenever she arrives
5. What a day
6. Not really
7. If you don't mind
8. Almost everyone
9. Someone should
10. Not right now

# 2

# A Closer Look at Subjects and Predicates

**Simple subjects** The subject without any modifiers or determiners is called the **simple subject**. The simple subject may consist of one word or more than one word. The simple subject with all its modifiers is called the **complete subject**. The complete subject may be identical to the simple subject or it may include more words.

simple subject
↓
The *girl* standing there is the best mechanic in the class.
complete subject

A simple subject is usually a noun—a naming word, such as *girl, Texas, clock,* or *freedom*. A simple subject may also be a pronoun—a word that takes the place of a noun. Some pronouns are *he, she, it,* and *they*.

**Simple predicates** The predicate without any modifiers or complements is the **simple predicate**. The simple predicate consists of the verb or the verb plus auxiliaries. The predicate verb with all its modifiers and complements is the **complete predicate**. The complete predicate may be identical to the predicate verb.

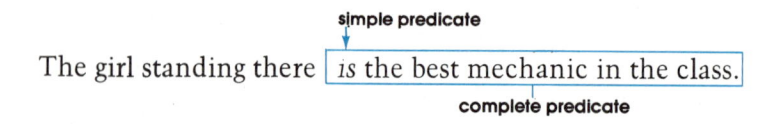

simple predicate
↓
The girl standing there *is* the best mechanic in the class.
complete predicate

A simple predicate is easy to identify because it is always a **verb**—a word that tells what something does or is. A simple predicate may be a one-word verb such as *jump* or *have,* or it may be a verb phrase such as *have been jumping* or *might have jumped*.

Sometimes a simple predicate is also the complete predicate, as in the following example.

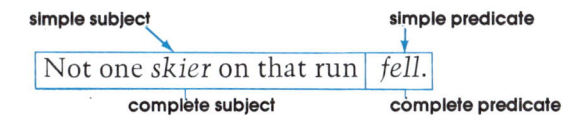

simple subject     simple predicate

Not one *skier* on that run | *fell*.

complete subject     complete predicate

Similarly, a simple subject may also be the complete subject.

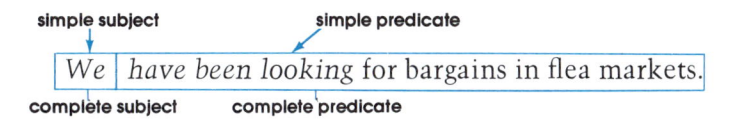

simple subject     simple predicate

We | *have been looking* for bargains in flea markets.

complete subject     complete predicate

**The understood you** In a command or a request sentence the subject is often understood rather than expressed. For example, the entire caption under the following cartoon is a predicate. You can find the subject by asking Who. The answer is the understood subject *you*. "(You) meet me at the spot."

Compound subjects and compound predicates   A sentence may have a compound subject. A **compound subject** is two or more simple subjects joined by *and, or, nor, yet,* or *but.* The following sentences contain compound subjects.

- Neither the *players* nor their *coaches* | have broken the rules.
- *Mary, Alice,* and *Bob* | applied to West Point.

A sentence may also have two or more simple predicates. Such a sentence is said to have a **compound predicate.** The simple predicates in a compound sentence are usually joined by *and, or, nor, yet,* or *but,* in the same way that simple subjects are joined. The following sentence contains a compound predicate.

- They | *are* experienced and *can cope* with it.

Some sentences have both a compound subject and a compound predicate. The following sentence is an example of such double compounds.

- *Ted* and *Rosa* and *Harvey* | *planned* and *scheduled* the tournament but *didn't participate.*

Contractions   We often speak and write with contractions of the simple subject and simple predicate (*I am = I'm; we are = we're; he is = he's; I have = I've*). In the following cartoon, for example, the subject of the sentence is *It,* and the rest of the sentence—[*i*]*s that man from the florist shop*—is the predicate.

"It's that man from the florist shop."

# EXERCISES

**A. Identifying subjects**  Write the numbers 1–10 on your paper. For each of the following sentences, copy the complete subject. Underline the simple subject.

EXAMPLE:   My oldest sister went camping for two weeks.
ANSWER:   My oldest <u>sister</u>

1. The woman in the first row found a wallet under the seat.
2. The two children took turns guarding the door.
3. Our club collected several hundred pounds of newspapers.
4. Yesterday I rearranged all the furniture in my room.
5. The volunteers who were dressed up as clowns gave each of the children a gift.
6. My cousin's dog is starring in a new television show.
7. American families often have reunions on Thanksgiving.
8. Very young children usually have trouble eating spaghetti.
9. My two cats prefer sleeping in a corner of the living room.
10. Both Pedro and I ran to the phone.

**B. Identifying predicates**  Write the numbers 1–10 on your paper. For each of the following sentences, copy the complete predicate. Underline the simple predicate.

EXAMPLE:   The monkeys in our zoo are very playful.
ANSWER:   <u>are</u> very playful

1. The woman in front of me won the lottery.
2. One of the men on the truck was waving to us.
3. Their oldest son has become an airline pilot.
4. The last book on the list is the best of all.
5. That dog and our cat play together all the time.
6. The man in the taxi is a famous author.
7. A very strange bird came to our bird feeder.
8. The hockey players cheered and waved when they won.
9. Our instructor and her assistant not only teach tennis but teach golf as well.
10. The coach told us to go home and rest.

**C. Forming compound subjects**  Write the numbers 1–10 on your paper. Develop the following predicates into sentences by adding an appropriate compound subject to each predicate. You may form the compound subject by joining two or more of the following subjects, or you may use ideas of your own.

| my friends | squirrels | my neighbors |
| monkeys | good skaters | young children |
| umpires | coaches | bear cubs |
| baseball players | teenagers | I |

EXAMPLE: _____ went to the movies.
ANSWER: Neither my friends nor I went to the movies.

1. _____ had a game last night.
2. _____ are good hockey players.
3. _____ like to climb trees.
4. _____ wear gloves.
5. _____ sometimes stop a game.
6. _____ often go hiking together.
7. _____ always win the sack race.
8. _____ grow excellent tomatoes.
9. _____ enjoy swinging on ropes.
10. _____ shouldn't play in the street.

# 3
# Word Order, Fragments, and Run-on Sentences

## Word Order

One of the ways to recognize a sentence is by the order of the words. In the following example, the meaning is destroyed by the illogical word order: *Working all were Saturday doctors the*.

Below are a number of ways that these same words can be rearranged to produce conventional English sentences.

- All the doctors were working Saturday.
- The doctors were all working Saturday.
- Saturday the doctors were all working.
- Saturday all the doctors were working.
- All Saturday the doctors were working.
- The doctors were working all Saturday.
- Were all the doctors working Saturday?
- Were the doctors all working Saturday?
- Were the doctors working all Saturday?

These rearrangements tell us three important facts about sentences.

1. Meaning is conveyed by word order.
2. A change in word order may produce a change in meaning.
3. A change in word order may produce no change in meaning but may shift the point of emphasis. For example, placing *Saturday* first in the sentence emphasizes the time element. Placing it last deemphasizes the time element and draws attention to what was happening.

## Fragments

A statement that is punctuated as a sentence but does not have both major sentence parts, subject and predicate, or has a subject and a predicate but lacks a complete thought, is called a **fragment**. The following groups of words are fragments.

- The man with the umbrella under his arm. (The predicate is missing.)
- Fell overboard and was lost at sea. (The subject is missing.)
- After dinner but before the dance. (Both subject and predicate are missing.)

## Run-on Sentences

Two sentences written and punctuated as though they were one sentence make what is called a **run-on sentence**.

RUN-ON:   I called several times he wasn't home.

You can correct a run-on by rewriting it and punctuating it as two separate sentences: *I called several times. He wasn't home.* Or, you can make the run-on into a **compound sentence**. A compound sentence is two complete sentences joined by *and, but, yet, or, nor,* or by a semicolon. The following sentences are compound.

- I called several times, but he wasn't home.
- I called several times; he wasn't home.

## EXERCISES

**A.** Changing word order   Write the numbers 1–10 on your paper. Change the meaning of the following sentences by repositioning one or more words in each sentence. Do not add or omit any words.

EXAMPLE:   Please guard that fire.
ANSWER:   Please fire that guard.

1. Some students have all the advantages.
2. The wholesale company had the merchandise.
3. You can't fool Maria and Joe.
4. All through the night the animals were restless.
5. John's mother understands problems.
6. Please ship the parts we use.
7. After the game we went to the movie.
8. They would crowd the train.

9. Did she really mark my mistake?
10. The two babies cooed at the pigeons.

**B. Changing fragments into sentences** Write the numbers 1–10 on your paper. Rewrite each of the following fragments as a sentence by adding a subject, or a predicate, or both a subject and a predicate.

1. The people on our block.
2. One day last spring.
3. Never heard from him again.
4. The people who are most anxious to criticize.
5. In the dead of the night, after all the lights were out.
6. Sitting in the middle of the road.
7. All the people you met on the trip.
8. Lost the only pet she had ever wanted.
9. Walked right into the room.
10. Not long after we had left the main road.

**C. Correcting run-on sentences** Write the numbers 1–10 on your paper. Rewrite each of the following run-on sentences as a compound sentence or as two separate sentences.

EXAMPLE: A storm came up suddenly we headed for shore.
POSSIBLE ANSWERS: A storm came up suddenly. We headed for shore.
A storm came up suddenly, and we headed for shore.
A storm came up suddenly; we headed for shore.

1. Their dog ran away all the neighbors helped look for it.
2. The scenery fell over no one was hurt.
3. She wins the dart games I win the chess games.
4. His shirts are attractive his shoes are a mess.
5. She wanted an aquarium she had no money.
6. My sister cuts the grass I have to rake the clippings.
7. It was a compact car all eight of us piled in.
8. Ice hockey can be dangerous it is still a great sport.
9. My tennis serve has improved my backhand needs a lot of work.
10. Cities are all right I prefer a farm.

# REVIEWING LESSONS 1-3

**A. Finding subjects and predicates in inverted sentences**   Write the numbers 1-10 on your paper. Copy each of the following sentences. Underline the simple subjects once and the simple predicates twice. If you have trouble, first put the sentence in its natural order.

EXAMPLE:   In the driveway <u>were parked</u> a <u>car</u> and a <u>motorcycle</u>.

1. Were you bowling with your mother last night?
2. On sale are men's and women's clothing and all shoes.
3. Leading the parade was an elephant.
4. Were the people in that store friendly to you?
5. Has a representative of that charity come to your home?
6. Next to me sat a very talkative but interesting child.
7. On your right are the two trees planted by my grandmother.
8. Hidden under the papers was the key.
9. Will you and your family stay at the shore this summer?
10. Perched on top of our car was my long lost parakeet.

**B. Distinguishing between sentences and fragments**   Write the numbers 1-10 on your paper. For each of the following groups of words write *S* if it is a sentence and *F* if it is a fragment. If it is a sentence, divide it into subject and predicate by drawing a vertical line at the end of the complete subject.

EXAMPLE:   S Each of you | will take this test.

1. The children on our block like to play street hockey.
2. Our world seems to be getting smaller.
3. The fans in the stands.
4. None of the people I know own three cars.
5. Because of the fire.
6. Don't go near that vacant house at night.
7. Trying to do what is fair and just.
8. That dress hanging in the window.
9. Behind the theater on Second Avenue.
10. Stop!

**C. Shifting the point of emphasis**   Write the numbers 1-10 on your paper. Change the point of emphasis in each of the following sentences by changing the word order. If your shift emphasizes time, write *T* after the rewritten sentence. If the shift emphasizes place, write *P*. If you emphasize action, write *A*.

EXAMPLE: There are no pictures in this book.
ANSWER: In this book there are no pictures. P

1. I feel uneasy at night.
2. Every Saturday night he bowls.
3. He had a different story yesterday.
4. If you have the time, stop by for a chat.
5. This plane will land in less than an hour.
6. A famous television actor sat across from me.
7. You will learn the truth about this sometime.
8. She and her brothers jog two miles every afternoon.
9. We always have a good time at your house.
10. There are lots of bargains in my uncle's store.

**D. Writing complete sentences** Write the numbers 1-10 on your paper. Answer each of the following questions by writing a complete sentence. Draw a vertical line between your complete subject and complete predicate.

EXAMPLE: Where was your mother born?
ANSWER: My mother | was born in Dallas, Texas.

1. What are your favorite foods?
2. Which sports do you enjoy most?
3. Who do you think studies more, students or teachers?
4. What do you like to do on Saturdays?
5. What do you think television can teach you?
6. What kind of animal do you think makes the best pet?
7. If someone paid all your expenses, where in the world would you most like to go?
8. Do you think a person's intelligence can be judged by school grades?
9. Do you think students should have after-school jobs?
10. What do you think is the greatest achievement in the twentieth century?

# NOUNS AND PRONOUNS

## 4

## Kinds of Nouns

A **noun** is a word or group of words that names an object, a person, or an idea. The name of the object you usually sit on is *chair;* so *chair* is a noun. Your friend's name is *Domingo Blanco;* so *Domingo Blanco* is a noun. The name of the tallest building in New York City is the *World Trade Center;* so these three words constitute one noun.

**Abstract or concrete?** Not all nouns name physical objects (objects that can be seen or touched). Nouns can be the names of things that cannot be seen or heard or felt. For example, we cannot see or hear or feel freedom, love, and hate, although we know of them. *Freedom, love,* and *hate* are nouns that name ideas; so they are **abstract nouns.** Nouns that name physical objects are called **concrete nouns.**

*Statue of Liberty is a concrete noun because a statue is a physical object. Liberty—the idea the statue represents—is an abstract noun.*

Compound nouns   Some nouns are **compound**; that is, they are made up of two words. Some compound nouns are written as two words joined. Some are written as two separate words. Still others are written as one hyphenated word. There is no general rule to follow because such words are in a constant state of change. When in doubt, check a recent dictionary for current usage. The following chart gives you some examples of the three ways compound nouns are written.

| Joined | Separated | Hyphenated |
|---|---|---|
| basketball | sergeant major | baby-sit |
| homework | ring finger | light-year |
| ladybug | grass roots | jet-propelled |

Collective nouns   Some nouns are **collective**. They appear singular in form but they name a group of persons or things. Following is a list of commonly used collective nouns.

| | | |
|---|---|---|
| family | board | bunch |
| jury | crew | brood |
| group | team | convey |
| crowd | band | litter |
| class | herd | swarm |
| committee | flock | pack |

Although collective nouns are singular in form, they may be either singular or plural in meaning. If you are using the noun to name a group, the noun is singular because you are referring to *one* group. If you use the noun to designate the members of a group, the noun is plural because you are referring to more than one member.

SINGULAR:   My family is living in Texas.
PLURAL:   My family are living in several different states.

Common or proper?   Another way to classify nouns is to call them common or proper. A **common noun** is a word that names a class of people or things. *Child* and *house* are common nouns. You don't capitalize a common noun, such as *woman*, because that is not the person's name. On the other hand, you do capitalize a proper noun. A **proper noun** is the name of a particular person, place, or thing, such as *Jennifer*.

The following chart compares common and proper nouns.

|  | Common | Proper |
|---|---|---|
| **Persons** | leader | Martin Luther King |
|  | soccer player | Pelé |
|  | skater | Peggy Fleming |
| **Places** | city | Atlanta |
|  | lake | Lake Superior |
|  | ball park | Astrodome |
| **Things** | car | Pinto |
|  | painting | Mona Lisa |
|  | book | *Moby Dick* |

## EXERCISES

**A. Identifying nouns in sentences** Write the numbers 1–10 on your paper. Identify the nouns in the following sentences. Copy only the nouns from each sentence. Remember that any noun of more than one word counts as one noun.

EXAMPLE: My friends and I went behind the scenery to find the stage manager.
ANSWER: friends, scenery, stage manager

1. Late that night the people in the barracks heard strange noises coming from the mess hall.
2. The pictures in our school newspaper caused both excitement and confusion in the principal's office.
3. Compassion and a sense of responsibility are demonstrated by the children in Louisa May Alcott's books *Little Women* and *Little Men*.
4. If time permits and the weather holds, the mayor of our city will talk to the visitors about our problems with hot rodders.
5. Illness and disease are robbers of humankind's time and energy.
6. She sat at her easel and studied the apple blossoms a long time before she made a stroke upon the canvas.
7. The Statue of Liberty stands in upper New York Bay not far from Ellis Island, a station where immigrants to this country were examined before entry.
8. The place mats were handmade by the man and the woman who own the shop next to the Empire Theatre.

**Compound nouns** Some nouns are **compound**; that is, they are made up of two words. Some compound nouns are written as two words joined. Some are written as two separate words. Still others are written as one hyphenated word. There is no general rule to follow because such words are in a constant state of change. When in doubt, check a recent dictionary for current usage. The following chart gives you some examples of the three ways compound nouns are written.

| Joined | Separated | Hyphenated |
|---|---|---|
| basketball | sergeant major | baby-sit |
| homework | ring finger | light-year |
| ladybug | grass roots | jet-propelled |

**Collective nouns** Some nouns are **collective**. They appear singular in form but they name a group of persons or things. Following is a list of commonly used collective nouns.

| | | |
|---|---|---|
| family | board | bunch |
| jury | crew | brood |
| group | team | convey |
| crowd | band | litter |
| class | herd | swarm |
| committee | flock | pack |

Although collective nouns are singular in form, they may be either singular or plural in meaning. If you are using the noun to name a group, the noun is singular because you are referring to *one* group. If you use the noun to designate the members of a group, the noun is plural because you are referring to more than one member.

SINGULAR:   My family is living in Texas.
PLURAL:   My family are living in several different states.

**Common or proper?** Another way to classify nouns is to call them common or proper. A **common noun** is a word that names a class of people or things. *Child* and *house* are common nouns. You don't capitalize a common noun, such as *woman,* because that is not the person's name. On the other hand, you do capitalize a proper noun. A **proper noun** is the name of a particular person, place, or thing, such as *Jennifer.*

The following chart compares common and proper nouns.

|  | Common | Proper |
|---|---|---|
| **Persons** | leader | Martin Luther King |
|  | soccer player | Pelé |
|  | skater | Peggy Fleming |
| **Places** | city | Atlanta |
|  | lake | Lake Superior |
|  | ball park | Astrodome |
| **Things** | car | Pinto |
|  | painting | Mona Lisa |
|  | book | *Moby Dick* |

## EXERCISES

**A. Identifying nouns in sentences** Write the numbers 1–10 on your paper. Identify the nouns in the following sentences. Copy only the nouns from each sentence. Remember that any noun of more than one word counts as one noun.

EXAMPLE: My friends and I went behind the scenery to find the stage manager.

ANSWER: friends, scenery, stage manager

1. Late that night the people in the barracks heard strange noises coming from the mess hall.
2. The pictures in our school newspaper caused both excitement and confusion in the principal's office.
3. Compassion and a sense of responsibility are demonstrated by the children in Louisa May Alcott's books *Little Women* and *Little Men*.
4. If time permits and the weather holds, the mayor of our city will talk to the visitors about our problems with hot rodders.
5. Illness and disease are robbers of humankind's time and energy.
6. She sat at her easel and studied the apple blossoms a long time before she made a stroke upon the canvas.
7. The Statue of Liberty stands in upper New York Bay not far from Ellis Island, a station where immigrants to this country were examined before entry.
8. The place mats were handmade by the man and the woman who own the shop next to the Empire Theatre.

9. Jane Austen was a great English novelist who wrote about manners in England in the late eighteenth century.
10. The first period of human culture is called the Stone Age.

**B. Using nouns to complete sentences** Write the numbers 1–10 on your paper. For each of the following sentences, write a noun for each blank. Try to use some proper nouns, some compound nouns, and some collective nouns.

1. After _____ the _____ went into the _____ and started a _____ of _____.
2. _____ and _____ are two important _____ that every _____ should have.
3. Some _____ enjoy playing _____ in the _____ with their _____.
4. The _____ in our _____ were _____ on the _____.
5. Not all _____ enjoy reading _____.
6. During the _____ two _____ came into our _____ and bought our _____ of _____.
7. If _____ saw her, why did he hide the _____ in the _____?
8. If I bring the _____, will you bring the _____?
9. His _____ ran into a _____ and broke his _____.
10. In every _____ there was a _____ of _____ lying on the _____.

**C. Choosing verbs for collective nouns** Write the numbers 1–10 on your paper. For each of the following sentences, write the collective noun and the correct form of the verb.

EXAMPLE:   After every dance a committee (is, are) needed for cleanup.
ANSWER:    committee is

1. Throughout the country the clergy (is, are) doing what they can to help the poor.
2. My class (was, were) ready for their test.
3. The board of trustees (is, are) arguing about the new rates.
4. This flock (gets, get) larger every year.
5. The band (has, have) all paid their dues.
6. My group broke up and (has, have) joined other activities.
7. The crew (is, are) very impressive in their new uniforms.
8. A bunch of kids (was, were) coming in all the side exits at the same time.
9. A pack of wolves (was, were) waiting in the shadows behind the barn.
10. Our brood (is, are) never willing to sit down at the same time for a meal.

**D. Naming with nouns** Write the numbers 1–10 on your paper. Look closely at the following photograph. Write ten nouns that name things in the photograph.

# 5
# Kinds of Pronouns

A **pronoun** is a word that takes the place of a noun or nouns, a noun phrase, or a noun substitute. The use of pronouns makes our speaking and writing less awkward and less repetitious.

- Joe wrecked the car when Joe drove the car off the road.
- Joe wrecked the car when *he* drove *it* off the road.

- If Lani has the books, will Lani let Jane use the books?
- If *you* have the books, will *you* let *her* use *them*?

- Mateo take Jack's, and Bill will take Carla's.
- *You* take *his*, and *I* will take *hers*.

There are three major types of pronouns—personal, possessive, and indefinite pronouns. A pronoun that denotes the speaker, the person spoken to, or the one spoken about is a **personal pronoun**. A pronoun that shows ownership is a **possessive pronoun**. An **indefinite pronoun** is a pronoun that does not identify its antecedent or referent specifically.

| Personal | Possessive | Indefinite |
|---|---|---|
| I, me | mine | any |
| you | yours | some |
| he, him | his | few |
| she, her | hers | all |
| it | its | several |
| we, us | ours | ____ one |
| they, them | theirs | ____ body |

Three other types of pronouns are the **interrogative pronoun** (used to ask questions), **demonstrative pronoun** (used to point out), and **relative pronoun** (used to associate an adjective clause with the noun it modifies).

| Interrogative | Demonstrative | Relative |
|---|---|---|
| who | this | who |
| whom | that | whom |
| what | these | which |
| which | those | that |

However, classification often depends on usage. Therefore, *who* can be either an interrogative or a relative pronoun.

INTERROGATIVE:   *Who* took my books?
RELATIVE:   The girl *who* helped you is my daughter.

The same is true of *whom* and *which*.

INTERROGATIVE:   *Whom* did you wish to see?
RELATIVE:   The man *whom* you met is Mr. Jacobs.

INTERROGATIVE:   *Which* do you want to buy?
RELATIVE:   The book *The Diary of Anne Frank, which* you borrowed, is mine.

*That* may be a demonstrative or a relative pronoun, depending on its usage.

DEMONSTRATIVE:   Please give me *that*.
RELATIVE:   The movie *that* we saw was fantastic.

The following examples show how a pronoun can take the place of a noun or nouns, a noun phrase or a noun substitute.

- All the patients enjoyed the beautiful flowers.
- *They* enjoyed *them*.
- Maria enjoys swimming.
- *She* enjoys *it*.
- Carlos needs the pen.
- *He* needs *that*.

The final pronoun you need to consider is the **compound personal pronoun:** *myself, ourselves, yourself, yourselves, himself, herself, itself, themselves.* A compound personal pronoun used to turn the action back onto the subject is a **reflexive pronoun.** A compound personal pronoun following a noun or another pronoun and used to add emphasis or force is an **intensive pronoun.**

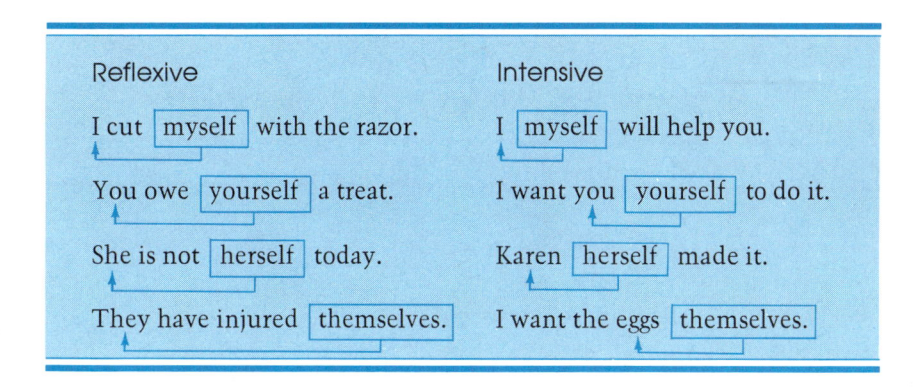

| Reflexive | Intensive |
|---|---|
| I cut **myself** with the razor. | I **myself** will help you. |
| You owe **yourself** a treat. | I want you **yourself** to do it. |
| She is not **herself** today. | Karen **herself** made it. |
| They have injured **themselves**. | I want the eggs **themselves**. |

Today informal usage permits moving the intensive pronoun to the end of the sentence: I'd rather do it *myself*.

## EXERCISES

**A. Identifying pronouns** Copy all the pronouns that you find in the following cartoon. Remember to separate the pronoun from any word with which it has been contracted. For example, in *I've*, only the word *I* is the pronoun.

**PEANUTS**

YOU KNOW WHAT BOTHERS ME THE MOST?

I FEEL THAT I'VE LET DOWN YOU PLAYERS WHO HAD FAITH IN ME AS YOUR MANAGER..

OH, WELL, IF THAT'S WHAT'S BOTHERING YOU, CHARLIE BROWN, JUST FORGET IT..

WE NEVER REALLY **HAD** ANY FAITH IN YOU!

**B. Identifying pronouns in sentences** Write the numbers 1–10 on your paper. Copy only the pronouns from each sentence. If a pronoun has been contracted with a verb, copy only the pronoun, as in the following example.

EXAMPLE: We who've done this before will show you.
ANSWER: we, who, this, you

1. Anyone who would swim in that river is braver than I.
2. What do they say will be done with ours if yours is accepted?
3. Trees that shade a house keep it cool in summer.
4. If they have any, let's borrow them.
5. Does anybody know which bus he got on?
6. Those who are supporting you will not let you down.
7. We asked what we could do, but she never answered us.
8. All players who've had their physicals report to me on the field.
9. Is there any doubt about who will win the meet this year?
10. What will you read after you have finished this?

**C. Using pronouns as substitutes** Write the numbers 1–15 on your paper. Rewrite the following sentences. Use a pronoun in place of every italicized noun, noun phrase, or noun substitute.

EXAMPLE: *My family* wanted *the Chings* to stay with *our family.*
ANSWER: We wanted them to stay with us.

1. *Pedro* asked *Jim* to bring *the records* for the dance.
2. For *what you have done, Lita* can stay home.
3. In place of *selling,* why doesn't *Mr. Zayas* try writing?
4. *Our parents* know that *their children* can be trusted.
5. If *Joel* uses *your car, yours truly* can use *Mother and Dad's.*
6. If *revenge* is what *those people* want, *our family* will avoid *those people.*
7. *Yours truly* wishes *our class* knew what *the graduates* want *our class* to do for *the graduates.*
8. Do *the people I'm talking to* know *which student* won *the medal*?
9. *The pictures my parents* admire are *the pictures my parents* buy.
10. When *Mrs. Levy* comes for *the package here,* be certain *Mrs. Levy* leaves a deposit for *the package.*
11. *The gardenia* was named for *Alexander Garden.*
12. *Americans* spell *traveler* with one l, but *the British* spell *traveler* with two ll's.
13. *The park* is near *my house.*
14. *Susan* went to *City College.*
15. *Julie* gave *Maggie* the paper.

**D. Using pronouns to complete sentences** Write the numbers 1–10 on your paper. Copy the following sentences and complete them by writing a pronoun in place of each blank. Use some reflexive and some intensive compound personal pronouns.

EXAMPLE: _____ hurt _____ when _____ fell out of the tree.
ANSWER: He hurt himself when he fell out of the tree.

1. _____ asked _____ to help _____ with the project.
2. If _____ will buy _____, _____ won't have to worry about _____ to do with _____.
3. Anita _____ has promised to help _____ with my tax returns.
4. The stranger _____ was walking behind _____ looked very suspicious to _____.
5. _____ did _____ think _____ would do with _____?
6. _____'ll be there by noon if _____ know _____ will feed _____.
7. Doesn't _____ know _____ put the salt in the sugar bowl?
8. _____ is a car _____ _____ would like to own.
9. _____ expects the mayor _____ to lead the parade.
10. If _____ ever see _____ again, please ask _____ if _____ knows my sister.

25

# Functions of Nouns and Pronouns

Nouns and pronouns do the same things in sentences. That is, nouns and pronouns have the same functions.

In sentences nouns and pronouns are often used as simple subjects. The simple subject of a sentence is easily found by asking *who* or *what* before the verb.

- After the game the *kids* came to our house. (Who came?)
- *They* made pizza. (Who made pizza?)
- All our *root beer* disappeared. (What disappeared?)

A noun or a pronoun can also be the **direct object** in a sentence, receiving the action from an active verb. You can easily find the direct object by asking *whom* or *what* after the verb.

- They built a *cabin* in the mountains. (Built what?)
- We saw *them*. (Saw whom?)
- My brother puts *tomatoes, pickles,* and *lettuce* in his sandwiches. (Puts what in his sandwiches?)

A noun or pronoun can also function as an indirect object. The **indirect object** tells *to whom* or *what,* or *for whom* or *what* something is done when the *to* or *for* is not expressed. The indirect object is placed between the verb and the direct object.

- We told *Mother* the news. (Told the news to whom?)
- She made *us* a chocolate cake. (Made a cake for whom?)
- Dad gave *Jim* and *me* our last warning. (Gave a warning to whom?)
- I gave *the horse* a carrot. (Gave a carrot to what?)

It is easy to convert the phrase *to someone* or *for someone* to an indirect object by dropping the *to* or *for* and repositioning the noun or pronoun.

- They gave a hard time *to the umpire.*
- They gave *the umpire* a hard time.

Nouns and pronouns also function as words of direct address. When a person addresses another person by name or by another term, this is called **a word (or words) of direct address** and is set off by commas.

*You* is the only pronoun that functions as a word of direct address, either by itself or in a phrase. The following sentences contain words of direct address.

- *Helen,* why don't you join us?
- All right, *Lefty,* you may go.
- *You* in the back, please leave.
- It is difficult, my *friends* and *classmates,* to say goodbye.

The **appositive** is a noun or noun phrase that explains and usually follows another noun. Most often an appositive is added information about a person, place, or thing. It is, therefore, set off by commas or dashes.

- Mary Beth Bleecker—*a friend of mine*—is the captain.
- I enjoy the works of Thomas Costain, *a novelist.*

If the appositive tells *which one,* do not set it off with commas.

- The poet *Wordsworth* was a lover of nature. (Which poet?)
- The book *Roots* became an outstanding television drama. (Which book?)

Appositives that follow personal pronouns are not set off by commas.

- We *girls* came along to protect you *boys.*

## EXERCISES

**A.** Identifying the function of nouns and pronouns   Write the numbers 1–10 on your paper. For the following sentences, copy each italicized word. Next to the word write its function in the sentence.

EXAMPLE:   The *people* in the *town* offered *us shelter.*
ANSWER:   people: simple subject; town: object of preposition; us: indirect object; shelter: direct object

1. *Friends,* will *you* please remove your *hats*?
2. Many *students* have *trouble* with this *word.*

3. If *you* will give *us* your *attention, we leaders* can help *you*.
4. Our *neighbors, those* who just moved in, are from *Seattle*.
5. The best *player* is the *goalie*, but *they* are all good *skaters*.
6. *Procrastination* has been your *downfall, Sue Ellen*.
7. If *Mr. Perez* won't give *us* the *information*, will *you*?
8. *That* was made for your *benefit, my friend*.
9. This *lamp*, a *gift* from my *uncle*, is made from *pieces* of *junk*.
10. Send *us* the *fee*, and *we* will make *you* a *member*.

**B. Changing phrases to indirect objects**   Write the numbers 1–10 on your paper. Change the italicized phrase in each of the following sentences to an indirect object and rewrite the sentence.

EXAMPLE:   He told the same story *to everyone* in the class.
ANSWER:   He told everyone in the class the same story.

1. Grandmother made a sled *for her grandchildren*.
2. Why don't you give some friendly advice *to him*?
3. Bruno brought the dessert tray *to us*.
4. The Cardonas offered a ride *to the Beitels*.
5. Last Valentine's Day my brother bought a pair of teddy bear hamsters *for his friend*.
6. Our community sent canned goods and clothing *to the flood victims*.
7. The manager sold the display equipment *to us*.
8. Why won't they mail the tickets *to us*?
9. The pitcher threw a fast ball *to the catcher*.
10. Before I enter the yard, I toss a bone *to the watchdog*.

**C. Identifying essential and nonessential appositives**   Write the numbers 1–10 on your paper. Copy each of the following sentences and underline the appositional word or phrase in each.

EXAMPLE:   I spend every summer with my uncle, a Texas rancher.
ANSWER:   I spend every summer with my uncle, <u>a Texas rancher</u>.

1. The poem *Evangeline* could easily be <u>made</u> into a movie.
2. We spent Sunday with the Fergusons, <u>our friends in Denver</u>.
3. Saturday, <u>my favorite day of the week</u>, is always too short.
4. The judges gave her first prize, <u>a trip to Mexico</u>.
5. Maria Russo—<u>our ceramics teacher</u>—is also an excellent writer.
6. We offered to take care of Thumper, <u>their big Manx cat</u>.
7. They made arrangements of forsythia and japonica—<u>two shrubs</u>.
8. We saw the "Pieta" and the "David"—<u>two of Michelangelo's statues</u>.
9. His sister <u>Angela</u> is smarter than the other two sisters.
10. The committee has chosen the colors <u>blue and green</u>.

# 7

# The Personal Pronoun

**Case** is a characteristic of nouns and pronouns, indicating grammatical function. The following are the three cases of the personal pronoun.

| Nominative | | Objective | | Possessive | |
|---|---|---|---|---|---|
| I | we | me | us | my, mine | our, ours |
| you | you | you | you | your, yours | your, yours |
| she, he, it | they | her, him, it | them | hers, his, its | their, theirs |

The difficulty for most people lies in choosing between the nominative and the objective forms of those pronouns. The following charts indicate when to use the nominative forms and when to use the objective forms of personal pronouns.

## NOMINATIVE CASE

### Simple Subjects

(I, we, he, she, it, they) has left.
(We) girls will help you.
Jim and (I, we, he, she, it, they) left.

### Subject Complements

The winner was (I, he, she).
The winners were (we, they).
The winners were Tony and (I, he, she, we, they).

### OBJECTIVE CASE

#### Direct Objects
He saw (me, us, him, her, it, them).
She saved Rae and (me, us, him, her, it, them).

#### Indirect Objects
Please give (me, us, him, her, it, them) a chance.
Please give Jon and (me, us, him, her, it, them) a chance

#### Objects of Prepositions
Please go with (me, us, him, her, it, them).
Wait here for Connie and (me, us, him, her, it, them).

When a pronoun is used as an appositive, it takes the same case as the noun or pronoun with which it is in apposition.

- The leaders—Cassandra and *I*—expect you. (apposition to subject)
- Let's *you* and *me* study together. (apposition to *us*)
- They are the two winners, Bert and *she!* (apposition to subject complement)
- Please give your friends—*him* and *me*—a chance. (apposition to indirect object)

## EXERCISES

**A. Choosing the correct pronoun**  Write the numbers 1–20 on your paper. For each sentence write the correct pronoun.

EXAMPLE:  They told it to Jan and (I, me).
ANSWER:  me

1. Carlos and (she, her) are working in a gas station.
2. They offered (us, we) students another chance.
3. The Vicentes and (we, us) drove to the shore yesterday.
4. The best person to represent us is (she, her).
5. We can always depend upon (he, him) for extra help.

6. When will the mayor and (he, him) arrive in town?
7. That company sent my sister and (I, me) the application forms.
8. The books I need are (they, them) on the top shelf.
9. Two students—Flo and (I, me)—became the leaders.
10. Why did you include the captain and (I, me)?
11. We were asked to sit with the Nakanos and (they, them).
12. The most valuable player should have been (she, her).
13. My friend and (we, us) hockey fans have our reservations.
14. The coach wants to talk to the pitcher and (I, me).
15. We mailed (she, her) the necessary forms and information.
16. Why do Hugo and (he, him) insist on coming along?
17. We stopped worrying because the next speaker was (she, her).
18. Please tell the class and (I, me) our test results.
19. The organizers of the rally are (they, them) in the red car.
20. We—Beth and (I, me)—will do what we can to help you.

*"It's elementary, Watson.
Carefully examine the case of the pronouns."*

**B. Using personal pronouns** Write the number 1–10 on your paper. For each of the following sentences write a personal pronoun for each blank.

EXAMPLE: The Ogdens and ———— attended the same party.
ANSWER: they

1. ———— and ———— heard the news late last night.
2. The clerk sold ———— and ———— the wrong sizes.
3. ———— in this class know what to expect.
4. The first to arrive were ———— and ————.
5. It is really the best solution for ———— all.
6. Did you really think it was ———— and ———— in the boat?
7. If ———— and ———— are willing to go, will you?
8. They told ————–Cora and ————–all about their accident.
9. If I had known it was ————, I would have helped.
10. When ———— arrives, please tell ———— the good news.

**C. Writing sentences with pronouns** Write the numbers 1–20 on your paper. Write an original sentence for each pronoun in the specified function.

EXAMPLE: *me*—object of a preposition
ANSWER: Would you do a favor for me?

1. *him*—indirect object
2. *they*—subject complement
3. *she*—simple subject
4. *us*—direct object
5. *we*—simple subject
6. *me*—indirect object
7. *her*—object of a preposition
8. *he*—subject complement
9. *them*—direct object
10. *they*—apposition
11. *I*—subject complement
12. *them*—indirect object
13. *me*—direct object
14. *we*—subject complement
15. *him*—object of a preposition
16. *her*—direct object
17. *us*—indirect object
18. *she*—subject complement
19. *me*—appositive
20. *them*—object of a preposition

# REVIEWING LESSONS 4-7

**A. Identifying nouns and their functions** Write the numbers 1-10 on your paper. Copy every noun from each of the following sentences. After each noun write its function in the sentence.

EXAMPLE: Now, class, here is your surprise—no more tests.
ANSWER: Class: direct address; surprise: simple subject; tests: appositive

1. A better route would have been the path through the woods.
2. The main speaker, Ms. Hanami, pointed out the real dangers.
3. During intermission, ushers, you may visit with your friends.
4. I was not the only person surprised by his departure.
5. They will give the students that kind of examination.
6. Mother, will you and Dad provide the cake for the party?
7. You runners can become the celebrities of the day if you win.
8. Not every person can admit such a mistake to the public.
9. Really, Franco, your tardiness is not the problem.
10. Your plants, the ferns and the violets, look quite healthy.

**B. Identifying pronouns and their functions** Write the numbers 1-10 on your paper. Copy every pronoun from each of the following sentences. After each pronoun write its function in the sentence.

EXAMPLE: We scouts will help you with the plans.
ANSWER: We: simple subject; you: direct object.

1. The two managers—he and she—will give you the equipment.
2. Some of us classmates don't understand his decision.
3. Everyone should be herself and not hurt her chances of winning.
4. He and I prefer these to those.
5. Who took the key from you after the show?
6. This is most definitely yours, Finnegan.
7. The twins, you, and I have the first four seats on the aisle.
8. The oldest ones—they in the red shirts—will help the others.
9. He has agreed to donate his services.
10. I myself will call the roll and check off their names.

**C. Using compound sentence parts** Write the numbers 1-15 on your paper. Write an original sentence for each of the compounds on the following page.

EXAMPLE: you and her: as appositives
ANSWER: He wants two volunteers, you and her.

1. her and her brothers: as direct objects
2. the Chiagos and we: as subjects
3. my best friend and me: as objects of a preposition
4. him and his new car: as direct objects
5. them and a few others: as indirect objects
6. we drivers and our passengers: as subjects
7. Jimmy Kwan and me: as indirect objects
8. the football captain and I: as subject complements
9. you and he: as appositives
10. they and the Nelsons: as subject complements
11. you and me: as indirect objects
12. the other members and I: as subjects
13. them and me: as appositives
14. he and she: as subjects
15. you and I: as subject complements

# VERBS AND THEIR HELPERS

## 8

## Verbs and Verb Phrases

The heart of every grammatically complete sentence is the verb. A **verb** is a word that shows action or existence.

**Action verbs**  Verbs that show action, called **action verbs**, include all the words for things we do, such as *see, hear, laugh, hit, swim, rotate, study,* and *imitate.*

**Auxiliary verbs**  Words that act as helpers for verbs are called **auxiliary verbs.** The *-en* and *-ing* forms of a verb must always have an auxiliary, or helper. Following is a list of the most frequently used auxiliary verbs.

| am | were | been | had | will | should |
| is | was | has | can | would | might |
| are | be | have | may | shall | could |
| did | being | do | does | must | |

**Verb phrases**  More than one auxiliary verb may be used at a time: *may be going, should have written, could have been heard.* A main verb and its auxiliary verbs make up what is commonly called a **verb phrase.** The simple predicate of a sentence may be a verb or a verb phrase.

The auxiliary verbs in a verb phrase may be separated from the main verb, as in the following sentence.

- Verbs *are* very often *used* with helpers.

A verb or its helper may be combined with *not* or its contraction *n't. Not* and *n't* are not part of the verb phrase.

- I *cannot go* with you because I *don't have* a ticket.

The following cartoon illustrates another attribute of auxiliary verbs. They can contract with the subject (I *will* = I'*ll*).

*"I'll avoid these economy cruises from now on."*

## EXERCISES

**A.** Identifying verbs and verb phrases   Write the numbers 1–10 on your paper. From each of the following sentences, copy every verb and every verb phrase.

EXAMPLE:   The workers were painting the barn while we slept.
ANSWER:   were painting, slept

1. Will you go with me to the movies on Saturday?
2. They have always been there when we needed them.

3. It hasn't been very long since your last visit.
4. Don't ever disturb her while she is napping.
5. You should have been warned about his moods.
6. They could always have stopped us before we entered.
7. There isn't anyone sitting there now.
8. Haven't you ever been caught off guard?
9. They are surely going to miss you when you leave.
10. She used to work with oils, but now she uses only pastels.

**B. Identifying verbs**  Write the numbers 1-10 on your paper. Copy all the main verbs from the following sentences. Write *A* after action verbs.

EXAMPLE:   She danced at the party.
ANSWER:    danced: A

1. I can't hear the music.
2. I have been to twelve states.
3. He was there years ago.
4. They ate all the fish.
5. The flowers wilted.
6. The dogs ran to their kennel for their dinner.
7. Give me that newspaper.
8. She's there now.
9. I'm not there now.
10. Where are you?

**C. Writing sentences with auxiliary verbs**  Write the numbers 1-10 on your paper. Use each of the following auxiliaries in an original sentence. Then underline the verb phrase.

EXAMPLE:   can be
ANSWER:    <u>Can</u> you <u>be reached</u> in the morning?

1. has
2. must have been
3. will be
4. may have been
5. did have
6. has been going
7. should have
8. is being
9. can be
10. were

**D.** Describing action with verbs   Write the numbers 1–5 on your paper. Look closely at the following picture. Write five verbs that describe actions or things that are happening in the picture.

# 9

# Tense

Verbs have more than one form, or tense. Verb **tenses** indicate time. For example, the verb *be* can indicate by its form the time someone or something exists. If you wish to indicate that someone exists now, you say "He *is*" or "Jack *is* my friend." To indicate past existence, you say "Eldora *was* ill" or "They *were* here."

The following are the six tenses of English verbs.

PRESENT: She *sees* who you are. (happening now)
He *walks* to work. (customary action)
The truth *is* best (timeless action)
PAST: He *injured* his knee during the game. (action completed before the present)
FUTURE: She *will drive* to Dallas tomorrow. (action sometime after the present)
PRESENT PERFECT: She *has helped* us before. (action in the indefinite past)
We *have lived* here ten years. (action begun in the past extending into the present)
PAST PERFECT: After she *had found* my wallet, I thanked her. (action completed before another past action)
FUTURE PERFECT: He *will have left* by the time you arrive. (action to be completed before another future action)

**Progressive form**  The six tenses of an English verb may express a continuing action by using forms of the verb *to be* as auxiliary verbs and adding *-ing* to the main verb.

PRESENT PROGRESSIVE:   She *is working*.
PAST PROGRESSIVE:   She *was working*.
FUTURE PROGRESSIVE:   She *will be working*.
PRESENT PERFECT PROGRESSIVE:   She *has been working*.
PAST PERFECT PROGRESSIVE:   She *had been working*.
FUTURE PERFECT PROGRESSIVE:   She *will have been working*.

**Regular verbs** Most English verbs are considered **regular** because their past form and their past participle form end in *-d* or *-ed*.

**Principal parts** The three **principal parts** of verbs—the **present, past,** and **past participle**—are the basic forms from which the tenses are built. The past participle is always preceded by *has* or *had*.

| Present | Past | Past Participle |
|---|---|---|
| walk | walked | walked |
| pitch | pitched | pitched |
| try | tried | tried |

**Irregular verbs** Verbs are considered **irregular** if they change forms for the past and past participle rather than add *-d* or *-ed*. The following chart illustrates many of these irregular verbs, grouped by similarity of changes.

| Present | Past | Past Participle |
|---|---|---|
| began | began | begun |
| drink | drank | drunk |
| ring | rang | rung |
| shrink | shrank | shrunk |
| sing | sang | sung |
| sink | sank | sunk |
| spring | sprang | sprung |
| swim | swam | swum |
| break | broke | broken |
| choose | chose | chosen |
| freeze | froze | frozen |
| speak | spoke | spoken |
| steal | stole | stolen |
| tear | tore | torn |
| wear | wore | worn |
| bite | bit | bitten |
| blow | blew | blown |
| draw | drew | drawn |
| drive | drove | driven |
| eat | ate | eaten |

| | | |
|---|---|---|
| fall | fell | fallen |
| fly | flew | flown |
| forgive | forgave | forgiven |
| give | gave | given |
| grow | grew | grown |
| know | knew | known |
| ride | rode | ridden |
| rise | rose | risen |
| see | saw | seen |
| take | took | taken |
| throw | threw | thrown |
| write | wrote | written |
| bring | brought | brought |
| catch | caught | caught |
| find | found | found |
| get | got | got |
| hang | hung | hung |
| lead | led | led |
| lose | lost | lost |
| say | said | said |
| swing | swung | swung |
| tell | told | told |
| burst | burst | burst |
| hit | hit | hit |
| hurt | hurt | hurt |

## EXERCISES

**A. Correcting errors in verb forms** Write the numbers 1–10 on your paper. For each sentence, correct any errors in verb form. If there is no error, write *C*.

EXAMPLE: The doctor done what she could to help us.
ANSWER: did

1. What have you brung us this time?
2. The balloon busted when it drifted into a tree.
3. The teacher was reading the papers that the students wrote.
4. We lived in that town for ten years.
5. My dog catched the ball when I threw it.

6. Last night we drive to the city and went to a movie.
7. Suddenly the lion sprung at the trainer.
8. The audience applauded when the horse dived into the pool.
9. She had eaten all of it before she knew what it was.
10. The two captains choosed their teams.

**B. Forming verb tenses**  Write the numbers 1–10 on your paper. Write the requested tense of the verb for each sentence.

EXAMPLE:  They (past of *hang*) the clothes up to dry.
ANSWER:  hung

1. Enrollment (future of *begin*) sometime next week.
2. All the plants in the garden (present perfect of *freeze*).
3. I couldn't hear because the bell (past progressive of *ring*).
4. The guides (present perfect of *lead*) the climbers to safety.
5. The child (past of *hurt*) himself when he fell.
6. She forgot to mail the letter she (past perfect of *write*).
7. The children (future perfect of *find*) him by then.
8. The clown (future progressive of *wear*) a red hat.
9. We (past of *see*) a huge truck going that way.
10. How all you (present perfect of *grow*)!

**C. Using tenses in sentences**  Write the numbers 1–12 on your paper. Write an original sentence for each of the following verb phrases.

EXAMPLE:  will have been
ANSWER:  At noon they will have been on the trail for six hours.

| | | | |
|---|---|---|---|
| 1. hung | 4. were bringing | 7. have fallen | 10. has been wearing |
| 2. bit | 5. has hurt | 8. has sprung | 11. will have broken |
| 3. shrank | 6. had sunk | 9. have drunk | 12. have been seeing |

# 10

# Voice

**Voice** is the relationship that exists between a verb and its subject. If the subject *does* the action, the verb is in the **active voice**. If the action is *performed upon* the subject, the verb is in the **passive voice**.

ACTIVE VOICE: The pitcher *threw* the ball.
PASSIVE VOICE: The ball *was thrown* by the pitcher.

To change from active to passive voice, you move the direct or the indirect object to the subject position. Then make the subject the object of the preposition *by*. (However, in some cases you may wish to drop the original subject.) The following pairs of sentences illustrate the changes from active to passive voice.

1. You may eliminate the direct object.

    ACTIVE: Joan has written the script.
    PASSIVE: The script has been written by Joan.

2. You may eliminate the indirect object.

    ACTIVE: The nurses gave me good care.
    PASSIVE: I was given good care by the nurses.

3. You may eliminate the doer of the action.

    ACTIVE: He has bought the car.
    PASSIVE: The car has been bought.

The passive voice always requires the use of an auxiliary verb. The auxiliary verb you choose depends upon the tense you wish to form.

PRESENT: Seafood *is* served every Wednesday.
PAST: Seafood *was* served every Wednesday.
FUTURE: Seafood *will be* served every Wednesday.

**Transitive and intransitive verbs** A verb is **transitive** if it has a direct object: *She writes poetry.* An active verb that does not have a direct object is **intransitive**: *She writes.* As you can see from the previous examples, a verb can be transitive in one sentence and intransitive in another. **Linking verbs** are always intransitive because they merely connect a subject with its complement: *She is a poet.*

## EXERCISES

**A. Changing from passive to active** Write the numbers 1–15 on your paper. Rewrite each of the following sentences by changing the voice of the verb from passive to active.

EXAMPLE: The bear was chased into the woods by the dogs.
ANSWER: The dogs chased the bear into the woods.

1. The team was followed onto the field by the cheerleaders.
2. The pies were put into the oven by the cook's helper.
3. You are being defeated by your own carelessness.
4. She was given a horse by her grandparents.
5. The invitations will be sent out by your committee.
6. The plants were grown and sold by the students themselves.
7. The cars were towed away by the police.
8. Your grades have been turned in by your teachers.
9. A home for the victims is being built by the townspeople.
10. The fire was discovered by a passer-by.
11. The directions will be given out by the coach.
12. New rules have been written for the game by Ms. Hernandez.
13. The car was being worked on by two mechanics.
14. The uniforms were designed by members of the Pep Club.
15. The winner was given a trophy by county sportswriters.

**B. Making verbs transitive** Write the numbers 1–10 on your paper. Rewrite each of the following sentences by adding a direct object to make the verb transitive.

EXAMPLE: Our students have entered every year.
ANSWER: Our students have entered the contest every year.

1. My grandmother painted for a living.
2. We were able to win only because we had practiced.
3. The farmer was still plowing after the sun had set.
4. Have you finished?

5. By next week everyone will have read.
6. The appointed committees have been planning.
7. Someone should be able to improve.
8. He can cook.
9. The custodians have cleaned.
10. Have the new nations signed?

**C. Distinguishing between active and passive** Write the numbers 1–10 on your paper. Copy the verb or verb phrase from each sentence. Indicate how the forms of the verbs are used by writing *active* or *passive* after the verb.

EXAMPLE: The European nations are ready for the changeover.
ANSWER: are: active

1. The scouts have been promised a trip this year.
2. Our parents have been waiting for our return.
3. The investigators will be prompt with their report.
4. Someone will be waiting there to meet you.
5. I am happy with the results.
6. Once a year I am ready for a long vacation.
7. All the mice were being counted as a precaution.
8. The children were being more patient than their parents.
9. She was discouraged from entering the races.
10. We were very discouraged by the results.

# REVIEWING LESSONS 8–10

**A. Correcting fragments by adding transitive verbs**  Write the numbers 1–10 on your paper. Rewrite each of the following sentence fragments into a fully expressed sentence by adding a transitive verb, its object, and any other phrases necessary for meaning.

EXAMPLE:  How many times will you?
ANSWER:  How many times will you make excuses for him?

1. All our neighbors have.
2. Evidently no one here will.
3. Not one hiker on the trail.
4. Someone in my family can.
5. Surprisingly enough, most visitors will.
6. A lonely traveler, far from home.
7. No one in the camp should.
8. With a few more hours of practice, I could.
9. People in that town used to.
10. The people on our block, after every snowstorm.

**B. Using correct verb forms**  Write the numbers 1–15 on your paper. Write the form of the verb in parentheses needed to complete each sentence.

EXAMPLE:  Every day she (drink) a quart of milk with dinner.
ANSWER:  drinks

1. What do you think my cat (drag) into the house yesterday?
2. I (know) you would be late for your appointment.
3. How often has that horse been (ride)?
4. He very carefully (weave) his initials into the pattern.
5. I wish they hadn't (choose) that song.
6. The crane (swing) from the deck of the ship to the dock.
7. Have you ever (dive) before?
8. They have (eat) almost everything in sight.
9. It's hard to believe she (grow) that much in one year.
10. Their parents (buy) them everything they needed for the trip.
11. Why do you suppose she (bring) that with her?
12. Who (burst) into the room while you were speaking?
13. We (do) what we had to do to save the situation.
14. Our coach (swim) with us while she was teaching us.
15. Have you ever (drive) that far alone?

**C. Making action progressive** Write the numbers 1-10 on your paper. Rewrite each of the following sentences. Make the action of the verb progressive but keep the same tense.

EXAMPLE: They will work in the mines all summer.
ANSWER: They will be working in the mines all summer.

1. He tried to stop the runaway horses.
2. What will you do next year at this time?
3. That new player is watched closely during every game.
4. How long have they stood in line for tickets?
5. The drivers had walked a picket line for three weeks.
6. He works as a volunteer in a children's hospital.
7. A new schedule is planned for the late entrants.
8. I do this out of loyalty, not fear.
9. What makes you so nervous?
10. Is a new plan of attack considered?

**D. Identifying verbs, their tense, and voice** Write the numbers 1-10 on your paper. Copy the verb or verb phrase from each sentence. After the verb, write its tense and voice.

EXAMPLE: Why have you removed your name from the list?
ANSWER: have removed: present perfect, active.

1. They will be sorry the rest of their lives.
2. The extra equipment was stored in the locker room.
3. Why have you been warned so many times?
4. You are certainly not helping with such an attitude.
5. Had she never accepted your advice before that time?
6. Wasn't the evidence destroyed in that last fire?
7. The food is then frozen in an airtight container.
8. How many autographs will you have collected by then?
9. I am being selected to represent all the minors.
10. Will they ever move back here?

# A LOOK AT ADJECTIVES

## 11

## Characteristics of Adjectives

An **adjective** is a word that describes a noun or its substitute. It often tells *what kind*.

- The *angry* man stormed out of the *quiet* room, stood in the *hot* street, and gazed at the *dark* sky.

**Placement**   An adjective need not precede a noun. It may also be positioned immediately after a noun or after a verb. Notice the positions of the adjectives in the following sentences.

- The *loose* bricks were a *dangerous* menace.
- The girls, *cold* and *hungry,* were *happy* to be home.
- The tracks on his lawn looked *odd* and *suspicious*.

### Kinds of Adjectives

The most common adjectives and the easiest to identify are **descriptive adjectives**: *tall, strong, neat, thin, sharp, young.*

Many descriptive adjectives are formed from other parts of speech through the use of adjective-forming suffixes. Following is a list of these suffixes with examples.

-able, (-ble, -ible): soluble, trainable, credible
-al: typical, annual, comical
-atic (-etic): pathetic, dogmatic, aromatic
-ful: harmful, shameful, beautiful
-ial: magisterial, custodial, menial
-ic: volcanic, oceanic, photographic
-ile: infantile, docile, fragile
-ish: bookish, reddish, childish

> -ive: creative, festive, pensive
> -less: careless, homeless, thoughtless
> -like: homelike, childlike, lifelike
> -ous (-ious): glorious, marvelous, hideous

Adjectives that *point out* are called **demonstrative adjectives.** They are the same words that can be demonstrative pronouns, but because they modify nouns, they are called demonstrative adjectives.

DEMONSTRATIVE PRONOUNS:   *This* is older than *that.*
DEMONSTRATIVE ADJECTIVES:   *This* statue is older than *that* painting.
DEMONSTRATIVE PRONOUNS:   I need *these,* but I like *those.*
DEMONSTRATIVE ADJECTIVES:   I need *these* shoes, but I like *those* boots.

Adjectives may also tell *how many.* When numbers are used as adjectives to tell *how many,* they are called **numerical adjectives.**

- *Four* boys and *six* girls sit in the *third* row.

Other adjectives that tell *how many* are **indefinite adjectives,** which indicate an indefinite amount or number.

- It took *many* members *several* days to earn a *few* dollars.

Some indefinite adjectives tell *how much.*

- It takes *more* time but no *less* effort to gain *some* respect.

Just as there are possessive pronouns, which tell *whose,* so there are **possessive adjectives** that tell *whose.* Possessive adjectives modify nouns while possessive pronouns take the place of nouns.

POSSESSIVE PRONOUNS:   Rover ran out of *ours* into *yours.*
POSSESSIVE ADJECTIVES:   Rover ran out of *our* yard to chase *your* cat.

An adjective that is used to ask a question is called an **interrogative adjective.**

- *Whose* car did you borrow?
- *Which* road did you follow?
- *What* time did you get home?

The smallest but the most common adjectives are the three that are called **articles**: *a, an,* and *the.* Their function is to signal the coming of a noun or a noun substitute.

- *A* person walked into *the* room and asked for *an* envelope.

Words sometimes function as adjectives but don't look like adjectives. For example, in the sentence "There were tire marks on the road," the word *tire* functions as an adjective. Out of context, however, the word may look like a noun to you. If you look up tire in a dictionary, you will find it classified as a noun or verb. Similarly, in the sentence "The falling rocks hit our car," the word *falling* functions as an adjective. It describes a noun—even though, out of context, it looks like a verb.

## EXERCISES

**A.** Identifying adjectives   Write the numbers 1–10 on your paper. Copy all the adjectives from each of the following sentences. After each adjective write *descriptive, demonstrative, numerical, indefinite, interrogative,* or *possessive.*

EXAMPLE:   At that moment we didn't feel very courageous.
ANSWER:   that: demonstrative; courageous: descriptive

1. The loose bricks in this old building are a dangerous menace.
2. The small dogs in her yard are frisky and noisy.
3. The yellow bird sat in the leafless tree.
4. What reason did your new employee give for her sudden disappearance?
5. Those people are the two nurses I told you about.
6. Which record would please a person with classical tastes?
7. The twenty-three sick tropical fish were put in a separate tank.
8. Her three youngest children have dark curly hair and blue eyes.
9. We followed the narrow, slippery path to the edge of a misty lagoon.
10. He felt ill and preferred to stay at home in his room.

**B.** Forming adjectives from other parts of speech   Write the numbers 1–20 on your paper. Add one of the adjective-forming suffixes to each of the following words to form an acceptable adjective. Check your spelling with a dictionary.

EXAMPLE:   memory—memorable

| | | | |
|---|---|---|---|
| 1. comfort | 6. nerve | 11. hilarity | 16. vindicate |
| 2. idealist | 7. sense | 12. consume | 17. allow |
| 3. care | 8. analogy | 13. villain | 18. optimist |
| 4. venom | 9. secretary | 14. combat | 19. baby |
| 5. joy | 10. zeal | 15. value | 20. acrobat |

**C. Adding adjectives to sentences** Improve the following sentences by adding interesting adjectives to modify the italicized nouns.

EXAMPLE: The *dog* crouched in the *corner* behind the *chair*.
ANSWER: The frightened little dog crouched in the dark corner behind the huge, overstuffed chair.

1. The *man* walked across the *street*.
2. The *stars* in the *sky* looked like *lights*.
3. The *people* in our *neighborhood* own *animals*.
4. The *children* left the *playground* early.
5. Her *home* is by the *river*.
6. The *books* are always found on the *shelves*.
7. *Activity* builds *muscles*.
8. A *stranger* came into *town*.
9. The *accident* was a *sight*.
10. The *girls* enjoy *games*.

**D. Describing with adjectives** Write the numbers 1–10 on your paper. Look closely at the following picture. Write ten adjectives that describe the tree.

# 12

# More About Adjectives

**Compound adjectives**   Many adjectives are formed by joining two or more words into a single descriptive **compound adjective**. Some of these compounds are written as one word; others are written with a hyphen to join the words. When you are not sure how to write a compound adjective, check a current dictionary. You cannot find all of them in a dictionary, however, because new ones are coined everyday. Following are some compound adjectives.

| breathtaking | far-reaching | high-hat |
| money-hungry | footloose | narrow-minded |
| deep-seated | hair-raising | handwoven |

**Comparison of adjectives**   An adjective can be used to describe a person or thing without comparison with another person or thing. Such an adjective is in the **positive degree:** *sweet*.

- This fruit drink is *sweet*.

But it is possible to compare the sweetness of the drink with another drink. To do this, you use the adjective in the **comparative degree,** which is usually formed by adding *-er* to the positive degree.

- This fruit drink is *sweeter* than that one.

You can also compare the quality of one thing with all the others in a group by using the adjective in the **superlative degree.** The superlative is usually formed by adding *-est* to the positive degree.

- This fruit drink is the *sweetest* one they sell.

If the adjective has more than two syllables or already has a suffix, the comparative degree is formed by using *more* or *less*. To form the superlative degree of such adjectives, precede them with *most* or *least*.

| Positive | Comparative | Superlative |
|---|---|---|
| happy | happier | happiest |
| sad | sadder | saddest |
| beautiful | more beautiful | most beautiful |
| zealous | less zealous | least zealous |

Some adjectives have irregular comparative and superlative forms.

| Positive | Comparative | Superlative |
|---|---|---|
| bad | worse | worst |
| good | better | best |
| little | less | least |
| many | more | most |

Use the comparative degree to compare *two* persons or things.

- He may be *stronger* than I, but I am *faster* than he.
- Which of the twins is *taller,* Mary or Beth?

Use the superlative degree to compare *more* than two persons or things.

- Today is the *longest* day of the year but not the *coldest.*
- That is our *most powerful* bow and our *most expensive.*

When you use the comparative degree to compare a person or thing with a group, you sometimes have to use *any other* to exclude from the group the person or thing being compared.

- This book is more interesting than *any* television program.
- This book is more interesting than *any other* book.

Some adjectives are absolute in their description and do not have comparative forms. For example, something can't be *rounder* than something else. To compare an absolute, use *almost, more nearly,* or *most nearly.*

POSITIVE: This apple is *almost round.*
COMPARATIVE: This apple is *more nearly round* than that one.
SUPERLATIVE: This apple is the *most nearly round* one of all.

Following are some other absolute adjectives.

| | | | |
|---|---|---|---|
| complete | full | pure | vacant |
| perfect | empty | dead | whole |

## EXERCISES

**A. Using hyphenated compound adjectives** Write the numbers 1–5 on your paper. Complete each of the following sentences by using a hyphenated compound adjective from the list.

*awe-struck*   *record-breaking*   *spine-chilling*
*half-baked*   *deep-sea*   *middle-aged*

1. Your idea is _____; it is not completely thought out.
2. The view is so beautiful that it makes me _____.
3. This ghost story is _____.
4. I love watching Jacques Cousteau's _____ adventures on television.
5. The temperature hit a _____ low today.

**B. Choosing the correct adjective form** Write the numbers 1–10 on your paper. For each of the following sentences, write the correct form of the adjective in parentheses.

EXAMPLE:   Her cold is (worse, more bad) than mine.
ANSWER:   worse

1. Which of the pair is (sturdiest, sturdier)?
2. Our gas tank is (fuller, more nearly full) than yours.
3. This picture is (prettier, more pretty) than that one.
4. Of the two books, this one is (more interesting, most interesting).
5. That mountain stream has the (purest, most nearly pure) water I have ever drunk.
6. She is the (powerfullest, most powerful) swimmer in the group.
7. That is the (worst, baddest) movie ever made.
8. He may be older than I, but I am (taller, tallest).
9. She is the (narrow-mindedest, most narrow-minded) person I've ever known.
10. This plant is (deader, more nearly dead) than that African violet.

**C. Making comparisons with adjectives** Write the numbers 1–10 on your paper. For each of the following sentences, write the comparative or superlative form of the adjective in parentheses.

EXAMPLE: My father is _____ than his brother. (old)
ANSWER: older

1. Jeanne is the _____ of the two girls. (wise)
2. Your accident was _____ than ours. (serious)
3. The oak is the _____ tree in our yard. (sturdy)
4. Her performance was _____ than his. (perfect)
5. My mother is the _____ of my parents. (young)
6. That cough is _____ than it was yesterday. (bad)
7. Most animals are _____ than most humans. (intelligent)
8. That is the _____ of all our worries. (little)
9. He seems to be _____ than he used to be. (childish)
10. _____ people attended on Saturday than on Sunday. (many)

# ADVERBS IN ACTION

## 13

## Characteristics of Adverbs

An **adverb** is a word that describes or modifies a verb by telling *how, when,* or *where*. The three types of adverbs are often referred to as **adverbs of manner** (how), **adverbs of time** (when), and **adverbs of place** (where).

### ADVERBS

| Manner | Time | Place |
|---|---|---|
| diligently | suddenly | there |
| silently | sometime | down |
| softly | then | here |
| carefully | soon | anywhere |
| fast | never | somewhere |
| well | always | forward |
| badly | presently | ahead |
| hard | often | away |

Look at the following sentences.

- Carlotta works
- Gabriel disappeared.
- My boss lives.

You could ask *how, when,* and *where* about all those sentences, and your questions could be answered with adverbs.

- Carlotta works *diligently*.
- Gabriel disappeared *suddenly*.
- My boss lives *there*.

A distinguishing sign of most adverbs of manner and some adverbs of time is the *-ly* ending, which has been added to an adjective to make it an adverb.

Another distinctive feature of many adverbs is their ability to be positioned in the beginning, the middle, or the end of a sentence.

- *Then* the crew repaired the road.
- The crew *then* repaired the road.
- The crew repaired the road *then*.

Intensifiers   There is a special group of adverbs that do not modify verbs. Instead, they modify adjectives or other adverbs. Some grammarians call them **intensifiers** because they strengthen (intensify) adjectives and other adverbs: *most* beautiful, *very* quickly. Following are other adverbs of this type.

| less | truly | actually |
| --- | --- | --- |
| least | rather | somewhat |
| quite | utterly | extremely |
| more | too | exceedingly |
| so | unusually | notoriously |

## EXERCISES

A. **Identifying adverbs in sentences**   Write the numbers 1–10 on your paper. Copy all the adverbs from each sentence. A sentence may have as few as one adverb or as many as four.

EXAMPLE:   Time passed slowly as we sat there and waited for them.
ANSWER:   slowly, there

1. Suddenly the door opened, and in walked a most unusual cat.
2. Angrily he pounded the table until everyone sat down.
3. Suddenly she turned around, put the book down, and walked out.
4. A heavy fog rolled in, and we were hopelessly lost.
5. Very young children always know when a holiday is near.
6. Work carefully so your paper will be neat and legible.
7. If you work well, you can expect a raise soon.
8. She came over to me and spoke softly about my being there.
9. Nowhere could I find a more exact reproduction.
10. It fits you perfectly, but you know it is too expensive.

**B. Adding adverbs to sentences** Write the numbers 1-10 on your paper. Complete each of the following sentences by writing adverbs in place of the blanks.

EXAMPLE: It was _____ evident to us that she was _____ our boss.
ANSWER: It was quite evident to us that she was now our boss.

1. _____ we go to the park and sit _____ for hours.
2. She is _____ sick to have visitors _____ .
3. Your suit is _____ beautiful but _____ practical.
4. She _____ can sing _____ even if she can't sing _____ .
5. The _____ poised host moved _____ among the guests.
6. _____ the wind picked it _____ and carried it _____ .
7. While you were _____ , did you go _____ or _____ ?
8. Come _____ and you will be able to hear _____ _____ .
9. We heard a noise _____ and went _____ to investigate.
10. I have it _____ hidden _____ in the attic.

**C. Forming adverbs from adjectives** Write the numbers 1-20 on your paper. Write the adverbs you form when you add -ly to the following adjectives. Check your answers with a dictionary if you are not sure about spelling changes.

EXAMPLE: weary
ANSWER: wearily

1. faithful
2. joyous
3. courteous
4. sincere
5. light
6. easy
7. true
8. simple
9. active
10. free
11. cheery
12. mild
13. beautiful
14. professional
15. angry
16. different
17. glad
18. visible
19. odd
20. speedy

# 14

## More About Adverbs

**Interrogative adverbs**  Just as you can use interrogative pronouns and adjectives to introduce questions, so can you use **interrogative adverbs**. The four interrogative adverbs that are used most often are *when, where, how* and *why*.

- *When* will I see you again?
- *Where* did you find it?
- *How* will you know the difference?
- *Why* do you really want to go?

**Not**  In a class by itself is the adverb *not*. Its chief use is to make a verb negative. *Not* is often used as part of a contraction.

- He is *not* going. He is*n't* going.
- I call her Bonnie, *not* Jean.

*Not* can also be used with an adjective or another adverb.

- *Not* many boys have his talent.
- She sings loudly but *not* well.

Since *not* is already negative, it should never be used with *no, none, nothing, only, scarcely,* or *hardly*. Use the following sentences as models.

- I have*n't any* paper.
- They *have scarcely* any room.

**Conjunctive adverbs**  A common use of the adverb is to form a *transition* between sentences, to *link* the idea of one sentence to the next. An adverb used in this way is called a **conjunctive adverb**.

- He had wanted to stay longer; *however,* we reminded him that the ride to the airport would take two hours. *Furthermore,* he hadn't bought his ticket in advance.

Following is a list of commonly used conjunctive adverbs.

| | | | | |
|---|---|---|---|---|
| moreover | further | furthermore | besides | likewise |
| similarly | therefore | accordingly | consequently | otherwise |
| thus | thereupon | meanwhile | still | |

**Comparison of adverbs**  An adverb has three degrees just as an adjective does: *positive, comparative,* and *superlative.* When you want to compare how two things or people do something, use the **comparative degree**.

- Jenny can run *faster* than Lisa if she starts *sooner.*

If the positive degree of the adverb has one syllable, form the comparative by adding *-er.* If the adverb has more than one syllable, use *more.*

    late, later    fast, faster    rapidly, more rapidly

Use the **superlative degree** of an adverb to compare how more than two things or people do something. For adverbs that end in *-er* in the comparative, use *-est* to form the superlative. For adverbs that have *more* in the comparative, use *most* to form the superlative.

    fast, faster, fastest    neatly, more neatly, most neatly

**Adverb or adjective?**  Many words in English can be either adverbs or adjectives. If the word modifies a noun or a noun substitute, it is an adjective. If it modifies a verb, an adjective, or another adverb, it is an adverb.

| Adjectives | Adverbs |
|---|---|
| This is a *better* book. | You are working *better* today. |
| That is a *hard* lesson. | Don't try so *hard* next time. |
| She is a *fast* runner. | She can really run *fast.* |
| Go to the *far* corner. | You don't have to run *far.* |

Use an adjective after a linking verb to modify the subject but an adverb to modify an action verb to tell *how, when,* or *where.*

- That *is* perfect. (linking verb)
- That *fits* perfectly. (action verb)

# EXERCISES

**A. Correcting errors in the use of adverbs** Write the numbers 1–10 on your paper. Rewrite the following sentences, correcting any errors in the use of adverbs.

1. I have used both brands, but I like this one best.
2. Your car runs more smoother than mine.
3. Of all the students in class, Maria writes better.
4. I talked with several people, but I enjoyed my conversation with her more.
5. The twins both study, but Meg concentrates best.
6. You couldn't have done it much worser.
7. She swims faster than any girl on her team.
8. They are working more harder now than they used to.
9. The three of them tried out, but Joel sang better.
10. They enjoy pizzas more than any food.

**B. Choosing between adjectives and adverbs** Write the numbers 1–10 on your paper. For each of the following sentences write the correct modifier from the parentheses.

1. A (heavy, heavily) built man stepped on my toe.
2. I am certain you feel (bad, badly) about this mistake.
3. She was so nervous she couldn't play very (good, well).
4. The two dogs fought (fierce, fiercely).
5. The girl was (beautiful, beautifully) in her graduation gown.
6. The man stared (angry, angrily) at the intruders.
7. The blind child felt (careful, carefully) along the stone wall.
8. The Iowa farmers grow corn very (good, well).
9. The flowers in the greenhouse grow (beautiful, beautifully).
10. The early corn tastes especially (sweet, sweetly).

**C. Using comparative forms** Write the numbers 1–5 on your paper. For each of the following sentences, write the correct form of the adjective or adverb in italics. If the modifier is already correct, write *C*.

1. I can work *easily* with you than with him.
2. The girl throws the ball *straight* than he.
3. They go on trips *often* than we.
4. Of all the animals, this one runs *fast*.
5. The guide gave *good* directions to them than to us.

# REVIEWING LESSONS 11-14

**A. Distinguishing between pronouns and adjectives** Write the numbers 1-15 on your paper. Copy the italicized word from each sentence. Then write whether it is a pronoun or an adjective. If it is an adjective, write the word it modifies.

EXAMPLE: *Whose* car is that?
ANSWER: whose: adjective, car

1. Would you please hand me *that* fork.
2. We have ordered *some* replacements.
3. Your tools are *these* on the bench.
4. I don't have *any* reason not to go.
5. *Which* of the two will last longer?
6. After the game they took *theirs*.
7. Only a *few* neighbors came to pay their respects.
8. I think I would give *ours* a second chance.
9. *Those* of you who are going will meet in the parking lot.
10. She can't decide *which* camera is the best buy.
11. *Seven* were in the car that I drove.
12. The cause of *that* is still a mystery to us all.
13. If you are sure you have enough, I'll take *some*.
14. *More* couples came to the party than we had expected.
15. I would like to buy *those* shoes in the window.

**B. Completing sentences by adding adjectives** Write the numbers 1-10 on your paper. Complete each of the following sentences by using appropriate adjectives for each blank.

EXAMPLE: _____ _____ students seem _____ and _____.
ANSWER: The new students seem friendly and cooperative.

1. _____ _____ brothers are working in _____ _____ mine.
2. _____ _____ animals hid in _____ _____ and wouldn't eat.
3. _____ gloves will look _____ with _____ _____ coat.
4. If _____ members drop out, _____ more can join.
5. _____ soup tastes _____ on _____ _____ day.
6. If you are _____, why don't you drink _____ _____ milk?
7. _____ _____ noises coming from _____ _____ house worried us.
8. _____ _____ children pressed _____ _____ noses against _____ _____ glass.

9. Then _____ _____ stranger entered _____ _____ room and disappeared.
10. _____ and _____ leaves fell from _____ _____ tree.

**C. Correcting errors in the use of adjectives** Write the numbers 1–20 on your paper. For each of the following sentences, correct all errors in the use of adjectives.

EXAMPLE: When I saw the two of them, I couldn't tell who was oldest.
ANSWER: older

1. The stronger boy in the group offered to help the others.
2. This suit fits me better than any I have tried on.
3. Why don't you take a apple for lunch?
4. Your diagram is more square than mine.
5. The news was more later than usual last night.
6. The baby's cold was worser yesterday.
7. Ralph is the oldest of their two sons.
8. The team played their most goodest game on Saturday.
9. I tried both toothpastes, and I like this one best.
10. She likes apples better than any fruit.
11. This was the taller of the three on the shelf.
12. He is the bashfulest of all our children.
13. My family likes our Irish setter better than any dog we have had.
14. Which of your feet is the biggest?
15. If you are comparing her with the principal, I think she is the best.
16. Of all the sports, I still like golf better.
17. She is the creativest member of our class.
18. That is the most homeliest dog I have ever seen.
19. Which of your two gifts do you like best?
20. That is the less objectionable of all your tricks.

**D. Correcting errors in the use of adjectives and adverbs** Write the numbers 1–20 on your paper. For each of the following sentences, correct any errors in the use of adverbs and adjectives. If a sentence contains no error, write *C*.

EXAMPLE: We have hardly no money left.
ANSWER: hardly any

1. She can jump as far as any boy.
2. The frost sparkled dim in the moonlight.

3. He can play good when he tries.
4. The team felt very badly about not winning the championship.
5. You are much younger than she.
6. The sun suddenly disappeared from our view.
7. You make your circles rounder than I do.
8. Which of the twins do you think is the most reliable?
9. No one is more disappointed than we.
10. The lost boy felt sadly as he walked along the street.
11. It looks much more prettier in that color.
12. She reached the shore more soon than he.
13. It was real kind of you to help us.
14. Surprisingly, the smallest of the two is stronger.
15. He is more alert than any boy in his scout troop.
16. Your coffee smells more strongly this morning.
17. More faster than an eagle it soared into the blue.
18. They really don't need no more food.
19. A rapid falling tree hit the car.
20. I can't hardly hear what you are saying.

**E. Using adjectives and adverbs** Write the numbers 1–15 on your paper. Complete each sentence by writing an adjective or adverb for each blank.

EXAMPLE: The _____ child seemed _____.
ANSWER: The youngest child seemed smart.

1. The dog, _____ and _____, leaped over the fence.
2. _____ all the children did the lesson _____.
3. They _____ study unless they think the test will be _____.
4. Do they use a _____ knife?
5. We haven't _____ tools to do the job _____.
6. _____ trees would make the place look _____.
7. _____ _____ animals were waiting to be fed.
8. They could _____ tell how _____ people there were.
9. There are _____ many chairs for a room _____ size.
10. When you have to work _____, dinner may be _____.
11. When she gets _____, she will be _____.
12. I have _____ one word of advice for you _____.
13. Quite _____ he turned _____ and walked out.
14. You will have to be _____ if you expect to be treated _____.
15. The car going _____ will be left _____.

# PREPOSITIONS

## 15

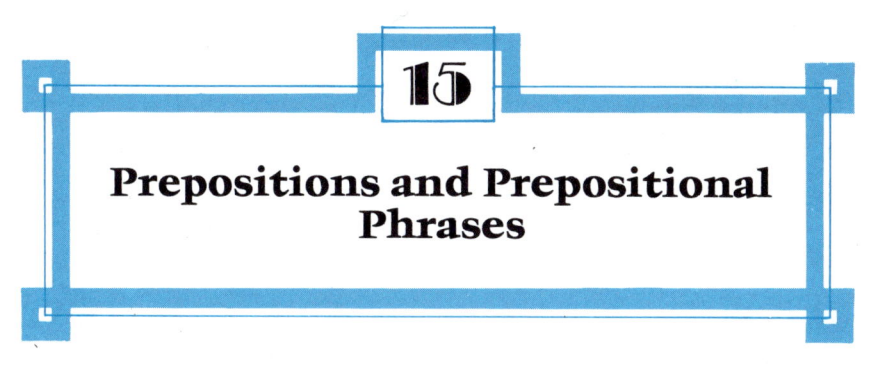

## Prepositions and Prepositional Phrases

A **preposition** is a part of speech used to link its object (a noun or noun substitute) with another part of a clause or sentence. For example, if you wish to tell where Ana *sat,* and *sofa* is the noun you wish to use, the only way to show the relationship between *the sofa* and *sat* is with a preposition.

- Ana sat *on* the sofa.

The noun or noun substitute that follows the preposition is called the **object of the preposition.** In the above sentence *sofa* is the object of the preposition *on.*

There are many prepositions in the English language. Since you cannot use a preposition unless it has an object, a good way to remember the most common prepositions is by thinking of them in relation to an object, such as a *desk.* Each of the prepositions in the following list can use *desk* as an object as in *on the desk.*

| above | at | beside | in | of | out of | toward |
| across | behind | by | into | off | over | under |
| against | below | except | like | on | through | upon |
| around | beneath | from | near | onto | to | with |

There are many other commonly used prepositions. Some of them are given in the following list.

| about | because of | during | on account of |
| after | before | for | since |
| along | between | in back of | together with |
| alongside | concerning | in front of | until |
| among | down | in regard to | up |

**Prepositional phrase** A preposition with its object and object modifiers is called a **prepositional phrase**. The following are some examples of prepositional phrases.

- during the early hours
- with Jo and her friends (two objects for one preposition)
- up and down the coast (two prepositions with one object)

You can use prepositional phrases to avoid writing short, choppy sentences. Prepositional phrases can make your writing and speaking smoother and more mature.

CHOPPY: She washed the car. She used a sponge.
SMOOTH: She washed the car *with a sponge.*

## EXERCISES

**A. Identifying prepositional phrases** Write the numbers 1–10 on your paper. Copy the prepositional phrase from each of the following sentences. Underline the preposition once and the object of the preposition twice.

EXAMPLE: Hang this on the wall.
ANSWER: on the wall

1. It's the remains of a ship.
2. We got into the canoe.
3. What's on that mountain?
4. I can't get the umbrella out of its case.
5. He keeps it beside the closet.
6. Put the envelope under the papers.
7. Above the clouds we flew.
8. Let's meet at the store or the luncheonette.
9. Let's meet at or before ten o'clock.
10. She went with us.

**B. Using prepositional phrases** Write the numbers 1–10 on your paper. Combine each of the following pairs of sentences into a single sentence by using a prepositional phrase.

EXAMPLE: She ran into the garage. She wanted a hammer.
ANSWER: She ran into the garage for a hammer.

1. All the students studied. Eli did not.
2. I visited my grandparents. They live in the country.

3. A woman came to see us. She was from the Mayor's office.
4. Buy yourself a car. Get one with dual carburetors.
5. She overpowered the thief. She used a broom.
6. The child was afraid. He feared snakes.
7. He left early. He had another appointment.
8. I saw an accident. It happened at our intersection.
9. The game was called off. It had started to rain.
10. Go the quickest way. Use the back streets.

**Finding prepositional phrases**   Read the following passage. Copy all the prepositional phrases that you find. There are thirteen of them. Do not include *of Wales* and *of England;* they are parts of titles.

> *The wild free ways of the plains were represented to the entire world by Buffalo Bill Cody's American Wild West show, which played to packed grandstands in Europe, England, and the United States for nearly thirty years. Star performer of the show, next to Cody himself, was Annie Oakley, "Little Sure Shot," the champion sharpshooter of all time, shown here being presented at London to Edward the Prince of Wales, later King of England, and Princess Alexandra. Born in Darke County, Ohio, Annie had never seen the prairie until the Wild West visited Omaha.* —Lucius Beebe and Charles Clegg

# 16

## Adverb, Preposition, or Verb?

Several words that are commonly used as prepositions can also be used as adverbs. However, if you remember that a word cannot be a preposition unless it has an object, you will be able to distinguish between adverbs and prepositions. The examples in the following chart show this difference.

| Adverbs | Prepositions |
|---|---|
| Her friends went *along*. | They walked *along the beach*. |
| Please keep *off*. | Please keep *off the grass*. |
| We went *across*. | We went *across the lake*. |
| They looked *around*. | They looked *around the tents*. |

In written sentences, the second word in a two-word verb may look very much like a preposition. However, if you examine the sentence closely, you will realize that you would change the meaning of the verb if you interpret the word as a preposition.

PART OF A TWO-WORD VERB:  Please look *over* my report.
PREPOSITION:   If you look *over the side* you can see the water.

Other two-word verbs are:

| | | |
|---|---|---|
| put forth (grow) | fall behind (lag) | hunt down (pursue) |
| put in (spend) | watch over (tend) | look up (locate) |
| put up (preserve) | turn up (find) | look out (be careful) |
| close out (exclude) | | throw out (remove) |

# EXERCISES

**A. Changing adverbs into prepositions** Write the numbers 1–10 on your paper. For each of the following sentences, change the italicized adverb into a preposition by building a prepositional phrase.

EXAMPLE: I saw you fall *down*.
ANSWER: I saw you fall down the ramp.

1. They decided to go *up*.
2. I've never seen her *before*.
3. Will you please keep *off*?
4. We will meet you *after*.
5. Try not to fall *behind*.
6. They pulled up *alongside*.
7. They were looking all *about*.
8. It will be safe *inside*.
9. Please be standing *near*.
10. Why don't you take a trip *over*?

**B. Identifying adverbs, prepositions, and verbs** Write the numbers 1–15 on your paper. For each of the following sentences, write whether the italicized word is used as an *adverb*, a *preposition*, or *part of a two-word verb*.

EXAMPLE: He certainly takes *after* his father.
ANSWER: part of a two-word verb

1. Please look *after* the children.
2. They plan to stop *over* in Chicago.
3. Turn the board *over* before you saw it.
4. It is not wise to come *between* friends.
5. I was sitting *between* two friends.
6. Please put *out* the lights.
7. Have you ever wanted to take *up* golf?
8. What goes *up* must come down.
9. Their dog chased our cat *up* a tree.
10. I hope she doesn't stay *out* late again tonight.
11. *Out* this window you can see the mountains.
12. I do hope everything will work *out* all right.
13. Do you think you can put *across* that idea?
14. If you come *across* one again, please get it for me.
15. We had to drive *across* the frozen lake.

**C. Replacing adjectives and adverbs with phrases** Write the numbers 1–10 on your paper. Rewrite each of the following sentences. Substitute a prepositional phrase for the italicized adjective or adverb.

EXAMPLE: A *southerly* breeze would be welcome.
ANSWER: A breeze from the south would be welcome.

1. She put a *leather* patch on each knee.
2. Make a *left* turn when you get there.
3. Work *speedily* and *accurately*.
4. Please sit *there*.
5. We started out *penniless*.
6. The *river* trout have a sweeter taste.
7. We have reason to envy the *country* people.
8. You will have to put it *somewhere*.
9. Children who go *here* should know better.
10. The *factory* wages are much higher.

# OTHER PARTS OF SPEECH

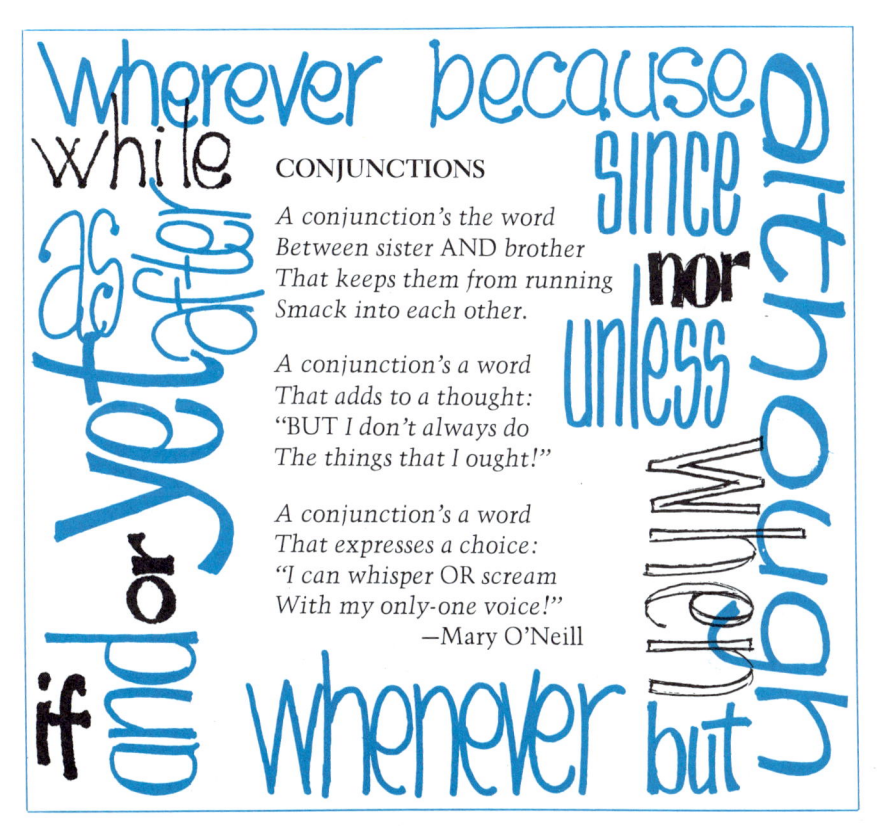

## 17 Conjunctions

**CONJUNCTIONS**

A conjunction's the word
Between sister AND brother
That keeps them from running
Smack into each other.

A conjunction's a word
That adds to a thought:
"BUT I don't always do
The things that I ought!"

A conjunction's a word
That expresses a choice:
"I can whisper OR scream
With my only-one voice!"
—Mary O'Neill

As the poem explains, a **conjunction** is a word that joins words or groups of words. The conjunctions that join words or groups of words of *equal rank* to form compounds are called **coordinating conjunctions**: *and, but, or, nor, yet.*

- The lions *and* tigers were in cages. (compound subject)
- He studied hard *but* failed the test. (compound predicate)
- The leader will visit Tony *or* Andrea. (compound object)

The coordinating conjunction may also join entire sentences to form a **compound sentence.** By building compound sentences you can avoid writing short, choppy simple sentences, as the following example illustrates.

- Marty apologized. Ramona still didn't forgive him.
- Marty apologized, *yet* Ramona didn't forgive him.

Some conjunctions may be used in pairs to connect words or groups of words. The pairs are known as **correlative conjunctions.**

- *Either* my father *or* I will be there to meet you.
- I will have *both* the lobster *and* the steak.
- We didn't know *whether* to laugh *or* to cry.
- They were *not only* pretty *but also* inexpensive.

Another type of conjunction is the **subordinating conjunction,** which is used to join words or groups of words of *unequal* rank. Following is a list of commonly used subordinating conjunctions.

| | | | | |
|---|---|---|---|---|
| as | whenever | because | since | while |
| if | where | though | after | until |
| when | wherever | although | before | unless |

A subordinating conjunction can make one group of words dependent on (or subordinate to) another word or group of words.

- She hid it *where no one can find it.*
- The children, *if they aren't late,* can eat first.
- *Until the law changes,* you are subject to arrest.

The purpose of subordinating conjunctions is to help a speaker or writer emphasize the main idea and subordinate the less important ideas. A common mistake is to make all ideas equal in importance either by writing only simple sentences or by using only coordinating conjunctions. A good rule is not to use a coordinating conjunction if you can use a subordinating conjunction.

POOR:   Diego was on a hike, *and* he lost his wallet.
IMPROVED:   Diego lost his wallet *when* he was on a hike.

# EXERCISES

**A. Using coordinating conjunctions**   Write the numbers 1-10 on your paper. Combine each of the following pairs of sentences into a single sentence by using a coordinating conjunction.

EXAMPLE:   Max washed the floors. He also polished them.
ANSWER:   Max washed and polished the floors.

1. Carla came in. She used my dictionary.
2. You should respect your mother. You should also respect your father.
3. Lily Mae washed the windows. She also scrubbed the floors.
4. Nancy stayed at school. Leilani walked home.
5. He is talkative at home. He is talkative in school.
6. Anita will build the model. Joe will paint it.
7. The president was not present. Neither was the secretary.
8. Skiing is one of her favorite sports. Golf is the other.
9. He was not successful in baseball. He was successful in basketball.
10. The chairs were not shipped. Neither was the table.

**B. Using subordinate conjunctions**   Write the numbers 1-10 on your paper. Rewrite each of the following sentences. Eliminate the coordinating conjunction and use a subordinating conjunction to make the less important idea dependent on the main idea. Make any other necessary adjustments.

EXAMPLE:   There was no breeze, and we didn't go sailing.
ANSWER:   We didn't go sailing because there was no breeze.

1. I cleaned the house, and at the same time Sam cooked the dinner.
2. Danny did not feel well, but he went on the trip anyway.
3. The storm may not let up, and we may not be able to go.
4. You may see her before I do, and would you please ask her to call me?
5. Finish washing the car, and please wax it.
6. Take a shower first, and then enter the pool.
7. She knew our telephone number, and she never called us.
8. My brother gets a cold, and he has to stay home three days.
9. We finished our shopping, and then we went to a movie.
10. The principal came into the room, and everyone greeted her.

**C. Choosing between coordination and subordination**   Write the numbers 1-15 on your paper. If you think that the ideas in each pair of tences are equally important, use a coordinating conjunction to combine them. If one idea is dependent on the other, join it to the other by using a subordinating conjunction.

EXAMPLE: Her fever was high. We took her to the doctor.
ANSWER: Because her fever was high, we took her to the doctor.

1. They both failed French. They had not studied.
2. We made her our captain. She is a good leader.
3. Carole sold her skates. She bought a pair of skis.
4. Finish what you are doing. I will talk with you.
5. She was very nervous. She gave her speech.
6. He catches a cold. He stays home.
7. She cut the grass. She trimmed the hedges.
8. We often see him. More often we see her.
9. You want to buy it. You will need more money.
10. Louise is our neighbor. So is her mother.
11. She may lose her voice. You will have to sing her part.
12. Tom and Ramona don't quarrel anymore. They have become friends.
13. He came in late. His parents were waiting for him.
14. It was raining. We waited on the corner anyway.
15. He tried to slip out of class. The teacher saw him.

**D. Identifying kinds of conjunctions** Write the numbers 1–10 on your paper. For each sentence label the conjunctions used as *coordinating, correlative,* or *subordinating*.

EXAMPLE: The guppies *and* the mollies were put in separate tanks.
ANSWER: coordinating conjunction

1. I knocked on the door, *but* nobody was home.
2. I read biographies *whenever* I get the chance.
3. *Neither* Johnny Chang *nor* Suzie Chang came to class today.
4. They didn't come *because* they have the measles.
5. Have you ever read any books by Twain *or* Welty?
6. He can't go there *until* this afternoon.
7. They were *not only* hungry *but also* tired.
8. I like music, *yet* I can't sing a note.
9. Birds *and* reptiles fascinate me.
10. Don't eat it *if* you don't like it.

# 18

# Interjections

An **interjection** is a word or group of words used to express emotion. It has no grammatical connection to the rest of the sentence. Strong interjections usually stand alone with an exclamation mark as in the poem below. Mild interjections are usually included in sentences. When an interjection is part of a sentence, it is usually set off by a comma.

- Well, I guess I can make arrangements to go.

It is not possible to list every interjection in the English language since speakers and writers often coin interjections to suit their purposes. The following list, however, includes some of the commonly used interjections.

| oh  | well | gosh | whew     | goodness' sake   |
|-----|------|------|----------|------------------|
| ah  | wow  | help | darn     | for land's sake  |
| hey | alas | rats | goodness | good grief       |
| my  | drat | what | gracious | good heavens     |

**INTERJECTION**

An interjection is an exclamation
Independent of grammatical relation,
Expressing strong feeling or claiming attention:
Horrors! It was too horrible to mention!
Darling! What a beautiful dress!
Jeepers! Isn't this room a mess?

—Mary O'Neill

## EXERCISES

**A. Supplying interjections** Write the numbers 1–10 on your paper. For each of the following, write the interjection you think would appropriately complete the sentence. Use the interjections listed in this lesson.

EXAMPLE: _____, it is getting late.
ANSWER: Goodness, it is getting late.

1. _____! Get your dirty hands off my coat!
2. _____, that's nothing to worry about.
3. _____, so that is where you hid it.
4. _____! I'll never invite you again!
5. _____, child! Where have you been?
6. _____! You failed again?
7. _____, it's only a small scratch.
8. _____, I guess there's nothing else we can do.
9. _____! What a runner he is!
10. _____, I'm not really concerned.

**B. Writing appropriate interjections** Write the numbers 1–10 on your paper. For each of the following, write an interjection that expresses the named emotion.

EXAMPLE: fright
ANSWER: Help!

1. joy
2. anger
3. pity
4. satisfaction
5. sorrow
6. terror
7. surprise
8. dislike
9. impatience
10. enthusiasm

# REVIEWING LESSONS 15–18

**A. Using prepositional phrases** Write the numbers 1–15 on your paper. Rewrite each of the following sentences by restructuring the italicized part of it into a prepositional phrase. If there is a pair of sentences, combine them by changing the italicized one into a prepositional phrase. Make any other necessary changes.

EXAMPLE: They showed *that they appreciated our hospitality.*
ANSWER: They showed their appreciation of our hospitality.

1. I admire *the love that they have for adventure.*
2. The questions *that pertained to summer trips* were interesting.
3. I really don't like the wallpaper *that this room has.*
4. We all enjoy a good soup *that has dumplings.*
5. My sister cuts her own hair. *She uses a razor.*
6. We found a basket on the porch. *Apples are in it.*
7. It was a long poem. *It concerned whaling boats.*
8. My dog plays tag. *He uses a ball.*
9. They accepted their assignments. *The assignments put them in classes.*
10. The news surprised us. *It concerned your award.*
11. A group came in for sodas. *There were ten people.*
12. I have everyone's reservation. *I don't have Daniela's.*
13. We decided to play some games. *The games took skill.*
14. The time *that she arrives* is still not known.
15. We covered the flower beds. *We used some old sheets.*

**B. Supplying prepositional phrases to complete sentences** Write the numbers 1–10 on your paper. Write a prepositional phrase in place of each blank.

EXAMPLE: The flowers _____ were grown _____.
ANSWER: in the court, from seeds

1. The sandwiches _____ are _____.
2. It rained _____ and flooded some _____.
3. Three _____ were placed _____.
4. Most _____ took the trail _____.
5. Swimming _____ is like swimming _____.
6. I enjoy working _____ and vacationing _____.
7. My dog brings bones _____ and hides them _____.
8. _____ we all went _____.
9. Don't step _____ as you come _____.
10. _____ we found a nest _____.

**C. Identifying adverbs, prepositions, and conjunctions** Write the numbers 1–10 on your paper. Write whether the italicized word in each sentence is an *adverb*, a *preposition*, or a *conjunction*.

EXAMPLE: She left a week ago, and we haven't seen her *since*.
ANSWER: adverb

1. Where will you be *after* the meeting?
2. You should practice *until* you can play it.
3. *Before* you go, I want to show you something.
4. You have *until* tomorrow.
5. We haven't gone back *since* we moved from there.
6. The teacher asked that I stay *after*.
7. I'll talk with him *before* the game.
8. It has been only three hours *since* lunch.
9. *After* she had said it, it was too late.
10. I have seen him *before,* but I don't know where.

**D. Combining sentences** Write the numbers 1–10 on your paper. Write a single sentence for each set of short, choppy sentences. Use coordinating conjunctions or subordinating conjunctions.

EXAMPLE: He was short. He was thin. The girls all liked him.
ANSWER: He was short and thin, but the girls all liked him.

1. The cave was cold. It was dark. We still used it for shelter.
2. He may stop by. Tell him where I've gone.
3. They painted the walls. They painted the ceiling. Then they laid a new carpet.
4. Judy came to see me. Pablo came with her. They didn't stay very long.
5. Everybody stopped. Everybody watched me. I was putting up the birdhouse.
6. They served dinner. Then they showed their movies of Switzerland. They also showed movies of Austria.
7. Who collected the money? Who bought the gift? I was away.
8. You should water this plant every week. You should also mist it every day. You may get some blooms.
9. They say they liked it. They say they will go there again. I can't go with them.
10. I jumped off the T–bar. I took a bow. Everyone was cheering.

# KINDS OF PHRASES

## 19

## More About Prepositional Phrases

A **phrase** is a group of two or more words that does not contain its own subject and predicate.

NOUN PHRASE: *A friendly old dog* came to our house.
VERB PHRASE: We *will be working* late.
PREPOSITIONAL PHRASE: We can't go *without a leader*.

**Prepositional phrases** The prepositional phrase may be used as an adjective or an adverb.

As an adjective, it is used to modify a noun or noun substitute by telling *which one* or *what kind*.

AS AN ADJECTIVE: The cat with the long whiskers is mine.

As an adverb, a prepositional phrase is used to modify a verb by telling *how, when,* or *where*.

AS AN ADVERB: I walked along the city streets.

You can use prepositional phrases to reduce wordiness and make your sentences more direct. Notice how the italicized part of each of the following sentences is shortened to a prepositional phrase.

- The chair *that has a broken leg* was thrown out.
- The chair *with a broken leg* was thrown out.
- We will meet again *when we have our next vacation*.
- We will meet again *during our next vacation*.
- The girl *who is in that room* is my sister.
- The girl *in that room* is my sister.

## EXERCISES

**A. Identifying prepositional phrases** Write the numbers 1–10 on your paper. Copy only the prepositional phrase from each of the following sentences. After the phrase, write whether it functions as an *adjective* or as an *adverb*. Then write the word or words the phrase modifies.

EXAMPLE: We found a box of old pictures.
ANSWER: of old pictures: adjective, box

1. Your excuses for your absence are not acceptable.
2. Three slept in the truck.
3. They will finish it by tomorrow.
4. She was riding in a carriage.
5. The first signs of spring are the crocuses.
6. The tuna was served in a casserole.
7. I can face any amount of trouble.
8. The first poem is one of his.
9. Not one fish in that tank is a guppy.
10. We stayed in the cottage.

**B. Reducing sentences** Write the numbers 1–15 on your paper. Write an improved version of each of the following sentences by reducing the italicized part of each sentence to a prepositional phrase.

EXAMPLE: We have a summer cabin, *which is in the mountains.*
ANSWER: We have a summer cabin in the mountains.

1. Our family won't eat a cake *that has no frosting.*
2. You will need a rake *that has a long handle.*
3. A person *who has a car* may volunteer.
4. They stayed alert *while the game was being played.*
5. The flowers, *which are in that bed,* are for seed.
6. A car *that had its lights off* was parked across the street.
7. We live in the house *that has the red roof.*
8. We could easily hear the ones *who were in the next apartment.*
9. I prefer to use the mower *when the bag isn't on it.*
10. You'll be more comfortable in a shirt *that has no sleeves.*
11. She bought a shirt *that has a big collar.*
12. The boy *who had the gloves* made the snowballs.
13. The cat, *which is on the chair,* is a Siamese.
14. The cat *that is on the chair* is Siamese.
15. The soup, *which is listed on the menu,* is watery.

**C. Identifying noun and verb phrases** Write the numbers 1-10 on your paper. For each of the following sentences, copy every noun phrase and every verb phrase. Underline the noun phrases once and the verb phrases twice.

EXAMPLE: I have planted one hundred bulbs.
ANSWER: <u>have planted</u> <u>one hundred bulbs</u>

1. Blue jays don't fly south.
2. My youngest sister was playing the violin.
3. America's endangered animals should be protected.
4. Grandma Moses's paintings are being exhibited here.
5. Holly trees were planted.
6. Don't they read the daily newspapers?
7. My favorite books are historical novels.
8. She doesn't eat meat everyday.
9. Lazaro's cousin has built up a fine reptile collection.
10. Ariella was made class president.

# 20

# Infinitives and Infinitive Phrases

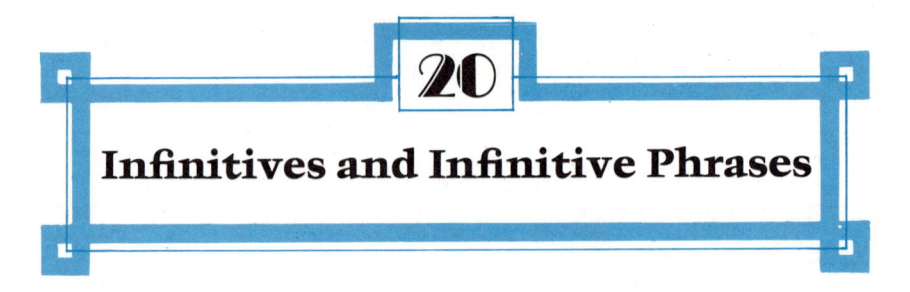

**Verbals** The chief function of a verb is to serve as the predicate of a sentence. However, there are verb forms that can serve as nouns, adjectives, or as adverbs. When any verb form substitutes as another part of speech, it is called a **verbal**.

**Infinitives** The most useful of the verbals is the **infinitive** because it can function as a noun, an adjective, or an adverb. You form an infinitive by using *to* with the base form of any verb: *to see, to hear, to become, to be*. If you want to form a *passive* infinitive, you use *to be* with a verb form: *to be seen, to be heard*.

The following sentences show how infinitives can be used as nouns.

SUBJECT: *To paint* requires talent.
SUBJECT COMPLEMENT: Her ambition is *to succeed*.
DIRECT OBJECT: I want *to win*.

The following sentences contain examples of how infinitives can be used as adjectives and as adverbs.

ADJECTIVE: The person to see is the president.

ADVERB: We came to learn

(Adverbial infinitives usually tell *why*.)

While a verbal substitutes as another part of speech, it loses none of its verb powers. It can still be modified and have objects or other complements. The verbal with its modifiers and complements is called a phrase. The following sentences include examples of **infinitive phrases** serving as other parts of speech.

NOUN: They tried *to change the flat tire*. (direct object)
ADJECTIVE: The person *to appoint to this job* is Mrs. Lee.
ADVERB: He went *to buy his friend a present*.

**Subjects of infinitives**  An infinitive or an infinitive phrase may have a subject. In the following sentence, *Mary* is the subject of the infinitive phrase.

- We wanted Mary *to win the election.*

When the subject of the infinitive is a pronoun, the pronoun must be in the objective case.

They told us to report early

## EXERCISES

**A. Identifying infinitive phrases**  Write the numbers 1–10 on your paper. For each of the following sentences, copy the infinitive phrase. Then write whether it is used as a *noun,* an *adjective,* or an *adverb.*

EXAMPLE:   The tool to use is a crowbar.
ANSWER:   to use: adjective

1. Our teacher asked us to decorate the gym.
2. Her ambition is to become a hospital administrator.
3. We have a right to question the witness.
4. She tried to give her cat a bubble bath.
5. We are working on Saturdays to raise money for the blind.
6. It is a shame to leave the animals alone that long.
7. To avoid the long lines, we attended an early show.
8. The best approach is to be friendly.
9. Our plan to take them along has our parents' approval.
10. The time to plant tulip bulbs is in the fall.

**B. Adding infinitive phrases to sentences**  Write the numbers 1–10 on your paper. Complete the following sentences by using infinitive phrases. Some structures will require that your infinitive have its own subject. Underline the infinitive phrases.

EXAMPLE:   We asked _____.
ANSWER:   We asked them to give us a ride.

1. It is natural for a child that age _____.
2. We watched _____.

3. I am not waiting any longer for _____.
4. The best place _____ is in a quiet room.
5. Does everyone in this class want _____.
6. We stopped at the store _____.
7. The girl wanted _____.
8. I'm looking for a person _____.
9. The best time _____ is in the evening.
10. His parents asked _____.

**C. Using infinitive phrases as specific parts of speech** Write the numbers 1–10 on your paper. Use each infinitive phrase in a sentence as the designated part of speech. Give some infinitives their own subjects.

EXAMPLE: to run your cars: adjective
ANSWER: That is not a good place to run your cars.

1. to eat lunch: adverb
2. to eat lunch: noun
3. to eat lunch: adjective
4. to write a report: noun
5. to write a report: adverb
6. to be on time: noun
7. to be on time: adverb
8. to treat a pet: adjective
9. to treat a pet: noun
10. to be heard easily: adverb

# 21

# Participles and Participial Phrases

A **participle** is a verbal that is used as an adjective. Like the infinitive, a participle can be active or passive. Unlike the infinitive, it can be used in different tenses. The present participle ends in *-ing*. The past participle most oftens ends in *-ed, -en,* or *-t*.

Because it is used as an adjective, a participle often precedes the noun or noun substitute it modifies.

- The *broken* dishes were lying on the floor.
- She won't eat *cooked* tomatoes.
- We followed the *winding* road.

A participle with modifiers and complements is called a **participial phrase**. If the phrase tells *which one* about the word it modifies, it is not set off with commas. If it does not tell *which one* but is only added information, it is set off with commas.

- The girl *carrying the suitcase* looks familiar. (Which girl?)
- Ms. Hona, *having completed her speech,* left the stage. (added information)

Participial phrases that can be set off with commas are sometimes positioned at the beginning or at the end of a sentence and set off with a comma. Although this can be an effective position for a participial phrase, you must be careful not to position it so that it modifies the wrong word or "dangles" without modifying anything.

MISPLACED:   I could hear strange noises, *sitting in my room.*
IMPROVED:   *Sitting in my room,* I could hear strange noises.
DANGLING:   The dinner tasted good, *having waited two hours.*
IMPROVED:   *Having waited two hours,* we enjoyed our dinner.

As a general rule, position a modifier as close as you can to what it modifies.

## EXERCISES

**A. Identifying participial phrases** Write the numbers 1–10 on your paper. Copy each of the following sentences. Underline the participial phrase, and circle the word it modifies.

EXAMPLE: The scouts collected the trash thrown from cars.
ANSWER: The scouts collected the (trash) thrown from cars.

1. Wanting a seafood dinner, we drove to the seashore.
2. That is a cake made without sugar.
3. The trees lining the street need to be trimmed.
4. My grandparents, needing a vacation, flew to Mexico.
5. The costumes worn in the class play were all handmade.
6. The student collecting the most labels will get a prize.
7. They are drinking a punch made with fresh strawberries.
8. Needing shelter for the night, the hiker crawled into a cave.
9. We like to eat steak marinated in soy sauce and ginger.
10. Threatened by the size of the dog, the intruder withdrew.

**B. Using participial phrases** Write the numbers 1–10 on your paper. Use each of the following participial phrases in a sentence. Use commas when necessary. Underline each participial phrase and circle the word it modifies.

EXAMPLE: looking out the car window
ANSWER: Looking out the car window, (I) could see the Rockies.

1. hanging on the trees
2. wearing the red shirt
3. having washed the car
4. being presented the trophy
5. having been ignored before
6. wanting to come in
7. delivered to your home
8. having aimed very carefully
9. needing extra help
10. having no need for a car

**C. Correcting dangling and misplaced participial phrases** Write the numbers 1–10 on your paper. Correct each of the following sentences. Reposition the participial phrase close to the word it modifies. In some cases, you will have to reword the entire sentence so that the participial phrase will have a word to modify.

EXAMPLE:   Being a teenager, the dance was really enjoyable.
ANSWER:    Being a teenager, I really enjoyed the dance.

1. Running for a touchdown, the crowd cheered the quarterback.
2. Barking wildly, I saw the dog run across the street.
3. Lifting the hood of the car, the engine was on fire.
4. Walking across the meadow, clouds could be seen in the sky.
5. Having been kept on the phone for an hour, my dinner was not eaten.
6. The game was not enjoyable, getting soaked by the rain.
7. The time was spent pleasantly, chatting in small groups.
8. The driver walked away from the car, shaking with fright.
9. Sitting on our front porch, the fireworks can be seen very easily.
10. The students should report to the nurse needing physicals.

# 22

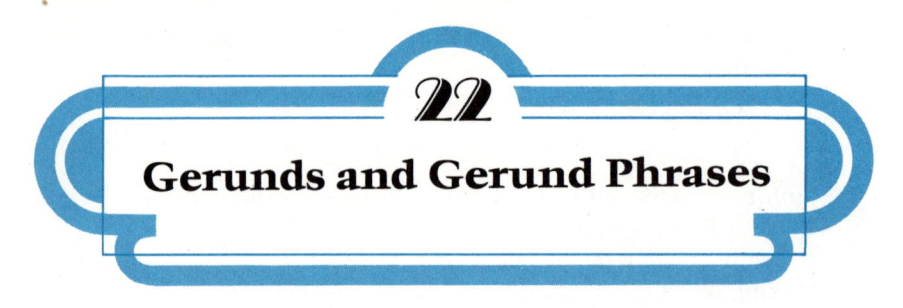

# Gerunds and Gerund Phrases

A **gerund** is a verbal that ends in -*ing* and functions as a noun. The uses of a gerund are shown in the following examples.

SUBJECT: *Swimming* is her sport.
SUBJECT COMPLEMENT: Her sport is *swimming*.
DIRECT OBJECT: She enjoys *swimming*.
INDIRECT OBJECT: She gives *swimming* her full attention.
OBJECT OF PREPOSITION: She never gets tired of *swimming*.
APPOSITIVE: She is good at her sport, *swimming*.
SUBJECT OF INFINITIVE: She wants *swimming* to be more popular.

Like the other verbals, the gerund can have modifiers and complements. The gerund with its modifiers and complements is called a **gerund phrase**. The gerund phrase has the same uses in a sentence as a gerund.

SUBJECT: *Winning another race this year* is his goal.
SUBJECT COMPLEMENT: The best sport is *chasing a white ball through eighteen holes*.
DIRECT OBJECT: We have tried *putting her in a kennel*.
INDIRECT OBJECT: Give *studying for this test* all your attention.
OBJECT OF PREPOSITION: You can win without *making a fool of yourself*.
APPOSITIVE: My hobby, *collecting poisonous spiders,* is dangerous.
SUBJECT OF INFINITIVE: I consider *attending class daily* to be necessary.

**Possessive case with gerunds** When you wish to tell who is doing the action of the gerund, you should make the noun or pronoun possessive.

- We are concerned about *Jim's* (not *Jim*) missing practice.
- We don't like *your* (not *you*) staying out late.

**Gerund or participle?** Since participles can also end in *-ing*, it is possible to confuse them with gerunds. You can tell the difference by the way the verbal is used in the sentence. A participle acts as an adjective. It is never preceded by a possessive noun or pronoun. A gerund acts as a noun. It may be preceded by a possessive noun or pronoun.

PARTICIPLE:   I saw them *standing there.*
GERUND:   Their *standing there* bothers me.

**Passive gerunds** Although gerunds are usually used in the active voice, it is possible to use a gerund in the passive voice. To make a gerund passive use *being* + the past participle: *Being left alone in that house terrifies him.*

## EXERCISES

**A. Identifying gerunds and gerund phrases** Write the numbers 1-10 on your paper. From each sentence, copy only the gerunds or gerund phrases.

EXAMPLE:   Seeing you again is like having a wonderful dream
ANSWER:   seeing you again, having a wonderful dream

1. His working in the city upsets his parents.
2. Catching a football is quite different from throwing it.
3. Writing this letter is harder than writing an essay.
4. It is a bad habit, coming home late every day.
5. Seeing is believing.
6. Eating ice cream before going to bed is my weakness.
7. Her hobby is collecting stamps from all parts of the world.
8. We enjoy swimming and diving from the high board.
9. You should give learning a foreign language a second try.
10. We consider being invited a real honor.

**B. Using gerunds and gerund phrases** Write the numbers 1-10 on your paper. Copy and complete each of the following sentences by using a gerund or gerund phrase.

EXAMPLE:   _____ has been a pleasure.
ANSWER:   Working with you this week has been a pleasure.

1. They reached California by _____.
2. _____ will never make you popular.

89

3. Most people enjoy ———.
4. ——— is the best way to lose weight.
5. His responsibilities are ———.
6. I am concerned about her ———.
7. Before ———, you should look at the headlines.
8. ——— gets boring after awhile.
9. I can't imagine their ———.
10. You can help people by ———.

**C. Using gerund phrases for specific noun functions** Write the numbers 1–10 on your paper. Use each gerund phrase in a sentence in the function designated.

EXAMPLE: giving the dog a bath: subject complement
ANSWER: My job is giving the dog a bath.

1. putting peanut butter on apples: direct object
2. taking a shortcut: object of a preposition
3. improving your spelling: indirect object
4. backing out of the driveway: subject complement
5. biting his nails: appositive
6. driving too fast: subject complement
7. broiling it over charcoal: direct object
8. standing in lunch line: subject
9. injuring anyone: object of a preposition
10. protecting the ocean: subject of an infinitive

# REVIEWING LESSONS 19-22

**A. Using prepositional and verbal phrases to complete sentences** Write the numbers 1-20 on your paper. Complete each of the following sentences by adding the kind of phrase requested in parentheses.

EXAMPLE: (prep. phrase) the students earn money by (gerund phrase).
ANSWER: On Saturdays the students earn money by washing cars.

1. (gerund phrase) is a worthy project (prep. phrase).
2. (participial phrase) she ran (prep. phrase).
3. A way (infinitive phrase) is (infinitive phrase).
4. Everyone (prep. phrase) began (gerund phrase).
5. (prep. phrase) our guide started (infinitive phrase).
6. The first three runners (infinitive phrase) will receive trophies (prep. phrase).
7. Anyone (participial phrase) will find it (participial phrase).
8. (gerund phrase) is not a job (infinitive phrase).
9. The cars (participial phrase) are preventing the snowplows from (gerund phrase).
10. A person (prep. phrase) has a better chance (infinitive phrase).
11. He began (gerund phrase) without our (gerund phrase).
12. The new animals (prep. phrase) were purchased (prep. phrase).
13. The shoes (prep. phrase) are not available (prep. phrase).
14. (prep. phrase) she decided (infinitive phrase).
15. All the clothing (participial phrase) will be given to the victims (prep. phrase).
16. (gerund phrase) can be dangerous (prep. phrase).
17. We saw their car (participial phrase) and waved (infinitive phrase).
18. The picture (participial phrase) was painted (infinitive phrase).
19. (prep. phrase) their one desire is (infinitive phrase).
20. The customers (participial phrase) like her (gerund phrase).

**B. Using prepositional and verbal phrases to improve writing** Write the numbers 1-10 on your paper. Improve each of the following sentences by changing the italicized part to the phrase named in parentheses.

EXAMPLE: Her greatest fear is *that she will lose this ring.* (gerund)
ANSWER: Her greatest fear is losing this ring.

1. Use a ladder *so that you can reach the top branches.* (infinitive)
2. The wind ripped the sheets *that were hanging on the line.* (participial)

3. They drove all night *and didn't stop.* (prepositional)
4. He works on a farm in the summer *so that he will keep in shape.* (infinitive)
5. *Because they were hoping to get good seats,* they waited in the ticket line all night. (participial)
6. I will paint the fence *that surrounds our property.* (participial)
7. The new uniforms *that were purchased for the band* should arrive soon. (participial)
8. *Because she is from Middletown,* Lani Emmons never misses a Flyers' home game. (passive gerund)
9. We bought her all new clothes *so that she could wear them on the class trip.* (infinitive)
10. The best view *that you can have of the parade* is the one from your sister's office on the sixth floor. (infinitive)

**C.** Finding verbals   Check through some old magazines, newspapers, and comic strips to find ten examples of verbals. Explain each verbal and how it is used. Following is an example.

"I don't ever want to hear the word 'baseball' again."

Explanation: The verbal *to hear the word "baseball" again* is an infinitive phrase used as a direct object.

# MORE ABOUT SENTENCES

## 24

## Basic Sentence Patterns

Although there are countless ways to arrange words into sentences, this lesson will examine four basic sentence structures. These structures are called **patterns**. Each contains the required subject and predicate. The differences in the four patterns are in the predicates.

**S + V pattern**   The most basic sentence pattern is that which contains only a subject and a verb. Both the subject and the verb may have modifiers, but the action of the verb must be self-contained (the verb must not require an object to complete its meaning). The following chart contains examples of **S + V** sentences and shows you how to diagram them. A **diagram** can help you to see the basic parts of a sentence and the relationship of modifiers to those basic parts.

SUBJECT + VERB:   S | V

- Ginger barked.

    Ginger | barked

- All the dogs barked wildly.

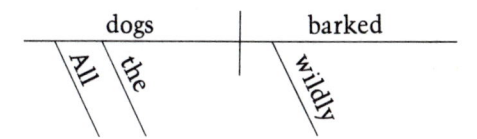

    dogs | barked
     \All \the    \wildly

- Some of the dogs never sleep during the night.

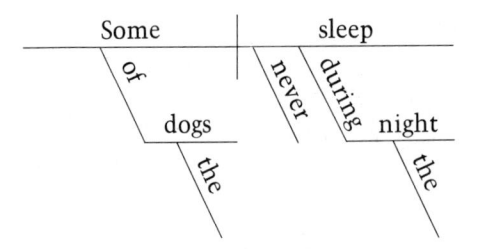

- Does that dog belong to you?

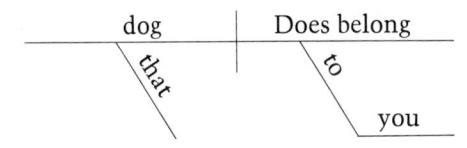

Either the subject or the verb may be compounded in any basic sentence pattern. It is also possible to compound modifiers without changing the basic pattern. The following diagrams illustrate the various kinds of compounding that can be done in a **S + V** sentence.

- The boys and girls in our class paraded on Saturday and Sunday.

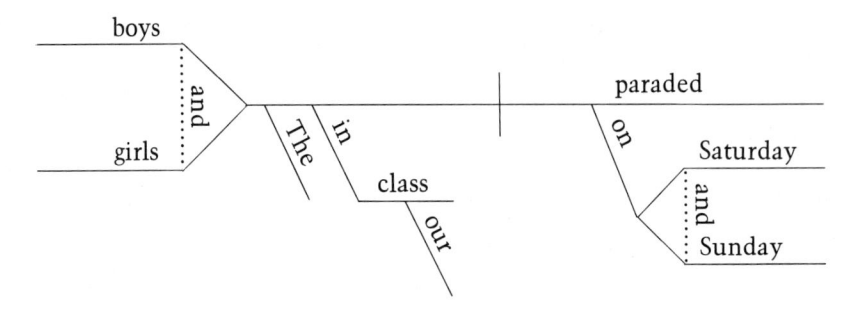

- The nervous but determined parents boldly walked in and sat down.

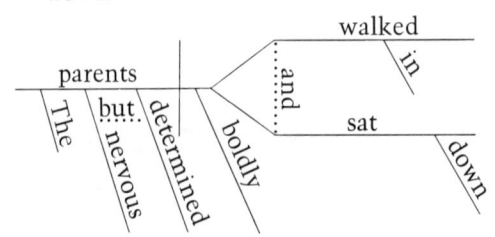

- After school come to the stage and help with the scenery for the play.

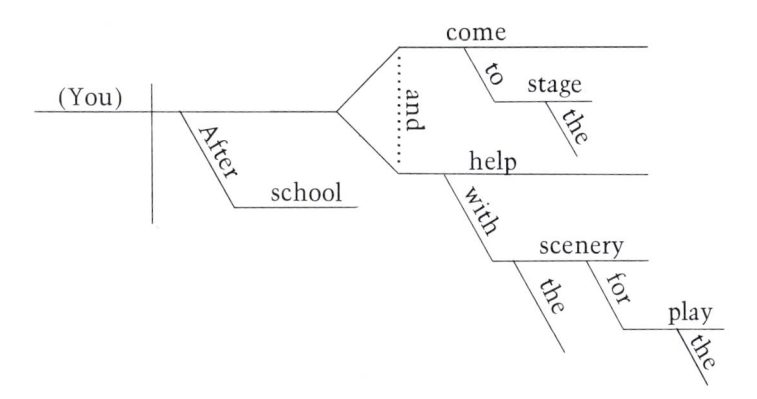

**S+V+O pattern**   The second basic sentence pattern is similar to the first. However, in addition to the subject and the verb, the S+V+O pattern includes a *direct object:* O. As in the S+V sentences, there may be any amount of modifiers attached to the basic parts of a S+V+O sentence. Also, there may be any amount of compounding or use of verbals.

SUBJECT + VERB + DIRECT OBJECT:   S | V | O

- She repairs watches.

- The fathers and their daughters caught sixty fish.

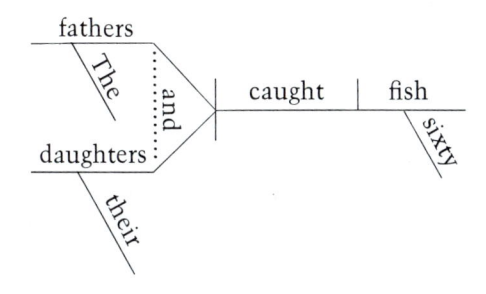

- The seniors and the juniors washed and waxed the cars for the parade.

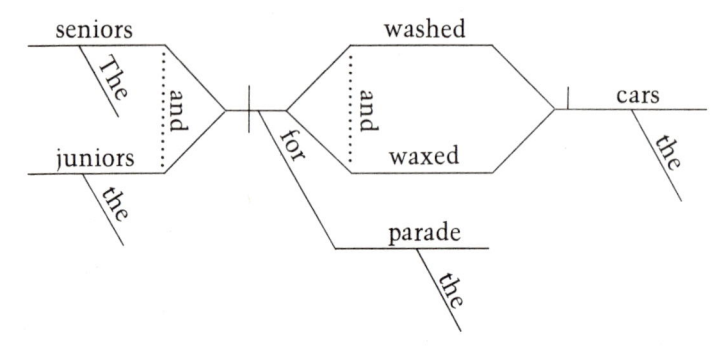

- Working with them has begun to tire and to bore me.

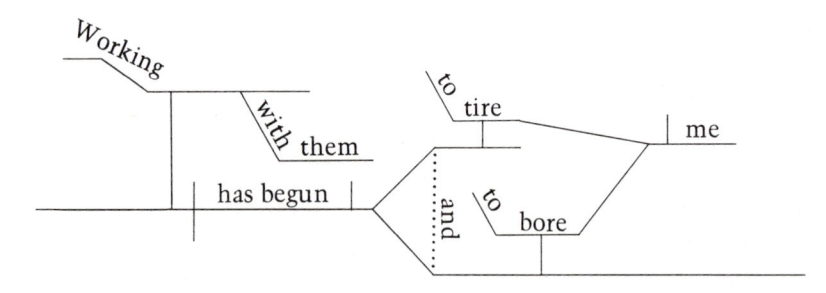

**S+V+IO+O pattern** The third basic sentence pattern has the basic elements of a **S+V+O** sentence plus one more basic part, the *indirect object:* **S+V+IO+O**.

SUBJECT + VERB + INDIRECT OBJECT + DIRECT OBJECT:

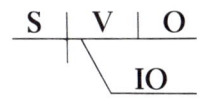

```
S | V | O
     \ IO
```

- We offered them friendship.

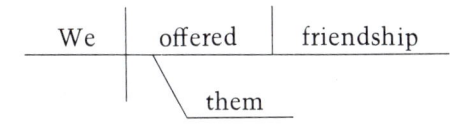

```
We | offered | friendship
         \ them
```

- Their parents gave them and us a ride.

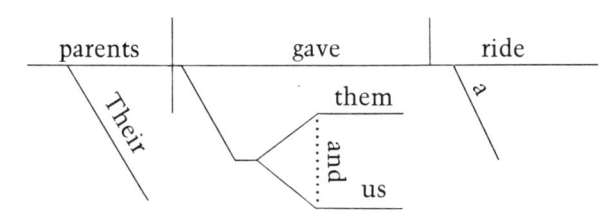

```
parents | gave | ride
  \Their    \them   \a
              \and
               \us
```

**S+LV+C pattern** The last basic sentence pattern to be considered in this lesson contains a subject, a linking verb, and a subject complement: **S+LV+C**. The subject complement may be a noun, a noun substitute, or an adjective.

SUBJECT + LINKING VERB + SUBJECT COMPLEMENT:  S | LV \ C

- Pat is captain.

```
Pat | is \ captain
```

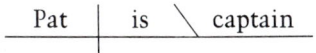

- The leaders of the parade will be Mark and Marta.

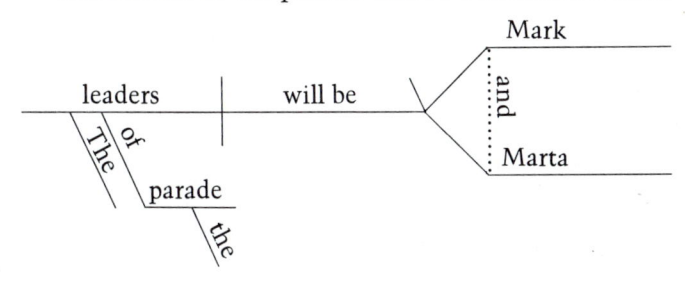

```
leaders | will be \ Mark
  \The              and
   \of              Marta
    \parade
     \the
```

- Your job is interesting.

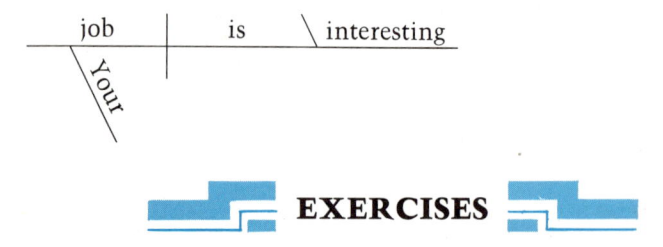

```
  job    |  is   \ interesting
\Your
```

# EXERCISES

**A. Identifying patterns** Write the numbers 1–10 on your paper. Remove all the modification from each of the following sentences and diagram only the basic parts. After each diagram, write its pattern.

EXAMPLE: A person with high ideals helps humanity.
ANSWER: person | helps | humanity : S+V+O

1. Very few people in my class have been to Bermuda.
2. Your partner will be Eldora.
3. This city doesn't offer us much excitement.
4. They had a party in the barn.
5. Some hungry children were standing on the steps.
6. She has been a teacher and a principal.
7. Reading in a dim light gives me a headache.
8. Gladys and Annie have skied during the last three winters.
9. The music sounded sad but beautiful.
10. The children threw their popcorn to the monkeys in the trees.

**B. Expanding basic sentence patterns** Write the numbers 1–10 on your paper. Write the pattern of each of the following sentences. Then write an expanded version of each sentence by adding a variety of modifiers to *each* basic part.

EXAMPLE: People show friends emotions.
ANSWER: S+V+IO+O: Almost all people try to show their closest friends their deepest emotions.

1. Residents have gardens.
2. Poverty exists.
3. Visitors give patients comfort.
4. Books are enjoyable.
5. Coaches give players strategies.
6. Audiences paid attention.
7. Corn grows tall.
8. Some give people service.

9. All sent parents cards.
10. Children have clothes.

**C.** Adding indirect objects and subject complements   Write the numbers 1–10 on your paper. To each of the following sentences add an indirect object or a subject complement. Write the basic pattern at the end of your completed sentence.

EXAMPLE:   He always gives a fair warning.
           She was with us last year.
ANSWER:    He always gives his opponents a fair warning. S+V+IO+O
           She was rather disappointed with us last year. S+LV+C

1. The thunder sounded in the distance.
2. That kind of corn grows in Iowa.
3. The new teacher gives long assignments.
4. The flowers are in the window boxes.
5. We couldn't offer another cent.
6. The grocer sells the best steaks.
7. You will be in this town for the rest of your life.
8. Why can't we stay?
9. The speaker has shown a new approach.
10. Have you ever sent postcards?

**D.** Writing patterned sentences   Write the numbers 1–5 on your paper. Study the accompanying picture carefully. Decide what is happening in the picture, who is involved, and when and where the action is taking place. Then write two **S+V** pattern sentences and one of each of the following pattern sentences about the picture: **S+V+O, S+V+IO+O,** and **S+LV+C.** Label each sentence according to its pattern.

# 24

# Kinds of Clauses

A **clause** is a group of words that has a subject and a predicate. An **independent clause** can stand by itself as a sentence. A **dependent clause**, sometimes called a **subordinate clause**, cannot stand by itself. A dependent clause is always connected to an independent clause.

INDEPENDENT CLAUSE: A storm was approaching.
DEPENDENT CLAUSE: *When it started to rain* we went home.

**Adjective clauses** A dependent clause used as an adjective is called an **adjective clause**. Like an adjective, an adjective clause modifies a noun or a noun substitute. Adjective clauses are usually introduced by a relative pronoun that refers the noun being described.

The people who bought our house have moved in.

Sometimes the relative pronoun is omitted.

The skiing (which) they do in Italy is quite different.

**Adverb clauses** An **adverb clause** is a dependent clause that modifies a verb, a verbal, an adjective, or an adverb. An adverb clause is introduced by a subordinating conjunction. It is not set off with commas unless it introduces a sentence or is in an unusual position, such as between the subject and its verb.

They will relax after they take this test.

After they take this test, they will relax.

**Noun clauses** A dependent clause used as a noun is a **noun clause**. It is used as a subject, a direct object, an indirect object, an object of a preposition, a subject complement, or an appositive. It can be introduced by a pronoun, a subordinating conjunction, or an adverb.

SUBJECT: *What you have done* concerns us all.
DIRECT OBJECT: Please give me *whatever you have written.*
OBJECT OF PREPOSITION: Hand this to *whoever is there.*
INDIRECT OBJECT  Give *whoever is there* this message.
SUBJECT COMPLEMENT: You can be *whatever you want.*
APPOSITIVE OF IT  It is a pity *that we can't go.*

## EXERCISES

**A. Identifying clauses** Write the numbers 1-10 on your paper. Write whether each italicized clause is *dependent* or *independent.*

EXAMPLE: People say *that they are very kind.*
ANSWER: dependent

1. Don't you know *who she is?*
2. We left *when it got dark.*
3. You can leave *if you wish.*
4. *You wash* and I'll dry.
5. Long after dark *we could still hear them singing.*
6. Don't leave without getting *what is coming to you.*
7. *It could have been worse,* but we can be thankful that it wasn't.
8. Are you going to buy one, or *do you want me to get it for you?*
9. Seeing all those lovely trees makes me wonder *if we should move to the country.*
10. *He sat beside the road* and spoke softly to the puppy lying in his arms.

**B. Identifying kinds of dependent clauses** Write the numbers 1-10 on your paper. From each sentence, copy only the dependent clauses. Identify each clause as a *noun, adjective,* or *adverb* clause.

EXAMPLE: What she has done cheers us.
ANSWER: what she has done: noun clause.

1. Please speak with whomever I send you.
2. I know that they are wealthy.

3. Unless you agree, I can't do anything.
4. People who smoke shouldn't offend other people.
5. It is a wonder that she doesn't leave.
6. When it rains, it floods the stream.
7. What makes you tick puzzle.
8. The truth is that I envy her.
9. The taxes are what keeps the county running.
10. If you can't be honest, say nothing.

**C. Building sentences by adding clauses** Write the numbers 1–10 on your paper. Complete the following sentences by adding the type of clause requested in parentheses.

EXAMPLE: The meteorologist says (noun clause).
ANSWER: The meteorologist says that we can expect snow today.

1. People (adjective clause) are usually very healthy.
2. (Adverb clause), be certain to include the zip code.
3. It was left here by someone (adjective clause).
4. I was very disappointed (adverb clause).
5. Who could possibly know (noun clause)?
6. The children, (adverb clause), look very innocent.
7. Why don't you choose a place (adjective clause)?
8. Why must you put your feet on (noun clause)?
9. Animals (adjective clause) make the best pets.
10. Is it a secret (noun clause)?

# Four Kinds of Sentences

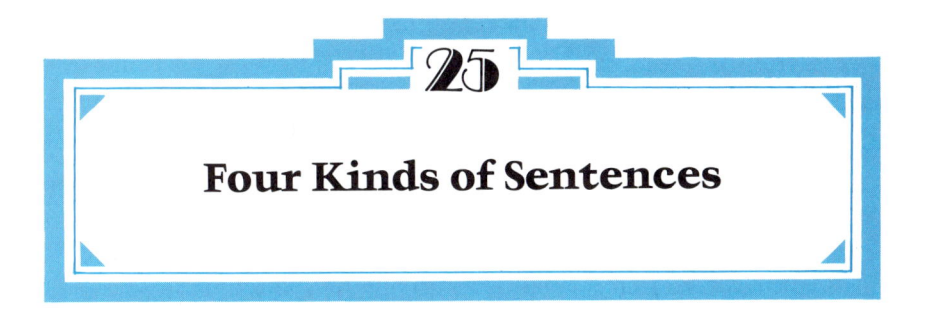

**The simple sentence**   A **simple sentence** is a sentence that has only one independent clause and no dependent clauses.

- We | took the dog and her pups to a kennel.
- The girls and their fathers | went on a fishing trip.

**The compound sentence**   A **compound sentence** contains two or more independent clauses but no dependent clauses. These independent clauses are usually joined by a coordinating conjunction or a semicolon. A semicolon may be used with a conjunction if either or both clauses already contain commas or are extremely long. Following are examples of compound sentences and their punctuation.

- She took the bus *but* I walked home. (short clauses with no commas)
- The seniors reported to the gym, *and* the juniors remained in their homerooms. (comma and conjunction)
- He lived in Gary, Indiana, for two years; *but* then his parents moved to Houston, Texas. (semicolon and conjunction)
- Arguing will do no good; that grade will not be changed. (semicolon only)

**The complex sentence**   A **complex sentence** is a sentence that has only one independent clause and one or more dependent clauses.

- We will go skating *when the ice is safe*.
- The book *that you want* hasn't been returned yet.

**The compound-complex sentence**   A **compound-complex sentence** is one that contains at least two independent clauses and one or more dependent clauses. If you were to connect an independent clause to an existing complex sentence by means of a coordinating conjunction or semicolon, the result would be a compound-complex sentence. Following are some examples of this structure.

- The bus pulled out, and we knew that we would have to walk.
- If you wish, you may see him; but there really is no need.
- We realized that we had lost; no one had to tell us.

Dependent clauses make it possible to show more exactly the relationships that exist between ideas in a sentence. Writing nothing but compound sentences or separate simple sentences makes it difficult to emphasize an idea or to show the true relationship between ideas. The following examples illustrate how dependent clauses can be used to combine simple sentences and to change compound sentences to complex sentences.

- Our neighbor is a surgeon, and she performed heart surgery.
- Our neighbor, who is a surgeon, performed heart surgery.
- You can't have a car. You don't have enough money for insurance.
- You can't have a car because you don't have enough money for insurance.

You can reduce a dependent clause to a phrase or even a single word if that reduction doesn't distort the meaning of the sentence. Most often, effective writing is clear and direct, uncluttered and uncomplicated. Following are two ways to express ideas more directly.

1. Use compound elements in simple sentences.

    - She wrote the paper. She folded it neatly. She handed it in.
    - She wrote the paper, folded it neatly, and handed it in.

2. Reduce clauses to phrases or single words.

    - Jersey is an island that is in the English Channel.
    - Jersey is an island in the English Channel.
    - Please throw out the dishes that are broken.
    - Please throw out the broken dishes.

# EXERCISES

**A. Changing simple sentences to complex**  Write the numbers 1–10 on your paper. Write one complex sentence from each of the following pairs of sentences by changing one of the sentences to a dependent clause.

EXAMPLE:   The girl found the lost dog. She has been rewarded.
ANSWER:    The girl who found the lost dog has been rewarded.

1. Everyone admired the room. We had decorated it.
2. The candidate lives in California. She will get the job.
3. We will sand the window sills. Then my mother will paint them.
4. The team won the championship. They were in perfect condition.
5. Here are the pictures. You left them in the cafeteria.
6. They delivered the groceries. We had ordered them.
7. Please read this book. It shows you how to prune roses.
8. You can weed the flower beds. At the same time I can be mowing the lawn.
9. You will come to the city this summer. Plan to stay with us.
10. We are very disappointed. You didn't ask us for help.

**B. Changing compound sentences to complex**  Write the numbers 1–15 on your paper. Change each compound sentence to a complex sentence by making one of the clauses dependent.

EXAMPLE:   I lost the wallet, but I have found it.
ANSWER:    I found the wallet that I lost.

1. He is still driving the car, and I sold it to him.
2. They dump sludge into the ocean, and it kills the fish.
3. We usually rent that cabin, but it has burned down.
4. She took a few lessons, and she began to improve.
5. I bought new shoes, and they are very comfortable.
6. We will wash the windows and then I will take you shopping.
7. Our friends were on the plane, and it flew to Dallas.
8. They will call your name, and you be ready to stand up.
9. You will be in Philadelphia, and you should see the Liberty Bell.
10. That was a mistake, and I will never make it again.
11. I have a dog, but it can't do tricks.
12. I play the piano everyday, and I play it well.
13. My sister is a lawyer, and she has many clients.
14. I wanted to borrow that book, but it has already been borrowed.
15. She lives near a lake, and she learned how to ice-skate.

**C. Reducing clauses to modifying words and phrases** Write the numbers 1–10 on your paper. Rewrite the following sentences, reducing each dependent clause to a modifying word or phrase.

EXAMPLE: The girl who is sitting in front of you can help you.
ANSWER: The girl sitting in front of you can help you.

1. Please hand in the assignments that have been completed.
2. The chair that is sitting in front of the fireplace is very comfortable.
3. The floors, which have been waxed, are very slippery.
4. The car that is in the driveway is my mother's.
5. Jeans that are ragged are not appropriate attire.
6. A candidate who has money stands a better chance of winning.
7. The storm, which was threatening, kept us home.
8. You should really get rid of those tires that are bald.
9. The players who are best are also the students who are best.
10. We are all happy because there will be a parade.

# REVIEWING LESSONS 23-25

**A. Identifying sentence patterns** Write the numbers 1–10 on your paper. Write the basic pattern of each of the following sentences.

EXAMPLE: They brought some very unusual toys.
ANSWER: S+V+O

1. They were hiking in the valley all week.
2. They were eating out of old army mess kits.
3. Both parents promised a trip in the fall.
4. All three of them had been playing all day.
5. We would be gathering in a few hours.
6. The strange visitor told some weird stories.
7. Didn't you mail the warranty?
8. We could be checking all night.
9. They very boldly drove onto our front lawn.
10. Has the company sent the checks yet?

**B. Varying sentence patterns** Write the numbers 1–10 on your paper. Vary the structure of each of the following sentences either by inverting the natural order or by repositioning modifiers.

EXAMPLE: Three yelping puppies dashed into the room.
ANSWER: Into the room dashed three yelping puppies.

1. An old-fashioned tire swing was hanging in the tree.
2. I will not give you one more chance.
3. A pole-sitter perched high above the stadium.
4. She stalked by with her nose high in the air.
5. We see a ray of hope in your last statement.
6. A very sad little boy crawled out from under the bed.
7. Almost anything grows in your garden.
8. They sat and waited for us, not knowing we had left already.
9. She looks like a jockey in that cap.
10. You will have to use real cream if you want it to be rich.

**C. Building dependent clauses into sentences** Write the numbers 1–10 on your paper. Build each of the dependent clauses on the next page into a complete sentence. The clause should function as the part of speech in parentheses.

EXAMPLE: that you were ill (noun)
ANSWER: We did not know that you were ill.

1. which you are wearing (adjective)
2. when they plan to sell the house (adverb)
3. when they plan to sell the house (noun)
4. that you plan to attend (noun)
5. that you plan to attend (adjective)
6. because no one invited us (adverb)
7. whom you met on the subway (adjective)
8. who has been protecting you (adjective)
9. if no one else can go (adverb)
10. that they have been well prepared (noun)

**D. Combining sentences** Write the numbers 1-15 on your paper. Combine each set of short, choppy sentences into one well written sentence. Reduce some sentences to dependent clauses and reduce others to modifying words or phrases. Use compounding whenever it is effective.

EXAMPLE: The night was long. It was dark. All through it she sat. She waited for some sign. She needed hope.

ANSWER: All through the long, dark night she sat and waited for some sign of hope.

1. We could save a lot of energy. We could do it easily. We could permit no businesses to be open on Sunday.
2. You met the man. He is a tourist. He is from Topeka, Kansas.
3. The leaves were red. They were yellow. They were gold.
4. You will meet my parents. You will come to my house. You will have dinner with us.
5. We planted seeds. We did it eight days ago. They have sprouted.
6. She cut the grass. She used a riding mower. She cleaned up the clippings. She used a lawn sweeper.
7. You are reading the book. It is a mystery. It is about Nancy Drew.
8. He hit one ball. It went into the water. He hit a second ball. It went into the water.
9. We are building a house. It is very modern. It is solar heated.
10. We will get to the top. We will stop. We will rest. We will do that for at least an hour.
11. He broke the cups. He swept them up. He used a broom.
12. We could not open the door. The snow had drifted against it.
13. It was a farm. They bought it. It had belonged to my grandparents.
14. These oranges are sweet. They are from Florida.
15. We will sing the song. We will do it in French.

# REVIEWING GRAMMAR

**A.** Identifying types of errors in sentence structures   Write the numbers 1–20 on your paper. Read each of the following sentences and determine whether or not it is effectively written. If it is effective, write *E* after the number for that sentence. If it is not well written, write one of the following symbols to indicate the type of error it contains: *F* (fragment), *RO* (run-on sentence), or *N CD* (needless or faulty compounding).

EXAMPLE:   They have a camper, and we will borrow it.
ANSWER:   CD

1. You need the book, and it is on the shelf.
2. Bring that with you it will come in handy.
3. No other city we have ever visited.
4. Don't do that now you will regret it later.
5. Whenever the roads are icy.
6. We cannot always have those things that we desire most.
7. After the sun had set and we were sitting around the campfire cooking our dinner of potatoes and steak.
8. We were on our way to the lake, and we had a flat tire.
9. There may be trouble we can't afford to be off guard.
10. Not knowing what to expect, we approached the cabin very cautiously.
11. Trying to crowd nine people into that car can be dangerous as well as uncomfortable.
12. Unless we are able to find a replacement and have it installed.
13. That is only one reason you think of a second one.
14. They are our best friends, and they live in San Francisco.
15. They have to make their own decisions, and they have to choose their own careers.
16. The relatives arriving from all parts of the country.
17. Giving them real responsibilities is preparing them for a realistic future.
18. That may be the wisest course of action we can't do anything else about the problem.
19. If there were more time and we had no other jobs to do.
20. What one says to hurt others usually returns to hurt oneself.

**B. Selecting the most effective sentence structure** Write the numbers 1–20 on your paper. Decide which sentence in each set of three sentences is written with the most effective structure and write its letter.

EXAMPLE:  A. She can practice, and she can improve her game.
B. She can improve her game by practicing.
C. Her game can be improved if she will practice.

ANSWER:  B

1. A. He is the tallest boy in his class.
   B. He is taller than any boy in his class.
   C. No boy in his class is taller than him.
2. A. We felt very well about our victory.
   B. We felt rather well about our victory.
   C. We felt good about winning.
3. A. We greeted the stranger who had entered.
   B. The stranger came in, and we greeted her.
   C. We greeted the stranger after she came in.
4. A. I don't have nothing for you but sympathy.
   B. Sympathy is all I have for you and nothing else.
   C. For you I have nothing but sympathy.
5. A. My sister is the one riding the horse wearing the green shirt.
   B. The rider in the green shirt is my sister.
   C. My sister is wearing the green shirt on the horse.
6. A. You could have come earlier so we could have used your help.
   B. We could have used your help if you had come earlier.
   C. Your earlier arrival would have benefited us with your help.
7. A. There isn't no other choice that we can make.
   B. That is the choice we will make because there is no other one.
   C. That is the only choice we can make.
8. A. All of us here want to help you.
   B. All of us who are here want to help you.
   C. All of us here have a desire to offer help to you.
9. A. Would you please show me the one that is in the window.
   B. Please show me the one in the window.
   C. Please show to me the one that is in the window.
10. A. We will walk in the garden after we have finished our dinner.
    B. After dinner is done, we will take a walk in the garden.
    C. After dinner, we will walk in the garden.
11. A. Needing a car immediately, the terms the dealer offered were acceptable to us.

  B. Needing a car immediately, we accepted the dealer's terms.
  C. The dealer offered us acceptable terms, needing a car immediately.
12. A. If you hadn't run so slow, you'd have won.
  B. You ran too slow, and you didn't win.
  C. You'd have won if you hadn't run so slowly.
13. A. She had lost the watch that he found.
  B. She lost the watch, and he found it.
  C. He found the watch that had been lost by her.
14. A. To the fair they brought the jellies that they had made at home.
  B. They brought their homemade jellies to the fair.
  C. They brought their jellies to the fair that they had made at home.
15. A. The birds, which were chirping, kept us awake.
  B. The chirping birds kept us awake.
  C. We were kept awake by the chirping of the birds.
16. A. She asked me if she could stay an extra night on the telephone.
  B. I was asked on the telephone if she could stay an extra night.
  C. When she telephoned me, she asked if she could stay an extra night.
17. A. You gave me the painting, and I hung it in my den.
  B. In my den I hung the painting that you had given me.
  C. In my den was hung the painting that you gave me.
18. A. At the age of three I took my son to the zoo.
  B. I took my son to the zoo, being only three years old.
  C. When my son was three, I took him to the zoo.
19. A. We didn't want to tell them about the cracked mirror.
  B. We didn't want to tell them about the mirror, which had been cracked.
  C. We kept the cracked mirror information among ourselves and didn't tell them.
20. A. All of us admire your test scores.
  B. Your test scores are admired by us all.
  C. We all admire the scores that you got on your test.

**C. Combining sentences** Write the numbers 1–5 on your paper. Combine each of the following sets of simple sentences into a single, well-structured sentence. Use a variety of clauses and phrases.

EXAMPLE: She sat down. She was on a bench. The bench was in a park. She tried to think. She needed an excuse.
ANSWER: She sat down on a park bench and tried to think of an excuse.

1. The man waited. He was sitting inside the truck. He was waiting for his buddy. It was cold. It was snowing. It was warm inside the truck.
2. She was half asleep. She thought about the mirror. It was framed in gold. It was valuable. It had been her mother's.
3. I left there two days ago. I was in Chicago then. I bought a ticket. It was for Detroit. I used the last of my money.
4. The puppy looked happy. He was carrying a large bone. It was freshly cooked. He kept looking behind him. He entered the alley.
5. It was dark night. It was raining. The lights were dim. There were a few red coals in the fireplace. I was alone. I sat in my chair. It was a big chair. It was made of leather. The leather was red.

Dialects in America    114
Sentence Sense    130
Choosing the Right Words    141
Language Pollution    172
Glossary of Usage    180
Reviewing Usage    206

# USAGE

# DIALECTS IN AMERICA

## 26
## Regional Dialects

You may wonder why a quiz as simple as the one on the opposite page would appear in a high school textbook. Answer the questions now, mentally.

You probably had no difficulty naming the objects and would have scored 100%—if we could only decide which six answers are right! If you compare your answers with those of your classmates, you may find some variation in the words they use in referring to the things on the quiz. If you could poll young people across the country, you would find even more variation. Add their parents and grandparents to your survey, and you might find all the following words mentioned:

1. frying pan, fry pan, skillet, spider, creeper
2. wishbone, breakbone, lucky bone, pull bone, pulling bone
3. sofa, lounge, couch, davenport, chesterfield
4. harmonica, French harp, mouth harp, harp, mouth organ
5. sweet corn, sugar corn, mutton corn, greencorn, roasting ear, table corn, corn on the cob
6. seesaw, teetering board, teeter-totter, dandle, tilt, tilts, ridy-horse, teeter-horse, see-horse, tiltamo

All thirty-eight names for these six everyday objects are "right" because, somewhere in the United States, a sizeable group of Americans uses them. There may be even more than thirty-eight possibilities. We may have missed some!

This simple quiz demonstrates two points about the language of Americans. First, Americans say the same thing in a variety of ways. Second, Americans who have lived together in a certain region for many years are likely to use language patterns that were established by previous generations who lived in that region.

Name the objects.

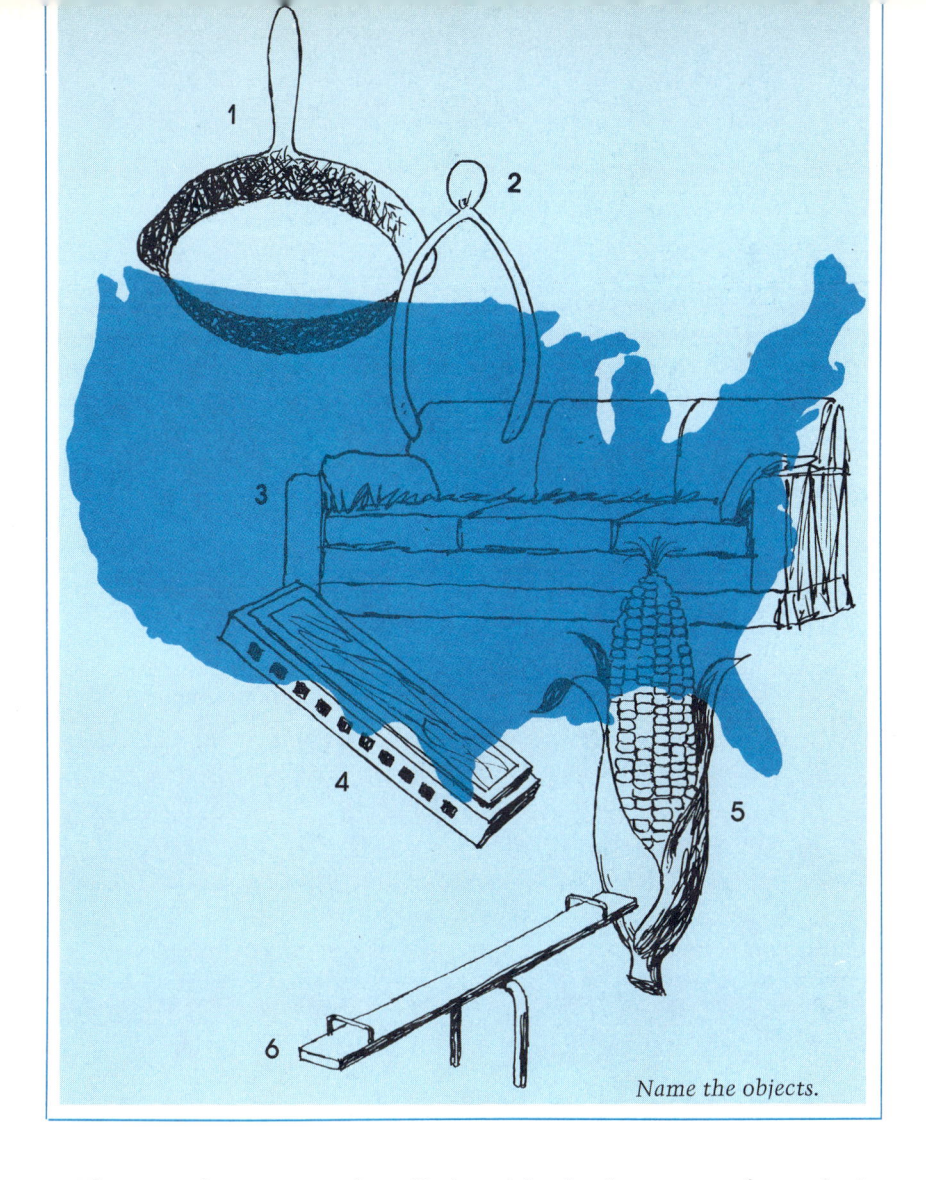

The speech patterns that distinguish the language of people in certain geographical areas are called **regional dialects.** A regional dialect consists of certain vocabulary, pronunciation, and grammar patterns in the speech of people who live together in a region. Normally, speakers gain their first regional dialect quite unconsciously when they learn to talk. They learn the dialect spoken by their parents, and, later, by other people in the community.

The first dialect is strongly established and, for many, is the dialect used throughout a lifetime. Moving to another region can affect one's language, of course. So can formal education and mass media such as television.

115

# EXERCISES

**A. Examining your regional dialect** Look at the following chart. Write the numbers 1–15 on your paper. Write the word or words in each group that you ordinarily use. If the word you ordinarily use is not listed, write the word that you do use. Compare your answers with those of your classmates. Try to discover why some students' responses differ from those of the majority of the class. Have any of them lived somewhere else for a long time? If not, have their parents lived elsewhere for a long time?

| Item | Choices |
|---|---|
| 1. Large open metal container for scrub water | pail, bucket |
| 2. Spout over a sink | faucet, hydrant, spicket, spigot, tap |
| 3. Vehicle for small baby | baby buggy, baby cab, baby carriage, baby coach |
| 4. Automobile device for making the car go faster | accelerator, gas pedal, throttle |
| 5. Limited access road | turnpike, toll road, freeway, parkway, pay road, tollway, thruway, expressway, interstate |
| 6. Grass strip in the center of a divided road | median, center strip, separator, divider, barrier, grass strip, boulevard |
| 7. Dog of mixed breed | common dog, cur, fice, feist, mongrel, no-count, scrub, heinz, sooner, mutt |
| 8. Carbonated drink | pop, soda, soda pop, tonic, soft drink |
| 9. Glass containing ice cream and root beer | float, black cow, Boston cooler |
| 10. Large sandwich designed to be a meal in itself | hero, submarine, hoagy, grinder, poor-boy |
| 11. Hit the water when diving | belly-flop, belly-buster |

| | | |
|---|---|---|
| 12. | Be absent from school | bag school, bolt, cook jack, lay out, lie out, play hookey, play truant, run out of school, skip class, skip school, slip off from school, ditch, flick, flake school |
| 13. | Time of day | quarter before eleven, quarter of eleven, quarter till eleven, quarter to eleven |
| 14. | Spinach makes me sick _____ my stomach | at, in, to, with |
| 15. | I have two _____ of shoes. | pair, pairs |

**B. Matching regional vocabularies** Write the numbers 1–10 on your paper. The numbered items are commonly used terms. Match them with the lettered regional terms. Use a dictionary if necessary.

1. pancakes
2. dragonfly
3. cottage cheese
4. chipmunk
5. disturbed, angry
6. lightning bug
7. chipped beef
8. algae
9. coincidence
10. pocket knife

a. roiled
b. glowworm
c. ground squirrel
d. frog spit
e. jackknife
f. happenstance
g. smearcase
h. flapjacks
i. jerky
j. darning needle

**C. Studying a dialect in literature** In their attempts to create authentic dialogue, American writers often use regional dialects. Study the following passage from Robert Peck's autobiographical novel, *A Day No Pigs Would Die*. It reflects the twentieth-century speech of the Shakers, a religious group living in Vermont. On your paper write down all the examples of regional usage that you find in the passage. Next to each item, write what *you* would normally say.

EXAMPLE:  You mending? — Are you feeling better?

At bedtime, Papa came upstairs with his big shoes kicking one of the risers, and brought me one of the last of the winter apples from the cellar. He pulled up a chair close to my bed and looked at me for a long time while I ate the apple with my left hand.

"You mending?"

"Yes, Papa."

"I ought to lick you proper for leaving the schoolhouse."

"Yes, Papa. You ought."

"Someday you want to walk into the bank in Learning and write down your name, don't you?"

"Yes, sir."

"I don't cotton to raise a fool."

"No, Papa."

I tried to move my right arm, but it made me wince up. I couldn't help but make a noise about it.

"She bit you up fair, that cow. Clear to bone."

"Sure did. I always thought cows don't bite."

"Anything'll bite, be it provoked."

"I guess I provoked old Apron. Boy, she sure did some provoking on me."
—Robert Peck

# 27

# Social Dialects

Most people are simply amused by or curious about the differences in regional dialects. Other kinds of language differences, however, may not be so easily dismissed. Certain pronunciations and word choices can cost us a great deal if they are used at the wrong time or in the wrong place. Consider these three sentences.

- Him and her ain't the ones who we's giving the party for.
- He and she aren't the ones we're giving the party for.
- He and she are not the ones for whom we are giving the party.

All three sentences say the same thing. What makes the sentences different is the speaker's choice of words: *him and her/he and she; ain't/aren't/are not; we's/we're/we are;* and *who/whom.*

The three sentences demonstrate different **levels of usage** that can be observed in the speech and the writing of Americans. Those levels of usage have little to do with geography. Instead, they convey messages about the speakers' or writers' education and the choices they make while using language.

The two basic levels of usage are called **standard English** and **nonstandard English.** Within standard English there are two separate levels, formal and informal usage.

## Standard English

**Formal standard English**  Language used on strictly formal occasions is called **formal English.** It is most often found in writing, especially in business and technical reports, legal documents, formal essays, editorials, and business correspondence. Occasionally it is used by speakers, too, as they deliver political addresses, preach sermons, or present their cases to a jury. Formal standard English is not appropriate in every situation, of course. If you use formal English in a conversation with friends in the school cafeteria, don't be surprised if they move to a table across the room!

**Informal standard English**   The language used in communicating with friends or a general audience is called **informal English**. Television interviews and committee meetings also are usually conducted in informal standard English.

Your written assignments in school, personal letters, and job applications require careful use of your knowledge of informal standard English. (Written informal English is less casual than oral informal English because writers often have more time to consider their choices than speakers do.)

## Nonstandard English

Nonstandard English is typically the oral language of English speakers whose formal education is limited.

Usage levels should not be labeled as "good" or "bad," "correct" or "incorrect," however, but as "appropriate" or "inappropriate." As you saw earlier, all three example sentences communicated the same idea. Though nonstandard English is less exact than standard English, nonstandard English serves many people very well. However, the use of nonstandard English may severely limit a person's opportunities. Our culture continues to respect standard English and those who use it appropriately.

There are comparatively few differences that separate the levels of usage. For instance, most of the words we use—words such as *job, friend, help,* and *important*—are used by speakers of both standard and nonstandard English. The following charts show the most common *kinds* of differences between standard and nonstandard English usage.

### VERBS

| Nonstandard | Standard |
| --- | --- |
| Fred *ain't* ready yet. | Fred *isn't* ready yet. |
| She had *went* home. | She had *gone* home. |
| Phyllis *done* her work. | Phyllis *did* her work. |
| Joe *be* tired. | Joe *is* tired. |
| Each of them *are* hungry. | Each of them *is* hungry. |

### PRONOUNS

| Nonstandard | Standard |
|---|---|
| *Us* three argued. | *We* three argued. |
| Did you see *them* shoes? | Did you see *those* shoes? |
| It was between *she* and *I*. | It was between *her* and *me*. |
| *Him* and *her* went to the dance. | *He* and *she* went to the dance. |
| Jim and *myself* agreed. | Jim and *I* agreed. |

### ADJECTIVES AND ADVERBS

| Nonstandard | Standard |
|---|---|
| He's a *real* nice person. | He's a *very* nice person. |
| Judy's the *most smartest* of all. | Judy's the *smartest* of all. |
| Ted hits the ball *good*. | Ted hits the ball *well*. |
| The dancer walks *graceful*. | The dancer walks *gracefully*. |
| This is the *best* hat of the two. | This is the *better* hat of the two. |

## Usage Today and Yesterday

It would be misleading to speak of usage as if the world stood still, as if language were as unchanging as the pyramids. Language choices are *not* for all time. One of the greatest writers in English, William Shakespeare, often wrote sentences that today would be red-penciled if they appeared on a high school composition.

> *Silence is the perfectest herald of joy: I were but little happy, if I could say how much.* —William Shakespeare

Time brings many changes in both speech and writing. Words change, expressions change, and sentence structures change. Language cannot be permanently "fixed," even though some people might wish that it could be.

In 1712 Jonathan Swift, the author of *Gulliver's Travels*, wrote a letter to the Earl of Oxford, proposing an academy of "qualified" persons to keep watch over language. Swift wanted this academy to "purify" the language and to standardize it. There were certain words in fashion that Swift didn't like. The word *mob*, instead of the Latin *mobile vulgus*, was one of them. *Banter, sham,* and *bamboozle* were others. He wanted to do away with these words, to throw them out of the English language.

Swift lost the battle. The words survived and are still used. No academy was established. But Swift didn't lose *all* his battles over words. Some of the words he objected to—*ult* (rather than *ultimate*), for instance, and *poz* (rather than *positive*)—didn't survive.

Look at the following example of an eighteenth-century advertisement from New England. Notice the early American English spellings and use of capital letters.

---

### DANIEL WALDO, jun.

*Has for Sale, at the* BRICK STORE, *a few rods South of the Court Houfe, in* WORCESTER,

AN Affortment of Nails, Tacks, and Brads, Window Glafs, Steel, Pewter and Brafs, Frying Pans, Flat Irons, iron Shovels, Carpenters' Hammers, Saws, Chiffels, Plane Irons, Locks, Hinges, Latches and Bolts, Buttons and Buckles, Saddlery Ware, Cabinet Ware, beautiful enamelled Clock and Watch Faces, with almoft every article in the Hard Ware line.

*A L S O,*

Broadcloths, German Serge, Shalloons, Tammies, Calimancoes, Calicoes, Shawls, Muflin, Lawn, Cambrick, Velvet, Corduroys and Fuftians, &c.

*LIKEWISE,*

Rum, Sugar, Wine, Tea, Chocolate, Coffee, &c. &c. with a great variety of articles not enumerated.

☞ Said WALDO affures his Cuftomers, that fince the Small Pox has been in Bofton, he has not received any Goods from that place, and that he determines not to bring any from thence while the diforder continues to prevail; fo that they may be fupplied by him without the leaft rifk to themfelves or their families.

*Worcefter, Sept.* 19, 1792.

# EXERCISES

**A. Identifying standard English**   Write the numbers 1–10 on your paper. Identify the example of standard English in each of the following pairs by writing *a* or *b* on your paper.

1. a. Who done it?
   b. Who did it?
2. a. They's nothing we can do about it.
   b. There is nothing we can do about it.
3. a. Harry brought that trouble on himself.
   b. Harry brung that trouble on hisself.
4. a. Them and us changed cars at Tenth and Franklin.
   b. They and we changed cars at Tenth and Franklin.
5. a. The balloon burst before it hit the sidewalk.
   b. The balloon busted before it hit the sidewalk.
6. a. My sister she never eats no breakfast.
   b. My sister never eats breakfast.
7. a. Could I have one of those tote bags?
   b. Could I have one of them tote bags?
8. a. You sang that song well.
   b. You sung that song good.
9. a. C.C. be working at night.
   b. C.C. works at night.
10. a. Learn me how to play the guitar before Friday.
    b. Teach me how to play the guitar before Friday.

**B. Changing nonstandard usage to standard usage**   Each of the following sentences contains at least one item of nonstandard usage. Some contain two or three. Write the numbers 1–15 on your paper. Rewrite the sentences so that they are examples of standard written usage.

1. The bell had rang, but Mr. Finch kept talking.
2. Patience and strength is what every doctor needs.
3. Have Brenda wrote you a letter yet?
4. There was two kittens laying on the bed.
5. Please leave me help you with them packages.
6. Him and Dorinda helped theirselves to most of the chocolate candy that we bought.
7. The turtle warn't nowhere around.
8. He ain't goin' to get a job nohow.
9. Could us students earn some extra credit points?
10. Father brung home the groceries.

11. We won't find no life on none of them other planets.
12. That girl who live above the Teagues' garage, she play tennis real good.
13. Will you and him be riding with her and I?
14. Sal had went to the game herself.
15. Being as you invited me, I'll go.

**C. Using appropriate English**  Rewrite each of the following passages in language that is appropriate for the situation indicated in italics.

1. *You are standing at the desk of your English teacher, asking for an extension of a deadline for an assignment.*

    My dear teacher, I beg that you heed my plea for additional time on this assignment. Try as I might, I could not obtain copies of the volumes that you suggested we peruse before we compose our essays. I contacted numerous peers, but they were unable to assist me. Consequently, I must seek your sympathetic understanding on this matter. I shall make every effort to complete the assignment before Friday.

2. *You are writing to the officer of a foundation that gives scholarships to deserving students.*

    Hey, folks! I heard tell that youse guys have some bread to give to we poor dudes who want to go to college. I've done good in all my subjects and have been pretty active at this here school. I mean, man, how many kids have a B minus average and can also play the cornet good? But I don't got no money. So check out my record good, and send the cash.

3. *You are sitting at a cafeteria table, trying to borrow a dollar from your best friend.*

    I am delighted to find you here. I trust that I am not disturbing your repast. I assure you that I would not interrupt so good a friend, were I not myself so disturbed. As you may recall, Ms. Burgess, our mentor, is administering a final examination to our history class this hour. It has been a decidedly difficult course, as you well know. Thirty minutes ago, I started to write the examination. I was doing exceedingly well when—alas!—my pen ran out of ink. Our dear teacher said that I might seek another writing utensil at my locker, but I found none there. Would you kindly loan me a dollar so that I can purchase another pen and hastily return to my examination? I will reimburse you tomorrow morning.

# 28

# Special Vocabularies

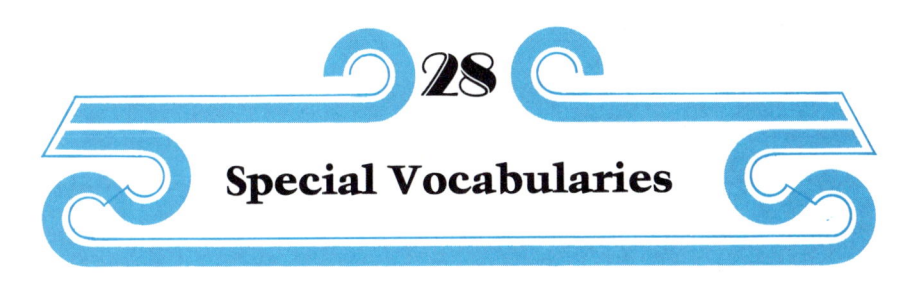

The language shared by members of an occupation or a special interest group is called **jargon.** People who repair automobiles, design clothes, drive trucks, practice medicine, or teach school often need to communicate with each other about objects and processes important to their jobs. They develop precise technical vocabularies which are almost universally understood among people who share the same occupations. Those outside an occupation seldom understand its jargon. The following chart shows examples from occupational vocabularies.

|  | Special Term | Standard Term |
|---|---|---|
| **Truck Drivers** | snore shelf | bed |
|  | handle | CB code name |
|  | motion lotion | gasoline |
| **Editors** | face | style of type |
|  | folio | page number |
|  | to bleed | to extend a picture to the edge of the page |
| **Stage Hands** | catwalk | work deck above a stage |
|  | flat | unit of scenery |
|  | to strike | to remove scenery |
| **Circus and Carnival Workers** | picture gallery | tattooed person |
|  | windjammer | musician |
|  | hoister | ferris wheel |
| **Railroad Workers** | hog mauler | locomotive engineer |
|  | louse cage | caboose |
|  | cow crate | cattle car |

People who enjoy certain sports, games, or hobbies use special vocabularies, too. Again, such language can be quite complex and technical. But long-term experience with the game or hobby usually leads to mastery of its special vocabulary.

## Slang

**Slang** is a special in-group language. It commonly originates among the young. It is lively, breezy language that often becomes popular among other age groups as well. Typically, slang is faddish language. It is introduced, spreads rapidly, is overused, becomes tiresome, and is dropped from the language. As slang words or phrases approach the end of this cycle, they often become tiresome and boring to listeners young and old.

Because the life span of slang is unpredictably short, it is of limited use to writers who want their work to be read very far into the future. In five years, today's slang will seem as dated as *jeepers creepers, peachy-keen,* and *neat-o* seem today. Also, much slang simply indicates approval or disapproval and so is not precise enough to serve a writer well. Words such as *neat, cool,* and *crummy* add little to style or meaning.

Sometimes slang is spread by the mass media. It is used widely by newscasters and columnists, for instance, and then enters general usage. *Lunch, hobo,* and *highbrow* are but three of hundreds of words that began as slang.

Slang is more appropriate in speech than in writing. Use it among friends, but do not overuse it. Be certain when you do use it that it is appropriate to your subject and to the tone you wish to establish. Slang should not be used in formal speech or formal writing.

## EXERCISES

**A. Matching sports vocabularies**   Label five columns with the names of these sports: *baseball, football, basketball, ice hockey,* and *skiing.* Under each heading, write three words from the following list that are part of that sport's special vocabulary. Use a dictionary for those items you do not know. Add a fourth term to as many of your lists as possible.

| | | |
|---|---|---|
| free throw | pitchout | slalom |
| T-bar | conversion | traveling |
| balk | keyhole | face-off |
| backfield | schuss | squeeze play |
| high-sticking | touchback | cross-checking |

**B. Exploring occupational vocabularies** Find at least five special terms that are often used by any one of the following persons. If you wish, you can choose a different occupation—especially one that you have personal knowledge about.

| | | |
|---|---|---|
| *auto mechanic* | *farmer* | *lawyer* |
| *airplane pilot* | *musician* | *soldier* or *sailor* |
| *poet* | *nurse* | *taxi driver* |

**C. Identifying out-dated slang terms** Write the numbers 1–12 on your paper. The words and expressions in the left-hand column were once in common use, some of them not long ago. Match the slang terms with their definitions shown in the right-hand column. Use a dictionary if you need help.

1. flummox
2. ten-carat
3. patootie
4. black cow
5. stickum
6. cancer stick
7. dillion
8. scroot
9. idiot box
10. jake
11. wampum
12. dagwood

a. sweetheart
b. a very large number
c. satisfactory, all right
d. big, remarkable
e. a dog
f. root beer and ice cream
g. cigarette
h. fail
i. money
j. glue
k. a very large sandwich
l. television set

# REVIEWING LESSONS 26-28

**A. Modernizing out-dated usage** All of the following sentences were written at least a hundred years ago in the standard English usage of the day. Rewrite each sentence according to modern standard usage.

1. Looke ere ye leape.—*John Heywood*
2. A Rose is sweeter in the bud than full blowne.—*John Lyly*
3. Methought I heard one calling "Child."—*George Herbert*
4. Ill news is wing'd with fate, and flies apace.—*John Dryden*
5. "Why speak ye so of the mirth that is in Heaven? Ye know it not, and ye have not been there, any more than we."—*Margery Kempe*
6. I do not know the method of drawing up an indictment against an whole people.—*Edmund Burke*

**B. Responding to a poem** Read the following poem. Then in a few sentences answer the questions that follow it.

### MOTTO
*I play it cool*
*And dig all jive—*
*That's the reason*
*I stay alive.*
*My motto,*
*As I live and learn*
      *is*
*Dig and be dug*
*In return.*
   —Langston Hughes

1. What do you think the poet means when he says, "I play it cool/And dig all jive"?
2. What does he mean by "That's the reason/I stay alive"?
3. What does this poem say to you about communication?

**C. Considering the nature of usage** Answer the following questions in a few sentences.

1. How is English usage like (a) table manners, (b) the way we dress, and (c) sportsmanship?
2. What happens if you break the "rules" in any of those areas?
3. Do the "rules" ever change? How? Who changes them?

**D. Comparing British and American English** The following picture shows the dashboard of a Rolls-Royce Silver Shadow. It is taken from the Rolls-Royce owner's handbook, published in England. Write the numbers 1–25 on your paper. For each British term write the term that would appear in a service manual for an American car. If the American term is the same as the British term, write *S*.

EXAMPLE: 1. Gear range selector lever
ANSWER: 1. Gear shift

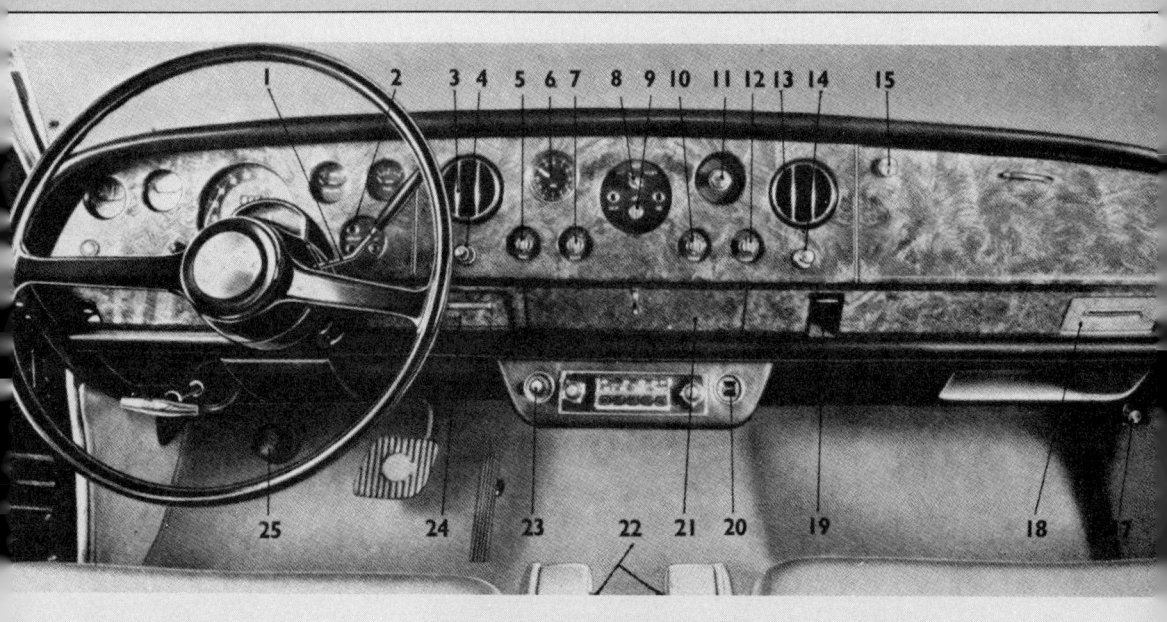

**Fig 3 DRIVER'S CONTROLS**

1. Gear range selector lever
2. Main warning lamp panel
3. Adjustable outlet for fresh or cold air
4. Control for adjustable outlet
5. Instrument lamps switch
6. Adjustment knob for hands
7. Windscreen wiper/washer switch
8. Main lighting switch
9. Ignition switch
10. Upper heating, ventilation and refrigeration switch
11. Cigar lighter
12. Lower heating and ventilation switch
13. Adjustable outlet for fresh air
14. Control for adjustable outlet
15. Facia compartment lock
16. Switch for passenger's roof lamp
17. Control for side scuttle wall outlet
18. Ash tray
19. Blower motors switch
20. Aerial switch
21. Air conditioning flap
22. Front seat switches
23. Loudspeaker balance control
24. Ash tray
25. Headlamp dipping switch

# SENTENCE SENSE

## 29

## Sentence Fragments

A piece of a broken phonograph record is a fragment. A portion of a broken dinner plate is a fragment. It follows then that a sentence fragment is a piece of a sentence, doesn't it? A **sentence fragment** is usually part of a complete sentence, but it is punctuated so that it resembles a complete sentence. Look at this example.

- Trisha ran to the tennis net. *Extending her arm to congratulate Tam.*

The italicized word group looks as though it were a sentence. It begins with a capital letter and ends with a period. However, a capital and a period do not necessarily mean that a word group is a sentence. Sentences must meet two tests: **(1)** they must have a subject and a verb, and **(2)** they must make sense by themselves. "Trisha ran to the tennis net" meets both requirements. "Extending her arm to congratulate Tam" meets neither requirement. It has no subject and no complete verb, and it does not make sense by itself. It makes us wonder who was extending her arm.

The writer probably intended the phrase "extending her arm to congratulate Tam" to modify the noun *Trisha*. If that is so, then the modifier belongs in the sentence that contains the word it modifies, *Trisha*. Sentence fragments such as this are easily corrected by attaching the fragment to the independent clause.

- Extending her arm to congratulate Tam, Trisha ran to the tennis net.

Sometimes sentences fragments contain subjects and verbs but do not make sense. Here is an example.

- The class left the room quickly. *When Ms. Rush dismissed them.*

The italicized word group is a dependent clause. It contains a subject, *Ms. Rush,* and a verb, *dismissed.* However, the adverb *when* signals an incomplete thought and keeps us from accepting the word group as a sentence. The fragment tells us when the class left, and it should be attached to the preceding word group, which is a sentence.

- The class left the room quickly when Ms. Rush dismissed them.

**Other kinds of fragments**   The preceding examples are but two kinds of fragments. Here are some others.

FRAGMENT:   She said she would drive me to school. *On Tuesday and Thursday mornings.* (prepositional phrase)
CORRECTED:   She said she would drive me to school on Tuesday and Thursday mornings.

FRAGMENT:   I have been pestering my parents. *To let me get a weekend job.* (infinitive phrase)
CORRECTED:   I have been pestering my parents to let me get a weekend job.

FRAGMENT:   I gave my report on Paul Zindel's *The Pigman. One of the best books I have ever read.* (appositive)
CORRECTED:   I gave my report on Paul Zindel's *The Pigman,* one of the best books I have ever read.

FRAGMENT:   My friends and I bought our lunches. *And set out for the lake.* (part of a compound verb)
CORRECTED:   My friends and I bought our lunches and set out for the lake.

You have probably noticed that in all of the examples of sentence fragments given so far the writer has cut off the last part of a complete sentence and then incorrectly punctuated it as a sentence. Sometimes a writer cuts off the first part instead as in the following fragment.

FRAGMENT:   *Walking toward the deserted mansion.* We tried not to seem frightened. (participial phrase)
CORRECTED:   Walking toward the deserted mansion, we tried not to seem frightened.

Sometimes writers create fragments that are confusing or meaningless because they have left out some important words.

FRAGMENT:   Chris, at first surprised by the centipede that was crawling along her arm.

In this case, the writer may have become so involved in writing the phrase beginning with *at first* that he or she forgot to finish the thought that inspired the sentence. Since we hate to leave Chris sitting there watching that insect, we will end the suspense—and the sentence.

CORRECTED:   Chris, at first surprised by the centipede that was crawling along her arm, began to count its legs.

Notice that we have spoken of sentence fragments as potential problems for writers. They seldom concern speakers. Most people—even masters of standard English—use sentence fragments frequently in their speech: "Which book?" "The brown one." "Probably not." Writers use fragments in writing dialogue. Advertising writers frequently use fragments in order to seem chatty.

But when informal or formal standard English is required, writers generally are careful to avoid sentence fragments because they do not want to confuse their readers. Careful proofreading of your writing will help you to eliminate sentence fragments.

## EXERCISES

**A. Identifying sentence fragments** Some of the following word groups are complete sentences and others are fragments. Write the numbers 1–10 on your paper. For each word group write *F* if it is a sentence fragment or *C* if the word group is a complete sentence.

EXAMPLE:   Seeing a girl that I knew.   F

1. Being excited as the game started.
2. After finishing my history assignment.
3. To buy an old Buick.
4. Playing tennis requires strong legs.
5. An old cat who knows a lot about our neighborhood.
6. Because it was raining and we had nowhere else to go.
7. Piloting a plane seemed exciting.

8. Reading the assigned book.
9. Hal playing the piano.
10. As the rain drummed on the metal roof of the shed.

**B.** Writing complete sentences   The following advertisement contains many sentence fragments. The passage makes sense, however, because it relies on a picture to get its meaning across.

Using complete sentences, rewrite the information given in the advertisement. Your essay should be one or two paragraphs long.

## Margie Adam.
## Songwriter.
## In Celebration.

**With**
E. Marcy Dicterow • Chris Hanson
Jerene Jackson • Diane Lindsay
Vicki Randle • Andrea Weltman

Presented by Women in Production

February 25, 26, 27
Palace of Fine Arts
Lyon and Bay Streets
San Francisco

March 4, 5
Longhorn Theatre
6230 Sunset Boulevard
Los Angeles

Child care provided. Workshops in each city.

For ticket information, write:
Women in Production
101 East Seventh Street
Davis, California 95616

Margie Adam, Songwriter available in records, tapes and songbooks:
Pleiades Records
P.O. Box D
Dixon, California 95620

For bulk rates:
Women in Distribution
P.O. Box 8858
Washington, D.C. 20003

Photo: Holly Hartman

**C. Correcting sentence fragments** Write the numbers 1–10 on your paper. Rewrite each of the following sentence fragments as part of a complete sentence.

EXAMPLE: Knowing the tune.
ANSWER: Knowing the tune, I sang along with the others.

1. Then slowly, going up the hill.
2. Arabela, often alert to problems of this sort.
3. And grinned from ear to ear.
4. To call that a good movie.
5. Before going to the museum.
6. Who coaches our team.
7. When we read about it.
8. On the chair in the corner of the green room.
9. Two of the nicest people I know.
10. But didn't need it.

## 30

# Run-on Sentences

Like a sentence fragment, a **run-on sentence** resembles a single complete sentence because it begins with a capital letter and ends with a period. Unlike a sentence fragment, though, a run-on sentence contains at least two complete sentences disguised as one. Sometimes writers put a comma at the end of the first sentence instead of a period. Sometimes they do not signal the end of a complete sentence at all. Regardless of which situation exists, run-on sentences often confuse readers.

Only a detective could love mystery sentences such as the following ones.

- Jack wanted to fly the airplane promised great adventure.
- Please plan to be here at 8:30 A.M. on Monday so that you can meet Ms. Selkirk, the principal, Mr. Baston, wants to meet all new students, too.

You probably had to read the run-on sentences above at least twice in order to decide what they meant. Run-on sentences are confusing and, in quantity, are frustrating to readers. Good writers take pains to avoid writing run-on sentences.

Run-on sentences seldom contain two random ideas. Instead, the two complete thoughts that share one capital letter and one period in a run-on sentence usually are closely related in meaning. They may seem to belong together. For instance, the second part of the run-on may give a reason for the statement that was made in the first part of the run-on.

RUN-ON:   Kara enjoys her gym classes, they give her a chance to be outdoors.
CORRECTED:   Kara enjoys her gym classes. They give her a chance to be outdoors.

Sometimes the second part of the run-on contributes a detail that is related to the statement made in the first part.

RUN-ON:   The concert was long, it lasted four hours.
CORRECTED:   The concert was long. It lasted four hours.

Sometimes the second part contrasts with the statement made in the first part.

RUN-ON:   Dan's old car is rusty and noisy, Bella's new car is shiny and runs quietly.
CORRECTED:   Dan's old car is rusty and noisy. Bella's new car is shiny and runs quietly.

**Words that often inspire run-on sentences**   The second part of a run-on sentence can begin with any kind of word. However, pronouns and conjunctive adverbs are often found in run-on sentences.

Pronouns are closely related to nouns. Their major function is replacing nouns in sentences. As you write and revise, check the following pronouns to see if they are the subjects of their sentences: *he, she, it, we, they.*

RUN-ON:   Those candles sell for fifty cents apiece, *they* used to be a dollar.
CORRECTED:   Those candles sell for fifty cents apiece. *They* used to be a dollar.

Conjunctive adverbs are adverbs that cannot ordinarily join two sentences without a semicolon. (Be here by noon; *otherwise* I'll mark you as late.) Writers often create run-on sentences when they use these adverbs incorrectly. Following is a list of conjunctive adverbs.

| also | furthermore | moreover | then |
| consequently | hence | nevertheless | there |
| finally | however | now | therefore |
| further | indeed | otherwise | thus |

RUN-ON:   I like shrimp, *however,* I dislike most other seafood.
CORRECTED:   I like shrimp. *However,* I dislike most other seafood.

RUN-ON:   The records from my old school came today, *therefore,* I won't need to write a letter to my former counselor.
CORRECTED:   The records from my old school came today; *therefore,* I won't need to write a letter to my former counselor.

Conjunctive adverbs should not be confused with coordinating conjunctions (*and, but, for, or, nor, yet, so*), which *can* be used to join two statements with a comma.

Correcting run-on sentences   One way to correct run-ons is to write each part as a separate sentence.

RUN-ON:   I went to the market for some flour, *then* I stopped at the drug store for my prescription.
CORRECTED:   I went to the market for some flour. *Then* I stopped at the drug store for my prescription.

When you want to emphasize the close relationship of the two statements in a run-on sentence, rewrite the run-on as a compound sentence. Use a semicolon to show where one statement ends and another begins.

CORRECTED:   I went to the market for some flour; *then* I stopped at the drug store for my prescription.

A third method is to create a compound sentence by using a coordinating conjunction to join the two statements.

CORRECTED:   I went to the market for some flour, *and then* I stopped at the drug store for my prescription.

## EXERCISES

**A.** Writing complete sentences   Write the numbers 1–10 on your paper. Copy each of the following word groups. Then, after each word group, write a complete statement that begins with the word in parentheses. The result may be one complete sentence or two complete sentences. Punctuate them appropriately.

EXAMPLE:   Bill was tired ... (he)
POSSIBLE ANSWERS:   Bill was tired. He had not slept for three days.
                    Bill was tired; he had not slept for three days.

1. Mrs. Garcia returned our themes ... (then)
2. I forgot my money ... (therefore)
3. Because no one knew the words ... (we)
4. Tennis is a fast game ... (however)

5. If you hurry to finish your work . . . (then)
6. We arrived late . . . (therefore)
7. Children seldom dislike school . . . (they)
8. I used to want to be a pilot . . . (now)
9. That song will not become popular . . . (it)
10. Although Jessie has taken lessons for years . . . (she)

**B. Correcting run-ons**  Write the numbers 1–10 on your paper. Rewrite each of the following run-on sentences as one complete sentence, or as two complete sentences.

EXAMPLE:  Her hands are large, she has trouble finding gloves.
ANSWER:  Her hands are large. She has trouble finding gloves.

1. I enjoy reading novels, they are better than television.
2. Mabel's painting is good, Paula's is not good.
3. We fished for hours, finally, we caught a trout.
4. It's too far to walk, furthermore, it's raining.
5. Maria wants to be an architect, I think she will be one.
6. I need a new coat, otherwise, I will have to borrow my sister's old one this year.
7. I couldn't sleep, therefore, I drank a glass of warm milk.
8. I like to read my sister's medical books, I think I'll study to become a doctor, too.
9. We went to the movies then we went to Cornelio's house.
10. Some people are afraid of spiders I'm not.

**C. Using conjunctive adverbs**  Write the numbers 1–10 on your paper. Write ten original compound sentences. Use a different conjunctive adverb in each sentence. Be sure to punctuate your sentences correctly.

EXAMPLE:  Send them this map; also, send the directions I wrote out for them.

# REVIEWING LESSONS 29–30

**A. Identifying sentence fragments and run-on sentences** Write the numbers 1–20 on your paper. If a group of words is a complete sentence, write *C* after its number. If it is a sentence fragment, write *F*. If it is a run-on sentence, write *RO*.

EXAMPLE:   Because I said so.   F

1. Although we never disagree.
2. Prepare your roller first, then mix the paint.
3. Unless you want to pay the heating bill, you will have to close the windows in your room during this blizzard.
4. Since Derrick is driving his Chevy and Susie will have her old Pinto.
5. Listening to the teacher whose directions were clear.
6. Tired after the long hike, both of us went to sleep in our chairs.
7. Several of the fall's new television shows have already gone off the air, they had low Nielsen ratings.
8. Because we could not afford the more expensive tickets that we wanted.
9. While we were waiting for Geraldo, Tony offered us a ride.
10. Cilla recommended S.E. Hinton's books, she said they are good stories about teenagers.
11. Forgetting to put his keys in his pocket before he locked the car and closed the windows.
12. This spray will kill weeds but not pets.
13. The scholarship committee, composed of a member from each homeroom.
14. Mr. Court told the same joke in class today, and no one laughed except Cathy, who was absent yesterday.
15. Salim should be here today, however, he was ill yesterday.
16. Trailing the blue Corvette through the crowded streets, sirens blaring and tires screeching.
17. It is possible that the sophomores will buy more yearbooks than the seniors this year, however, since the sophomore class is so large.
18. People have grown tired of the Blitz-o commercials they have heard them too often.
19. Paying no attention to their coach's warning, the Stingrays lost four yards on the play.
20. I read the question too quickly, therefore, I didn't give the right answer.

**B.** Correcting sentence fragments and run-on sentences   The following passage contains several sentence fragments and run-on sentences. Rewrite the passage, correcting those sentence errors. Do not change the meaning of the passage.

### THE BIRTH OF FRANKENSTEIN

Mary Shelley was the wife of the famous poet, Percy Bysshe Shelley, she was only eighteen when she wrote Frankenstein. A supernatural tale which has fascinated readers since a nightmare inspired her to write it in 1816.

The night that she got the idea for the story, she was staying with friends in a gloomy Swiss chateau. Which belonged to another poet. Lord Byron. The weather created a spooky setting, lightning flashed through the night and thunder crashed as the friends gathered before bedtime. Inspired by the foul weather and sitting before a flickering fire. They told ghost stories for a long time. They agreed that each of them would write a ghost story to share with the group, however, Mary was the only one to write one. In the middle of the night she was awakened by a nightmare. So frightening that she could not go back to sleep.

Early in the morning she sat down to write, she began to record the events of her bad dream. Frankenstein and his monster were born that morning. The story about a medical student who uses the parts of corpses to build a monster that destroys its creator.

Almost everyone knows the story now, millions have read the book. Or seen one of the many film versions of the eerie tale that started as a real nightmare.

# CHOOSING THE RIGHT WORDS

## 31

## Subject–Verb Agreement

Here are some pairs of sentences similar to those that you speak, hear, read, and write every day. As you examine each pair, compare their subjects and verbs, which are in italics.

- That *picture reminds* me of you.
- Those *pictures remind* me of you.

- The *customer was* right.
- The *customers were* right.

- The *train is running* late tonight.
- The *trains are running* late tonight.

You should have observed that the subject of the first sentence in each pair of sentences (*picture, customer, train*) is singular. The subject of the second sentence in each pair (*pictures, customers, trains*) is plural. You probably observed, too, that the verbs are different in each pair of sentences. Singular subjects are followed by singular forms of verbs. Plural subjects are followed by plural forms of verbs.

None of this should surprise you. It merely reviews a basic language principle: *In standard English, the subject and the verb agree in number.*

### When Subjects and Verbs Are Separated

Verbs do not always immediately follow their subjects, however. Sometimes other words stand between the subject and the verb. When that happens, speakers and writers are tempted to choose a form of the verb that agrees with the nearer word.

For instance, which verb would you choose for the following?

- One of the tires (was, were) low.

If you are tempted to choose *were,* it is probably because a plural noun, *tires,* stands closest to the verb. *Tires* is not the subject of the sentence, however. It is the object of the preposition *of. One* is the subject of the sentence. It is singular and therefore requires the singular verb form *was.*

- *One* of the tires *was* low. (singular subject)
- *Two* of the tires *were* low. (plural subject)

Sometimes the opposite situation occurs. A singular noun that is not the subject of the sentence precedes the verb and tempts a speaker or writer to make the wrong choice.

NONSTANDARD:  Several clerks at our hardware store has not been paid yet.
STANDARD:  Several *clerks* at our hardware store *have* not *been paid* yet.

The subject of the sentence determines whether you should choose a singular or plural verb form.

## When Sentences Have Compound Subjects

**Subjects joined by and**   Generally, compound subjects joined by *and* require plural verb forms.

- The *singer* and the *guitarist were* the winners.
- *Math* and *history require* most of my study time.

Occasionally, a compound subject refers to only one thing or to two things thought of as one. In such cases, the singular verb form is appropriate.

- My best *friend* and greatest *critic is* Emily.
 (*Friend* and *critic* refer to the same person.)

**Subjects joined by or, nor**   The following sentence may appear to have two subjects, but it does not.

- *Vic* or *Beth is* the culprit.

While there are two people named, the word *or* signals that only one of the people is the culprit. Therefore, the singular verb form is appropriate.

When the parts of a compound subject are both plural, a plural verb form should be used.

- Cookies and pies *are sold* at each bazaar.
- Neither medals nor trophies *were given*.

When a compound subject consists of a singular part and a plural part, the verb should agree with the part that is nearer to it.

- *John* or the *twins are* washing the dishes tonight.
- A few *cloves* or a *pinch* of cinnamon *is* all you need to add to make this plain cake spicy.

## When Subjects Follow Their Verbs

Another problem of subject—verb agreement occurs when a verb precedes its subject.

Two types of constructions deserve careful attention: (1) statements beginning with *there* or *here,* and (2) questions. In both cases, if the subject is going to be singular, choose a singular verb form. If it is going to be plural, choose a plural verb form.

SINGULAR:    Here *is* my *mother* now.
                     There *is* a matching *scarf* or *sash* somewhere.
                     Where *was* the *glue*?
PLURALS:     Here *are* the *stamps*.
                     Here *are* the *envelope* and the *stamp*.
                     Where *are* the *snapshots*?

**Plural form, singular meaning**   Some nouns are plural in form but usually singular in meaning. *Mathematics, physics,* and *measles* are three examples. They generally require singular verb forms.

- Mathematics *seems* easier this year.
- Physics *is* offered to seniors only.
- Measles *was* a dangerous disease.

Words stating weights, measurements, periods of time, and amounts of money are usually singular, though they appear to be plural.

- Two weeks *is* not long to wait for a letter.
- Three blocks *is* as far as I'll walk.
- *Is* seventy cents a reasonable price for a school lunch?

**Titles** When the subject of a sentence is the title of a single book, poem, story, film, or painting, use a singular verb form even if the title contains plural nouns.

- *Star Wars was* noted for its special effects.
- "Three Women Warriors" *is* one of my favorite poems.

**Collective nouns** Collective nouns name groups of people or objects. *Class, team, faculty, committee, group, band,* and *family* are collective nouns. Such nouns can take either singular or plural verb forms, depending upon their meaning.

- The *band was* excellent last night.
- The *band were* selling their quotas of chocolate bars.

**Indefinite pronouns** The following indefinite pronouns have singular meanings and require singular verb forms in standard English.

|  |  |  |
|---|---|---|
| anybody | somebody | one |
| anyone | someone | each |
| everybody | nobody | either |
| everyone | no one | neither |

- *Everybody is expected* to attend.
- *Each* of the plans *has* some merit.

Several indefinite pronouns have plural meanings and therefore require plural verbs: *both, few, many, several.*

- *Several* of us *are* eligible for prizes.
- *Few* people ever *gain* admission to that school.

**None** When you use the pronoun *none* to indicate *how much*, choose a singular verb form.

- *None* of the ice cream *remains.*
- *Is none* of my story believable?

Otherwise, your choice of singular or plural verb form with *none* will depend upon what meaning you intend.

- Although four students from our school are finalists, *none is* talented enough to win. (*None* is used to mean "not one of them" and so is considered singular.)
- *None* of the faculty *like* her. (*None* is used to mean "not any part of the group" and so the plural verb is appropriate.)

**Number varies with meaning** Several other words such as *all, half, part, some, more,* and *most* may take either a singular or a plural verb. When you use them to refer to *how much*, choose the singular verb.

- *Most* of the cake *was* gone.
- *Half* of my time *is* spent correcting the mistakes of others.

When you refer to *how many*, choose the plural verb.

- *Most* of the sophomores *were* at the game.
- *Half* of the points *were* scored in the first eight minutes.

# EXERCISES

**A. Matching the verb to the subject**  Write the numbers 1–15 on your paper. For each sentence, write the verb that agrees in number with the subject of the sentence.

1. A set of keys (was, were) found in the parking lot. *was*
2. One of the show's stars (is, are) ill. *is*
3. His spelling of the sisters' names (was, were) incorrect. *was*
4. Your reasons for seeking a transfer (surprises, surprise) me. *surprise*
5. The school's supply of paper towels (is, are) low. *is*
6. Only one of Jan's errors (was, were) evident. *was*
7. Eduardo, like his two brothers, (reads, read) science fiction constantly. *reads*
8. The list of necessary props for the play (was, were) posted in the drama classroom. *was*
9. A guarantee covering all moving parts (comes, come) with that robot. *comes*
10. Sylvia together with her sister and brother (plans, plan) to go to San Francisco for Christmas. *plans*
11. The costs of education (continues, continue) to rise each year. *continue*
12. Each one of these tickets (takes, take) you to a different place. *takes*
13. Lois Ashike, unlike the other teachers, (works, work) at school until five. *works*
14. A large box of science books (was, were) found in the cafeteria. *was*
15. Nina's ability to remember jokes (fascinates, fascinate) me. *fascinates*

**B. Dealing with compound subjects**  Write the numbers 1–10 on your paper. For each sentence write the verb that agrees in number with the compound subject of the sentence.

1. The hunting and fishing (is, are) excellent at Guntersville. *are*
2. Either a red scarf or a small pin (look, looks) good with that blouse. *looks*
3. Tennis and track (keeps, keep) Melissa busy after school. *keep*
4. Tennis or track (keeps, keep) Melissa busy after school. *keeps*
5. Neither Davis High nor Woodlawn High (is, are) likely to have a strong team this year. *is*
6. Pork and beans (is, are) my specialty. *is*
7. Neither Levi nor T.J. (is, are) staying to clean up after the dance. *is*
8. Neither the book nor the magazines (has, have) been moved from the table. *have*
9. Neither the magazines nor the book (has, have) been moved from the table. *has*
10. The magazines and the book (is, are) still on the table. *are*

**C. Deciding whether subjects are singular or plural** Write the numbers 1–25 on your paper. For each sentence write the verb that agrees in number with the subject of the sentence.

1. There (was, were) no spelling errors in the letter.
2. (Does, Do) this box of books belong in this room?
3. Here (is, are) the list of our demands.
4. Three years (seems, seem) like a long time.
5. None of your articles (has, have) been published.
6. How much (does, do) that shirt and pair of pants cost.
7. In Iowa there (is, are) a lake and a town named Clear Lake.
8. There (wasn't, weren't) enough seats on stage for the band.
9. Where (is, are) the people who volunteered earlier?
10. Every test she gives her classes (contains, contain) at least one essay question.
11. The principal thinks that shorter lunch shifts (is, are) the answer to the cafeteria problem.
12. The only evidence (was, were) the cookie crumbs on the table.
13. Everyone in the chorus (was, were) supposed to sell eight concert tickets.
14. *The Defenders* (is, are) an old TV series.
15. The largest item in Pedro's budget (is, are) his lunches.
16. Pedro's lunches (is, are) the largest item in his budget.
17. There (was, were) too many fouls called during that game.
18. (Is, Are) either of those clocks accurate?
19. Neither of the boys (has, have) any swimming ability.
20. Half of my English assignment (remains, remain) unfinished.
21. Physics (deals, deal) with matter and motion.
22. Neither of the plans (provides, provide) enough time.
23. Forty pounds (is, are) too much for a cat to weigh.
24. Some of the gasoline (has, have) been siphoned out.
25. Two days (is, are) enough time to finish this assignment.

# 32

# Pronoun Reference

**Agreement with antecedents** A pronoun takes the place of a noun, a phrase, or a clause. The word or group of words that a pronoun replaces is called its **antecedent**. A pronoun should agree with its antecedent in number and gender.

**Number** refers to the singular and plural forms of pronouns and their antecedents. Singular forms of pronouns normally follow singular antecedents. Plural forms of pronouns follow plural antecedents.

SINGULAR: *Libby* gave *her* report first.
PLURAL: The *scouts* gave *their* reports on Tuesday.

Several pronouns also communicate the sex or **gender** of their antecedents.

FEMININE: *Nina* found *her* paint when *she* lifted *her* canvas.
MASCULINE: When *Roland* stood to give *his* report, *he* forgot *his* introduction.
NEUTER: Don't judge the *book* by *its* cover.

Matching the number and gender of pronouns and their antecedents probably comes automatically to you now. However, most people will occasionally use a plural pronoun in a sentence in which the antecedent requires a singular pronoun.

WRONG: If a *person* does not succeed at first, *they* should try again.
IMPROVED: If a *person* does not succeed at first, *he or she* should try again.
IMPROVED: If *people* do not succeed at first, *they* should try again.

**Indefinite pronouns** Some indefinite pronouns are singular in number. When they are antecedents, one of the singular pronoun forms should follow.

- *Each* of the scouts has *his* assigned duty. (*Each* is singular. The group consists only of males.)
- *Someone* on the girls' basketball team forgot to leave *her* completed questionnaire. (*Someone* is singular. The group consists only of females.)
- *Everyone* in our class read *his* or *her* prediction aloud. (*Everyone* is singular. The group consists of both females and males.)

In informal conversation, plural pronouns are often used in place of singular pronouns, but that usage is inappropriate in written work.

SPOKEN:  *Everyone* should report to *their* homeroom.
WRITTEN: *Everyone* should report to *his* or *her* homeroom.
         *Students* should report to *their* homerooms.

Occasionally the meaning of an indefinite pronoun is clearly plural. Using the singular pronoun in such cases produces absurd sentences.

- After *everybody* arrived, *he* began to dance with each other.

In informal English, replace *he* with *they*.

INFORMAL: After *everybody* arrived, *they* began to dance with each other.

In formal English, rephrase such sentences to avoid the problem.

FORMAL: After *all the guests* arrived, *they* began to dance with each other.

Compound antecedents   When two or more antecedents are joined by *and,* you should choose a plural pronoun for agreement.

- Clyde *and* Chris brought *their* assignments in late.
- Mrs. Watson *and* her daughter asked me to ride with *them*.

When two or more singular antecedents are joined by *or* or *nor,* choose a singular pronoun for agreement.

- Either Miguel *or* Ralph will bring *his* guitar for our presentation of *Our Town*.
- Neither Anna *nor* her sister has had *her* tonsils out.

However, if one of the antecedents joined by *or* or *nor* is plural and the other is singular, you should choose the pronoun that agrees with the antecedent that is nearer.

- Neither Dolores nor her *partners* had paid *their* lab fees.

Unclear antecedents   Occasionally a speaker or writer fails to make clear what the antecedent of a pronoun is. The result can be confusion for those who hear or read the sentence.

1. The antecedent is implied but not stated.

    UNCLEAR:  We spent the day aboard a fishing boat but didn't catch *any*.
    CLEAR:  We spent the day aboard a fishing boat but didn't catch *any fish*.

    UNCLEAR:  When Andy finished writing, he put *them* on the teacher's desk.
    CLEAR:  When Andy finished writing, he put *his finished pages* on the teacher's desk.

2. *It* and *they* may need specification. In informal conversation we often use the pronouns *it* and *they* carelessly, without antecedents. Sometimes we do so because we don't know who "they" are or what "it" is. In formal speech and all writing, however, we must be more specific.

    UNCLEAR:  Though Farah had wanted to be an engineer, she didn't enjoy *it*.
    CLEAR:  Though Farah had wanted to be an engineer, she didn't enjoy *her work*.

    UNCLEAR:  When I started work, *they* told me that I would be paid every Friday.
    CLEAR:  When I started work, *the manager and the personnel manager* told me that I would be paid every Friday.

3. When two nouns are present, the pronoun may not clearly refer to its intended antecedent.

    UNCLEAR:  Hal and Mario were working on *his* car.
        (Whose car were they working on?)
    CLEAR:  Hal and Mario were working on *Hal's* car.

UNCLEAR: The coaches told the players that *they* weren't ready to meet the Bulldogs on Friday. (Who weren't ready, the players or the coaches?)
CLEAR: The coaches said that the players weren't ready to meet the Bulldogs on Friday.

4. Clauses beginning with *who, which,* and *that* can also be ambiguous.

UNCLEAR: Maureen finished her act, which amazed us. (What was amazing—Maureen's act or the fact that she finished it?)
CLEAR: Maureen finished her amazing act.

## EXERCISES

**A. Choosing correct pronouns** Write the numbers 1–15 on your paper. For each of the following sentences write the correct pronoun or pronouns.

1. Everyone has (his or her, their) own opinion about cafeteria food.
2. Both fire fighters received awards for (his, their) heroic acts.
3. One of the singers dropped (his, their) music in mid-performance.
4. Each of the sales representatives wrote (her, their) own letters to prospective clients.
5. Either Dee or Stephanie will take you home in (her, their) car.
6. Neither of the fellows heard (his, their) name when it was announced.
7. Nobody is to park (his or her, their) car in the faculty lot this week.
8. If a player moves (his or her, their) foot over this line, (he or she, they) will forfeit a turn.
9. Three of us boys forgot (his, our, their) fishing tackle.
10. Mr. Wong let each of the tardy boys tell (his, their) sad tale.
11. Neither Christy nor Alicia played (her, their) best in the preliminary round.
12. If a person doesn't understand the scoring system, (he or she, they, you) should confer with the referee.
13. Return each of these books to (its, their) proper shelf.
14. Neither Latrice nor her sisters lost (her, their) English books in the fire.
15. Everyone should check (his or her, their, your) spelling of the contestants' names before posting the lists.

**B. Checking for pronoun-antecedent agreement** Write the numbers 1–10 on your paper. In the following sentences some of the pronouns agree with their antecedents and some do not. If the pronouns in a sentence agree with their antecedents, write *C* after the number on your paper. Otherwise, rewrite the sentence according to *formal* usage.

1. Neither player did their best.
2. Both girls brought their tennis rackets.
3. No one who values his or her life will come tomorrow without the completed assignment.
4. Did anybody turn in their reports early?
5. Neither of the actors knew his lines.
6. I'm sure that either Jack or Luis will be glad to show you their projects.
7. After the assembly, everyone left their programs scattered throughout the gym.
8. Neither Keith nor Timoteo thought that Mr. Bell liked them.
9. Each of the forwards did his best during Friday's game.
10. Anyone wanting to be a color guard member should submit their application before 4:00 P.M. Wednesday.

**C. Clarifying antecedents** Write the numbers 1–10 on your paper. Rewrite the following sentences so that there is no confusion regarding the antecedents of the pronouns.

1. When I put my elbow on the glass tabletop, it broke.
2. Mr. Godfrey told Bonita that she acted courageously.
3. When Lorie ran into Becky, she dropped her books.
4. Leon played well but didn't win it.
5. They say school will be dismissed after lunch.
6. If teachers would talk to parents, they would learn a lot.
7. Twenty minutes after I put the pie into the refrigerator, it disappeared.
8. The council has passed a resolution against smoking in public buildings, which bothers me.
9. Dexter gave Bob his watch.
10. Since six accidents have occurred there this month, they have installed stop lights at Sixth and College.

# 33

# Case of Pronouns

In English, personal pronouns have three forms or cases. The nominative case is used when the pronoun is the subject of the sentence. The objective case is used when the pronoun is the object of a verb or a preposition. The possessive case shows ownership.

|  | Nominative | Possessive | Objective |
|---|---|---|---|
| **Singular:** | I | my, mine | me |
|  | you | your, yours | you |
|  | she, he, it | her, hers, his, its | her, him, it |
| **Plural:** | we | our, ours | us |
|  | you | your, yours | you |
|  | they | their, theirs | them |

Pronoun form is rarely a problem when the subject or the object requires only one pronoun. Few people choose the wrong pronoun for sentences like the following.

- *She* brought her lunch. (nominative case)
- Tyrone helped *her*. (objective case—direct object)
- Bea gave *him* my book. (objective case—indirect object)
- Mr. Cortez came with *them*. (objective case—object of the preposition *with*)

On the other hand, compound subjects and compound objects requiring personal pronouns are troublesome to many people. Sometimes nonstandard sentences like the following are constructed.

NONSTANDARD: *Him and her* chased the thief.
NONSTANDARD: Paco called *Glen and she*.

153

NONSTANDARD:   Cathy gave *Neil and I* some tickets.
NONSTANDARD:   Gene rode with *Mr. Messina and I.*

When you use pronouns in pairs, use the same form you would use if the pronouns were being used singly.

STANDARD:   *He and she* chased the thief.
*He* chased the thief.
*She* chased the thief.

STANDARD:   Paco called *Glen and her.*
Paco called *Glen.*
Paco called *her.*

STANDARD:   Cathy gave *Neil and me* some tickets.
Cathy gave *Neil* some tickets.
Cathy gave *me* some tickets.

STANDARD:   Gene rode with *Mr. Messina and me.*
Gene rode with *Mr. Messina.*
Gene rode with *me.*

Subject complement   A subject complement follows a linking verb. Look at the following sentences.

- She is the best *gymnast.*
- Leon and he are the *champions.*
- They must be the *winners.*

The verbs in these sentences—*is, are,* and *must be*—are forms of the verb *be.* The italicized nouns which follow those verbs are the subject complements. Each of the subject complements means the same thing as the subject of its sentence: gymnast = she, champions = Leon and he, winners = they.

Since the subjects and the subject complements mean the same thing, we can reverse them without altering the meaning of the sentences.

- The best gymnast is *she.*
- The champions are *Leon and he.*
- The winners must have been *they.*

However, in informal standard speech and writing, "It's me" has replaced the formal "It is I."

**Making comparisons**   Assume that Brett works math problems faster than anyone in her class. If you wanted to compare her speed to that of Paul, you might say: Brett works math problems faster than Paul works math problems.

Because the last three words are unnecessary to the meaning of the sentence, people seldom say or write them. They say instead: Brett works math problems faster than Paul.

Knowing about such omitted phrases in sentences can help you to decide which pronoun form to choose. Choose the pronoun form that you would choose if the omitted phrases were maintained in those sentences.

SUBJECT FORM:   Brett works math problems faster than *he* (works math problems).
SUBJECT FORM:   Paul doesn't work math problems as fast as *she* (works math problems).
OBJECT FORM:   Jeff's piano playing bothers his mother more than (it bothers) *him*.
OBJECT FORM:   You told Lisa more than (you told) *them*.

**Possessive pronouns**   When we want to use pronouns to show possession, we need no apostrophes. Instead, we choose one of the possessive forms of pronouns.

- That pen is *mine*.
- *Hers* are on that shelf.
- The cat washed *its* paws.
- *His* hat is brown.

Note that while all of the possessive forms shown above except *mine* end in *s*, they show possession without apostrophes.

INCORRECT:   Are those *our's* or *your's?*
CORRECT:   Are those *ours* or *yours?*

Probably the possessive form most often abused is *its*. Remember that *it's* is the contraction for *it is*.

INCORRECT:   *It's* fur is soft.
CORRECT:   *Its* fur is soft.
INCORRECT:   *It's* not hard to teach a dog to obey *it's* owner.
CORRECT:   *It's* not hard to teach a dog to obey *its* owner.

**Who and whom** Like personal pronouns, *who* has several forms.

NOMINATIVE: *Who* bought your bicycle?
OBJECTIVE: *Whom* will you select?
POSSESSIVE: *Whose* keys are those?

When *who* is used as the object of a verb or a preposition at the beginning of a sentence or clause, informal standard English generally uses the nominative case. Formal standard English uses the objective case *whom*.

FORMAL: *Whom* did you prefer? (object of *did prefer*)
INFORMAL: *Who* did you prefer?

FORMAL: To *whom* should we send it? (object of *to*)
INFORMAL: *Who* should we send it to?

When the pronoun functions as the object of a verb or preposition in a relative clause, as it does in the following examples, formal English uses *whom*. In informal English, the pronoun is often omitted or *that* is substituted.

FORMAL:   Katy is a person *whom* we can respect.
INFORMAL:   Katy is a person we can respect.
INFORMAL:   Katy is a person *that* we can respect.

The possessive form *whose* sometimes perplexes people because, like possessive personal pronouns, it has no apostrophe. *Who's* is sometimes mistakenly used. *Who's* is the contraction for *who is*.

NOT:   *Who's* cycle is that?
BUT:   *Whose* cycle is that?

**-self and -selves**   The words *hisself* and *theirselves* are nonstandard. Use *herself, itself, himself,* and *themselves.*

- When Prentice saw *himself* in the mirror, he laughed. (Do not use *hisself.*)
- Stan and Eugenia will have to find a ride *themselves.* (Do not use *theirselves.*)

**We and us**   Deciding whether to use *we* or *us* in a sentence like the following is a relatively simple matter.

- *We* sophomores would like to see the principal.

Choose the word that you would use if *sophomores* were not in the sentence.

- *We* would like to see the principal.

**Them and those**   In standard English the demonstrative pronoun *those* is used for pointing to or singling out persons or objects. The personal pronoun *them* is not used for that purpose.

NOT:   *Them* are the shoes I want.
BUT:   *Those* are the shoes I want.

**Unnecessary pronouns**   The pronouns in the following sentences are unnecessary.

- My father *he* likes to fish.
- The twins *they* like to fool people.

Pronouns take the place of nouns. Since the nouns *father* and *twins* appear in these sentences, the pronouns *he* and *they* are unnecessary and should be omitted.

157

**Putting yourself last** Traditionally, speakers and writers of standard English have placed pronouns referring to other people before pronouns referring to themselves.

- *H.W. and I* sneaked out together. (not *I and H.W.*)
- The *Cardonas and we* are neighbors. (not *We and the Cardonas*)
- Becky ran toward *him and me*. (not *me and him*)

## EXERCISES

**A. Using compound subjects and compound objects** Write the numbers 1–15 on your paper. For each of the following sentences copy a compound subject or a compound object from the list. Do not use any compound more than once. Two of the compounds listed are nonstandard. Do not use them.

1. _____ are not speaking to each other.
2. Mrs. Horton invited _____.
3. Ken brought enough milk for _____.
4. Shall I call _____?
5. The only ones who got there on time were _____.
6. Laura came to the party with _____.
7. It was _____ who brought up the idea.
8. My birthday present from _____ came yesterday.
9. Ms. Betts asked _____ what they had said about her.
10. The ones who left early were _____.
11. Do you blame _____ for not saying anything?
12. Should it be _____ who tells Smoky about Joni?
13. Mr. Taylor handed _____ the wrong exams.
14. Those lunch tickets belong to _____.
15. Either _____ will go there.

| Dena and I | Tracy and me | him and her |
| them and us | Bill Strong and I | Garth and me |
| you and me | him and I | Carlos, T.C., and me |
| she and them | him or her | Carlos, T.C., and I |
| he and Chris | the Parkers and her | he or she |
| Peggy or her | they and we | my friend and me |

**B. Using who and whom** Write the numbers 1–15 on your paper. For each of the following sentences decide whether *who* or *whom* would be appropriate in formal usage.

1. From _____ did you receive those instructions?
2. Vote for Beth Cohen, _____ even the teachers trust!
3. The actor _____ played the role of the captain is now dead.
4. The students _____ were given awards have become popular.
5. _____ did they say won the game?
6. Dr. Thurston, _____ everyone respects, will retire soon.
7. With _____ should we register?
8. Nobody knew _____ he really was.
9. Ms. Alley, _____ none of us knew, was appointed our new sponsor.
10. She is the person _____ we most admire.
11. Edward and I were the only ones _____ got Cs.
12. It is he _____ we should honor.
13. Most of the juniors _____ we asked are undecided about college.
14. Chaim Potok, _____ several of you met last year, is the author of several acclaimed novels.
15. Molly is the student _____ was chosen.

C. **Choosing appropriate pronouns** Write the numbers 1–20 on your paper. For each of the following sentences write the pronoun that is appropriate in standard usage.

1. Is he younger than (she, her)?
2. (Her's, Hers) is a newer model than (their's, theirs).
3. Jill and Hal can type faster than (we, us).
4. Three of (we, us) boys will be a little late for class.
5. A local service club will donate new blazers for (we, us) chorus members to wear.
6. (Who's, Whose) the lucky kid (who's, whose) aunt left her a fortune?
7. Dad gives my little sister more allowance than he gives (I, me).
8. They built the camper (themselves, theirselves).
9. Eduino, (who's, whose) dog hurt (it's, its) paw, also owns a thirty-pound turtle.
10. Why don't (we, us) sophomores sponsor a disco dance?
11. Mr. Mills said that (we, us) girls could have the gym at four o'clock.
12. (Them, Those) are like the ones I wanted.
13. Julio made (hisself, himself) a milkshake.
14. That new hairstyle suits you better than (I, me), doesn't it?
15. Hank bet he could stay under water longer than (she, her).
16. I finished my assignment long before (he, him).
17. Troy, (who's, whose) tray fell to the cafeteria floor when Bill hit his arm, felt betrayed.
18. Eli weighs more than (I, me), but I am taller than (he, him).
19. These are reasonable, but (them, those) are too expensive.
20. You write as well as (he, him).

# 34

# Irregular Verbs

Verbs express action, and they also tell *when* action occurs. When someone tells you that Gina cleaned out her desk, you know what she did and that she did it sometime in the past. The *-ed* ending on the verb *cleaned* tells you that. If, instead, you are told that Gina will clean out her desk, you know that she will do it sometime in the future. The auxiliary verb *will* tells you that.

These are but two of the tenses that a verb can assume. Tense means "time." In all, there are six verb tenses.

PRESENT:   I *clean* my room once a week.
 Al *cleans* his suit before he wears it.
PAST:   Gina *cleaned* out her desk on Monday.
 Phil *did clean* the floor before you asked him to.
FUTURE:   Anna *will clean* the fish she caught.
PRESENT PERFECT:   She *has cleaned* house twice this spring.
 They *have cleaned* their boots and may enter.
PAST PERFECT:   Someone *had cleaned* out the refrigerator before snack time.
FUTURE PERFECT:   The kids *will have cleaned* out the candy dish before supper.

**Principal parts**   A verb has three basic forms. Because all of the tenses are made from those three forms, they are called the principal parts of the verb.

| Present | Past | Past Participle |
|---------|------|-----------------|
| clean   | cleaned | (have) cleaned |
| drop    | dropped | (have) dropped |
| mark    | marked  | (have) marked  |

Most verbs are regular; that is, they follow a regular pattern. Their past and past participle forms are exactly alike. Both forms end in *-ed*. Regular verbs present few problems for speakers or writers, except perhaps for spelling. Remember to change *y* to *i* before adding *-ed* for verbs like *pity/pitied*. Double the final consonant before adding *-ed* for verbs like *prefer/preferred* and *stop/stopped*.

Some verbs do not follow the pattern of the regular verbs, however. Irregular verbs deviate from that pattern in several ways. Compare the forms of the irregular verbs in the following chart with those of the regular verbs.

| Present | Past | Past Participle |
|---------|------|-----------------|
| do | did | (have) done |
| drink | drank | (have) drunk |
| find | found | (have) found |
| freeze | froze | (have) frozen |
| go | went | (have) gone |
| see | saw | (have) seen |

You probably observed that irregular verbs do not form their past tense by simply adding *-ed* to the present form, and that the past and past participle forms of most irregular verbs are not identical.

Fortunately, the list of irregular verbs is relatively short. Nevertheless, those verbs can be very troublesome for people who wish to use standard verb forms in their speech and writing. For one thing, we hear nonstandard forms of some of these verbs so often that they sound "right." Standard forms may sound strange or wrong at first.

Learning standard forms requires some effort—including, for some people, memorization of the principal parts of irregular verbs. To make that task easier, learn the following rules.

1. The forms of the past tense are always used alone.

    - He *did* his best. (not *has did*)
    - The child *drank* his milk. (not *has drank*)

2. The forms of the past participle are always used with auxiliary verbs, such as *has, have,* and *had*.

    - We *have done* our best. (not *done*)

## EXERCISES

**A. Testing yourself**  Cover the second and third columns of the following chart with a sheet of paper. For each verb say to yourself the principal parts that you think appear in columns two and three. Then move the paper down a line so that you can check yourself immediately. When you make an error, write the verb on your sheet of paper.

When you have completed that process, write two sentences for each of the verbs whose principal parts you did not know well. Use the past form alone in one of your sentences. Use the past participle form with an auxiliary verb in the other. Say your sentences to yourself several times so that the standard verb forms will begin to sound "right" to you.

| Present | Past | Past Participle |
| --- | --- | --- |
| beat | beat | beaten |
| become | became | become |
| begin | began | begun |
| blow | blew | blown |
| break | broke | broken |
| bring | brought | brought |
| burst | burst | burst |
| catch | caught | caught |
| choose | chose | chosen |
| come | came | come |
| do | did | done |
| draw | drew | drawn |
| drink | drank | drunk |
| drive | drove | driven |
| eat | ate | eaten |
| fall | fell | fallen |
| fly | flew | flown |
| forbid | forbade, forbad | forbidden |
| forgive | forgave | forgiven |
| freeze | froze | frozen |
| get | got | got, gotten |
| give | gave | given |
| go | went | gone |
| grow | grew | grown |
| know | knew | known |
| mistake | mistook | mistaken |

| | | |
|---|---|---|
| ride | rode | ridden |
| ring | rang | rung |
| run | ran | run |
| say | said | said |
| see | saw | seen |
| shake | shook | shaken |
| shrink | shrank | shrunk |
| sing | sang | sung |
| sink | sank, sunk | sunk |
| speak | spoke | spoken |
| spring | sprang, sprung | sprung |
| steal | stole | stolen |
| swim | swam | swum |
| take | took | taken |
| tear | tore | torn |
| throw | threw | thrown |
| wear | wore | worn |
| write | wrote | written |

**B. Choosing correct verb forms** Write the numbers 1–20 on your paper. For each of the following sentences write the appropriate past or past participle form of the irregular verb in parentheses.

EXAMPLE: She has _____ her report. (give)

ANSWER: given

1. Miguel and I _saw_ the Mets game yesterday. (see)
2. I have _known_ about the secret passageway for a long time. (know)
3. No one but Carrie could have _chosen_ that color combination. (choose)
4. Either she bought the wrong size or those jeans have _shrunk_ in the wash. (shrink)
5. The basketball team _did_ their best to win. (do)
6. When her horse _threw_ her, Alice broke her arm. (throw)
7. Have you _forgiven_ me for being late yesterday? (forgive)
8. Dex had _____ the winning basket. (sink)
9. If you had asked, I would have _____ to school today. (drive)
10. Has the team _____ out for their warm-up yet? (come)
11. I was so _____ by the accident that I couldn't remember my name. (shake)
12. My father _____ Mr. Gomez for Mr. Thorne at open house. (mistake)
13. The Tigers have often _____ the Blue Devils. (beat)

163

14. You must have _____ Vinnie leave the office. (see)
15. Has our mascot been _____ again? (steal)
16. Ms. Teng has emphatically _____ us to talk during test periods. (forbid)
17. The Bible had been _____ to Karen by her grandmother. (give)
18. The milk _____. (freeze)
19. The girls had _____ to school together for years. (go)
20. "America" was _____ with spirit during the assembly. (sing)

**C. Correcting mistakes in verb usage** Write the numbers 1-10 on your paper. Read the sets of three sentences after each number below. Most of the sets contain one sentence that has a nonstandard irregular verb form. Rewrite each nonstandard form as it should be in standard usage. If a set contains only examples of standard usage, write *C* next to the number of that set.

1. They had caught the plane. He drunk the whole glass of milk. My sweater had shrunk.
2. We had sang the anthem. They were forbidden to laugh. All of them rode the roller coaster.
3. We began that tradition. You have grew three inches. They chose me captain.
4. He had been shook by the bad news. Holly drew the cover. He writes well.
5. They rang the bell. Larry had forgave Maria. The Bulldogs had been beaten.
6. He has spoke to us before. Suzi threw the ball to first base. She had drawn Harvey's name.
7. The balloon burst. She sings well. Her jacket was tore.
8. Nina has went to the grocery store. They drank six cokes. Have you seen the dog?
9. The meal had been eaten. Her voice shook. The water main had sprung a leak.
10. They had did their best. Tim and Chris saw us first. She has already gone.

# 35

# Troublesome Verb Pairs

Six pairs of verbs are especially tricky for many people: *lay–lie, set–sit, raise–rise, let–leave, bring–take,* and *learn–teach.*

**Lay and lie**   This pair is the most challenging of the troublesome verb pairs. It is also the most abused.

Examine the following sentences. They are alike in two ways: (1) they contain forms of the verb *lay,* which means "to put or place," and (2) they contain direct objects—that is, someone or something receives the action expressed by the verb.

PRESENT:   I always *lay* my *keys* on that table.
PAST:   Bella *laid* her *dollar* on the counter.
PAST PERFECT:   Somebody *had laid* a wet *umbrella* on the sofa.

Use a form of *lay* in sentences that tell who or what is placed somewhere. Forms of *lay* usually appear in Subject + Verb + Object (**S+V+O**) sentences. The past and past participle forms are identical and they end in *d.*

Each of the following sentences contains a form of the verb *lie,* which means "to recline" or "to rest in a flat position." Note that *lie* does not take an object.

PRESENT:   Grandpa *lies* down for a nap after lunch.
PAST:   Tim *lay* in the ditch for an hour before someone found him.
PAST PERFECT:   That old board *had lain* in our yard for years.

Use a form of *lie* in sentences that tell about someone or something reclining or resting in a flat position. Do not use a form of *lie* as the main verb in a Subject + Verb + Object (**S+V+O**) sentence.

NONSTANDARD:   I'll *lay* here for a while.
STANDARD:   I'll *lie* here for a while.

NONSTANDARD:   Your notebook *is laying* on the kitchen table.
STANDARD:   Your notebook *is lying* on the kitchen table.

NONSTANDARD:   That dime *has laid* on the TV set since Tuesday.
STANDARD:   That dime *has lain* on the TV set since Tuesday.

**Set and sit; raise and rise**   These two troublesome verb pairs function much as *lay* and *lie* do. *Set* and *raise* usually take direct objects. *Sit* and *rise* do not take objects.

PRESENT:   *Set* the *milk* on the table. (*Milk* is the object.)
PAST:   She *set* the *thimble* down. (*Thimble* is the object.)
PAST PERFECT:   She *had set* the *casserole* too close to the table's edge. (*Casserole* is the object.)

PRESENT:   *Raise* the entrance *fee*. (*Fee* is the object.)
PAST:   We *raised* the *flag* at dawn. (*Flag* is the object.)
PAST PERFECT:   The club *had raised* enough *money* for its trip. (*Money* is the object.)

PRESENT:   I *sit* in the front row in math class.
PAST:   Una *sat* silently throughout our discussion.
PAST PERFECT:   They had *sat* in the counselor's office for an hour.

PRESENT: The sun *rises* earlier each day now.
PAST: Barbara *rose* from her chair.
PAST PERFECT: The full moon *had* already *risen* by the time we started out.

**Let and leave**  Some people use forms of *leave* in sentences that require *let*. *Let* means "to permit" or "to allow."

- *Let* me help. (Not: *Leave* me help.)
- My parents *let* me get a summer job. (Not: My parents *leaved* me get a summer job.)

**Bring and take**  Whether you choose *bring* or *take* as you speak and write should depend upon the direction of the motion you are describing. If the motion is toward the speaker, choose *bring*.

- *Bring* me the newspaper.
- Shelley *brought* us souvenirs from Mexico.

If the motion is away from the speaker, choose *take*.

- *Take* this cup to the kitchen.
- Damita *took* the note to the principal's office.

**Learn and teach**  People *learn* through study and experience. People *teach* by giving knowledge to others. Standard English observes that difference.

- Barry *taught* me to play bridge. (Not: Barry *learned* me to play bridge.)
- We *learned* the new routine quickly.

## EXERCISES

**A. Using lay and lie**  Write the numbers 1–20 on your paper. For each of the following sentences write the appropriate form of *lay* (*lay, laying, laid, laid*) or *lie* (*lie, lying, lay, lain*).

1. Where did I ___lay___ the scissors?
2. Go ___lie___ down for a few minutes before dinner.
3. Grandma had ___lain___ awake most of the night.

167

4. Coach Nakano __laid__ a cold cloth on the quarterback's forehead.
5. Why don't you __lie__ in the sun this morning?
6. Susie's left slipper had __lain__ under her bed for a week before she rescued it.
7. That winter coat has been __laid__ aside for someone else.
8. The two cats are __lying__ side by side on the porch.
9. The miser's money had __lain__ under his mattress for many years.
10. You shouldn't be __lying__ in that cold room very long.
11. I had __laid__ the meat out to thaw.
12. Last Saturday we just _____ there watching TV all day.
13. Roberto had _____ his cards on the table before I could stop him.
14. After she collected our homework, Ms. Chong _____ the papers on her desk.
15. Your check book is probably still _____ where you dropped it.
16. The sod had been _____ for weeks before it took root.
17. The workers were _____ the last row of bricks this morning.
18. I'll just _____ down while you are _____ the linoleum.
19. While you were _____ on the sofa, I _____ on my bed.
20. Before the new carpet could be _____ in place, our dog was _____ on it.

**B. Using troublesome verbs**  Write the numbers 1–15 on your paper. For each of the following sentences write the appropriate form of *lay/lie, set/sit,* or *raise/rise.*

1. The price of bread has (raised, **risen**) two cents this month.
2. Will you (set, **sit**) on the porch with me?
3. Dad always (sets, **sits**) in that chair while he works crossword puzzles.
4. Tony (sits, **sets**) the table before his mother gets home from work.
5. The courthouse (lays, **lies**) near the center of town.
6. As Tadeo (**lay**, laid) in bed, he wondered where he had put his science book.
7. The hem of those slacks should be (risen, raised) at least one inch.
8. Let Aunt Grace (sit, set) in that chair by the window.
9. After we painted the screens, we (set, sat) them in the sun to dry.
10. Mom doesn't need to (rise, raise) her voice to show me that she's angry.
11. "Someone has been (lying, laying) in that pile of leaves," said Polly.
12. Who was (setting, sitting) next to Xavier when he dozed off?
13. Our family has often (sat, set) out on the porch until midnight.
14. On the count of three, (rise, raise) up from your chair and walk toward me.
15. Our band director (lies, lays) down the same rules every September.

C. **Choosing the appropriate verb** Write the numbers 1–10 on your paper. For each of the following sentences write the appropriate verb form.

1. Mother must have (let, left) the twins go to the baseball game after all.
2. Chen's brother (took, brought) all of us to the shopping center last night.
3. Why did Mr. Braun (leave, let) Ed go there?
4. Ms. Nichols knows a lot about economics, but she hasn't (taught, learned) us much so far.
5. Will you (let, leave) me carry some of your packages?
6. Coach Finn said she would (learn, teach) us a new dive.
7. Let's not (let, leave) the lights on while we're gone.
8. Since I'm busy here, please (take, bring) your fee money to the other secretary.
9. Don't (let, leave) a child play with medicine bottles.
10. (Leave, Let) the water run until it's warm enough for your bath.

# REVIEWING LESSONS 31–35

**A. Checking for agreement** Write the numbers 1–20 on your paper. If a sentence is written in standard English, write *C* after its number. Rewrite any sentences written in nonstandard English.

1. There was no numbers on the mailbox.
2. Each contestant must pay their own entry fee.
3. Here are the names of some volunteers.
4. Either the doctor or one of the nurses are ready to see you now.
5. Ellen said it wasn't her who complained to Mr. Wauneka.
6. Neither of the swimmers appear to be at their best today.
7. Is there any refunds on this sale merchandise?
8. One of the girls left her purse on the table.
9. The price of tires have increased 20 percent in six months.
10. Neither Aaron nor Vincent is quick enough to win this event.
11. Alana, like her parents, pinch every penny.
12. Neither Kim nor her sisters want to work in the family's shoe store.
13. Each of these books is by John Steinbeck.
14. Neither of the boys were willing to drive Harvey's old car.
15. Which one of these buttons control the electric windows?
16. Nobody should forget to bring his or her lunch for tomorrow's field trip.
17. Either her mother or her father buy her anything she wants.
18. Your ability to draw cartoon figures pleases me.
19. Either of the girls can be very charming if she tries to be.
20. Did anyone bring their donation for the rummage sale today?

**B. Changing tenses** Write the numbers 1–10 on your paper. For each of the following sentences write the appropriate form for each of the italicized verbs.

1. Mother *tear* the buttons from the dress that had *shrink*.
2. When Angela *bring* the cookies, she nearly *freeze* as she *stand* on my porch.
3. I should have *know* that the Cougars would be *beat* in the final seconds!
4. After we *eat* the whole pie, we *write* a note of apology to my family and *leave* the house.
5. Though Tina had *swim* in deep water many times, she had never *dive* as deep as she did when she went after the treasure that had *sink* centuries earlier.

6. Yesterday when the whistle *blow,* the competitors *spring* from their starting blocks and *begin* their long run.
7. During the hour that you *lie* sleeping on the sofa, I *lay* the carpet in the bedroom.
8. I have often *sit* at this window while the sun *rise* over those distant trees.
9. The writer had *drink* some broth and had *write* some poetry before he *rise* from his desk and *sing* a lullaby to the sleepy kitten that *lie* at his feet.
10. Alan's mother had *forbid* him to wear again the suit he had *buy* from the army surplus store and had *wear* to his cousin's wedding.

**C.** Correcting pronoun forms   Write the numbers 1–14 on your paper. Most of the following sentences have one or more nonstandard pronoun forms. Copy the sentences, substituting standard forms for nonstandard ones. If a sentence contains no nonstandard forms, write C next to its number on your paper.

1. After us boys saw the accident, we told he and Casandra about it.
2. Anyone who drives their cycle on the grass will lose their school parking permit.
3. Them are the same iron-on emblems you bought for we girls and him.
4. That sweater fits Oliverio better than Jeff or me.
5. Libby she would rather see a movie with Mary and him than go skating with you and I.
6. When we boys played tennis, Steve and his brother challenged me and my cousin, who plays better than me.
7. The only ones to speak up were they and we.
8. Us students thought it was him who needed help.
9. Where did you and them go after the play?
10. When it comes time for we sophomores to vote, I hope we will not elect Tim Budd or any of the people who he wants in office.
11. Few of the teachers are as hard to fool as Mr. Begay or him.
12. Her and Maya told me theirselves.
13. He is a better speaker than I, but I am a better writer than he.
14. Ann, who no one trusts, won't admit that the culprits were she and Carolyn Marks, who is even less trustworthy than her.

# LANGUAGE POLLUTION

## 36

## Redundancy and Verbosity

Most of us are aware of the serious problem created by air pollution and water pollution. Today some people feel that we have a problem with language pollution as well.

In this lesson we will be concerned with one form of language pollution—wasted words. By the time you finish the lesson, you should be able to recognize wasted words. More important, you should be able to eliminate wasted words from your own speaking and writing.

*"I always maintain that anything written on two sides of a mountain could be said just as well on only one side of a mountain!"*

## Redundancy

**Redundancy** is the needless repetition of an idea. Some redundancies are so common that you may use them unconsciously. Here is a list of common redundancies.

| | | |
|---|---|---|
| add another | both together | join together |
| adequate enough | famous celebrity | newer, more modern |
| advance planning | completely surrounded | true fact |
| all-time record | free gift | unusual quirk |

Some clauses, sentences, and even whole paragraphs are redundant. You have to listen closely and read carefully to tell the difference between redundancy and intentional repetition for effect. For example, popular song lyrics and poems frequently contain repetition for effect.

## Verbosity

People who want to show that they really know their subject sometimes become **verbose**. They use extra words or roundabout expressions. Writers who do not revise their first drafts for conciseness and directness are often verbose. **Verbosity** is wordiness.

Compare the following two sentences.

- Ms. Chiang will endeavor to communicate with you by telephone before she departs from the office.
- Ms. Chiang will try to call you before she leaves the office.

The second sentence is more concise and probably easier to understand because the words *endeavor, communicate,* and *departs from* have been replaced by *try, call,* and *leaves.* Replacing "communicate with you by telephone" with "call you" also created a shorter sentence.

Occasionally a big word *does* convey meaning that a small word does not, so of course you must be alert to shades of meaning as you choose words. Generally, though, if you choose direct language, you will find it easier to speak or write streamlined sentences.

VERBOSE: It is not often the case that we have to sell anything at half price.

In order to make such a sentence more direct, try using a different subject in your revision.

173

CONCISE: We seldom have to sell anything at half price.

Here is a summary of ways to make yourself clear by saving words.

1. Don't use a long word if a short one will do as well. American astronauts and CB radio operators use *affirmative* and *negative*. For the rest of us, *yes* and *no* will do.
2. Don't use two words if one will do as well. *In order to* usually means *to; by means of* usually means *by; give consideration to* means *consider*.

VERBOSE: the dog *with the spots*
CONCISE: the *spotted* dog

3. Don't use a clause if a phrase or word will do as well.

VERBOSE: Cheer for the team that has the orange jerseys on.
CONCISE: Cheer for the team in the orange jerseys.

4. Don't use a sentence if a clause or phrase will do as well.
5. Don't use a paragraph if a sentence will do as well.
6. Don't overuse words that are vague and add little meaning: *rather, pretty, nice, a little, kind of, sort of*.

## EXERCISES

**A. Eliminating redundancies** Write the numbers 1–10 on your paper. Each of the following sentences contains a redundant word or phrase. Rewrite each sentence, eliminating any unnecessary repetition.

1. She will meet us in the lobby at twelve noon.
2. A huge throng had gathered at the park.
3. The Espinozas stayed on an island surrounded by water during their two-week stay.
4. In my opinion, it seems to me that the club should meet every week.
5. Many new innovations are advertised first on television.
6. The flames rose higher, and the house was soon a flaming inferno.
7. It's clearly obvious that she isn't coming here.
8. The end result of their action was higher wages but fewer jobs.
9. Memorize the basic fundamentals that are absolutely essential, so that you can apply them quickly when you take the test.
10. Ms. Devereaux never found out the name of the student from whom she got the flowers from.

**B. Revising verbose sentences** Write the numbers 1–10 on your paper. Rewrite the following sentences, cutting out as many unnecessary words as possible. Also eliminate big words that are inappropriate. Do not change the meaning of any sentence.

1. Monetarily speaking, I am insolvent.
2. Rene is 5'6" in height, has eyes that are blue, and has hair that is bright red.
3. What I want you to do is to leave this room immediately.
4. The way that young lion cubs get their food is by waiting for their female mother lion to kill it.
5. Tennis is one of my favorite sports, and I like to play golf in addition to tennis.
6. The way you win this game is by getting rid of all of your cards before any of your adversaries get rid of theirs.
7. Every time I devour a giant chocolate bar I berate myself for having so indulged.
8. It is always the case that I am ready to return to school in the fall.
9. The reason that the car wouldn't start was because we were out of petroleum.
10. Mr. Piper, your son Tom has an inclination to take the property of others and to prevaricate when truth is sought.

**C. Getting rid of needless words** Rewrite the following paragraph. Eliminate all unnecessary words. Be sure to keep the essential ideas, however.

> Let us all give consideration to one of today's pretty serious contemporary problems. The problem is that some people contribute to the pollution of language. They add additional needless and unnecessary words and phrases to their oral conversations and their written papers. You know what I mean? You know, they use a number of words when only one would be adequate enough. Some of the perpetrators of this nefarious act are well known personalities from that old "boob tube," television. You know some of the ones I mean. Some of them are on the late evening conversational interview shows. Others who pollute language may be found among local and national politicians who hold political offices locally and nationally, you know. And see, we really ought to attempt to do something about this kind of modern linguistic language pollution problem before it inundates us all totally altogether, you know.

# 37

# Clichés and Pet Phrases

## Clichés

**Clichés** are figures of speech or other phrases that as a result of overuse have lost their freshness. At one time, for example, *green with envy* probably seemed a clever phrase used to describe a jealous person. Drawn by its originality, people adopted the phrase and used it ... and used it and used it. Now its originality has faded; it has become commonplace and stale. That expression and others like it may annoy people who value freshness in language.

Clichés usually fall into one of three categories.

1. *Tired figures of speech:* light as a feather, clear as day, dull as dishwater, pretty as a picture, shaking like a leaf

2. *Overworked quotations and proverbs:* better late than never, sadder but wiser, where there's a will there's a way, haste makes waste

3. *Fatigued phrases:* easier said than done, venture an opinion, in broad daylight, now or never, on bended knee, by leaps and bounds

Clichés are found in the speech of almost everyone. They seem to arise automatically during the rapid thought process that speech requires. Writers, however, should try to avoid using clichés. Frequent use of clichés, no matter how unintentional, may communicate that a writer is inexperienced with language. Also, readers may ignore a good idea if it is written in dull, clichéd language.

As you revise your written work, look for clichés and replace them. Replace stale figures of speech with literal terms or with original comparisons. Replace overworked quotations with quotations from your own reading. When trite quotations are mere space-fillers, omit them.

*"Therefore, for better or worse, let me venture the opinion that one can not have one's cake and eat it. Too many irons in the fire will knock the bottom out of the best laid plans..."*

## Pet Phrases

Like clichés, pet phrases can become annoying. Most of us have pet phrases like *y'know* or *I mean,* but we don't realize how much we overuse them. People of all ages and levels of education are guilty of using meaningless interruptors that break the flow of thought from speaker to listener.

A well-known weekly magazine reported on a survey of three late-night talk shows on television. On one show there were 219 *y'know's* and 31 *I mean's*. The author concluded that a person watching this show for a year would hear 11,788 *y'know's*. *And–uh, great, really, okay,* and *cool* are other pets.

Pet phrases, like slang, slip in and out of favor quite rapidly. Recent pets include *that dude, for sure,* and *flake off*.

Pet phrases seldom appear in writing, except where the writer is trying to achieve a very informal tone. Speakers needing extra time to process a thought or construct a sentence often use them as time fillers. When they appear too often in one's speech, they become distracting and annoying. Where they are used as fillers, a simple pause would be preferable.

## EXERCISES

**A. Identifying clichés** Write the numbers 1–10 on your paper. The following phrases have been repeated so often that you should have no trouble filling in the words that have been left out. Write each complete phrase on your paper.

1. now or _____
2. last _____ not _____
3. raining _____ and _____
4. better _____ than _____
5. as _____ as molasses
6. in _____ daylight
7. can't see the _____ for the _____
8. growing by _____ and _____
9. snug as a _____ in a _____
10. _____ as a fiddle

**B. Identifying trite figures of speech** Write the numbers 1–10 on your paper. All of the following trite figures of speech can be completed with the name of an animal. Write the name of the appropriate animal on your paper.

EXAMPLE: as sly as a _____
ANSWER: fox

1. as quiet as a _____
2. as slow as a _____
3. as proud as a _____
4. as hungry as a _____
5. as stubborn as a _____
6. as free as a _____
7. as gentle as a _____
8. as clumsy as a _____
9. as strong as a _____
10. as wise as an _____

C. **Finding substitutions for clichés** Write the numbers 1–10 on your paper. Rewrite each of the following sentences. Substitute direct language or fresh figures of speech for the clichés that you find.

1. Jobs like this are few and far between.
2. Evaleen is as smart as a whip.
3. Each and every one of us owes a debt of gratitude to our parents.
4. Paula beat a hasty retreat.
5. If I may venture an opinion, I'd say that Deven is as sharp as a tack.
6. Usually happy as a lark, Maria seemed down in the dumps on Tuesday.
7. It goes without saying that students like Johnny Ling who progress slowly but surely through their lessons are as scarce as hen's teeth.
8. Though they were lost and hungry as wolves, the campers remained as cool as cucumbers.
9. We stayed until the bitter end, when the search party threw in a towel; then we returned to our home sweet home.
10. Shaking like a leaf and scared out of his wits, Christopher reached for the flashlight.

# GLOSSARY OF USAGE

In the following glossary you will find short entries for many usage items. Some entries will deal with usage problems that you have not previously studied. Other entries will review problems with which you are already familiar.

This glossary may be used in at least two ways: (1) you may study all its entries and complete the accompanying exercises, or (2) you may use it as a handbook for solving specific usage problems.

As you use this glossary, remember that *formal standard English* is the language that well-educated people use on formal occasions, most often in writing. *Informal standard English* is used in communicating with friends or a general audience. It is the social dialect taught in classrooms. *Nonstandard English* is typically the oral language of people whose formal education is limited. It is mainly a spoken dialect because those who use it seldom find it necessary to write.

a, an   Use *a* before words beginning with *h,* if the *h* is sounded: *a* hospital, *a* house. If the *h* is not sounded, use *an: an* hour, *an* honest person.

accept, except   *Accept* is a verb. It means "to agree to" or "to receive willingly." *Except* is most commonly a preposition meaning "but." *Except* is also a verb meaning "to exclude" or "to leave out."

- Will more than thirty people *accept* your idea? (agree to)
- Everyone *except* Carrie will be out of town. (but)
- Students having medical excuses will be *excepted* from physical education requirements. (excluded)

affect, effect   *Affect* is always a verb, meaning "to influence" or "pretend to have or feel." *Effect* is chiefly a noun meaning "result" or "consequence." *Effect* is also a verb meaning "to bring about or make happen."

- Diet *affects* alertness. (influences)
- Stephanie *affected* disinterest in Lola's joking with her. (pretended)
- Punishment had no *effect* on Robert's behavior. (result)
- Through punishment, Ms. Furumoto hoped to *effect* a change in Robert's behavior. (bring about)

**ain't**  *Ain't* is regarded as nonstandard usage. Always use *am not* or *is not*.

**all ready, already**  *All ready* is a two-word term meaning "completely ready." *Already* is one word meaning "at that time" or "by that time."

- The cast is *all ready* for the curtain to go up.
- I have *already* bought my ticket.

**all right, alright**  *Alright,* a common misspelling of *all right,* is nonstandard.

**all together, altogether**  *All together* usually means "as a group." *Altogether,* an adverb, means "completely" or "on the whole."

- The Hansens sit *all together* in church. (as a group)
- I find it *altogether* impossible to meet his expectations. (completely)
- *Altogether,* smoking is an undesirable habit. (on the whole)

**allusion, illusion**  An indirect reference to something is an *allusion.* A false impression of reality is an *illusion.*

- The comedian's routine contained many *allusions* to people and events in Washington, D.C.
- The fog gave the *illusion* of ghosts in the woods.

**among, between**  *Between* relates to two things. *Among* relates to three or more things.

- We must choose *between* two fine candidates.
- How will she recognize Ms. Farnsworth *among* all of the people getting off the airplane?

**amount, number**  *Amount* is used when referring to things that can be measured or weighed: a small *amount* of cinnamon, a large *amount* of cement. *Number* is used when referring to things that can be counted: a small *number* of boats, a larger *number* of french fries.

**anyplace, anywhere**  Other compounds of *-place,* or *-where* are *everyplace, everywhere; noplace, nowhere; someplace, somewhere.* The *-place* words are often used informally instead of the *-where* words. The *-s* form of the *-where* words is not acceptable in standard English.

NONSTANDARD:  Have you seen the cat *anywheres*?
INFORMAL:  Have you seen the cat *anyplace*?
FORMAL:  Have you seen the cat *anywhere*?

**bad, badly**  *Bad* is an adjective; *badly* is an adverb. Linking verbs, including *feel, smell, look,* and *taste,* use the adjective form *bad.*

NONSTANDARD: The cream smells *badly*. (Literally, this sentence means that the cream has a poor sense of smell.)
STANDARD: The cream smells *bad*. (adjective)
STANDARD: She plays tennis *badly*. (adverb)

*Feel badly* is used in speech, but *feel bad* is preferred for written work.

## EXERCISES

**A.** Write the numbers 1–10 on your paper. For each of the following sentences, write the word in parentheses that completes the sentence in standard English.

1. No (amount, number) of coaxing could convince me to tell you how (bad, badly) I played that bridge hand.
2. When it came time to choose (among, between) doing dishes and sweeping, Carla was (nowheres, nowhere) around.
3. When the lawyer sought (a, an) heir to the Stockworth fortune, no one (accept, except) Jim Tweed could be found.
4. Will it be (all right, alright) for us four to sit (all together, altogether)?
5. Any (amount, number) of people can play Monopoly.
6. Was that an (allusion, illusion), or did I see Derrick doing his homework before watching TV?
7. The weather looked (bad, badly) and I played tennis (bad, badly).
8. The weird sound (affects, effects) in that movie really (affected, effected) my brother, who kept covering his eyes.
9. Those who have (already, all ready) served on the committee will be (accepted, excepted) from clean-up duty on Saturday.
10. Finding a reference to *Alice in Wonderland* (among, between) all these (allusions, illusions) to Bible events is nearly impossible.

**B.** Write the numbers 1–10 on your paper. Some of the following sentences contain mistakes in usage. Rewrite those sentences correctly. Write *C* next to the numbers of sentences that are already correct.

1. I won't except the responsibility to choose among green or blue walls for your kitchen.
2. If you want to affect a change in school policy, you must go through channels all ready set up.
3. Alright, I'll go anywheres you want to go, but I ain't going nowheres without my sister.
4. No amount of warnings could convince Aunt Bonita that smoking would make her feel badly and effect her lifespan.

5. Forty-three students is altogether too many for any teacher to accept in one class.
6. Your illusion to an historical event that occurred here in our state will impress a large amount of your readers.
7. I think that Kristi looks so badly these days because she has all together too many problems.
8. How can you effect pleasure when Mr. Sutton reads that poetry so badly?
9. Is it all right if I put a larger amount of salt in this recipe, or will it affect the taste too much?
10. Everyone accept Luellen excepted the low wages and the small amount of fringe benefits that the job offered.

being as, being that  Both phrases should be avoided. Use *because* or *since* instead.

    NONSTANDARD:  *Being as* we had never met before, I approached the old man cautiously.
    STANDARD:  *Since* we had never met before, I approached the old man cautiously.

beside, besides  *Beside* means "next to" or "at the side of." *Besides* can mean either "except (for)" or "in addition to."

- Bradley sits *beside* me in biology class. (next to)
- No one *besides* Matilde knew about the trap door. (except for)
- *Besides* money, I spent a lot of time. (in addition to)

between, among  See *among, between*.

bring, take  *Bring* refers to motion toward the speaker. *Take* refers to motion away from the speaker.

    NONSTANDARD:  Will you *bring* me away from this place?
    STANDARD:  Will you *take* me away from this place?
    STANDARD:  *Bring* your tests to my desk and hand them to me.

brought, have brought  The principal parts of *bring* are *bring, brought,* and *(have) brought*. In nonstandard English *brung* and *have brung* are often used as the simple past and past participle.

    NONSTANDARD:  He *brung* his sister to school.
    STANDARD:  Harry *brought* us souvenirs.
    STANDARD:  Mr. and Mrs. Montoya *have brought* their slides.

**broke, broken** *Broke* is the simple past of *break;* (have) *broken* is the past participle. *Breaked, busted,* and *have broke* are nonstandard forms.

   NONSTANDARD:   Tracy *busted* her tooth.
   STANDARD:   Hal *broke* the silence with his hearty laugh.

   NONSTANDARD:   Because he *has broke* the law, he must be punished.
   STANDARD:   The baby *has broken* the volume dial again.

**burst** The principal parts of *burst* are *burst, burst,* and *(have) burst. Bust* and *bursted* are nonstandard forms.

   NONSTANDARD:   When little Ben *busted* his balloon, he cried.
   STANDARD:   When the water main *burst,* we were without water at our house for two hours.

*Bust a bronco,* and *bust a trust* are most often classed as slang. However, they are so often used in informal English that they may be considered standard.

**can, may** In informal English, both spoken and written, *can* is used to express permission as well as ability.

- *Can* I go to the lake? (permission)
- He *can* run fast. (ability)

In formal English, *can* is used only to express ability. *May* is generally used to express permission.

- You *may* delay payment until June 1. (permission)

**come, came** The principal parts of *come* are *come, came,* and *(have) come. Come* as simple past tense and *have came* as past participle are nonstandard.

   NONSTANDARD:   They *come* over to our house yesterday.
   STANDARD:   They *came* over to our house yesterday.

   NONSTANDARD:   Grandpa *has came* for dinner every Sunday for years.
   STANDARD:   Grandpa *has come* for dinner every Sunday for years.

**compare to, compare with** To *compare* one thing *to* another is to point out general similarities in unlike things. To *compare* a thing *with* another is to examine specific points of difference or likeness.

- *Compared to* Dracula, you are handsome.
- How do those biscuits *compare with* your mother's in taste?

**comparison of adjectives** For most adjectives of one or two syllables, add *-er* to form the comparative degree and *-est* to form the superlative degree. For adjectives of more than two syllables, form the comparative degree by placing *more* before the positive degree, and form the superlative degree by placing *most* before the positive degree. A few adjectives are compared irregularly.

### COMPARISON OF ADJECTIVES

|  | Positive | Comparative | Superlative |
|---|---|---|---|
| **One or two syllable** | slow<br>pretty | slower<br>prettier | slowest<br>prettiest |
| **More than two syllables** | beautiful<br>interesting | more beautiful<br>more interesting | most beautiful<br>most interesting |
| **Irregular** | good, well<br>bad, ill<br>far<br>many, much<br>some<br>little | better<br>worse<br>farther<br>more<br><br>less | best<br>worst<br>fartherest<br>most<br><br>least |

Avoid the double comparison.

NONSTANDARD: The train is *more slower* than the plane.
STANDARD: The train is *slower* than the plane.

In contrasting one person or object with all the others of its kind, insert the word *other* before the noun that designates the classification, or use the word *else*.

- Jack is taller than *any other* boy in his class.
- Jack is taller than *anyone else* in his class.

comparison of adverbs   Adverbs ending in *-ly* are preceded by *more* and *most* in the comparative and superlative degrees. Most adverbs not ending in *-ly* form the comparative and superlative degrees by adding *-er* and *-est*. A few adverbs are compared irregularly.

### COMPARISON OF ADVERBS

|  | Positive | Comparative | Superlative |
|---|---|---|---|
| **-ly form** | quick | more quickly | most quickly |
| **One syllable** | fast | faster | fastest |
| **Irregular** | badly<br>well<br>little<br>much | worse<br>better<br>less<br>more | worst<br>best<br>least<br>most |

**could of, should of, might of**  These phrases are mistakes caused by the sound of the contractions for *could have* (could've), *should have* (should've), and *might have* (might've). In informal English contractions may be used. But formal English requires the use of the two words.

NONSTANDARD:   You *might of* caught a cold.
INFORMAL:   You *might've* been killed by that car!
FORMAL:   We *might have* made Silas angry.

# EXERCISES

**A.** Write the numbers 1–10 on your paper. For each of the following sentences, write the word in parentheses that completes the sentence in standard English.

1. (Being that, Since) you are busy, should I (bring, take) my purchase to another clerk?
2. Jan is the (most smart, smartest) person in my math class and, (beside, besides) that, she is (more attractive, attractiver) than Vickie.
3. Compared (to, with) golf, tennis is a (more fast, faster) game.
4. You should (of, have) (brung, brought) some cups that weren't (broke, broken).
5. (Beside, Besides) Mrs. Trent, I can't think of anyone who can play the clarinet, (can, may) you?
6. She (brung, brought) the (broke, broken, busted) watch in for repair this morning.
7. I might (of, have) known that you would get here (more rapidly, rapider) by bus.
8. Her senior picture was taken (beside, besides) an azalea that had just (bursted, busted, burst) into bloom.
9. No patient who has (come, came) to me has had a (worse, worser) cough.
10. If I (may, can), I would like to show you a house that you (may, can) afford.

**B.** Write the numbers 1–10 on your paper. Some of the following sentences contain mistakes in usage. Rewrite those sentences correctly. Write *C* next to the numbers of sentences that are already correct.

1. Her illusion to Mother Goose led to a discussion.
2. I should of came over yesterday, but I had nowheres to leave the baby.

3. When Leif's appendix bursted last week, we brung him from here to the hospital more faster than you can imagine.
4. By noon the baby had all ready broke a window.
5. You can avoid any number of penalties if you will accept the responsibility to double-check reports that are brought to you.
6. Compared to our cat, yours is a tiger!
7. When Sadie come by here for coffee yesterday, she was limping bad on the leg she breaked last year.
8. If it's alright, I'll wait until you're already before I go out to start the car, being as it's raining hard now.
9. No one beside Emily has served a meal to the amount of people likely to be there tomorrow night.
10. If I must choose between Greg, Mike, and Luis, I will choose the most pleasantest boy.

different from, different than  In general, *different from* is preferred to *different than*. *Than* is used with *better*.

- Your class ring is *different from* mine.
- The children's play was *better than* we expected.

dived, dove  Either word may be used as the past tense of *dive*. In writing, *dived* is most common.

do, did, done  The principal parts of *do* are *do, did,* and *(have) done.* Using *done* as the simple past tense and *have did* as the past participle should be avoided.

- He *did* his best to pass chemistry.
- They *have done* everything they could to help us.

doesn't, don't  These contractions for *does not* and *do not* are widely accepted in informal writing. However, users of standard English are careful to use *doesn't* with a third person singular subject and *don't* only with a plural subject or with *I* or *you*.

NONSTANDARD:  He *don't* like spinach.
STANDARD:  She *doesn't* like asparagus.
STANDARD:  They *don't* refuse dessert, however.

double negative  Avoid using two negative words to express a single negative meaning. Such constructions are nonstandard English.

NONSTANDARD:  I did*n't* get *no* mail today.
STANDARD:  I did*n't* get *any* mail today.

Also avoid double negatives that include the adverbs *hardly, scarcely,* and *barely.*

NONSTANDARD: She could*n't hardly* see the road.
STANDARD: She *could hardly* see the road.

e.g.   See i.e., e.g.

either . . . or   See or, nor

emigrate, immigrate   *Emigrate* means "to leave one's country in order to live elsewhere." *Immigrate* means "to come into a new country to live." The prefixes are helpful clues to the meanings: *e-* (or *ex-*) means "out from," *im-* means "into."

- Many refuges from Germany *emigrated* from their homeland.
- Some of them *immigrated* to the United States.

etc.   *Etc.* is the abbreviation for *et cetera,* which means "and so forth." Avoid using *etc.* to suggest a completion of your thoughts. Instead, say what you mean.

POOR: Her dialect was compared to that of Cindy, *etc.*
IMPROVED: Her dialect was compared to that of Cindy, Peter, and Candee.

When introducing a list with *including, such as,* or *for example,* do not end the list with *etc.* or *and etc.* The introduction indicates that the list is not meant to be complete. *And etc.* is incorrect at all times. Since the *et* in *et cetera* means "and," *and etc.* would mean "and and so forth." Note the spelling: *etc.*, not *ect.*

except   See accept, except

farther, further   *Farther* refers to physical distance, while *further* refers to abstract relationships of degree or quantity.

- I can't run any *farther.*
- He would say nothing *further* about my grades.

fewer, less   Use *fewer* with things that can be counted. Use *less* with things that cannot be counted. *Less* is also used with words such as *money, time,* or *weight.*

- Let's have *less* talking and more listening.
- She had *less* weight to lose than I.
- She has eaten *fewer* ice cream cones than I.

former, latter   *Former* refers to the first of two items mentioned. *Latter* refers to the second of two items mentioned.

- The president and the treasurer of the student council spoke to the assembled students. The *former* spoke about the council's goals. The *latter* spoke about needed financial support.

Using *former* and *latter* sometimes confuses the reader. Rather than use *former* or *latter,* rewrite the sentences so that the words are not needed.

- At this morning's assembly the president of the student council spoke about the council's goals. The treasurer spoke of needed financial support.

## EXERCISES

**A.** Write the numbers 1–10 on your paper. For each of the following sentences, write the word in parentheses that completes the sentence in standard English.

1. (Fewer, Less) than four out of one hundred American residents (immigrated, emigrated) here within the past twelve years.
2. The puppy (could, couldn't) hardly walk before it (did, done) its first clever trick.
3. Give me (less, fewer) potatoes and (less, fewer) meat than you gave Martha.
4. Carlos and Ed (don't, doesn't) like the song, and Brenda (don't, doesn't) like it either.
5. Our new house is (farther, further) from school than the house we lived in before.
6. Sheryl said she (don't, doesn't) want (any, no) interruptions while she does her math homework.
7. Have you ever (did, done) a math problem and not gotten an answer different (than, from) mine?
8. Since Venezuela is warm all year, let's (emigrate, immigrate) to Venezuela!
9. We would have (fewer, less) accidents if (fewer, less) drinkers would insist on driving.
10. Beulah's science project is better (from, than) mine.

**B.** Write the numbers 1–8 on your paper. Some of the following sentences contain mistakes in usage. Rewrite those sentences correctly. Write *C* next to the numbers of sentences that are already correct.

1. I cannot accept any answer besides the one in the teacher's manual.
2. The amount of suffering among our elderly poor is heartbreaking.

3. He feels so badly that he don't want to be anywheres but home.
4. When Grandma took the axe to her TV set, she said she should of busted it sooner.
5. Though the wounded cowboy wasn't hardly conscious, he reached for the rope that lay besides him.
6. No amount of discussion would affect Alice's decision, for her mind was already made up.
7. This is the year's worse issue of the school paper.
8. It contains all together too many errors that staff members should of corrected.

gave, given   The principal parts of *give* are *give, gave,* and *(have) given. Have gave* is nonstandard.

> NONSTANDARD:   The staff *had gave* her a farewell party already.
> STANDARD:   The staff *had given* her a farewell party already.

get, got   The principal parts of *get* are *get, got,* and *(have) got* or *gotten.* While both *got* and *gotten* are acceptable past participle forms, *gotten* is used more frequently.

- In the past we *have gotten* (or *got*) permission to use the auditorium for our fashion show.

In informal speech, *have got* is sometimes used instead of *have* in order to emphasize obligation or possession. The usage is avoided in formal English.

> INFORMAL:   I *have got* to do my homework. (obligation)
> FORMAL:   I *have* to do my homework.

> INFORMAL:   *Have* you *got* a cold? (possession)
> FORMAL:   *Have* you a cold? *Do* you *have* a cold?

go, went, gone   The principal parts of *go* are *go, went,* and *(have) gone.* However, in nonstandard usage, *went* often appears as the past participle.

> NONSTANDARD:   They *have went* to the grocery store.
> STANDARD:   They *have gone* to the grocery store.

In informal usage, *go and* is commonly used for emphasis. This usage is not appropriate for most writing.

> INFORMAL:   My sister will *go and* get A's in math.
> FORMAL:   My sister will get A's in math.

**good, well** *Good* is an adjective. *Well* can be used as either an adjective or an adverb. As an adjective, *well* implies good health. As a subject complement *good* implies a sense of well-being or satisfaction. *Good* should not be used as an adverb. In nonstandard English *good* is often used in place of *well*.

NONSTANDARD: You dance *good*.
STANDARD: You dance *well*. (adverb)

STANDARD: We've done a *good* job. (adjective)
STANDARD: The cake tastes *good*. (subject complement)
STANDARD: She feels *good*. (satisfaction)
STANDARD: She feels *well*. (good health)

**had ought, hadn't ought** *Had ought* and *hadn't ought* are nonstandard forms of *ought* and *ought not*.

NONSTANDARD: Do you think there *had ought* to be a four-day school week?
STANDARD: Do you think there *ought* to be a four-day school week?

NONSTANDARD: The children *hadn't ought* to play there.
STANDARD: The children *ought not* to play there.

**hardly, scarcely** The mistake often made in using these words involves forming a double negative. *Hardly* and *scarcely* are already negative. Do not use the word *not* with *hardly* or *scarcely*.

NONSTANDARD: The food is so hot that we ca*n't hardly* eat it.
STANDARD: The food is so hot that we *can hardly* eat it.

**healthy, healthful** In formal English, *healthful* means "giving health" or "good for the health"; *healthy* means "having or showing good health."

- How can you expect to be *healthy* if you don't eat *healthful* food?

In informal English, *healthy* frequently replaces *healthful*.

- This city is not a *healthy* place for people with allergies.

**i.e., e.g.** The initials *i.e.* represent *id est,* Latin words meaning "that is." An explanation follows *i.e.* The initials *e.g.* represent *exempli gratia,* Latin words meaning "for example." An example follows *e.g.*

- Use only triangles; *i.e.*, three-sided figures.
- The fair will offer many amusements, *e.g.,* pony rides and a pie eating contest.

When you write, avoid using *i.e.* and *e.g.* Write out the words *that is* or *for example*.

**if I was, if I were** When an *if* clause relates to the past, use the verb *was* for singular subjects.

- *If I was* there, I don't remember it.

When an *if* clause relates to a wish rather than a fact, use *were*.

- *If I were* in charge, I would set higher standards.
- *If Mrs. Cortez were* my counselor, I would seek her advice.

**imply, infer** *Imply* means "to suggest something rather than say it directly." *Infer* means "to conclude or interpret something."

- The principal *implied* that he was displeased with the resolution.
- I have *inferred* from several books I've read that the "good old days" weren't as good as Grandma says.

The noun forms of *imply* and *infer* are *implication* and *inference*.

- The *inference* we draw from your *implication* is that you dislike motorcycle clubs.

**in, into** *In* is used to indicate location; *into* to indicate motion.

- The plant is *in* the corner of the room. (location)
- We stepped *into* the store. (motion)

In informal English, *in* is often substituted for *into*.

**its, it's** *Its* is a possessive pronoun like *hers*, *his*, *theirs*, and *mine*. *It's* is the contraction for *it is*.

- I read the book twice, once for *its* plot and once for *its* language.
- If *it's* Tuesday, *it's* time for a soup and sandwich supper.

## EXERCISES

**A.** Write the numbers 1–10. For each sentence, write the word in parentheses that completes the sentence in standard English.

1. If I (was, were) as (healthy, healthful) as you, I wouldn't complain.
2. Are you (inferring, implying) that our treasurer is dishonest?
3. Since I (can, can't) hardly see the blackboard, I (ought, had ought) to get my eyes checked.
4. The dog played (its, it's) part (good, well), in the film.
5. For your father's sake, we have to move to a (more healthful, healthier) climate.
6. If I (was, were) late it was because my watch has not been keeping time (good, well) lately.

7. We (ought not, hadn't ought) to eat any of the pie, but (its, it's) aroma is making me hungry.
8. I have (gone, went) over your letters again; from them I (imply, infer) that you regret your recent decision to change jobs.
9. You type (good, well); this paper has scarcely (no, any) errors.
10. Although you are (implying, inferring) that you do not feel (good, well), you certainly look (healthful, healthy).

**B.** Write the numbers 1–10 on your paper. Some of the following sentences contain mistakes in usage. Rewrite those sentences correctly. Write C next to the numbers of sentences that are already correct.

1. Is it all right to give a speech on a subject beside Insects?
2. I have been sleeping good, though I get less hours of sleep each night than I used to.
3. If I was principal of this school, it would be the most cleanest school in the country.
4. Lucio affected interest in Ms. Kirby's lesson, though he wanted to burst out laughing about how well his practical joke had succeeded.
5. Am I correct in implying from your campaign speeches that you think we should of encouraged more people to emigrate to our country?
6. You are not healthful because you do not follow the advice I have gave you.
7. Jill don't need to eat so many junk food.
8. After he had went in the house, we looked everywheres for the tools we needed to repair the bird feeder he busted.
9. Besides the chaperones, fewer than one hundred came to the dance.
10. I hadn't ought to do bad in this event.

kind of, sort of  *Kind of* and *sort of* are singular. They take singular modifiers and singular verbs. In informal English plural forms are used with *kind of* and *sort of*.

INFORMAL:  These *sort of* vacations *are* restful to me.
FORMAL:  This *sort of* vacation *is* restful to me.

INFORMAL:  I always liked *those kind of* cookies.
FORMAL:  I always liked *that kind of* cookie.

When the plural nouns referred to are of different types, *kinds of* and *sorts of* may be used.

- He met all *kinds of* people while he was in New York City.

*Kind of* and *sort of* are used informally to mean "somewhat" or "rather." However, it is better to write out what you mean.

POOR: Doing those problems was *kind of* difficult.
IMPROVED: Doing those problems was difficult because I missed class yesterday when they were explained.

POOR: The meeting was *sort of* dull.
IMPROVED: The meeting was dull because all we did was review amendments to our constitution.

The use of *kind a* and *sort a* is always nonstandard.

**lay, lie**   See lie, lay.

**learn, teach**   *Learn* means "to acquire knowledge." *Teach* means "to give or impart knowledge."

NONSTANDARD: Will you *learn* me to play the guitar?
STANDARD: I will work hard to *learn* what you *teach* me.

**leave, let**   *Leave* means "to go away" or "to abandon." *Let* means "to permit" or "to allow."

NONSTANDARD: *Leave* me go there now.
STANDARD: *Let* me go there now.

*Leave* and *let* are used interchangeably in one sense.

- *Leave* me alone. *Let* me alone.

**less, few**   See few, less.

**lie, lay**   The verb *lie* means "to recline." *Lie* never has a direct object. The principal parts of *lie* are *lie, lay,* and *(have) lain.*

- Please *lie* down for a short nap.
- For a week the lost keys *lay* in the grass unnoticed.
- Your mail *has lain* on your dresser for two days now.

The verb *lay* means "to put or place something somewhere." *Lay* usually takes a receiver of action, which may be the object or the subject of the sentence. The principal parts of *lay* are *lay, laid,* and *(have) laid.*

- *Lay* the mail on the counter. (*Mail* is the direct object.)
- The mail *had been laid* on the counter. (*Mail* is the subject of a passive verb.)
- I do not know where Beth *laid* her glasses. (*Glasses* is the direct object of *laid.*)
- I *have laid* aside my plans to open a book store. (*Plans* is the direct object of *have laid.*)

**like, as** *Like,* a preposition, means "similar to" and introduces a phrase. *As* is a conjunction meaning "such as." It is used to introduce a clause.

- Eating this pizza is *like* chewing on cardboard.
- We sang *as* Ms. Chang had asked.

In informal English, *like* often replaces *as.*

INFORMAL: We sang *like* Ms. Chang had asked.

**loose, lose** *Loose* is an adjective or adverb meaning "not tight," or "free." *Lose* is a verb meaning "to misplace."

- The *loose* bulb caused the light to flicker. (adjective)
- The hinge came *loose.* (adverb)
- Don't *lose* those concert tickets! (verb)

**misplaced modifiers** An adjective phrase or modifying clause should immediately precede or follow the noun or pronoun that it modifies. Misplaced modifiers can result in sentences that are both confusing and absurd.

POOR: I took my watch to the jeweler *with the broken spring.* (Does the watch or the jeweler have a broken spring?)

IMPROVED: I took my watch *with the broken spring* to the jeweler.

POOR: We sold the jewelry *at the fair* that we had made. (Did you make the jewelry or the fair?)

IMPROVED: *At the fair* we sold the jewelry that we had made.

**neither . . . nor** See or, nor

**off, off of** *Off of* has the same meaning as *off.* Do not use *of* with *off.*

- She stepped *off* the ladder.

*Off* or *off of* is sometimes mistakenly used for *from.*

NONSTANDARD: I borrowed an umbrella *off of* Leanor.
STANDARD: I borrowed an umbrella *from* Leanor.

**or, nor** *Or* and *nor* are coordinating conjunctions that connect words, phrases, or clauses of equal grammatical value. *Nor* signals negative meaning.

- I'll have peas *or* corn. (words)
- We will watch TV *or* listen to records. (phrases)
- I will not write to him, *nor* will I call him. (clauses)

When the singular parts of a compound subject are connected by *or,* a singular verb is used.

- Roberto *or* Chris *provides* something for us to talk about everyday.

Used in pairs, *either...or* and *neither...nor* are correlative conjunctions. They emphasize that two items are involved. They also signal the need for a singular verb when they connect singular parts of compound subjects.

- *Either* the scarf *or* the sash *adds* just the touch of color that you need with that outfit.

A plural verb is necessary when both parts or only the second part of a compound subject is plural.

- *Either* the sophomore officers *or* the junior officers *need* to reserve the gym by Friday. (Both parts of the compound subject are plural. Therefore, the verb is plural.)
- *Neither* Tyrone *nor* his teachers *have* reported his Friday absence. (The second part of the compound subject is plural. Therefore, the verb is plural.)

pronouns (needless)  In nonstandard usage an unnecessary pronoun often follows immediately after its antecedent. The structure does not appear in standard English.

NONSTANDARD:   My *sister she* bought a new Triumph.
STANDARD:   My sister bought a new Triumph.

pronouns (subject and object)  The subject form of a personal pronoun is used when the pronoun is the subject of a sentence or clause. The object form is used when the pronoun is the object of a verb or a preposition.

### FORMS OF PERSONAL PRONOUNS

|  | Subject Form | Object Form |
|---|---|---|
| **Singular** | I | me |
|  | you | you |
|  | he | him |
|  | she | her |
|  | it | it |
| **Plural** | we | us |
|  | you | you |
|  | they | them |

All of the subject form pronouns can be used as subjects in this sentence: _____ saw Lynn. All of the object form pronouns can be used as objects in these sentences: Lynn saw _____. Lynn gave _____ a quick smile. Lynn talked to _____.

Compound subjects and objects requiring personal pronouns are more troublesome. When you use pronouns as part of a compound subject or a compound object, use the same form you would use if the pronouns were being used singly.

NONSTANDARD: *Him and her* saw Sam. (subject)
STANDARD: *He* saw Sam. *She* saw Sam. *He and she* saw Sam.

NONSTANDARD: Vicki passed *he and I* without smiling. (direct object)
STANDARD: Vicki passed *him*. Vicki passed *me*. Vicki passed *him and me* without smiling.

NONSTANDARD: She gave *Ricardo and I* a piece of the cake. (indirect object)
STANDARD: She gave *Ricardo* a piece of the cake. She gave *me* a piece of the cake. She gave *Ricardo and me* a piece of the cake.

NONSTANDARD: The coach rode with *he and Toby*. (object of the preposition *with*)
STANDARD: The coach rode with *him*. The coach rode with *Toby*. The coach rode with *him and Toby*.

Pronouns that follow a form of the verb *be* should be subject forms because those complements are equal in meaning to the subjects of their sentences.

- *She and I* are the winners. (subject)
- The winners are *she and I*. (complement)

## EXERCISES

A. Write the numbers 1–10 on your paper. For each of the following sentences, write the word in parentheses that completes the sentence in standard English.

1. (She, Her) and (I, me) will pick up some bread on the way home.
2. If you will (leave, let) me have the car now, I will mow the lawn this afternoon.
3. I find it hard to (lie, lay) down this kind of book once I've started reading.
4. Try not to (lose, loose) any of this (lose, loose) change.
5. The letter was addressed to (he, him) and (I, me).
6. Mr. Cortez (learned, taught) me how to read that Spanish newspaper that is (laying, lying) on the table.
7. He looks (as, like) his father, except he has more hair to (lose, loose)!

8. I did (like, as) you told me and gave Uncle Cheung the tools that have (laid, lain) in the utility room for so long.
9. (Leave, Let) Billy stay to play with Maria, and I'll take (he, him) and (she, her) to the playground this afternoon.
10. Right after Mr. Harper (lay, laid) the last piece of carpet we found him (laying, lying) asleep in the middle of it!

**B.** Write the numbers 1-10 on your paper. Some of the following sentences contain mistakes in usage. Rewrite those sentences correctly. Write *C* next to the numbers of sentences that are already correct.

1. If I was to choose an all-star team, it would include she and him.
2. We hadn't ought to buy less than six extra bulbs.
3. Until you are already to go, I'll just lay here on the sofa.
4. No one can sing as good as Monte can; he never sings bad.
5. Do you mean to infer that our working conditions aren't none of our business?
6. Julia she bought a box of chocolates for her boyfriend that weighed five pounds.
7. People who don't know anything about that kind of motor should leave this motor alone.
8. I am trying to choose between Spanish, French, or German and would like to know which is easier.
9. Him and I put the squirrels in the garage that we shot.
10. The play turned out well; we all felt good about the size of our audience.

raise, rise    *Raise* means "to lift up something" and is followed by a direct object. *Rise* means "to go up" or "to get up." Rise is not followed by a direct object.

- We will *raise* the price of electricity this year.
- The price of electricity *rises* each year.

ran, run    The principal parts of the verb *run* are *run*, *ran*, and *(have) run*. In nonstandard usage, *run* is often used as the simple past tense and *ran* is used as the past participle.

NONSTANDARD:   Yesterday he *run* the distance in one minute.
STANDARD:   Yesterday he *ran* the distance in one minute.

NONSTANDARD:   She *has ran* all over the state.
STANDARD:   She *has run* all over the state.

real, really   *Real* is an adjective meaning "true" or "genuine." Some people use *real* as an adverb meaning "very," but *really,* meaning "truly," should be used instead.

> NONSTANDARD:   He was *real* happy to see her.
> STANDARD:   We were *really* (or *very*) happy, too.

reason is because   The expression *reason is because* is redundant. *Because* should be replaced by *that.* If the use of *that* creates an awkward sentence, then the sentence should be rewritten.

> REDUNDANT:   The *reason* this phrase is in the glossary *is because* it is redundant.
> IMPROVED:   The *reason* this phrase is in the glossary *is that* it is redundant.
> IMPROVED:   This phrase is in the glossary *because* it is redundant.

respectively, respectfully   *Respectively* means "in the previously mentioned order." *Respectfully* means "with respect."

- The first, second, and third races were won by Smith, Nakai, and Hing, *respectively.* (in the order named)
- We *respectfully* request that you reconsider your recent decision concerning the athletic program at our school. (with respect)

The use of *respectively* often forces the reader to go back and sort out which is which. Therefore, *respectively* should be avoided.

- Smith won the first race; Nakai won the second; Hing won the third.

said, says   In the present tense, *says* is the appropriate form of *say* to use with a third-person singular subject: *he says, she says, it says, the teacher says. Say* is used with all other singular and plural subjects: *I say, you say, we say, they say, the teachers say. Said* is the appropriate past tense and past participle form for all subjects, singular and plural.

> NONSTANDARD:   He *say* we won that round.
> STANDARD:   He *says* we won that round.
>
> STANDARD:   Yesterday he *said* we won that round.
> STANDARD:   He *has said* repeatedly that we won the round.

saw, seen   The principal parts of *see* are *see, saw,* and *(have) seen.* In nonstandard usage, *saw* and *seen* are frequently interchanged.

> NONSTANDARD:   They *seen* him coming over the hill.
> STANDARD:   They *saw* him coming over the hill.
>
> NONSTANDARD:   We *have saw* all we need to see.
> STANDARD:   We *have seen* all we need to see.

**-self, -selves** Pronouns ending in *-self* or *-selves* serve two functions: (**1**) they turn the action of the verb back to the subject (reflexive pronouns) or (**2**) they emphasize the nouns or pronouns that they follow (intensive pronouns). The suffix *-self* is added to singular pronouns: *myself, yourself, himself, herself, itself, oneself.* The suffix *-selves* is added to plural pronouns: *ourselves, yourselves, themselves.*

- They forced *themselves* not to laugh. (reflexive)
- He vowed to make the dinner *himself.* (intensive)

The forms *hisself, ourself, theirself,* and *theirselves* are nonstandard.

**shall, will** Formerly, *shall* was used for the simple future tense in the first person and to express determination in the second and third persons. Today, however, it is acceptable to use *will* in all persons for both simple future tense and to express determination.

- I *will* eat with you. (simple future)
- He *will* sign your pass. (simple future)
- The children *will* certainly be there. (determination)
- I *will* not agree to that condition. (determination)

Sometimes, however, *shall* is the only logical word to use.

- *Shall* we go to the movies? (*Will* would change the meaning.)

**set, sit** *Sit* usually means "to place oneself in a seat." *Sit* seldom takes a direct object. Its principal parts are *sit, sat,* and *(have) sat. Set* usually means "to place or put something somewhere." *Set* generally does take a direct object. Its principal parts are *set, set,* and *(have) set.*

- She *sits* on the porch for awhile every day. (no direct object)
- He *set* the aquarium on the bookcase. (aquarium is a direct object)

There are a few special cases when *sit* takes a direct object and *set* takes no object.

- Joe *sits* the baby in the high chair when it's meal time.
- The sun *sets* over those trees.

Hens, paint, and concrete also can *set* without an object.

## EXERCISES

**A.** Write the numbers 1–10. For each sentence, write the word in parentheses that completes the sentence in standard English.

1. While the bread (raises, rises), I'll (sit, set) here and chat with you.
2. They have only (theirselves, themselves) to blame for those errors.

3. I'm (real, really) glad to have (saw, seen) you again.
4. After the group of scouts (raised, rose) the flag, they (run, ran) to the mess hall for breakfast.
5. The reason no one called you is (that, because) everyone (says, said) you were out of town for a month.
6. There (sat, set) my grandma, my Aunt Delma, and my Uncle Gil, who live in Chicago, Los Angeles, and Tucson, (respectfully, respectively).
7. Marvin had never before (saw, seen) (himself, hisself) in a tuxedo.
8. Mr. Morgenstern (says, say) that we should leave now.
9. Guess who I (run, ran) into today that I hadn't (saw, seen) for years.
10. The sun that (raises, rises) in the east this morning will (sit, set) tonight in the west.

**B.** Write the numbers 1-10 on your paper. Some of the following sentences contain mistakes in usage. Rewrite those sentences correctly. Write *C* next to the numbers of sentences that are already correct.

1. My cousin he seen the children when they come out of the drugstore.
2. Sandy has all ready went to Cleveland to except first prize for her essay.
3. Don't you think you and me had ought to pay for the ceramic cat that we busted?
4. He say that its alright to leave fifteen minutes early this afternoon.
5. The reason we were late was because we stopped to give Jan and she a ride.
6. If we lay our coats on these speakers, will they affect the music?
7. If he was to set hisself realistic goals, do you think he could achieve them?
8. I really doubt that Mario laid out in the sun that long; you know how good he can tell tall tales.
9. No one from Ohio beside Rosabel and I was among the semifinalists accept one fellow from Columbus.
10. Being that him and Rudy have broke the record all ready, they should of made plans to be in the Olympics.

slowly, slow   *Slow* is both an adverb and an adjective. *Slowly* is always an adverb. However, the use of *slow* as an adverb should be avoided.

POOR:   Walk *slow* past the counselor's office. (adverb)
IMPROVED:   Walk *slowly* past the counselor's office. (adverb)
■ After a *slow* start, the team played hard. (adjective)

sort of, kind of   *See* kind of, sort of.

take, bring   *See* bring, take.

teach, learn   *See* learn, teach.

than, then   *Than* is used to make comparisons. *Then* is an adverb that tells *when*.

- I know more about English usage now *than* I did in September. (comparison)
- *Then* I knew a little about usage; now I know a lot. (adverb telling *when*)

that there, this here   *There* and *here* should not be used with *that* and *this*.

NONSTANDARD:   Give me *that there* cup.
STANDARD:   Give me *that* cup.

NONSTANDARD:   Do you want *this here* coat?
STANDARD:   Do you want *this* coat?

these, those   In standard English the demonstrative pronouns *these* and *those* are used for pointing to or singling out persons or objects. Nonstandard English often uses the personal pronoun *them* instead of *these* and *those*.

NONSTANDARD:   *Them* are the team captains.
STANDARD:   *Those* are the team captains.

there is, there are   When *there* introduces a sentence or clause in which the subject is singular, a singular verb follows *there*. When the subject is plural, a plural verb follows *there*.

- *There is* a man waiting in your office.
- *There are* three dozen pencils in this box.
- In the drawer *there were* two old books and a pen.

When the first part of a compound subject following *there* is singular, a singular verb is often used.

- In the drawer *there was* a pen and two old books.

Sentences that begin with *there is* delay the subject and thus are often less emphatic than they might be. Repeated use of this structure should therefore be avoided. In rephrasing such a sentence, begin with its subject.

POOR:   *There were* few scientists who supported the old man's theories.
IMPROVED:   Few scientists supported the old man's theories.

**threw, thrown**   The principal parts of *throw* are *throw, threw,* and *(have) thrown.* Nonstandard English often uses *throwed* as the simple past tense and *have threw* as the past participle.

> NONSTANDARD:   Sal *throwed* a big party at his house Saturday.
> STANDARD:   Sal *threw* a big party at his house Saturday.
>
> NONSTANDARD:   Sal *has threw* a party about once a month so far this year.
> STANDARD:   Sal *has thrown* a party about once a month so far this year.

**took, taken**   The principal parts of *take* are *take, took,* and *(have) taken. Have took* is nonstandard.

> NONSTANDARD:   You *have took* enough pictures already.
> STANDARD:   You *have taken* enough pictures already.

**toward, towards**   *Toward* is the preferred usage.

**way, ways**   Use *way* rather than *ways* when referring to distance.

> NONSTANDARD:   We have come a long *ways* together since October.
> STANDARD:   We have come a long *way* together since October.

**well, good**   See *good, well.*

**who, which, that**   *Who, which,* and *that* are relative pronouns when they introduce relative clauses. In general, *who* refers only to people, *which* refers only to things, and *that* refers to either people or things.

- The giant *who* was at the top of the beanstalk, *which* reached above the clouds, gave Jack a scare *that* he would not soon forget.

*Which* should be used for nonrestrictive clauses (clauses that, if eliminated, would not change the meaning of the sentence). *That* should be used with restrictive clauses (clauses necessary to the meaning of a sentence).

- The porch, *which* was old and very tired, leaned westward.
- The record *that* we had set in March was broken in April.

**who, whom**   In spoken English *who* and *whom* are often used interchangeably. *Who* is often substituted for *whom,* especially when it appears near the beginning of a clause. In written English, however, certain distinctions are still observed.

*Who* and *whoever* are used as the subject of a sentence or clause. *Whom* and *whomever* are used as the object of a verb or preposition. An exception to this rule occurs when a preposition and its object are widely separated.

STANDARD: *Who* gave you that? (subject of the sentence)
He saw the man *who* makes skis. (subject of the clause)
Mr. Mallory is the man *whom* I saw. (object of *saw*)
FORMAL: Will you tell me *whom* you came here with?
INFORMAL: Will you tell me *who* you came here with?

To avoid problems, put the pronoun after the preposition and use the objective form *whom*.

- Will you tell me *with whom* you came? (object of preposition *with*)

If the clause follows a preposition, *whom* is sometimes wrongly used as the object of the preposition. Instead, the pronoun *who* is the subject of the clause.

- Give this package to *whoever* answers the door. (*Whoever* is the subject of the clause. The whole clause, not just *whoever,* is the object of *to.*)

**will, shall** See shall, will.

## EXERCISES

**A.** Write the numbers 1–10 on your paper. After each of the following sentences, write the word in parentheses that completes the sentences in standard English.

1. There (is, are) many people here.
2. If you walk (slow, slowly) past Ms. Mason's room, you will see a substitute teacher rather (than, then) Ms. Mason.
3. As Uncle Gaspar walked (toward, towards) me, I saw that he was wearing one of those (kind, kinds) of shirts that I like.
4. (This, This here) sign is a landmark telling us that we have a long (way, ways) to go yet.
5. There (is, are) few other trails we could have (took, taken).
6. (Them, Those) are the young women (who, whom) I recruited for minor league play.
7. No one else has worked so (slow, slowly) nor (took, taken) so much time to make a set of bookends!
8. (Than, Then) we knew that the car cost more (than, then) we were prepared to pay.
9. I think there (is, are) a set of headphones on the table; plug it into (that, that there) receiver.
10. Angered by his own mistakes, the actor had (threw, thrown) a tantrum in front of the director (who, whom) he most admired.

B. Write the numbers 1–10 on your paper. Some of the following sentences contain mistakes in usage. Rewrite those sentences correctly. Write *C* next to the numbers of sentences that are already correct.

1. The man to whom you spoke has been with the firm fewer than thirty days.
2. That there is the person who come by here yesterday to complain that her new ceiling fan turns too slow.
3. I have gave you and she the albums.
4. The man which I thought was your uncle seemed real friendly.
5. When him and I drove his old Chevy to Montgomery by ourself, it seemed like a long ways.
6. I can't hardly believe its my birthday since its been one of the worse days of my life.
7. Eat healthy food and lay down for a short nap.
8. If you let me borrow a pen, I promise that I won't lay it down somewhere and loose it.
9. These kind of sweaters ain't nothing like the ones I bought Dad; they don't fit as good.
10. The reason I left the meeting early was because I had to meet Jeff and her more then a kilometer away from where we were meeting.

# REVIEWING USAGE

**A. Writing complete sentences** Write the numbers 1–20 on your paper. Copy each word group below. Then, after each group, write a complete statement that begins with the word in parentheses. The result may be one complete sentence or two complete sentences. Punctuate them appropriately and capitalize letters where necessary.

EXAMPLE:  Mrs. Cortez called roll . . . (then)
REVISIONS:  Mrs. Cortez called roll. Then she took up our assignments.
Mrs. Cortez called roll; then she took up our assignments.

1. Although I forgot to call on Geraldo . . . (he)
2. I didn't see Mr. Barber . . . (therefore)
3. Some came by bus . . . (others)
4. Because she knew the city . . . (she)
5. Whenever I skip lunch . . . (I)
6. If you hurry, you can finish your work by noon . . . (then)
7. I don't care who called this meeting . . . (I)
8. We don't usually allow students to use this phone . . . (however)
9. I finished my sandwich, cleared the table, and rinsed off my dishes . . . (finally)
10. Realizing that some team members would be absent . . . (the coach)
11. Because she had chosen *A Separate Peace* for us to read . . . (we)
12. Playing golf requires patience . . . (therefore)
13. After buying Mark's old Buick . . . (however)
14. Tadeo is funny . . . (he)
15. When they see sad movies . . . (they)
16. Several left early . . . (others)
17. When she was there . . . (she)
18. I like rain . . . (but)
19. I saw it . . . (and)
20. You can swim . . . (or)

**B. Improving sentences** Write the numbers 1–15 on your paper. The following sentences suffer a combination of ills. In revising them, remove all symptoms of verbosity, redundancy, cliché, and inappropriate usage. Most of your revised sentences should be shorter than the originals.

1. The thing that I wonder about is whether or not Reginald can win.
2. When you have a moment that you can spare, will you be so kind as to get me a cup of coffee?
3. Due to the fact that our performance is this afternoon at 4:00 P.M., I am in a state of nervousness.
4. Are you going to verbalize what transpired at Ninita's party, or must I hypothesize and then interrogate other guests at that event?
5. I get tired of watching television commercials for new innovations that are repeated over and over again.
6. A horse that was beautiful won the race that was held first.
7. The child was injured, and he was taken to a hospital that was nearby. An ambulance came and took him.
8. Chocolate cake is one of my favorite foods that I like a lot, and, in addition, I like butterscotch pudding, too.
9. What I want you to tell me is how you can eat like a horse and still stay as light as a feather.
10. I told my father that the reason we were excessively tardy in the return of his automobile was because our supply of petroleum had become depleted between Auburn and Alex City.
11. It is our hope that by the time Cindy Lou reaches the point of graduation from Anne School, we will have been successful in terminating her inclination to be slovenly and sloppy in her attire.
12. It goes without saying that, after all is said and done, businesses that advertise will grow by leaps and bounds, while businesses that hide their lights under a bushel will progress at a snail's pace.
13. My sister goes to a college of higher learning.
14. Us students find the lesson hard and difficult.
15. Lie the in the upper desk draw of my desk.

**C. Identifying standard usage** Write the numbers 1–30 on your paper. For each of the following sentences write *C* if the sentence is in standard usage. If it contains nonstandard usage, write *N* next to its number. All of the usage items tested in this exercise were treated in the Glossary of Usage.

1. You took the biggest half!
2. If I were twenty, I would apply for that job.

3. They allowed theirselves only twenty minutes to get to school.
4. Be certain to set the alarm clock before you leave.
5. That baseball bat has lain on our front lawn for three days.
6. Can I borrow a dime off of you?
7. Armando's absence had little affect on his test grade.
8. The chairperson appointed Ricardo and me to the committee.
9. Gina sings badly.
10. Millions emigrated to the U.S. during the nineteenth century.
11. By noon we were all ready to go to the picnic.
12. Rise from your seat and walk toward the windows.
13. That's a real pretty scarf lying on the counter.
14. No one besides Maria knew about Miss Brewster's engagement.
15. Leave me go to the game with my friends.
16. I laid down because I did not feel well.
17. He plays the tuba well.
18. When Andy's balloon burst, he cried.
19. Mr. Potts gave him and I a chance to defend ourselves.
20. I didn't mean to imply that I dislike your painting.
21. The class discussed ways that TV affects children.
22. The phone book is somewheres in this drawer.
23. They couldn't hardly see the road ahead.
24. John dived into the pool and swum toward the screaming child.
25. To who did I give the answer book?
26. The centipede crawled across the driveway very slowly.
27. There is a pair of gloves and two jackets in the front closet.
28. Of the three boys, Chip was the worse dancer.
29. Who do you think will win first prize?
30. That kind of shirt is on sale at Sears.

**D. Taking a usage test**   Write the numbers 1–20 on your paper. Find the underlined example of nonstandard usage in each of the following sentences and write its letter on your paper. No sentence contains more than one error. If you find no example of nonstandard usage among the underlined parts, write *E* on your paper. The format of this exercise is similar to those found in standardized tests on usage, like the SAT (Scholastic Aptitude Test).

1. After the man had drank a cup of coffee and eaten a piece of pie, he
                         (A)                          (B)
   laid a dollar on the counter and left. No error.
   (C)                               (D)   (E)

2. It <u>was</u> <u>him</u> and Mr. Sanchez <u>whom</u> we asked to help <u>us</u> scouts when
   (A) (B)  (C)  (D)
   our canoe tipped over. <u>No error.</u>
   (E)

3. If I <u>was</u> happy then, the reason was <u>because</u> I had not yet <u>seen</u> what
   (A)  (B)  (C)
   wealth and power can do to people <u>who</u> are not ready for it. <u>No error.</u>
   (D)  (E)

4. <u>Do</u> either of your parents <u>care</u> if <u>he</u> and <u>I</u> stay for lunch? <u>No error.</u>
   (A)  (B)  (C) (D)  (E)

5. Each of <u>us</u> girls <u>have</u> chosen a friend <u>who</u> will escort <u>her</u> to the stage.
   (A)  (B)  (C)  (D)
   <u>No error.</u>
   (E)

6. After my brother and <u>I</u> had <u>drunk</u> all the milk in the refrigerator, we
   (A)  (B)
   remembered that Mom had <u>forbid</u> <u>us</u> boys to touch it. <u>No error.</u>
   (C)  (D)  (E)

7. <u>Being as</u> <u>it's</u> cloudy now, we will take that umbrella that somebody
   (A)  (B)
   <u>laid</u> <u>beside</u> my coat. <u>No error.</u>
   (C)  (D)  (E)

8. Although physics <u>was</u> easier for Karen and <u>me</u> than biology had been,
   (A)  (B)
   neither of us <u>did</u> <u>good</u>. <u>No error.</u>
   (C)  (D)  (E)

9. <u>Among</u> the members of the student council only <u>he</u> and Tony <u>could</u>
   (A)  (B)  (C)
   <u>of</u> convinced us sophomores to <u>lay</u> aside our plans. <u>No error.</u>
   (D)  (E)

10. Larry James, to <u>whom</u> the Green Thumb Award was <u>given</u>, always
    (A)  (B)
    harvests bigger and <u>better</u> tomatoes than <u>us</u>. <u>No error.</u>
    (C)  (D)  (E)

11. Barb, <u>whom</u> everyone likes, won't admit that either <u>she</u> or Anna <u>is</u> the
    (A)  (B)  (C)
    one <u>who</u> sent the telegram to the choir. <u>No error.</u>
    (D)  (E)

12. I find it impossible to <u>lay</u> down <u>these</u> kind of <u>book</u> once I have <u>begun</u>
    (A)  (B)  (C)  (D)
    reading the first chapter. <u>No error.</u>
    (E)

13. He and Julia play the piano better than I, but I play the guitar better
    (A)      (B)                      (C)
    than them. No error.
         (D)   (E)

14. There are less people in the audience today than there were when
          (A) (B)                                (C)
    Paula and I were in charge of the program. No error.
             (D)                                (E)

15. When we girls play tennis, no one wants to challenge Kaulana or her
         (A)                       (B)
    brother; she won the school's tournament, and he is even better than
                                                            (C)
    her. No error.
    (D)  (E)

16. Nick, like his brothers, is willing to help anyone who needs help. No
          (A)                 (B)                       (C)  (D)        (E)
    error.,

17. Are them the books that you and he brought for us girls to read after
        (A)                      (B)              (C)
    we have done our homework? No error.
              (D)               (E)

18. Charles sat at the piano ready to accompany Becky and me; he played
               (A)                                          (B)
    well, but we sang bad. No error.
    (C)              (D)  (E)

19. One of the girls whom I know promised to set up an interview be-
                     (A)         (B)        (C)
    tween her boss and me. No error.
                       (D)  (E)

20. Compared to Lawrence, you play the accordion badly, but you do
                (A)                               (B)
    dance better than him. No error.
          (C)       (D)   (E)

§ COMPOSITION

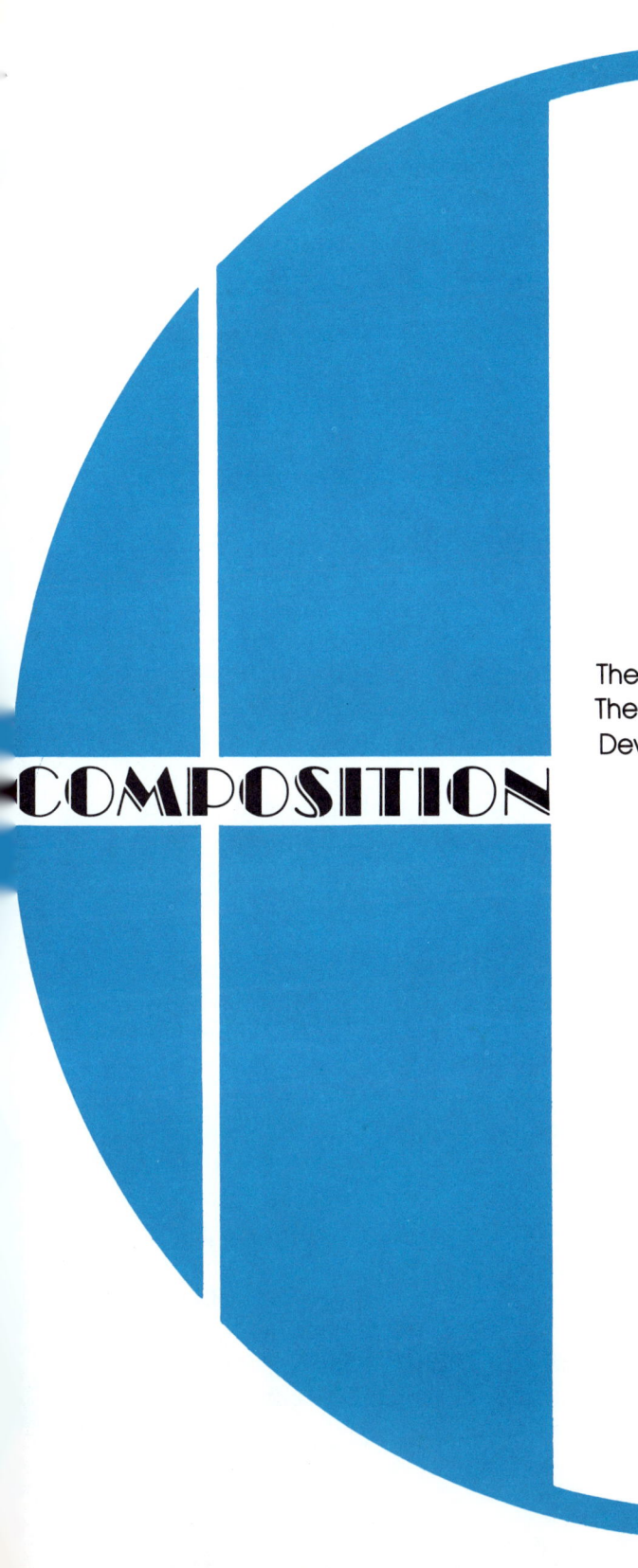

The Art of Explanation   212
The Whole Composition   227
Developing Your Writing   241

# THE ART OF EXPLANATION

## 38

## Getting Started

Writing isn't easy. It's great to *have* written something. But getting started and actually doing the writing can be difficult for both students and professional authors.

"Writing, when properly managed (as you may be sure I think mine is)," said Laurence Sterne in his novel *Tristram Shandy,* "is but another name for conversation." That's true. But notice that he says "properly managed." Writing, unlike much of our casual conversation, has to be organized.

When we talk to one another, we can rephrase statements or reexplain points if we haven't made them clear. But writing can't be immediately added to or clarified for the reader. Writing must be so organized as to be clear the first time it's read. This is the art of explanation.

If you want to write, then, how and where do you begin? The most common excuse for not getting started is "I don't have anything to say." Nonsense. In the first century, Pliny the Younger refuted this excuse in a letter to the Roman Emperor Trajan. "There is nothing to write about, you say. Well, then, write and let me know just this—that there *is* nothing to write about."

Everybody has thoughts, feelings, memories, and experiences. You need not lead a particularly exciting life in order to write well. Nor do you need to always be with brilliant or adventurous people, or to visit exotic places. The best source for writing ideas is yourself. If you observe and think about the world around you, you will have no trouble finding things to write about. Therefore, the next time you find yourself putting off writing because you think you have nothing to say, take a good look at your thoughts, feelings, and experiences.

# EXERCISES

**A. Organizing thoughts** The following list is a jumble of impressions a person might have on going to a rock concert. Prepare the list for written communication by grouping related details together into smaller lists.

*New songs*
*Expensive tickets*
*Sitting near stage*
*Music loud*
*Large theater*
*Seats uncomfortable*
*Great drummer*
*Crowded ticket line*
*Golden oldie songs*
*Good bass guitarist*
*Smoky air*
*Velvet curtains*
*Multicolored lights*
*High ceiling*
*Various ages in audience*
*Constant movement of people*
*Purple costumes on band*
*New lead guitarist*
*Occasional strobe light*
*Tall person sitting in front*

**B. Selecting related ideas** Below is a list of ideas about gardening. From that list, copy the sentences you might use if you were going to write about *vegetable* gardening.

- *Rabbits destroy lettuce crops.*
- *Radishes take two weeks to grow.*
- *Tulips start from bulbs.*
- *Green pepper plants have white flowers.*
- *Deer eat squash and must be fenced out of gardens.*
- *Corn grows better in groups.*
- *Peas must be planted in early spring.*
- *Roses make lovely bouquets.*

**C. Preparing to write** Write down an idea or opinion you believe in. Under that, list three or more reasons why you believe your statement is true. If possible, include examples to support each of your reasons.

# 39

# The Structure of an Expository Paragraph

The one form of writing that you will undoubtedly use more than any other, both in school and as an adult outside of school, is **exposition,** or expository writing. This form of writing can be defined very simply as writing that *explains* something. When you write a report or a term paper, you are writing exposition. An encyclopedia, a newspaper article, a how-to manual, a recipe, this textbook—all are examples of expository writing.

The topic for an expository paragraph must be narrow enough for you to deal with it completely. At first you may think of a topic wide enough to cover many books in a library. But then you must narrow the topic to paragraph size. Look at the graph below. Reading across the first row of blocks, you will find that the topic wide

|  | Packing a Picnic Basket | Planning a Picnic | Safe Barbecuing | Camp Cookery | Plain and Fancy Cooking | Food Around the World |
|---|---|---|---|---|---|---|
| Wide enough for a library |  |  |  |  |  | ● |
| Wide enough for a bookshelf |  |  |  |  | ● |  |
| Wide enough for a book |  |  |  | ● |  |  |
| Narrow enough for a chapter |  |  | ● |  |  |  |
| Narrow enough for a composition |  | ● |  |  |  |  |
| Narrow enough for a paragraph | ● |  |  |  |  |  |

enough for a library is "Food Around the World." As you read down the graph, the dotted squares show how the topic can be narrowed. When you get to the bottom row, the topic narrow enough for a paragraph is "Packing a Picnic Basket." You would not need a whole library or even a shelf of books to write about that topic.

Having decided on a topic, you must organize or give structure to your paragraph. A paragraph of exposition is often a mini-composition, composed of a beginning, a middle, and an end. The paragraph focuses on *one* main idea and is developed through details and examples that support the main idea. This is the organizational or structural aspect of the paragraph.

The paragraph also has a certain "look," or visual appearance. It starts with an indented line, which signals that the writer is starting a new thought and also gives readers an "eye break" from a solid page of print. Newspapers and magazines often break a long paragraph into short paragraphs to make the page seem less crowded with type, and to help us read faster and easier.

Regardless of the length of a paragraph, the most important thing for you to remember is that each sentence should bear a logical relationship to the next one.

The following model illustrates how each sentence should help develop the main idea of a paragraph.

**Main Idea**
↓

*Civilized humans who live in cities are constantly receiving complicated signals and interpreting them correctly without the use of words.* A red light, a green light, or the gestures of a traffic officer—all these are the equivalents of imperative or permissive sentences. A bell which rings a certain number of times will announce to students a change of classes, to workers a shift in jobs, to persons on a party wire of a telephone the summons to a conversation with a friend. The bells on shipboard are highly conventionalized signals marking the passage of a day of maritime work. A trumpet call in the Tuileries garden of Paris warns visitors that they must part. The dirge of a funeral and the chimes of a wedding tell a whole story without words. A green line painted on the ceiling of the New York subway station at Forty-second Street conveys the message: "Follow me, all you who would shuttle over to the West Side trains." The red line, pointing contrariwise, guides the tense and hurrying throngs eastward.

—Margaret Schlauch

## EXERCISES

**A. Identifying guidelines to exposition** Reread the Margaret Schlauch passage. Tell why that paragraph is an example of the expository paragraph. Then list the details in the paragraph that support the main idea.

**B. Narrowing a topic** Each topic below is too broad for one paragraph. Choose one topic. Make a graph like the one on page 214. Show how you would narrow the topic from library size to paragraph size.

*High school basketball*
*Movie stars*
*Health food*
*Part-time jobs*

**C. Organizing a paragraph** Use your paragraph topic from Exercise B. List five details you would use to develop the main idea into an expository paragraph.

**D. Identifying expository paragraphs** Look through magazines and newspapers and clip out two expository paragraphs. Paste these clippings on a sheet of paper. Below each one, state the main idea and list the details that develop the main idea.

# 40

# Using a Topic Sentence

The main idea of an expository paragraph is often stated in one sentence, called the **topic sentence**.

The following model is an example of an effective expository paragraph that uses a topic sentence.

**Topic Sentence**

*The automatic dishwasher is in many ways an economical machine.* It saves time for whoever in the family has to clean up after meals—every year there is an average of 40,000 glasses, dishes, pots and pans to do. Dishwashers are water misers besides, using about 15 gallons per full load, less than the amount generally required by a hand-wash job. And the operating cost is low—the electricity used is less than you use in making waffles and bacon for the family breakfast. —Editors of Time-Life Books

The topic sentence may be written in the form of a question. The paragraph is then developed by specific details that answer the question.

**Topic Sentence**

*Why should you be interested in a station wagon that looks like a bus?* Well, first of all, because it has more cargo space and shorter overall length than wagons based on sedan chassis. The seating arrangement is more versatile. And the vehicle is more maneuverable in tight spots, due to its tight turning circle and boxy shape.
—Jan P. Norbye and Jim Dunne

A topic sentence is usually the first sentence of the paragraph (as in the models above), although it *can* occur elsewhere. Some writers merely imply the subject and main idea of a paragraph. Until you become a more experienced writer, however, it is a good idea to use a topic sentence.

217

# EXERCISES

**A.** Identifying the topic sentence   Read the following passages. Write down the topic sentence for each paragraph, and in your own words, state the main idea.

1.  Water has many ways. It is fog and mist and rain, it is snow and sleet and ice. It is the filmy veil of a waterfall and the polished mirror of a lake. It is the bubbling trill of a brook and the crystal lace of snowflakes. Water is our humble servant and precious treasure. Held in trust high on the mountain it runs down hill to give us light and heat and power. It fills our lakes and reservoirs and brings life to the thirsty land. Continually a mist rises to fall again as rain and never a drop is lost. Sustaining and cleansing all things water returns to its original purity.   —Arizona Highways

2.  Some people feel that we should use water of different qualities for different purposes. They have said that there should be three different qualities of water piped into homes. Grade A might be for drinking and cooking only. Grade B might be for washing dishes, clothes, and human bodies. And Grade C might be used for washing floors, windows, walls, the family car, and the dog. What do you think of this idea? How much would it change your way of life?—Edna A. Anderson

**B.** Writing an effective topic sentence   Write a topic sentence of your own for the following passage. Make sure that it states the main idea of the passage.

Below is a floor plan of the plane you are in. Familiarize yourself with the location of the exits. Note particularly the exits nearest you. Study how they are opened and also the protective position you should assume during an emergency landing. When leaving, move to the exits immediately. Do not go back for coats, purses, or other personal items.   —United Airlines

**C.** Identifying statements that reinforce the main idea   Write the numbers of the sentences that *best* explain the main idea expressed in the topic sentence (1) of the following passage.

(1) America has been going suburban. (2) The city moving out and the country moving in have met and mingled in this new melting

pot—the urban belt. (3) *According to a United States census, the suburban population increased approximately thirty per cent between 1930 and 1940, against little more than seven per cent for the country as a whole. (4) In the decade between 1920 and 1930, the suburbs grew five times faster than the rural districts and three times faster than the cities they encompassed. (5) Many people in this country live in metropolitan areas, with a disproportionate number in nineteen centers, such as Greater New York, Chicago-land, and Greater Los Angeles. (6) Small towns, the traditional citadels of American provincialism, have become enveloped in some metropolitan area or another, and have become citified. (7) Highway 67 is now the extension of Main Street, and the corner grocery has given place to the A&P.*  —Carl von Rhode

**D.** Choosing a topic sentence   The list below contains three topic sentences. From the list, write the topic sentence that *best* relates to the corresponding photograph.

- *Throughout her career, she has continued to help others.*
- *Julie wanted to be a lawyer.*
- *Julie is a fine doctor.*

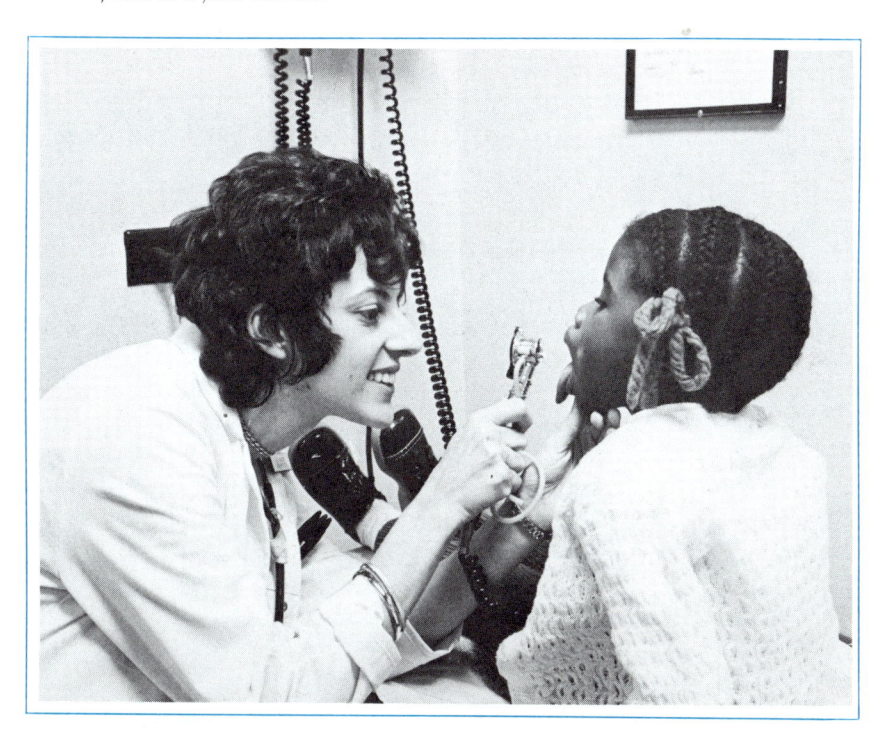

# 41

## Explaining a Process

A good expository paragraph has supporting details that describe or explain the main idea of the paragraph. To be effective, these details must be arranged in the logical order. The need for presenting details in order is clearly shown in paragraphs that explain a process.

A **process** is a set of actions or operations through which something is made or done. The procedure involved in cooking an omelet, the movements that enable a stork to fly, the chain of explosions that cause an engine to work—all these are types of processes.

Quite often you are forced to assemble certain things you have bought from a store. The instructions are usually illustrated in steps such as those shown in the illustration below.

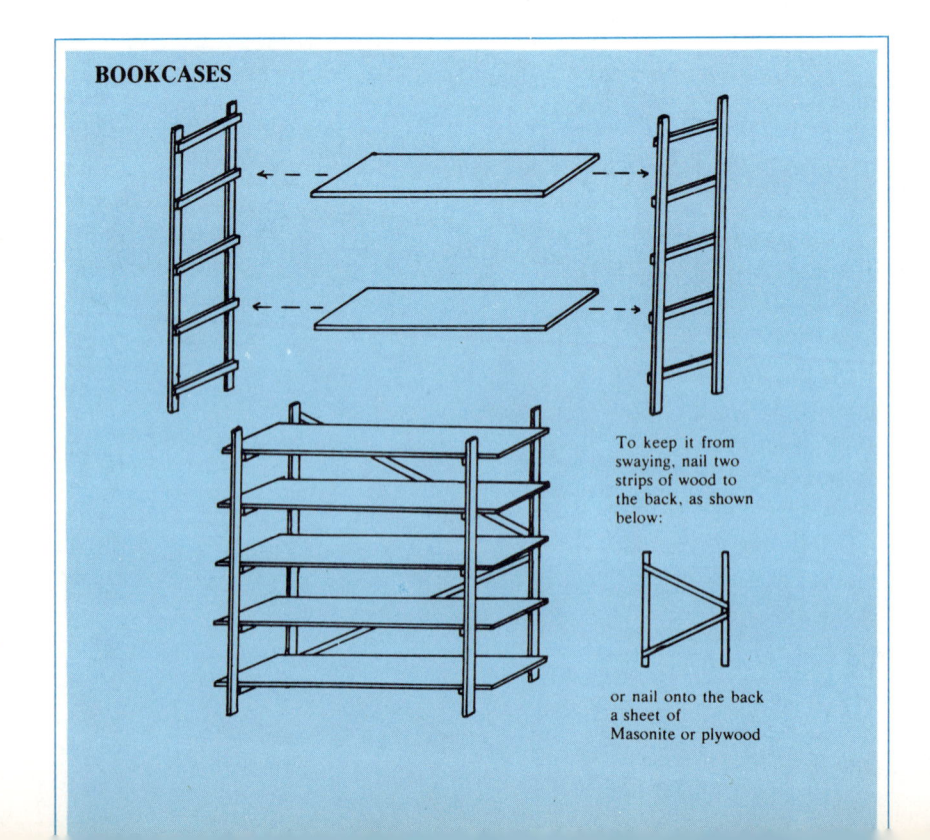

**BOOKCASES**

To keep it from swaying, nail two strips of wood to the back, as shown below:

or nail onto the back a sheet of Masonite or plywood

Explaining a process does not always need illustrations. Notice the way a process is explained in the following paragraph.

**Main idea is expressed in a topic sentence.**

**Step 1** → To get compact, bushy house plants with many flowers, pinch off the ends of new stems, using your thumbnail to sever the stem if needed. Pinch as close as you can to the top leaves without injuring the tiny buds below. The energy that the tip would have put into flowering now goes to the buds, producing new branches, all of which can bear flowers. Repeat the process on the new stems, if needed, to control the plant's shape.

**Details are in order.**

**Step 2** →

—James Underwood Crockett

## EXERCISES

**A. Writing a set of instructions** Write a clear, specific set of directions that would help a stranger in your town or area get from your school to your home.

**B. Identifying order** Look again at the illustration. Write each step of the pictured process in its proper sequence.

**C. Describing a process** Write a paragraph explaining how to do something with which you are familiar. Present each step in its proper order.

**D. Putting steps in order** Make a list of the steps necessary to do one of the things below. Then write a paragraph on the process you chose. Begin with a topic sentence and develop it with relevant details.

- How to hoist a sail
- How to roller-skate without falling
- How to change an automobile tire
- How to make a piecrust
- How to housebreak a dog or cat
- How to hold a fork and knife

# 42

# Developing a Paragraph Through Examples

Expository paragraphs are often developed by the use of examples. The writer may list a number of facts or incidents, or may present in detail a single fact or incident.

Suppose your main idea is that air pollution is dangerous to our health. How would you convince your reader that this idea is true? You would need to cite one or more facts about the effects of air pollution or to describe an incident or two in detail to prove that air pollution is indeed dangerous. In short, you would develop your idea through examples.

Notice how the Margaret Schlauch paragraph on page 215 is developed by examples. Here is another paragraph developed in the same way.

> When we listen to music, we can listen in a number of ways. We can listen passively, paying little or no conscious attention to the music. Much listening is done this way, because the presence of music is so universal and inescapable. On a higher level, we may listen for sheer aural pleasure. Our response, if we are listening in this way, is likely to be something like, "That's a pretty song." But there is at least one other way we may listen. We may actively participate in the listening experience. —Charles H. Ball

## EXERCISES

**A.** Supporting main ideas through examples  Read the following paragraphs. For each, write the main idea. Under the main idea, list the example or examples that best illustrate or support the main idea.

1. The signs of change are everywhere. Eastern Airlines distributes a newsletter, Businesswoman, to the 60,000 women executives who fly Eastern each year. Women now climb telephone poles as well as tend switchboards for AT&T, trade stocks on the floor of the New York

*Stock Exchange, assemble cars in Detroit and sit on the boards of the largest corporations—all highly visible symbols of the New Woman.**
—Newsweek

2. Most incoming messages travel through more than two cells before there is a response. For example, suppose someone asks you who your favorite football player is. Nerves from your ears carry that message to your brain. But then that message may travel through several thousand cells. Eventually a message will go out to muscles in your throat and lungs. Then you can give some kind of answer to the question. —George G. Mallinson

**B.** Developing a paragraph through example   Choose one of the following topic sentences and develop a paragraph from it through the use of examples.

- *Some toys are very dangerous for young children.*
- *I have never encountered such a traffic tie-up.*
- *Every student should learn to type.*
- *Dancing is an excellent form of exercise.*

**C.** Writing a paragraph by using examples   Collect facts, incidents, or ideas from a newspaper to illustrate a topic that interests you. Write a paragraph based on the material you collected.

*Copyright 1976 by Newsweek, Inc. All rights reserved. Reprinted by permission.

# 43

# Using Cause-and-Effect Relationships

The topic sentence may state an **effect** that has been produced. In this case, the paragraph would be developed by listing the causes or reasons that have produced this effect. The following passage by John Steinbeck gives his reasons for being interested in junk. The paragraph organization is that of *effect-to-cause*.

> If I seem to be over-interested in junk, it is because I am, and I have a lot of it, too—half a garage full of bits and broken pieces. I use these things for repairing other things. Recently I stopped my car in front of the display yard of a junk dealer near Sag Harbor. As I was looking courteously at the stock, it suddenly occurred to me that I had more than he had. But it can be seen that I do have a genuine and almost miserly interest in worthless objects. My excuse is that in this era of planned obsolescence, when a thing breaks down, I can usually find something in my collection to repair it—a toilet, or a motor, or a lawn mower. But I guess the truth is that I simply like junk.
>
> —John Steinbeck

In some paragraphs, a topic sentence may also state a **cause**. The paragraph is then developed by presenting the effects produced by the given cause. Notice how a *cause-to-effect* relationship is illustrated in the following passage.

> The desert is the battleground of the primeval elements of fire and water, and their effects on the land can everywhere be seen. The fires of the sun have baked the bare rocks and sands, sucked the moisture out of plants and left them shriveled. It has created dry washes, where streambeds fill with water only

*following a rain and then disappear abruptly. It has cast upon the land a pitiless heat, and at noonday the desert appears barren.* Cause 2 → *Water,* Effect 2 → *on the rare occasions when it comes, brings the desert suddenly to life. The plants grow quickly and burst into bloom; many kinds of animals produce young during the fleeting periods of abundant water. Fire and water occasionally battle to a draw, as can be seen on those summer days when black clouds roll across the desert, bringing promise of rain. But no rain reaches the desert surface; the heat of the sun evaporates it before it can moisten the dry sands.*

—Peter Farb

A paragraph may also use *both* effect-to-cause *and* cause-to-effect relationships. In the following paragraph, for example, a whole chain of causes and effects is given.

Here is one of the most familiar forms of the vicious circle of poverty. The poor get sick more than anyone else in the society. That is because they live in slums, jammed together under unhygienic conditions; they have inadequate diets, and cannot get decent medical care. When they become sick, they are sick longer than any other group in the society. Because they are sick more often and longer than anyone else, they lose wages and work, and find it difficult to hold a steady job. And because of this, they cannot pay for good housing, for a nutritious diet, for doctors. At any given point in the circle, particularly when there is a major illness, their prospect is to move to an even lower level and to begin the cycle, round and round, toward even more suffering.   —Michael Harrington

## EXERCISES

**A. Identifying cause and effect**   Read the following paragraph. In your own words, explain the *effect-to-cause* relationship in the passage. Then briefly explain the *cause-to-effect* relationship. Be sure to label each relationship.

The exaggerated view of baboon and macaque ferocity arose from the failure to realize just how much a monkey's behavior changes when the monkey is kept in captivity. A captive monkey is simply not a normal monkey. It does not even have to be kept in a cage for its behavior to become abnormal. Whenever monkeys are subjected to unnatural conditions—when they are fed, for example, by humans—they are liable to become unusually competitive and aggressive. It is not hard to see why. In the wild, every monkey forages for itself, and competition over food is rare. But if a whole troop of monkeys is obliged to feed out of the same bin, their competitiveness comes out. The closer their confinement, the more aggressive the monkeys will be. They are very much like humans, who become more irritable in a crowded place like Manhattan than in the wide-open spaces of Wyoming. Even the peaceful monkeys such as Indian langurs, are more nervous and irritable in confined areas around villages than they are in the roomy spaces of the forest.

—Sarel Eimerl and Irven DeVore

**B.** Identifying cause and effect   Look at the drawing below. After you have examined it closely, write a paragraph, using the cause-and-effect relationship illustrated in the drawing.

**C.** Writing an effect-to-cause paragraph   Choose one of the following effects. Decide what its causes are. Then write a paragraph that explains this effect-to-cause relationship.

- A student's failure in school
- The success of an athletic team
- Family squabbles
- The popularity of your favorite entertainer

# THE WHOLE COMPOSITION

## 44

## Developing a Good Composition

Although a composition may have only one paragraph, most of the writing you do will contain more than one paragraph.

A longer composition has much in common with an expository paragraph. Like a good paragraph, a composition must stick to the point. It must be arranged in a sensible order. And, like a paragraph, its sentences should flow into each other. In other words, an effective composition must have unity, structure, and coherence.

**Unity** No matter how many paragraphs a composition has, every paragraph—in fact, every sentence—must develop the main idea of the composition.

**Structure** The whole composition must have structure just as a paragraph has. The structure of a composition is basically a simple, three-part structure that consists of an introduction, a middle, and an end—each part performing a special function. In other words, an effective composition has an *introductory paragraph,* one or more *developmental paragraphs,* and a *concluding paragraph.*

**Coherence** A composition has coherence when its sentences and paragraphs flow into one another and the parts hold together. The following techniques can help you write a smoother composition.

- Use words that tell the reader the *order* of ideas and events:

    *first, second, third, finally, now, soon, before, after, as, then, eventually, presently, earlier*

- Use transitional words that *connect* one idea to another:

    *also, furthermore, in addition, subsequently, still, besides, moreover, further, again, thus, certainly, clearly, then, obviously, in fact, indeed, to be sure, undoubtedly*

- *Repeat key words:*

    Some etiquette books talk at length about <u>telephone</u> manners without getting down to fundamentals, like the fact that it's unwise to press the <u>telephone</u> to your rib cage while making a frank aside to someone in the room. Nearly always, this can be heard at the other end of the line.

    How <u>telephone</u> sounds carry is mysterious, anyway. For instance, if there's so much noise at your end of the line that you can't hear, cover the mouthpiece—not your unemployed ear—and you'll hear better.                    —Peg Bracken

- Use *pronouns* and *synonyms* for words you have used in preceding sentences and paragraphs:

    Last year my cousin Peter hiked through Oregon's Eagle Cap Wilderness Area. <u>He</u> had never been to the park before but <u>he</u> had no trouble making <u>his</u> way through the woods.      —Margaret Grund

- Use words that *compare* or *contrast:*

    *but, however, nevertheless, on the other hand, both, as a result, like, therefore, on the contrary, although, because, even so*

## EXERCISES

**A.** Identifying transitional words and phrases   Read the following passage. Then write the transitional words and phrases.

There was only one way known of avoiding a severe case of smallpox. Since ancient times, people in Asia and the Middle East had noticed that anyone who had smallpox and recovered never had it again. Therefore, they reasoned, if they could have a mild attack, it would protect them without harming them. So they took a little of the liquid from the sores on the skin of someone who had smallpox and put it into healthy people through a scratch. This gave the *healthy people smallpox. It was never possible to make sure it would just be a mild attack. But by choosing a time when the person receiving the smallpox was healthy, they tried to take as little risk as possible. Nevertheless, people sometimes died as a result.*—Navin Sullivan

**B. Building a composition**  The sentences below can be structured to form a three-paragraph composition. Using the techniques mentioned in this lesson, write the composition. You may add your own details.

   a. My father and I had an argument.
   b. I was furious.
   c. I decided I would live with my grandmother.
   d. My grandmother had a bigger house and more yard.
   e. Most of all, my grandmother seemed to me, at that moment, an infinitely nicer person to be with than my father.
   f. I sat down to write her a letter.
   g. Halfway through the letter, it dawned on me that my grandmother was probably too old to take care of me.
   h. I might even have to take care of her.
   i. I stopped writing.
   j. I sat there at my desk feeling very dejected.
   k. My father strolled into the room.
   l. We talked over our argument.
   m. We became friends again.
   n. Staying home seemed to be the best solution to the problem.

# 45

# The Introductory Paragraph

The first paragraph of a composition should
1. attract the attention and interest of the reader,
2. introduce the subject of the composition, and
3. include or imply a thesis statement that pinpoints the main idea of the composition.

The **thesis statement** of a composition should present a general view of the subject. Since each paragraph after the first one will have its *own* main point, the thesis statement should be general enough to include the main points of all the paragraphs that follow it.

The following models of introductory paragraphs are meant only as suggestions for helping you write effectively. Keep in mind that there are other ways to introduce a composition.

- Begin with a *question:*

    What do you think of as American music—folk songs? jazz? spirituals? rock? all those are American, of course, but none so truly American as Indian [Native American] music—the music of the first Americans. —Louis W. Ballard

- Begin with a *startling statement:*

    "Get out of that office, Fred, or it will surely kill you," a concerned family doctor told him. Frederick Kent Truslow was fifty-three.
    —*Audubon* Magazine

- Use *analogy;* explain something unfamiliar by *comparing* it to something familiar:

    The biologist George Wald once compared his work on an exceedingly specialized subject, the visual pigments of the eye, to "a very narrow window through which at a distance one can see only a crack

*of light. As one comes closer the view grows wider and wider, until finally through this same narrow window one is looking at the universe."*
—Rachel Carson

- Start with a *definition:*

    *In the United States, a city is, by law, a unit of government with a charter from the state in which it is located. The charter describes the city's boundaries and the powers of its government. A city may make changes in its charter, with the state's permission. A city may also expand its boundaries, growing larger by annexing, or taking over, neighboring areas. Different states have different requirements for becoming a city.*
    —Edna A. Anderson

- Relate an *incident:*

    *More than three million men waited. They waited on ships, tossing and turning in the storm-tossed harbors of England. They waited in tents, lashed by wind and rain and cold, and in thousands of staging area barracks. They were the men in the wings, awaiting the great drama of June 6, 1944: D-Day, the invasion of Europe.*
    —Gordon T. Morris, Jr.

## EXERCISES

**A. Writing an introductory paragraph**  Write an opening paragraph for one of the following topics or a topic of your own. Use one of the five techniques discussed in this lesson.

- *Television Programs That Should Be Censored*
- *Should Books Be Censored?*
- *Why Pass-Fail Grades Should Apply for All Courses*

**B. Classifying passages**  Classify the following passages according to these labels: *Definition, Startling statement, Question, Analogy.* Write the subject and the main idea about the subject.

1. What can you say about a 21-year-old lefthander who has control of a fastball that explodes in all directions? If you are Boog Powell, you can say: "He throws harder than Sandy Koufax did. He has an effortless motion, a smooth, compact delivery. He goes out for nine innings and doesn't seem to weaken."
—Roy Blount

2. You wouldn't think mere spelling was that important. Yet, American business firms are spending millions of dollars every year, just to remind the public to start certain words with a capital letter.
—Will Bernard

3. The Rocky Mountains are the greatest range of mountains in the United States today. They are part of a long chain stretching from the tip of South America all the way to the Arctic regions of Alaska. In the United States they extend from the Mexican to the Canadian border through the states of Arizona, New Mexico, Colorado, Utah, Nevada, Wyoming, Idaho, and Montana. Jagged and beautiful, they are a young mountain range geologically, but water, wind, and ice have sculptured them into bare peaks, ridges, and lovely deep canyons. They have slopes covered with majestic spruce and pine trees. They have broad, grassy valleys. The range is 3,000 miles long and up to 300 miles wide.
—Francis Smith

**C. Focusing on a topic**  Using the general topic of friendship, write an introductory paragraph for a composition. Be sure to narrow your topic to a specific aspect of friendship. Include a good thesis statement and let it serve as a guide to prevent you from wandering from your topic. (Save the paragraph; you will need it for an exercise in the next lesson.)

**D. Writing analogy**  Choose one item from Column A that can be likened to one from Column B. Then take that pair of words and write an introductory paragraph involving the analogy you have chosen.

| Column A | Column B |
|---|---|
| a. kite | 1. flower |
| b. freedom | 2. ribbon |
| c. girl | 3. storm |
| d. birth | 4. open door |
| e. highway | 5. spring |
| f. anger | 6. bird |
| g. human body | 7. camera |
| h. dreams | 8. cancer |
| i. pollution | 9. machine |
| j. eye | 10. kaleidoscope |

# 46

# Developmental Paragraphs

The function of the developmental, or middle, section of a composition is to develop the main idea, or thesis, set forth in your introduction. Since these paragraphs follow the introductory paragraph, you are saying to your reader: "I have *told* you what I want to say, and now I will *explain* what I mean by expanding on my subject."

You can see, therefore, how important your developmental paragraphs are. They must be relevant to the main idea of your composition and must flow smoothly and logically into each other so that your reader is able to follow your train of thought. Think of the middle paragraphs as the "meat" of your paper—each paragraph having continuity, and being organized around *one major point* of the composition's thesis.

Using an outline   When you are writing a composition that has several paragraphs, it is best to start with an outline. An outline will help you set up the structure of your composition.

The simplest outline is the topic outline. A **topic outline** is the arrangement of the main topics of the composition into their proper order. Look at the following topic outline.

> THESIS: There is a charm about medieval manuscripts.
> Main topics
> I. The individuality of hand-done manuscripts
> II. The personality of one particular manuscript

The sentence outline   A sentence outline is more detailed than a topic outline. Notice how the following sentence outline carefully maps out what the writer wants to say. Also notice how the thesis, "There is a charm about medieval manuscripts," is expanded into a thesis statement that gives more details about the main idea of the composition.

233

THESIS STATEMENT: There is a charm about a medieval manuscript that a printed book can never have.

**Main topics** → I. No two old manuscripts are alike.
**Major subtopics** → A. The lambskin pages have been cut by hand.
→ B. The lettering is done by hand.
II. One particular manuscript I remember possessed a dual personality.
    A. The first paragraph began bravely.
**Minor subtopics** → 1. The letters were perfectly shaded and spaced.
→ 2. The lines marched down the page with mathematical exactness.
    B. After three pages the letters seemed to have become tired and slumped together.
    C. Then came an obvious change.
        1. The lines again were orderly and perfect in detail.
        2. The penmanship was not quite the same.
        3. Some other person had written the rest.

The number of paragraphs you use in your middle section is less important than the way you present them. Remember to make use of transitional words and phrases to connect one point to another. Present your material by example, by analogy, by quotation, or by any other logical arrangement you think develops your topic effectively.

# A MEDIEVAL MANUSCRIPT

*There is a charm about a medieval manuscript that a printed book can never have.* Books that come by the thousands from power-presses have a sleek machine-made air.

Of old manuscripts, however, no two are alike. The lambskin pages have been cut by hand. Their beauty lies in their slight imperfectness. The hand-done lettering shows the writer's painstaking concentration. The initial letters—red, gold, blue, and black—are often exquisitely done. But the slip of the old writer's pen, which placed a wavering line where it should not have been and changed the design, suddenly shows us the humanness of that medieval writer.

One particular manuscript I remember possessed a dual personality. The first paragraph began bravely. The letters were perfectly shaded and spaced. The lines marched down the page with mathematical exactness. But after about three pages the letters seemed to have become tired. They lost their uprightness and slumped together, crowding and pushing in wobbly lines. Then came an obvious change. The lines again were orderly and perfect in detail, but the penmanship was not quite the same. The first writer had not been permitted to continue the manuscript. Some other person had written the rest. The following pages showed this same firm, sure lettering. In looking over this manuscript, anyone would feel the personalities of these two writers. One is firm, decided, and skilled. The other is eager and willing in spirit but weak in the actual doing.

I cannot read either this fourteenth century manuscript or any other of medieval times, but I do like to hold them in my hands. I like trying to understand a word here and there. I like to picture in my mind the lives of those curious and interesting persons who wrote so many hundreds of years ago.   —Susan Moody

# EXERCISES

**A. Analyzing a composition**  Reread "A Medieval Manuscript." Then answer the following.

1. How do you know that this composition is an example of expository writing?
2. Which paragraph is developed by examples?
3. Which paragraph relates an incident?
4. What techniques has the writer used to give the composition coherence? Give examples for each technique.
5. Name one of the cause-to-effect relationships in the third paragraph.

**B. Writing an outline**  Look back at the introductory paragraph on Friendship that you wrote in the previous lesson, Exercise C. Read it over now. Then write a sentence outline for a composition on Friendship.

**C. Writing developmental paragraphs**  Reread the introductory paragraph you wrote in the previous lesson, Exercise C. Add to it a good developmental paragraph. Use the outline you wrote for Exercise B of this lesson. (Save your work. You will use it in the next lesson.)

**D. Developing your paragraphs by details**  Read the following statements. Select one as your thesis statement or main idea. Then choose any of the other sentences that relate to the main idea. Use them as topics to develop a brief composition. You may use some or all of the sentences.

- *Fear makes us tense.*
- *Stress can affect our health.*
- *My mother worries about her job.*
- *My mother performs well under stress.*
- *My father often gardens to relax.*
- *Worry can interfere with our lives.*
- *Some forms of stress are good for us.*
- *Stress is caused by many things.*
- *An athlete or a performing artist usually is under great stress.*

# 47

# The Concluding Paragraph

The last paragraph of a composition should
1. Leave the reader with an impression of wholeness and of completion,
2. sound like the end, and
3. make the reader feel that the thesis sentence has now been coherently explained and logically supported.

Although there are no right rules about how to conclude a paper, here are some suggested types of conclusions for you to follow.

- *Restate your thesis,* using fresh, new wording to summarize your main idea:

    *Finally—and most important in light of current medical knowledge—the athlete should avoid tobacco in any form. Smoking works against all the things you are trying to do in a training program. It irritates the tissues of the heart muscle, thus making it difficult for them to work harder under stress conditions; it overstimulates the sympathetic nervous system, causing the heart to beat faster even when the extra blood supply is not needed; it robs the body's other muscles of their energy; it prevents the lungs from getting a full supply of oxygen; and it reduces the oxygen-carrying capacity of the bloodstream. Add to this the well-known fact that smoking can lead to lung cancer, and you have several good reasons why tobacco should have no place in the life of an athlete.* —Stanley L. Englebardt

- End with a *quotation:*

    *Or, as my mother used to say, "Don't jump to conclusions: You never know the why of what another person does."* —Debbie Pruce

- Use an *analogy:*

    *We were on top again. As always, again. We survived. The depths had been icy and dark, but now a bright sun spoke to our souls. I was* no longer simply a member of the proud graduating class of 1940: I was a proud member of the wonderful, beautiful Negro race.

—Maya Angelou

- Pose a *question:*

    So we need protein, but two basic questions still face us: how much and what kind? The answer to the question, "how much?," depends in part, on "what kind?."  —Francis Moore Lappé

- Use a *startling statement* or *emotional expression,* or a *plea for action:*

    And so, my fellow Americans; ask not what your country can do for you: ask what you can do for your country. My fellow citizens of the world: ask not what America will do for you, but what together we can do for the freedom of man.  —John F. Kennedy

## EXERCISES

**A.** Analyzing a concluding paragraph   Read the following paragraph and then answer the questions.

1. Does the paragraph *sound* like an ending? Why?
2. What do you think is the thesis of the whole composition, judging from the concluding paragraph?
3. Judging from this paragraph, what points do you think were developed in the middle paragraphs of the composition?
4. What are some of the techniques used to make this ending effective?

    All this is not to say there is no insect problem and no need of control. I am saying, rather, that control must be geared to realities, not to mythical situations, and that the methods employed must be such that they do not destroy us along with the insects.  —Rachel Carson

**B.** Recognizing good concluding paragraphs   Look through newspapers or magazines and find two articles that contain examples of effective concluding paragraphs. Discuss why the conclusions are effective.

**C.** Completing the composition   Using the introductory and developmental paragraphs you wrote on Friendship in Lesson 45 and Lesson 46, write a concluding paragraph for your composition. Be sure to follow the outline you made in Exercise A of the previous lesson.

# 48

# Choosing an Effective Title

Some writers may be able to choose a good title before they start to write. However, it is often better to select a title when you know for sure what you plan to say and how you plan to say it.

Ideally, your composition title should attract the reader's attention and give a hint about your subject.

If you are writing a humorous piece, your title will probably be lively or humorous. On the other hand, if you are explaining a process or imparting a piece of information, it is best to write a short, specific title that leaves no doubt in the reader's mind about the subject.

"What do I consider the most important thing in writing a book? The title!"

The best source of title ideas is your own imagination. "But," you might say, "it's not always easy to think of a good title." True. But not all good titles need be original. Quite often they are *found*. Sometimes a phrase from the composition itself will work. Sometimes the thesis can be implied (the thesis should be *stated* only in the introductory paragraph).

Many writers use *Bartlett's Familiar Quotations*, the Bible, or lines from famous poems and songs as sources for titles.

No matter where your title comes from, however, it should be a distinct and important part of the composition.

## EXERCISES

**A. Understanding the role of titles** Read the following list of titles. Then answer the questions that follow.

"Clocks"
"America and Americans"
"Standing Firmly on a Cloud"
"Gods, Graves, and Scholars"
"Let My People Go"
"Journey Toward Freedom"
"The Jet That Crashed Before Takeoff"
"My War with the Twentieth Century"
"Really the Blues"

1. Which titles are too wide for a composition?
2. Which titles hint at a humorous composition?
3. Which titles state the subject of the composition?
4. Which title do you find most interesting? Why?

**B. Writing titles** Study the list of general topics below. Then write two effective titles for *each* idea. Make sure your title is narrow enough for a short composition. For example, you might narrow a topic such as cars to fit a composition that will tell how you feel about pollution caused by cars: "Traveling Pollution Makers."

1. Pets
2. Music
3. Seasons
4. Television
5. Parents

**C. Completing the composition** Now for the composition you completed in the previous lesson, Exercise C, what title are you going to give it?

# DEVELOPING YOUR WRITING

## 49

## Starting a Journal

An excellent way to develop your writing ability is to keep a **journal**. Many writers keep a daily journal, or record of day-to-day incidents. Each day they jot down *something*—a story idea, a colorful phrase, an observation, an opinion, an impression.

A journal of this kind is more than a private diary. It is rather like a testing ground on which to try out your ideas and plans. It's a special place in which to *save* sights, insights, sounds, tastes, facts, feelings, reactions, impressions—any experience at all.

A well-kept journal notebook provides handy material to draw upon—entries that you can expand into longer pieces of writing. If you jot down entries in your notebook every day, you'll get valuable practice in the technique of writing.

An inexpensive bound notebook and a pencil are the only equipment you need, and since no one but you will read your private jottings, you can feel free to write whatever you want.

The diary entries that follow were written by a young girl, Sallie Hester, in the 1800s. She and her family left Indiana to hit the teeming California Trail, seeking a new life in the West.

> *June 3. Our tent is now pitched on the beautiful Platte River, 315 miles from St. Joe. The cholera is raging. A great many deaths. Graves everywhere. We are all in good health. Game is scarce; a few antelope in sight. Roads bad.*
>
> *Fort Laramie, Wyoming. June 19. This fort is of adobe, enclosed with a high wall. The entrance is a hole in the wall just large enough for a person to crawl through. The impression you have on entering is that you are in a small town. Men are engaged in all kinds of business from blacksmith up. We camped a mile from the fort, where we remained a few days to wash and lighten up.*

September 8. Traveled fourteen miles. Crossed Truckee twelve times.

September 11. Made eighteen miles. Crossed Truckee River ten times. Came near being drowned at one of the crossings. Got frightened and jumped out of the carriage into the water. The current was very swift and carried me some distance down the stream. In jumping I expected to reach the shore; instead I landed in the water, but was rescued in time all right.

Yuba Valley [California]. We are now 108 miles from Sutter's Fort [where gold had been discovered the year before].

Monday, September 17. Lay by two days. Had preaching under the pines at night.

September 21. Reached Bear Valley by descending a tremendous hill. We let the wagons down with ropes. Left one of our wagons and the springs of our carriage. Cut down trees for our cattle to browse on.

—Sallie Hester

# EXERCISES

**A. Keeping a journal**  Keep a journal for at least one week. Record your experiences, feelings, and observations. Your entries need not be lengthy, but make sure you write something each day.

**B. Writing spontaneously**  For five minutes, jot down anything that comes into your head about the picture below. It is not necessary to worry about using complete sentences. This type of writing is only meant for recording thoughts and feelings.

**C. Writing from notes**  Reread what you wrote for Exercise B. Then use those notes to write a paragraph that communicates your ideas or feelings. Use complete sentences, paying attention to correct punctuation and grammar.

**D. Finding ideas**  Make a list of five ideas from your journal and develop one of them into a composition.

## 50

# Telling What Happened

In writing exposition you *explained* your ideas and information to your readers. Another way to communicate through writing is to put your ideas into story form. This kind of writing is called **narration**.

Narration is an account of something that has occurred. It could be something that happened to you. Or it might have happened to someone else, who told you about it. Or it might be something you read about in a newspaper, magazine, or book. Write down in your notebook exactly what happened.

Narration, like exposition, must have structure. Narrative structure is usually the **chronological order** of events—what happened, what happened next, and what happened after that. From beginning, to middle, to end, your reader should be carried along by your story, with each sentence moving the narrative to its conclusion.

The following is a student's account of a personal experience, written from notes made in a journal.

> When the coach sent in orders to go for the long one, I got pretty confused. We were third down with three to go on the 40-yard line. The score was 8 to 6 with three minutes left to the game. Ordinarily we would have ground out the necessary yards, but I guess the coach was more concerned than usual. But I was more worried than he. I had to catch the ball.
>
> Suddenly the huddle broke. We came out, and the count ran down. Over one and straight on through—down field—close shave with three tackles—and a fast defense at my heels. The ball came. The old cliché about "the bomb" had fresh meaning, for either I or my pursuer would be demolished.
>
> It was a long arching throw, a perfect spiral. It seemed to be headed well beyond me. On we sprinted with me just managing to stay ahead but not quite fast enough to meet the predetermined target of the ball. And suddenly the ball landed. With more effort than I

thought was in me, I was there with the ball. But somehow my hands weren't, and the ball went on through.

The crowd roared its disapproval, and I was mad. Why was such a call made in the first place? Third down and three to go. The coach panics. And I take the beating. Oh well, that's just the way it goes sometimes. —Marty Nystrand

The person who wrote the account you just read was an active participant in the event described. However, some narrations are the views and reactions a person has about people and situations observed. Notice how the following narrative is developed.

Ben Duggar is my favorite failure. He proved to me that getting fired or retired can be man's noblest moment. "Doctor Duggar," botany professor, was 70 in 1943 when the University of Wisconsin told him he was through.

Duggar said he couldn't be through. He was 70, but a young 70. He bowled every week. He took long walks, played golf.

The faculty listened. They heaped praise on him. However, the university had a rule: mandatory retirement at 70.

A few of Duggar's graduates were working at Lederle Laboratories, the pharmaceutical house. They read about the old prof's retirement and spoke to the top boss at Lederle. Yes, he said, he could use an old professor. Duggar got a nice letter and traveled to Pearl River, N.Y., for talks. He was hired as a consultant and to do independent research.

In the labs, there were thousands of small drawers in rows, each labeled as a sample of earth from a particular place in the world. The samples would have to be cross-matched in tiny doses and placed in clinical flasks.

They would be nurtured into a growing mold. After numberless tests, Ben Duggar might find a cure for something—or for nothing. With 6000 drawers, there would be a minimum of 36 million cross-matchings.

Ben didn't have that much time. He started work. Nothing happened the first year, but one day when he was 73 he looked into one of the flasks and saw a golden mold. It almost spoke to him. It said, "I'm something." Hands shaking, Duggar isolated an antibiotic. He gave it a name—aureomycin. The old prof lived to see it control more than 50 grave maladies.

"But wait!" Ben said. "From this I can get another antibiotic." He did—tetracycline—the most widely prescribed broad-spectrum antibiotic in the world. It controls, among other things, streptococcus, pneumonia, staphylococcus, and typhus.

Ben Duggar died at 84. He may well have helped more people to live than any physician in the world. He's my favorite failure.

—Jim Bishop

## EXERCISES

**A. Writing from personal experience** Think about an interesting experience that you have had or have observed. Then make a list of details that answers these questions:

1. When and where did the event occur?
2. Who were the people involved?
3. What happened?

After you have completed your list, write a *brief* narrative, using your list as a guide. The structure of your story should be based on the order of events.

**B. Writing a story** Write a short narrative that follows the plan below. Your story can be based on a personal experience or on another's experiences.

### TITLE

I. Introduction

SETTING
- Describe the *place*.
- Tell what was happening at that *time*.

CHARACTERS
- Tell who was involved.

II. Development
- Relate the incidents in chronological order.
- Develop suspense and/or emotion through vivid details.

III. Conclusion
- Tell the effects or outcome of the incident.
- Tell the point of the story or your feelings about the outcome.

**C.** Writing about a factual incident  Read the passage below. Then write the story as you would tell it to a friend. Your composition need not be lengthy.

### FAMOUS TEARS

*Graham Washington Jackson was waiting for a funeral cortege to pass on April 12, 1945, when a photographer took his picture. The photo became world famous.*

*It showed Mr. Jackson, then a chief petty officer in the Navy, playing an accordion and crying bitterly as the body of President Franklin D. Roosevelt was borne from the Little White House in Warm Springs, Ga. The photo came to symbolize the nation's grief at the time.*

*Mr. Jackson, who was one of President Roosevelt's favorite musicians and played often for him, treasures that picture today.*

—New York Times

# 51
# Writing About Your Private World

Young writers are often told, "Write from your own experience." Many of your experiences take place in your *inner* world. These experiences include your private thoughts, your emotions, and your dreams.

Your inner world involves not only yourself, but others as well. A chance meeting with a particular person, a problem at home, or a success in school might trigger a whole chain of thoughts and feelings.

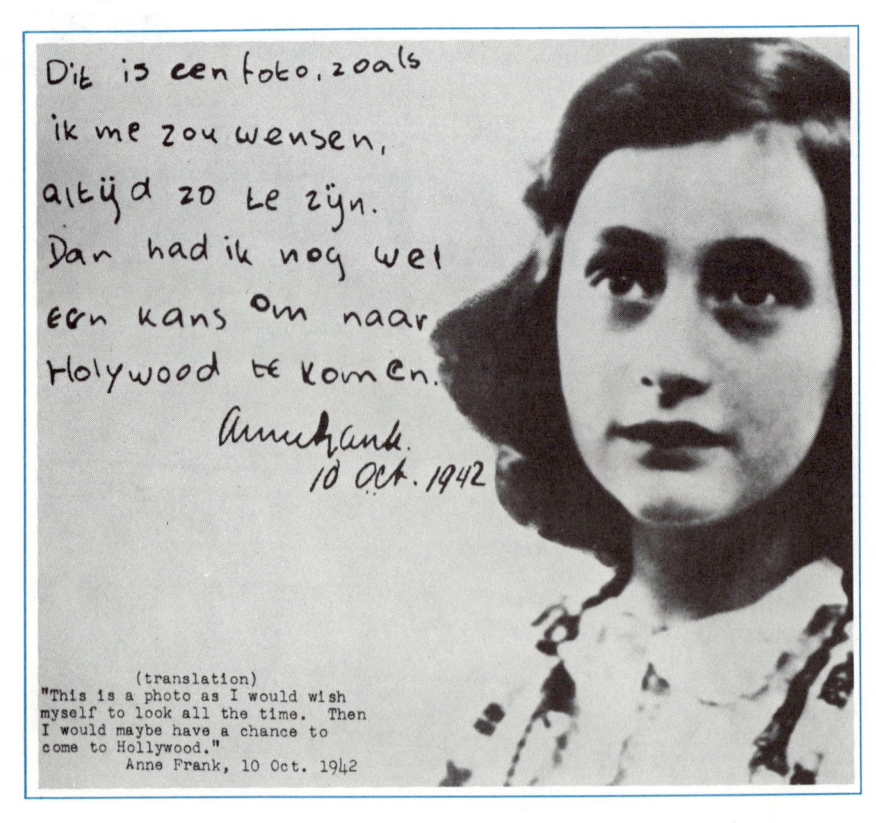

Dit is een foto, zoals ik me zou wensen, altijd zo te zijn. Dan had ik nog wel een kans om naar Holywood te komen.

Anne Frank.
10 Oct. 1942

(translation)
"This is a photo as I would wish myself to look all the time. Then I would maybe have a chance to come to Hollywood."
Anne Frank, 10 Oct. 1942

During the Second World War, Anne Frank, a teen-age Jewish girl hiding from the Nazis, wrote down her fears and her hopes about the future of the world. The following is from an entry in her diary, published after her death.

> It's really a wonder that I haven't dropped all my ideals, because they seem too absurd and impossible to carry out. Yet I keep them, because in spite of everything I still believe that people are really good at heart. I simply can't build up my hopes on a foundation consisting of confusion, misery, and death. I see the world gradually being turned into a wilderness, I hear the ever-approaching thunder, which will destroy us too. I can feel the sufferings of millions and yet, if I look up into the heavens, I think that it will all come right, that this cruelty too will end, and that peace and tranquility will return again. —Anne Frank

## EXERCISES

**A.** Writing about your predream world   Many writers say that their imaginations are most active just before they fall asleep. Write a composition about *your* predream world. You may use the following three questions as guides.

- *What is it like to be very tired?*
- *What are some of the things that suddenly pop into your mind when you can't go to sleep?*
- *How is your predream world sometimes different from reality?*

**B.** Writing about your private world   Write a composition about your experiences in the private world of thought, feeling, imagination, or dreams.

**C.** Using your imagination   Use your imagination to answer one of the following questions in an essay of about 200 words.

1. If you are sometimes fed up with the planet Earth, what kind of planet would you want instead?
2. How would you react as a flight crew member if your plane were hijacked?
3. What might your life be like when you reach age thirty?

# 52

# Audience and Purpose

In writing for an audience, two elements must be considered: (1) your reader, and (2) your purpose in writing. In other words, why do you want this particular audience to listen to your "written voice"?

Specific purposes may vary, but there is one general purpose: to produce an effect on the reader. The specific purpose will depend on the particular effect you want to achieve—to entertain, to arouse a certain feeling, to persuade, to explain something, or to define something that may be unfamiliar.

In order to produce the desired effect and to reach your reader, you must first ask yourself these questions: Who is my audience? Am I writing to a general audience or to a special group? Do the educational and cultural backgrounds of my readers vary? Do they share a common interest? Am I writing for a certain age group? Do I know my readers personally, or are they strangers? Are they likely to be a receptive, or a hostile, audience?

As you read the following passages, notice how the levels of vocabulary and sentence structure vary for the different audiences and purposes of the passages.

> As a retired person you've got something going for you that you may not have realized.
> Many an organization looking for interesting speakers is finding out that the retired person has the asset of experience in work, at hobbies, in human relations and in living. —Ken and Pat Kraft

> There are three general routes that pathogens can take to enter your body. The first route that we will discuss is the aerial route. Pathogens enter the body along with the air that you breathe. The actual pathway is through the respiratory passages: the nose and mouth, throat, trachea, bronchial tubes, and lungs. As you might

*imagine, many of the pathogens that use this route also cause disease in the respiratory passages. However, there are some that gain entrance through the respiratory system, but proceed into the bloodstream and cause their damage in different organs and systems.*
—William L. Smallwood and Edna R. Green

A man named Stephen Austin was the first American to settle in Texas. When Austin went to Texas in 1821, it was still a part of the Spanish Empire. The Spanish government was glad to give him land. Spain never had enough colonists to protect her empire and wanted to get more. By 1835 more than 30 thousand Americans were living in Texas. But by that time, the Spanish Empire had been broken by revolutions, and Texas was part of the new Republic of Mexico.
—Jay Glanzrock

# Are we killing our roads with silence?

Everybody gripes about the terrible shape of many of our roads. But instead of griping to our families and friends, let's tell it to the people in a position to really do something about it.

There's plenty to gripe about. Our roads are deteriorating 50% faster than we are maintaining them. From age, constant heavy use, and lack of funds for an adequate maintenance program. Even though we're putting more traffic and heavier vehicles on our roads each year, we're spending less of the GNP to maintain them than we did in the 30's!

Your taxes helped pay for a magnificent $425 billion dollar road system that speeds your way to work, to school, to stores, and assures effective fire and police protection. So speak up. Now. To the people in your community, state, and national government who can help preserve this bargain in effective transportation. Let's not kill our roads with silence. When it's so easy to put in a good word for them.

## ROAD PRESERVATION...A TRANSPORTATION BARGAIN.

As a motorist, shouldn't you take a stand on this vital issue now? Remember...when the roads go, we won't! For a free information booklet on the problem, write to: The Asphalt Institute, College Park, Maryland 20740.

## EXERCISES

**A. Identifying audience and purpose**  Choose one passage from this lesson. Describe the audience for whom it was written and state the writer's purpose.

**B. Writing for an audience**  Using the information on the chart below, complete two of these assignments:

1. Write a newspaper article informing the readers of the facts in the chart.
2. Write a paragraph or two aimed at cigarette smokers. State your views about cigarette smoking.
3. Assume that your audience is composed of fifth-grade students. Write a paragraph or two describing the relationship between smoking and health. Your purpose is to persuade.
4. Write a letter to a cigarette manufacturer, urging the company to introduce a harmless tobacco substitute.

- One out of every seven deaths this year will be linked to cigarette smoking.
- Up to ten times more cigarette smokers die of lung cancer than do nonsmokers.
- About 3,200 children and teenagers start smoking every day. If this continues, about one million children now in school will die of lung cancer by age seventy.
- *Every* smoker is injured. Smoking kills some, makes others very ill, and gives all smokers far more than their share of minor illness and loss of workdays.

# 53

# Point of View

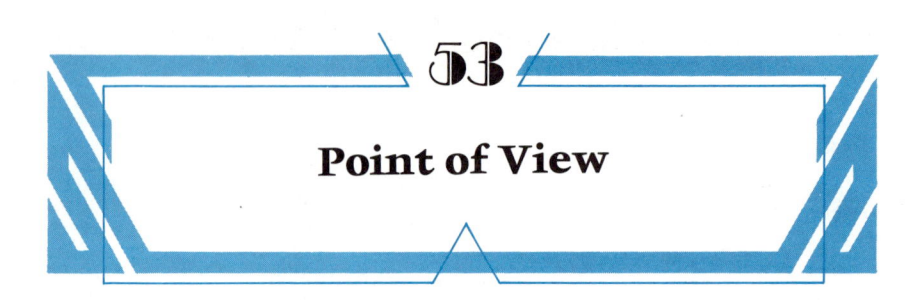

Writers often use different methods of narration to express their ideas or tell their stories. Sometimes they use their own voice to narrate, or tell, the story.

The writer is then using the **first-person point of view**. The pronoun used is "I." This method is useful when the writer

- wants her or his own voice to be heard, or
- wants the reader to feel acquainted with the author, or
- wants to write subjectively in order to express the writer's emotions or impressions, or
- is speaking for a group. (The pronoun used is "we.")

In the following passage a student uses the first-person point of view to tell about a way to relax.

> *When my life gets too hectic and I need a vacation from my everyday problems, I visit my old friend—Nature. Just relaxing under a tree, watching the birds and insects go about their business, helps me regain a proper perspective on my life.* —Katherine Mary Wright

An author may decide to use the **third-person point of view**, sometimes referred to as **third-person omniscient**. The word *omniscient* means "having complete knowledge." As its name implies, this point of view permits the narrator to *know all and tell all* about the events and characters in the story. Notice how the third-person point of view is presented in the following passage.

> *There was a woman who was beautiful, who started with all the advantages, yet she had no luck. She married for love, and love turned to dust. She had bonny children, yet she felt they had been thrust upon her, and she could not love them. They looked at her coldly, as if they were finding fault with her. And hurriedly she felt she must cover up some fault in herself. Yet what it was that she*

*must cover up she never knew. Nevertheless, when her children were present, she always felt the center of her heart go hard. This troubled her, and in her manner she was all the more gentle and anxious for her children, as if she loved them very much. Only she herself knew that at the center of her heart was a hard little place that could not feel love, no, not for anybody. Everybody else said of her: "She is such a good mother. She adores her children." Only she herself, and her children themselves, knew it was not so. They read it in each other's eyes.*
—D. H. Lawrence

Whatever the point of view you decide to use in your writing, make sure that you are *consistent* within each piece of writing. In other words, whatever point of view you start with, you should stay with.

## EXERCISES

**A. Using a fictitious narrator** Select a newspaper article about a recent event involving several people. Imagine that you are one of the people involved in that event. Write a brief account of the event, using "I" as the narrator.

**B. Writing in the first-person** Write a brief account of a personal experience that has made an impact on your life.

**C. Using the third-person point of view** Examine the photograph below. Concentrate on one person in the picture and tell about his or her feelings, thoughts, and role in the scene. Write in the third person.

# 54

# Tone in Writing

No matter which point of view you choose, first person or third, your writing will convey a definite tone to the reader. **Tone** is a reflection of the writer's attitude toward the subject matter and toward the reader.

The first step in communicating tone is to decide how *you feel* about your topic. The second step is to select those words and details that best express your feelings and opinions. For example, if your aim is to convey a feeling of panic, you might write a sentence like this: "He ran blindly and breathlessly, like a hunted animal, into the dark alley, aware that his legs could carry him no farther."

Tone can usually be described by an adjective: "The tone of that story is *sad* (or *witty* or *eloquent*)." Here are some more adjectives commonly used to describe tone.

| | | | |
|---|---|---|---|
| *amiable* | *jubilant* | *hopeful* | *affirmative* |
| *angry* | *lonely* | *satirical* | *apprehensive* |
| *alienated* | *critical* | *ironic* | *condescending* |
| *formal* | *nostalgic* | *happy* | *impersonal* |
| *hilarious* | *personal* | *pompous* | *confidential* |
| *objective* | *negative* | *serious* | *reminiscent* |
| *humorous* | *romantic* | *chatty* | *matter-of-fact* |

## EXERCISES

**A. Identifying words and details that express tone**  Some words express tone very clearly. Read the following passages. For each passage, write an adjective that describes the tone of the passage. Next to your answers, write those words or phrases from the passage that help express the tone.

1.   *The town itself is dreary; not much is there except the cotton mill, the two-room houses where the workers live, a few peach trees, a*

church with two colored windows, and a miserable main street only a hundred yards long. On Saturdays the tenants from the near-by farms come in for a day of talk and trade. Otherwise the town is lonesome, sad, and like a place that is far off and estranged from all other places in the world. —Carson McCullers

2. For many years Red Farm, by King Philip's Pond, the home of Mr. J. E. Chamberlin and his family, was my home. I remember with deepest gratitude the kindness of these dear friends and the happy days I spent with them. The sweet companionship of their children meant much to me. I joined in all their sports and rambles through the woods and frolics in the water. The prattle of the little ones and their pleasure in the stories I told them of elf and gnome, of hero and wily bear, are pleasant things to remember. —Helen Keller

**B.** Conveying tone  Write a short narrative that conveys the tone of the following picture. Circle the words and phrases in your narrative that create this tone.

# 55

# Using Figurative Language

Writers often use figurative language to make analogies and to lend force and originality to their writing. A **figure of speech** is a departure from the normal use of words; its purpose is to describe something vividly. Simile, metaphor, and personification are common figures of speech. The first two, **simile** and **metaphor**, are comparisons of two unlike things. Only the simile uses *like* or *as* to make a comparison; the metaphor simply states that one thing is or has the qualities of another thing. Notice how effective they can be in some cases.

SIMILES:
- He is *as* graceful as a cougar.
- Her smile is *like* the rising sun.
- Reading that book is *like* wading in mud.

METAPHORS:
- That test is the one cloud in my sky.
- The baby has a rosebud mouth.
- Our players were lions in that game.
- Terry's eyes were riveted to the television set.
- Dr. Rosen was always our security blanket when anyone in the family became ill.
- Have you hired Ms. Herkshaw as a private eye?
- Margaret shot from the room when she heard the news.

**Personification** is a figure of speech in which an object, a quality, or an idea is represented as a person.
- Death stood waiting for us at every curve.
- Night spread its blanket of darkness over the city.
- Anger wrapped tight fingers around his throat and made him speechless.
- Fear grabbed me, turned me around, and made me run for my life.

Notice how the simile in the first sentence of the passage below is expanded into personification in the rest of the passage.

> *A painting, like a person, has a life span; pigments fade, varnish cracks, and canvas rots. A particularly vulnerable part of most paintings is the linen-canvas base. Flax dries and crumbles, and without fresh support the paint it holds will flake off. Louvre technicians were among the first to perfect the incredible operation of tranferring old masters to new canvas.*
>
> *I watched with excitement as men in spotless white wheeled a patient into the bright light of the operating room. They had covered the painting with special paper, held on with wheat-flour paste so that not the tiniest sliver of surface paint could move. They laid the ailing picture face down on the operating table. Painstakingly wielding scalpels and tweezers, they flayed the canvas thread by thread—unwove it, so to speak—from the back.*
>
> *Then they applied new fabric and fastened it with an adhesive. Turning the patient over, they gently dissolved the paper from the surface with a mixture of liquids, and voilà—the old master had a new lease on life.* —Hereward Lester Cooke, Jr.

## EXERCISES

**A. Identifying similes and metaphors**  Write the number of each expression below and tell whether it is a simile or a metaphor.

1. The cemetery was a dark shelf about the town.
2. The chimney branched like coral in the upper blue.
3. Life was a holiday for Blake and me.
4. Dorothy was as agile as a jungle cat.
5. Misery is cold French fries.

**B. Identifying figures of speech**  Read the selection below. Copy each underscored word or phrase and identify it as *simile*, *metaphor*, or *personification*.

> Behold <u>the gem strung towns and cities</u> of the good, green East, <u>flung like stardust</u> through <u>the field of night</u>. That <u>spreading constellation</u> to the north is called Chicago, and <u>the giant wink that blazes in the moon</u> is the pendant lake that it is built upon. Beyond, <u>close-set and dense as a clenched fist</u>, are all <u>the jeweled cities</u> of the

eastern seaboard. There's Boston, ringed with <u>the bracelet of its shining little towns</u>, and all the lights that sparkle on the rocky indentations of New England. Here, southward and a little to the west, and yet still coasted to the sea, is our intensest ray, <u>the splintered firmament</u> of the towered island of Manhattan. Round about <u>her, sown thick as grain</u>, is the glitter of a hundred towns and cities.

—Thomas Wolfe

**C. Writing figures of speech** Study the following photographs carefully. Choose three of the photographs and write a figure of speech for each one.

# 56

# Other Writers' Styles

One way for you to develop your writing ability is to study the styles of great authors. By observing how they use tone, point of view, rhythm, and sentence structure, you will improve your own use of language.

*What* you say (content) is important, or course. But *how* you say it (style) determines the effect your writing will have on your reader. Whether your story or article will strike your reader as being dull or exciting or beautiful depends on your style.

Style can be learned. Ralph Ellison, the author of *The Invisible Man,* said: "At night I practiced writing and studied Joyce, Dostoevski, Stein, and Hemingway. Especially Hemingway; I read him to learn his sentence structure and how to organize a story." By observing how the "greats" combined those elements that resulted in their distinctive writing styles, you too can develop a special style of your own.

The following passage is by a nineteenth-century author whose style is still admired today. Notice the effect he achieves by the repetition of the words *emphasis* and *square,* and by the use of similes and metaphors.

> The scene was a plain, bare, monotonous vault of a schoolroom, and the speaker's square forefinger emphasized his observations by underscoring every sentence with a line on the schoolmaster's sleeve. The emphasis was helped by the speaker's mouth, which was wide, thin, and hard set. The emphasis was helped by the speaker's voice, which was inflexible, dry, and dictatorial. The emphasis was helped by the speaker's hair, which bristled on the skirts of his bald head, a plantation of firs to keep the wind from its shining surface, all covered with knobs, like the crust of a plum pie, as if the head had scarcely warehouse room for the hard facts stored inside. The

*speaker's obstinate carriage, square coat, square legs, square shoulders—nay, his very neckcloth, trained to take him by the throat with an unaccommodating grasp, like a stubborn fact, as it was—all helped the emphasis.* —Charles Dickens

Here is an imitation of the Dickens passage, written by a student. Notice the effect she achieves by the use of figures of speech and the rhythm she creates by repetition of sentence patterns.

*The station was a squalid, dingy, deserted outpost of the subway, and the waiting girl's tight posture betrayed her fear by stiffening every time the noise of a distant tram was heard. The fear was apparent in the girl's hands, which were clenched, bloodless, and trembling. The fear was apparent in the girl's mouth, which was strained, thin, and unmoving. The fear was apparent in the girl's eyes, which darted from the otherwise frozen face, two searchlights to detect trouble before it got too near, surrounded with pale skin, like the pallor of a sick man, as if the eyes hardly had courage to move within the stillness of the surrounding face.* —Deirdre Hovne

## EXERCISES

**A. Imitating a style**   Choosing your own subject and words, write a sentence that imitates the flowing, poetic style of the following sentence.

*Hear the nocturnal sounds and voices of the sleeping, holy Jerusalem, weaving in whispers through the rolling land.*   —Kristen Lems

**B. Examining a style**   Study James Baldwin's style in the passage below. Then try out some of Baldwin's techniques by writing a paragraph about your interests.

*About my interests: I don't know if I have any, unless the mortal desire to own a sixteen-millimeter camera and make experimental movies can be so classified. Otherwise, I love to eat and drink—it's my melancholy conviction that I've scarcely ever had enough to eat (this is because it's impossible to eat enough if you're worried about the next meal)—and I love to laugh. I do not like bohemia, or bohemians, I do not like people who are earnest about anything. I don't like people who like me because I'm a Negro; neither do I like people who find in the same accident grounds for contempt. I love America more than any other country in the world, and, exactly for this reason, I insist on the right to criticize her perpetually. I think all theories are suspect, that the finest principles may have to be modified, or may even be pulverized by the demands of life, and that one must find, therefore, one's own moral center and move through the world hoping that this center will guide one aright. I consider that I have many responsibilities, but none greater than this: to last, as Hemingway says, and get my work done.*

*I want to be an honest man and a good writer.*    —James Baldwin

**C. Completing a passage**   Read the following passage. Write another paragraph as a continuation of the story, keeping the subject matter and style the same as the original.

<u>*I wonder if they're as scared of me as I am of them*</u>*. She smiled brightly.*

*"Good morning, children. I am Miss Richards." As if they don't know—the door of the third-grade room had a new sign pasted above it with her name in bold black capitals: and anyway, a new teacher's name is the first thing that children find out about on the first day of school. Nevertheless, she wrote it for their benefit in large white letters on the blackboard.*

*"I hope we will all be happy working and playing together this year."* <u>*Now why does that sound so trite?*</u>   —Mary Elizabeth Vroman

**D. Analyzing elements of a style**   Read the following passage. Then answer each of the following questions in a complete sentence.

1. What is the tone of the passage?
2. What is the point of view?
3. What is the purpose?
4. What specific words or phrases make the style special?

*All at once the whole open sky could be seen—she had come to the river. A quiet fire burned on the bluff and moving as far outward as she could see was the cold blur of water. A great spiraled net lay on its side and its circles twinkled faintly on the sky. Veil behind veil of long drying nets hung on all sides, dropping softly and blue-colored in the low wind and the place was folded in by them. All things, river, sky, fire, and air, seemed the same color, the color that is seen behind the closed eyelids, the color of day when vision and despair are the same thing.*   —Eudora Welty

# 57

# Writing Dialogue

An excellent way to liven up your narrative is to include dialogue. A **dialogue** is a written conversation between two or more characters in a story.

When it is well-written, dialogue makes characters come alive and helps carry the story along. Writing interesting, natural-sounding dialogue is one of the best ways to keep your readers reading.

The important things to remember when writing dialogue are these:

1. Dialogue should move along at a lively pace. This can be accomplished by writing *short* exchanges between characters.
2. Dialogue should sound like real conversation. When writing dialogue you may use contractions, one-word sentences, or short phrases—whatever imitates natural conversation.
3. A character's speech should always be in keeping with his or her immediate emotions, personality, or role in the story. A person who is frightened should *sound* frightened. A stuffy person should sound stuffy; a witty person should joke.
4. A character should have a reason for speaking. All speech should either further the story or tell something about the characters.
5. Dialogue form calls for a new paragraph each time a different person speaks. For more guidelines on dialogue form, turn to "Punctuating Direct Quotations" on pages 00–00 of this book.
6. Dialogue structure, like the structure of straight narrative, is usually the chronological order of events.

The following dialogue is the ending of Saki's story "The Interlopers." The characters, Georg and Ulrich, have been pinned under a fallen tree in a forest. Wounded and helpless, they are waiting to be rescued by their foresters.

> *Presently, as the wind dropped for a moment, Ulrich broke silence. "Let's shout for help," he said. "In this lull our voices may carry a little way."*
>
> *"They won't carry far through the trees and undergrowth," said Georg, "but we can try. Together, then."*
>
> *The two raised their voices in a prolonged hunting call.*
>
> *"Together again," said Ulrich a few minutes later, after listening in vain for an answering hallo. "I heard something that time, I think," said Ulrich.*
>
> *"I heard nothing but the pestilential wind," said Georg hoarsely.*
>
> *There was silence again for some minutes, and then Ulrich gave a joyful cry. "I can see figures coming through the wood. They are following in the way I came down the hillside."*
>
> *Both men raised their voices in as loud a shout as they could muster.*
>
> *"They hear us! They've stopped. Now they see us. They're running down the hill towards us," cried Ulrich.*
>
> *"How many of them are there?" asked Georg.*
>
> *"I can't see distinctly," said Ulrich. "Nine or ten."*
>
> *"Then they are yours," said Georg. "I had only seven out with me."*
>
> *"They are making all the speed they can, brave lads," said Ulrich gladly.*
>
> *"Are they your men?" he repeated impatiently, as Ulrich did not answer.*
>
> *"No," said Ulrich with a laugh, the idiotic chattering laugh of a man unstrung with hideous fear.*
>
> *"Who are they?" asked Georg quickly, straining his eyes to see what the other would gladly not have seen.*
>
> *"Wolves."*
>
> —Saki

## EXERCISES

**A. Analyzing a dialogue** Reread the Saki dialogue. Then answer the following five questions in a few sentences.

1. What words and phrases does Saki use to tell the reader that time is passing?
2. Why does the dialogue move along so quickly?

3. What devices does Saki use to make the dialogue sound like real conversation?
4. What words and phrases does Saki use to convey the changes in his characters' emotions?
5. What point of view does Saki use? Why couldn't he have used any other point of view?

**B.** Telling a story   Using dialogue, write a short narrative about an adventure you've had. Use the narrative outline on page 246, Exercise B as your guide. You may imitate Saki's style if you wish.

**C.** Writing a conversation   Look at the following photograph. Write a short conversation that might have taken place between the people in the picture. Try to bring out the "personalities" of the characters through their speech.

What Is Language     268
From Latin and Greek     286
Words From Many Sources     304
Building Your Vocabulary     316
Reviewing Vocabulary     330

# VOCABULARY

# WHAT IS LANGUAGE?

## 58 Language Beginnings

No one is certain where human speech began—or precisely when it began. People have been around for more than half a million years, but the earliest written records of human language are only about six thousand years old. By the time language was available for us to study in its written form, it was a fully developed system, the product of thousands of years of oral use. We can only guess what happened to language during those hundreds of prehistoric generations.

Uncertainty has not kept people from exploring the origin of human speech, though. In fact, many scholars have ideas, or **theories,** that attempt to explain how human language began.

**The Instinctive Theory** Some early **linguists,** or scholars of language, believed speech was not learned, but was an instinct that people were born with, just as birds have the instinct to fly. These linguists noticed that babies make noises that sound like "Ouch," "Oh," "Ah," and "Sh." Therefore, the linguists said, those sounds must have been the first cries of humans. Such sounds, they said, were the beginning of language.

However, though such sounds do seem to be **instinctive,** or automatic, they make up only a very small group of words in any language, and they are really among the least important. So the instinctive theory is no longer taken very seriously.

**The Imitative Theory** Another popular theory was that speech began when people imitated the sounds of nature. This was known as the **imitative theory,** or the "bow-wow" theory. According to this theory, words like *moo, caw, hiss,* and *murmur* came from sounds made by birds and other animals.

Other theories    There are several other theories on how language began. The "ta-ta" theory suggests that speech began when prehistoric people made their cave drawings, or when they butchered animals. While working, the people moved their jaws, lips, tongues, and teeth—much as we often do when we cut with scissors—and escaping breath formed those first words. According to the "yo-he-ho" theory, language arose out of shouts or grunts produced as people went about their work, pursuing a wild animal perhaps, or picking nuts and berries.

   These theories and many others, some with amusing names such as "goo-goo" and "sing-song," lost favor because they did not explain many of the words in any language—and because we now realize that the truth about language origin lies lost in prehistory.

## EXERCISES

**A. Testing two theories of language origin** Write the numbers 1–20 on your paper. After each number write the word and either *instinctive* or *imitative* to explain the word's origin.

EXAMPLE:  moo—imitative

1. aha
2. buzz
3. hiss
4. humph
5. wow
6. bah
7. squeak
8. hah
9. pop
10. squeal
11. spank
12. ahem
13. chatter
14. hey
15. whippoorwill
16. crack
17. swish
18. ouch
19. ugh
20. fizz

**B. Writing imitative words** Some imitative words share a common sound. For each numbered item below, write imitative words that begin or end with the letters shown.

1. sq_____
2. sw_____
3. _____ash
4. _____ump
5. _____umble
6. _____ingle

**C. Exploring foreign imitative words** See how many of the following foreign words you can identify even though you may not know the languages. Write the numbers 1–5 on your paper. Next to each number write the letter of the word that you think corresponds to the numbered word.

1. miau (German)
2. gakgak (Turkish)
3. jodeln (German)
4. omumu (Tahitian)
5. how-how (Hebrew)

a. duck
b. yodel
c. bark
d. murmur
e. sound a cat makes

# 59

# Language Family Trees

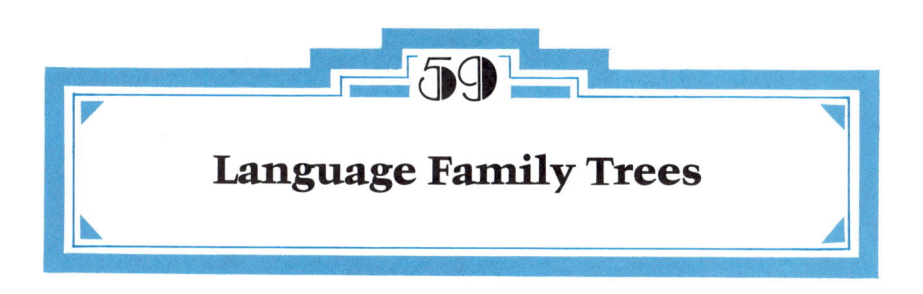

Linguists have sorted the approximately 2,800 languages of the world into a dozen or more larger groups, which they call **language families.** All the languages within each family are linguistically related to each other.

Here are three of the largest language families, with a few of the languages that are included in each.

INDO-EUROPEAN FAMILY: English, French, German, Spanish, Italian, Russian, Portuguese, Latin, Greek, Swedish.
SINO-TIBETAN FAMILY: Chinese, Tibetan, Burmese, Lao
SEMITIC FAMILY: Hebrew, Arabic

Were you surprised to find that Russian is related to English? The fact that languages are related or that they are similar does not mean that a person who can speak one of the languages within a family can automatically understand a person who speaks another language within the same family. Someone who speaks Hebrew, for example, will not understand Arabic unless he or she has learned Arabic.

Languages within the same family are different languages, certainly, but they are related linguistically. This means that we have discovered, through comparative studies, that they have descended from the same parent language.

The number of people who speak each of the languages of the world varies widely. Some languages are in danger of disappearing because they are spoken by only a small number of people. Others are spoken by millions of people. You may be interested to know how English and some other Indo-European languages rank among the major languages of the world. The following chart shows the thirteen most widely used languages and the number of people who speak them. Notice that each of the languages listed is spoken by more than fifty million people.

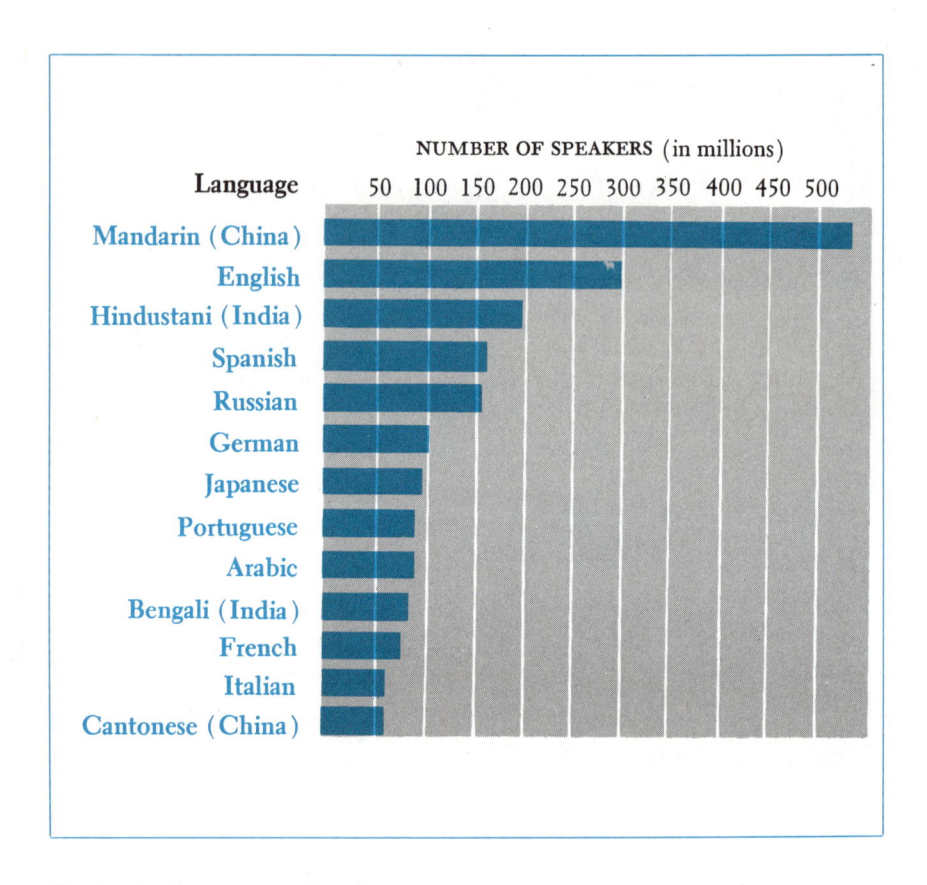

| Language | NUMBER OF SPEAKERS (in millions) |
|---|---|
| | 50  100  150  200  250  300  350  400  450  500 |
| Mandarin (China) | ▬▬▬▬▬▬▬▬▬▬ |
| English | ▬▬▬▬▬ |
| Hindustani (India) | ▬▬▬ |
| Spanish | ▬▬ |
| Russian | ▬▬ |
| German | ▬ |
| Japanese | ▬ |
| Portuguese | ▬ |
| Arabic | ▬ |
| Bengali (India) | ▬ |
| French | ▬ |
| Italian | ▪ |
| Cantonese (China) | ▪ |

**The Indo-European family** Sometime before 2000 B.C., a language called Indo-European was spoken by a small tribe of people who lived somewhere in central or southeastern Europe. As this group kept expanding, smaller groups began to branch out in different directions. They traveled into all parts of Europe—north, south, west, and east as far as India. Sometimes they migrated as peaceful immigrants, other times as conquering hordes. All the while their language kept changing, adapting itself to the new life-experiences of each group. Different versions of the Indo-European language developed. Eventually, after the groups had lived apart for centuries, separate languages developed, but all of the languages retain traces of the original parent language, Indo-European.

A chart of the Indo-European family of languages can be drawn in a number of ways. Here is a sample, simplified for the purpose of our study. By looking at it you can see why charts showing the relationships in a language family are often called **language trees**.

## EXERCISES

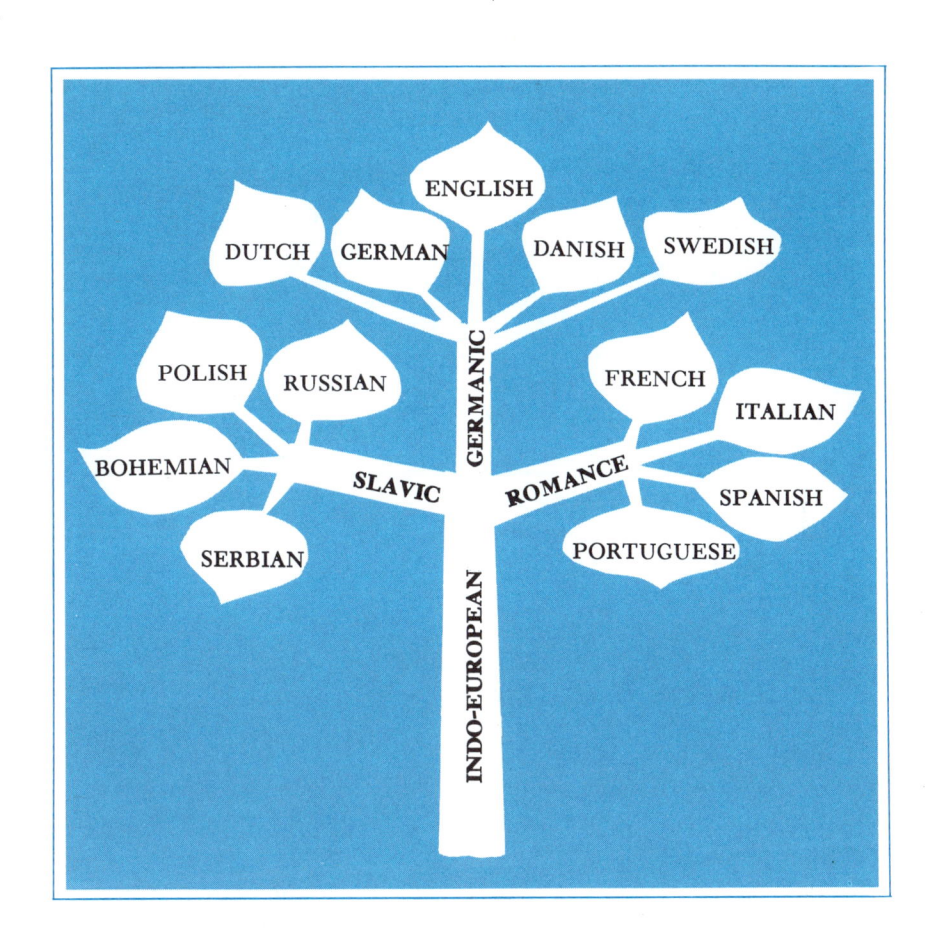

**A. Identifying Indo-European languages** From the following list of languages, copy the names of the languages that belong to the Indo-European group. Refer to the language tree for help.

*Danish      Dutch        Polynesian*
*Korean      Spanish      French*
*Japanese    Bantu        Hungarian*
*Polish      Italian      Hebrew*
*Turkish     English      Arabic*
*Russian     Bohemian     Serbian*
*Swedish     Portuguese   German*

**B. Comparing Germanic languages with Romance languages** Look at the following chart. Then answer the questions.

| Germanic Languages | | Romance Languages | |
|---|---|---|---|
| **English** | **German** | **Italian** | **Spanish** |
| mother | Mutter | madre | madre |
| night | Nacht | notte | noche |
| life | Leben | vita | vida |
| summer | Sommer | estate | estio |
| hand | Hand | mano | mano |

1. Which two words are most similar in *all* the languages?
2. Which word changes the most from the Germanic group to the Romance group?
3. Which word is the same in German and English?
4. Which two words are the same in Spanish and Italian?
5. To which of the languages is English most closely related?

**C. Seeing relationships between German, French, and English** The following list of words includes modern German and French words. Write the numbers 1–10 on your paper. Then write what you think is the English word for each of the German and French words.

1. Werk (G)
2. oncle (F)
3. Barbier (G)
4. manoeuvre (F)
5. magnifique (F)
6. triomphe (F)
7. famille (F)
8. musique (F)
9. Bluse (G)
10. ya (G)

# 60

# Characteristics of Language

**Verbal language**—or language using words, either spoken or written—is humankind's main instrument of communication. Language is therefore probably humankind's greatest invention. Other animals do indeed communicate successfully. However, they do not use the methods that make human verbal language so flexible, dynamic, and specific.

Following are several characteristics that define verbal language.

1. *Language consists of sounds that are symbolic.* The sounds that we make when we talk have no real relationship to the objects or ideas that we talk about. Those sounds form words that represent, or symbolize, objects or ideas. Juliet is right when, in Shakespeare's *Romeo and Juliet,* she says:

   *What's in a name? That which we call a rose
   By any other name would smell as sweet.*

   Juliet suggests that a name—*rose*—is only a symbol used to refer to an object or an idea. There is certainly nothing more "roseish" about the sound of the English word *rose,* for example, than the sound of the Arabic word *wur'dee,* which names the same flower.

2. *Language is arbitrary.* Why certain sounds were used to name certain things is still a mystery. We must assume that names are given to objects somewhat arbitrarily; that is, without there being any reasonable connection between the object and the name given it. Had the first person who called the flower a rose thought that it looked more like a *frim,* we might be phoning the florist on Mother's Day to order some red frims for Mom.

3. *Language is systematic.* In order to speak a language, we must learn to use many systems.

When we are born we have the potential for using many more sounds and sound combinations than our native language will ever demand that we develop. Languages use selected groups, or systems, of sounds rather than all the sounds that a human can produce. Systems of sounds differ from language to language. For instance, since you are a speaker of English, you will be able to decide which of these words could be an English word and which is definitely non-English: *ngilkgrlipf, cantraibic.*

The letters *ng* do not begin English words, though they do appear at the ends of words such as *long.* The letters *ng* often begin words in African languages, however.

The grammar and syntax of a language are systems of word arrangements that communicate meaning. In English, word order, or **syntax,** greatly affects meaning, while it is less important in other languages.

Notice how word order affects meaning in these sentences:

- Harold devoured the chiliburger.
- The chiliburger devoured Harold.

4. *Language must be learned.* We are not born knowing how to speak a particular language. We are born with the capacity to learn any language. Since we become a part of a specific group of people as children, we learn the language of that group.

5. *A language reflects the culture that uses it.* **Culture** refers to all of the ways of living built up by one group of people and passed down from one generation to another. It includes religious beliefs, marriage and child-rearing customs, music—and language. Language is an especially important aspect of a culture because it is necessary for the handing down of that culture from one generation to another.

All languages are equally easy for native speakers to learn. The fact that a speaker of English finds it easier to learn Spanish than Chinese has nothing to do with the complexity of any of those languages. It is the family relationship between English and Spanish that makes the difference.

6. *The vocabularies of languages meet the needs of the people who use them.* People within a culture create a body of words that al-

lows them to express specific messages about their environments and the things they value. Since environments and values vary from culture to culture, it is not surprising that the dictionaries of different languages vary so much in length. In English, for instance, we have one word for the color *black*. In Turkey, on the other hand, people "see" two different kinds of black. Therefore, Turks have two separate words referring to black: *siyah* is the black found in hair, clothes, and furniture; *kara* is the black of the Black Sea (*Kara Deniz*).

A large vocabulary, however, does not make a language better than a language with fewer words. In fact, no language is better than another. All languages are perfectly suited to the purpose for which they exist: to allow the people who share the same culture to communicate about life in that culture.

## EXERCISES

**A. Exploring language change** Assume that a people existed who spoke a language called Sopholingua. About a hundred years ago, because of famine and disease, they split up and moved in several directions.

> Group 1 moved to uninhabited desert country surrounded by treacherous mountains.
> Group 2 moved to a little populated, lush and productive land on a seacoast.
> Group 3 moved to a large city populated by many tribes.
> Group 4 was captured by a large tribe of barbarians and was taken to serve the barbarians in forest caves.

Write the numbers 1–4 on your paper. Then answer the following questions.

1. Which group probably developed many words for forest?
2. Which group probably developed many words for desert?
3. Why will the great-great-grandchildren of Group 4 probably *not* be able to speak Sopholingua.
4. Which two groups have the greatest chance of keeping the Sopholingua language, and why?

**B.** Using the systems of English   The words in each of the following groups can be combined to form an English sentence. Unscramble the word groups and write the sentences on your paper.

1. makes the Tanya's her score winner
2. left silent twenty the students room
3. had three them C.C. dollars between Phil only and
4. were Hiroshi both I dinners their when Kin arrived and eating
5. need I a new mug

**C.** Relating vocabulary to culture   The fact that Turks have two words for black tells us something about how they see their environment. Write down the name for something in our environment that we "see" in several ways. After that, write down at least five synonyms for that word.

EXAMPLE:   cloud—fog, smog, smoke, haze, mist

# 61

# Nonverbal Communication

Verbal language is only one means that people have for communicating with each other. They also use many nonverbal methods. While **nonverbal communication** contains some of the traits of verbal language, it does not possess all of them. On the next few pages you will explore nonverbal methods of communication.

Paralanguage   You can tell quite a bit about speakers without listening to or understanding any of their words. By listening to the voice of a stranger at the other end of your telephone line, for example, you can often identify the speaker's sex with little difficulty. You can tell something about the speaker's age, too—certainly whether he or she is a young child, a young adult, or a senior citizen. You can often detect something about the speaker's emotional state of mind—perhaps whether he or she is happy, angry, or confused. Often the speaker's voice betrays a certain attitude toward the subject of the telephone call or toward you.

Such clues, called **paralanguage**, may be only indirectly related to the speaker's message, but they can be sources of very crucial information. Speakers who want to disguise their voices in order not to communicate any of these paralinguistic clues sometimes have a hard time doing it.

Facial expression   Human beings use parts of their faces for communicating important messages. Mouths and eyes are particularly expressive.

Sometimes the messages conveyed by facial expressions contradict the words that accompany them. You have probably seen parents smiling while they scolded their very young children for acts that seemed at the same time naughty and funny.

Usually, however, facial expressions and the words or acts that accompany them are perfectly matched.

Gestures  People also communicate through movements of their hands, arms, shoulders, and head. Such movements are called **gestures**. Gestures usually accompany speech, but they sometimes occur separately and convey a message of their own.

Sign "languages" are made up of symbolic gestures. They are used (1) by people who do not share a language, (2) by people who cannot hear or speak, and (3) by those who are in a situation where spoken language would not be appropriate.

Most of us often use commonly understood gestures in place of words. We wink, we nod our heads, or we point at objects with a forefinger. Other people understand the messages and respond appropriately. Such gestures come to have only one meaning or a limited number of related meanings because people within a culture agree to use them to convey certain messages.

But meaningful gestures are very frequently bound to particular cultures. Nodding the head up and down means "no" instead of "yes" in some cultures while the wink is not meaningful at all in others.

While gestures bear messages themselves and thus make words unnecessary at times, speakers sometimes also use gestures to emphasize their words.

Strictly unconscious gestures often accompany our speech, too. We may wave our arms or wiggle our fingers. We may shuffle our feet. We may change our posture as we shift roles as speaker or listener. Scientists interested in gestures are making careful studies of movement. Some scientists feel that our gestures make up something called "body language." These scientists agree that we use our bodies to convey messages about ourselves to others. They do not always agree on what messages we are sending, however. Does that give you a clue as to why "body language" is not a language at all, according to our definition of language?

Signs   Highway signs, traffic lights, and the painted lines that define traffic lanes are designed to convey messages quickly to drivers who must understand the messages and control their vehicle at the same time.

Because our national parks attract foreign visitors as well as Americans, the United States Department of the Interior decided that signs in the parks should carry nonverbal symbols—codes that everyone can understand, regardless of the language spoken. Here are some of the nonverbal symbols that are gradually replacing the words on the signs in our national parks.

Animal communication   Whether or not we are the only talking animals is an issue that has not been settled. For years naturalists and other scientists have observed animals in order to decipher animal codes of communication. While animal communication remains largely a mystery, scientists are making discoveries all the time. They have found that some of the ways in which animals communicate are quite complex.

Among the most interesting experiments are those of Karl von Frisch, a well-known German scientist. Through his observations of honeybees, he realized that these insects actually communicate with each other concerning the location of food. When a bee finds food, it returns to the hive to share its information with the other bees by performing different kinds of dances. The kind of dance it performs depends on the information it wants to convey. Von Frisch gave each of these dances a name, linking each name to the type of information given. The bee's "round dance" tells the other bees that food is very near the hives. The "waggle dance," in which the bee wags its abdomen back and forth, indicates that food is farther away. The speed of the wagging and the number of times the bee performs the dance tell the others both the distance and the direction they have to fly to find the food. Monkeys, dolphins, certain birds, and fish have also been subjects of research on animal communication.

For the present, most scientists believe that sounds made by animals are instinctive responses to what is going on around them, not language as we know it. A goose sensing danger makes warning sounds that immediately alert the rest of the flock, and the flock takes off to seek safer ponds. But so far as we know, the geese cannot discuss the danger they have just escaped, nor can they talk about the hunter who was hiding behind the reeds the day before, and who may be back tomorrow.

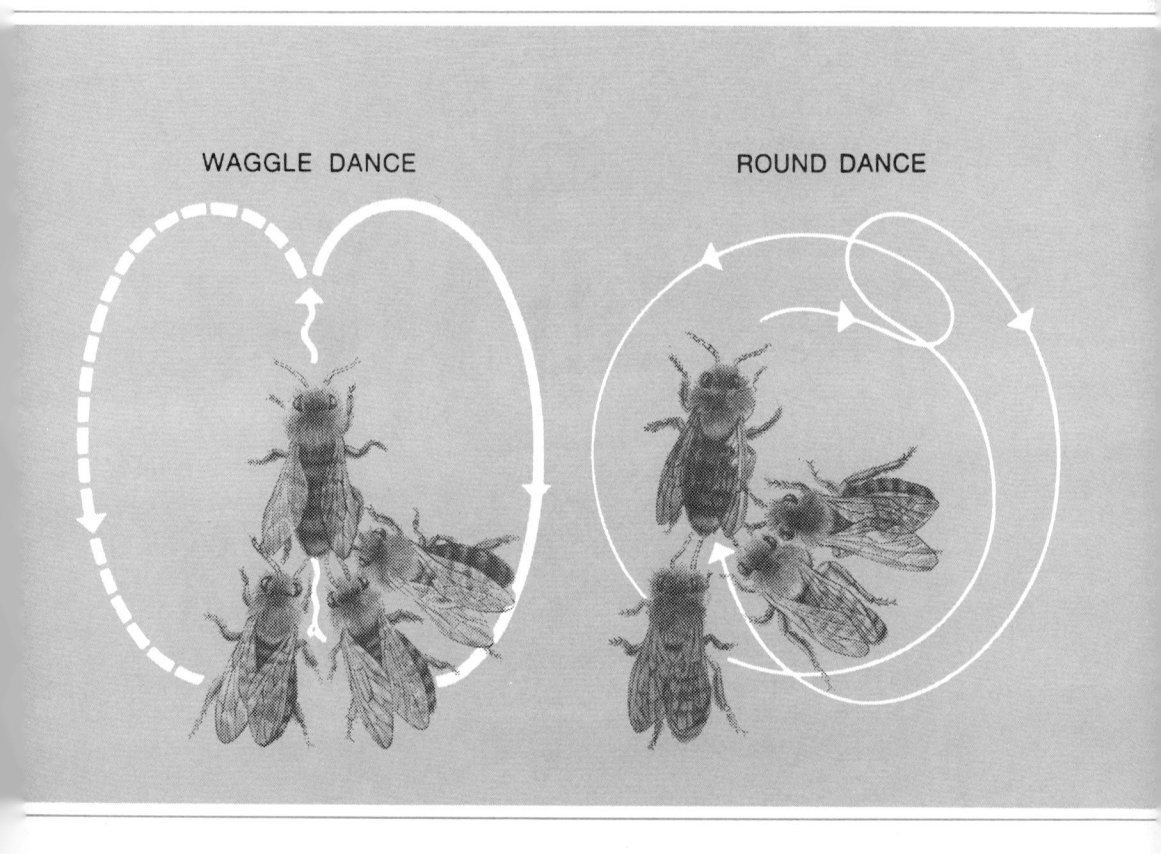

WAGGLE DANCE        ROUND DANCE

# EXERCISES

**A. Learning the importance of gestures and paralanguage** When Dr. Albert Maehrabian made the statement which follows, he used three numbers which add up to 100 in the places where we have left blanks.

*People convey feelings _____% because of the words actually said, _____% through tone of voice, _____% through expressions and posture.* —Albert Maehrabian

Decide what proportions you would assign to each aspect. Compare your answers with those of your classmates.

**B. Reading signs that have no words** Look at each of the following symbols. Write the meaning of each symbol next to the appropriate number on your paper.

**C.** Reading ''body language'' Examine the following photograph. Write a description of the message that the person's "body language" conveys to you. Compare your answer with your classmates' answers.

# FROM LATIN AND GREEK

## 62

## Latin Roots

Most of us feel the need to become acquainted with more words than we know right now. Each day brings new challenges to our command of the **lexicon,** or total vocabulary, of the English language. There are so many words that we can never hope to memorize the meanings of all of them. Furthermore, we are told that English is constantly growing to meet the needs of the societies that use it. A dynamic language such as English is not likely to stop growing and changing so that we can catch up with it. However, knowing ways in which our lexicon has grown will help us to increase our vocabularies without having to memorize every new word that challenges us.

One way in which our language has grown is through borrowing. Speakers of English have always borrowed words from other languages when they needed them. Invasions, conquests, and foreign trade offered many chances for early settlers living in what is now England to borrow from the Germans, the Norse, the French, and others. Latin, the language of ancient Rome, affected all of those languages and thus affected English. For centuries Latin was the language of education, religion, and science throughout Europe. There, books were printed and academic classes were taught only in Latin. The influence of that language remains with us, for English has borrowed thousands of words directly from Latin.

Perhaps more important to vocabulary building than the words borrowed directly from Latin are the **roots** of Latin words. Those roots have allowed speakers of English to create new words.

For example, the Latin word *audire* meant "to hear" when the Romans used it. English-speaking people have used the root *aud* in building many new words whose essential meanings are related to hearing. Some of them are *auditorium, audio-visual,* and *audible.*

Once we know the meanings of a generous handful of Latin roots, we have information that can help us to figure out the meanings of many unfamiliar words based on them.

## LATIN ROOTS

| Root | Meaning | Examples |
| --- | --- | --- |
| ann, enn | year | annual, anniversary |
| aud | hear | audible, audience |
| cred | believe | incredible, credit |
| dic, dict | speak, say | dictate, benediction |
| duct | lead | conduct, deduce |
| finis | end, limit | finish, infinite |
| mal | bad, evil | malicious, malady |
| miss, mit | let go, send | mission, permit |
| port | carry | import, transport |
| scrib | write | description, manuscript |
| spec, spect | look at | spectator, spectacular |
| tempor | time | temporary, tempo |
| tract | draw | attract, distract |
| vers, vert | turn | reverse, convert |
| vit | life | vitamin, vitality |

**A. Relating meanings of Latin roots to familiar words** Write the numbers 1–20 on your paper. Look at the chart of Latin roots. Select any ten roots whose example words you think you can define. For each example word you choose, write down a definition that shows the word's relationship to the meaning of its root.

EXAMPLE: aud—hear
ANSWERS: 1. audible—can be heard
2. audience—a group of people who hear a performer

**B. Writing words from Latin roots** Write the numbers 1–15 on your paper. Write a third example for each of the roots listed in the chart on Latin roots. List your information in two columns: one column for the roots and one column for your additional example. Underline the root that appears in each of your additional words. Use your dictionary for help.

EXAMPLE: aud—<u>aud</u>itorium

**C. Using context clues** Each of the following sentences provides an additional word for one of the roots listed in the chart on Latin roots. Write the numbers 1–10 on your paper. Next to each number, write (a) the root-based word that appears in the sentence, and (b) a word that will correctly fit in the blank. Refer to the chart for help.

EXAMPLE: On his inscribed plaque Gerardo found his name _____ in gold letters.
ANSWER: (a) inscribed, (b) written

1. I prefer a portfolio to that big briefcase because it is easier to _____.
2. Extemporaneous speeches are fun to hear because people have little _____ to organize them.
3. Before she extracted my tooth the dentist told me that _____ it out would not hurt.
4. A person with good diction will _____ very clearly.
5. The company's treasurer makes a seminannual report twice each _____.
6. I will divert Bill's attention from Melisenda by getting him to _____ away from her.
7. The specter that haunts our attic is one I would rather not _____ again soon.
8. Tadeo's tuba emits sounds more horrible than I thought a musical instrument could _____ out.
9. Grendel the monster stared at Beowulf malignantly—a stare that reflected the monster's _____ intentions.
10. Marta was incredulous when Mr. Begaye complimented her on her speech. She simply could not _____ what he said.

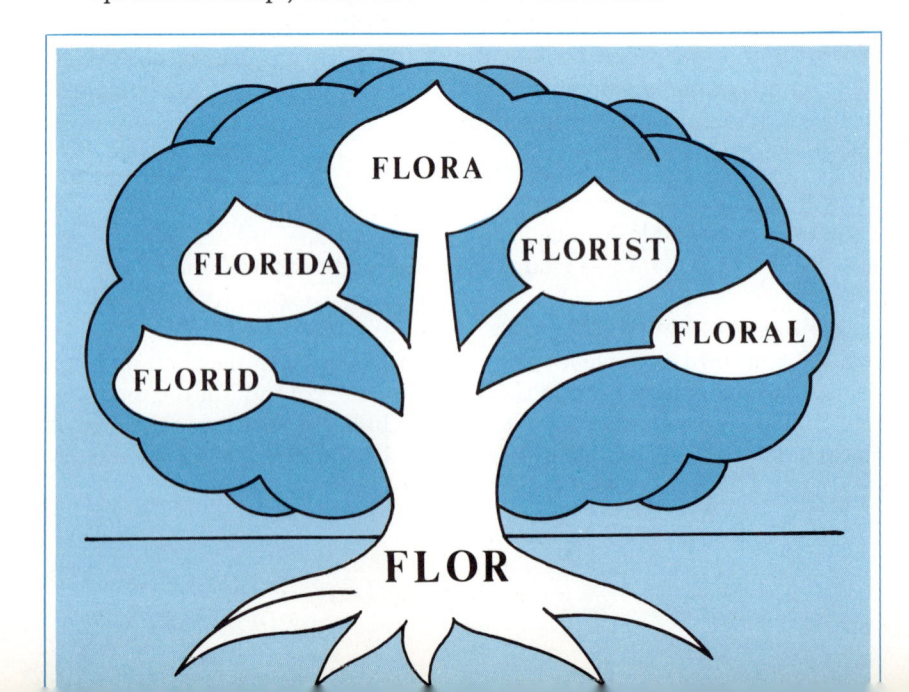

288

D. **Discovering meanings of Latin roots** Write the numbers 1-10 on your paper. Following is a list of Latin roots. Next to each root is a series of three words in which that root may be found. Compare those words and decide what the meaning of the root is. Write that meaning. You may use a dictionary.

EXAMPLE: du   dual, duplicate, duplex
ANSWER: two

| Root | Examples |
| --- | --- |
| 1. aqua | aquarium, aquaplane, aquatic |
| 2. cap, capit | captain, capital, capitulate |
| 3. cent | century, centennial, percent |
| 4. flor | florist, flora, floral |
| 5. fort | fortitude, fortify, fortress |
| 6. grat | grateful, congratulate, gratitude |
| 7. leg | legal, legislate, legitimate |
| 8. magn | magnify, magnificent, magnitude |
| 9. man | manual, manicure, manufacture |
| 10. pop | population, populace, popular |

# 63

# Greek Roots

Greek preceded Latin as the most influential language in Europe. When the Romans came to power, they borrowed heavily from the Greek language. Later, both Latin and Greek contributed generously to French. Speakers of English have borrowed directly and indirectly from those three languages more than from any others. Some scholars estimate that about half of our English vocabulary has been acquired from Greek, Latin, and French sources.

Greek roots, like Latin roots, can help us as we meet unfamiliar English words and try to build our vocabularies. Though there are fewer commonly used Greek roots than Latin roots, they are often clues to the meanings of words used in scientific and technical subjects. Fifteen useful Greek roots are included in the following chart.

## GREEK ROOTS

| Root | Examples |
| --- | --- |
| auto | automatic, autograph |
| bio | biography, biology |
| chron | chronological, synchronize |
| cycl | bicycle, cyclone |
| deca | decimal, decade |
| geo | geography, geology |
| graph | graphic, stenographer |
| hydr | dehydrate, hydrant |
| log, logy | dialogue, prologue |
| log, logy | mythology, biology |
| mon, mono | monorail, monotonous |
| phon, phone | phonograph, saxophone |
| psych | psychology, psychiatrist |
| tele | telephone, telegram |
| therm, thermo | thermometer, thermos bottle |

# EXERCISES

**A. Discovering meanings of Greek roots** Look again at the chart on Greek roots. Note that the meanings of those roots are not given there. Study the two examples given for each root. Then write the numbers 1–15 on your paper. Copy each Greek root. Then copy its meaning from the following list. You may use a dictionary.

| | | |
|---|---|---|
| *mind* | *fire* | *self* |
| *man* | *earth* | *science of; study of* |
| *water* | *heat* | *small* |
| *life* | *time* | *word or speech* |
| *march* | *write* | *wheel or circle* |
| *teach* | *ten* | *sound* |
| *one, single* | *guilt* | *distance* |

**B. Writing words from Greek roots** Write the numbers 1–15 on your paper. Write one additional word for each root in the chart of Greek roots. You may use a dictionary, but be sure to read the word's entry to make certain that the word is actually based on the appropriate root.

**C. Using context clues** Each of the following sentences provides an additional word for one of the roots listed in the chart on Greek roots. Write the numbers 1–10 on your paper. Next to each number, write (**a**) the root-based word that appears in the sentence, and (**b**) a word that will correctly fit in the blank. Refer to the chart for help.

EXAMPLE:  A psychopath suffers from a disorder of the _____.
ANSWER:   (a) psychopath, (b) mind

1. A chronic smoker is one whose habit has lasted for a long _____.
2. Psychology is the _____ of the mind.
3. When children study phonics, they are studying the relationships between _____ and the symbols that represent them.
4. Orthography is the study of how words are _____, or spelled.
5. Bionics is the study of how the _____ processes of humans and animals can be applied to machines. (Notice that *bionics* is a combination of *biology* and *electronics*.)
6. An athlete who is entered in the decathlon must compete in _____ field and track events.
7. A thermofax machine uses _____ in order to produce copies of printed materials.
8. A monologue is a speech delivered by _____ person.

291

9. Telepathy is said to be a means by which two minds can communicate though they are _____ away from each other.
10. An autonomous group is independent and _____-governing.

**D.** Relating unfamiliar words to the meanings of Greek roots   Write the numbers 1–5 on your paper. Copy each of the following words. Underline the Greek root or roots that appear in it. Then look up each word in your dictionary. In your own words, rewrite the dictionary's definitions that are related to the meaning of the root.

EXAMPLE:   tele photo—a picture sent a long distance by wire or radio

1. monopoly
2. anachronism
3. autobiography
4. hydrotherapy
5. geocentric

# 64

# Latin and Greek Prefixes

The root words you have been working with in this unit rarely stand alone when they appear in English. Occasionally two roots have been combined to form a single new word, as in *psychology* or *monologue*. More often, though, those roots contribute basic meanings that are enriched or modified by affixes. **Affixes** are word parts (usually single syllables) that are attached to roots in order to create new words.

di*vert*   in*cred*ulous   *fort*ify   *flor*ist

In the preceding words, everything except the italicized roots are meaningful affixes. The root *vert* means "turn"; but *divert* means "to turn aside." *Cred* means "believe," while *incredulous* refers to not believing. *Fort* means "strong," while *fortify* refers to the act of making something strong. *Flora* means "flowers," while *florist* names one who sells those flowers. It is easy to see why affixes are said to enrich or modify roots.

There are two kinds of affixes: prefixes and suffixes. **Prefixes** are placed at the beginning of a word, in front of the root. **Suffixes** follow the root.

The following chart shows some commonly used prefixes, which come to us from Latin and Greek.

| Prefix | Meaning | Examples |
| --- | --- | --- |
| a–, an– | without, not | amoral, anharmonic |
| ab–, abs– | from, away | abduct, absent |
| anti–, ant– | opposite, against | antifreeze, antacid |
| bene– | well, good | benefit, benediction |
| bi– | two, twice | bicycle, bisect |

| | | |
|---|---|---|
| co– | with, together | copilot, cooperate |
| con– | together | concert, convention |
| contra–, counter– | against, opposed to | contradict, counteract |
| de–, di– | down, away, reversal | decrease, depart, divert |
| dia– | across, through | diagonal, diameter |
| dis– | away, removal, not | dismiss, dissatisfied |
| ex–, e– | formerly, beyond, out | ex-President, exceed, erase, exit, exclude |
| in–, il–, im–, ir– | not, in, or into | invisible, include, illegal, improper, irregular |
| inter– | among, between, together | interfere, international |
| mis– | wrong | misbehave, misunderstand |
| post– | after | postpone, postwar |
| pre– | before, ahead of | preview, prehistoric |
| pro– | forward, in favor of, in place of | propel, pro-labor, pronoun |
| re– | back or backward, again | retrieve, recall |
| semi– | half, partly | semicircle, semiconscious |
| sub– | under or below | submarine, submerge |
| super– | over or above | superhuman, superior |
| syn–, sym– | with, together, like | synonym, sympathy |
| trans– | across or over | transfer, transparent |

The negative prefix *in–* sometimes changes its spelling. Look at the following words and notice how the spelling of the prefix changes.

*il*legal  *im*movable  *im*proper  *ir*regular

Placed in front of roots beginning with the letter *l*, the prefix generally becomes *il–;* in front of roots beginning with *m* or *p,* the prefix becomes *im–;* and in front of roots beginning with *r,* the prefix becomes *ir–*. Otherwise, the *in–* spelling is used.

# EXERCISES

**A. Relating the meanings of prefixes to familiar words** Write the numbers 1–15 on your paper. In each of the following sentences there are (a) a word that contains a prefix that appears in the prefix chart, and (b) a word or phrase that has the same meaning as the prefix in that word. Write the prefixed word on your paper and underline its prefix. Next to it write the word or phrase that also appears in the sentence and has the same meaning as the prefix. Refer to the chart whenever you need to.

EXAMPLE: International trade among free nations increased last year.
ANSWER: international—among

1. Like all bicycles, mine has two wheels.
2. Paula is seldom absent from basketball practice.
3. Insert tab A into slot 34.
4. Gino preheated the oven before he put in the TV dinner.
5. When you depart, my dear, go away with a smile on your face.
6. I'll recall the name when I hear it again.
7. Bernabe's gesture of dismissal told me to go away and never come back.
8. The fringe benefits of my job at the leather jacket factory are good for all the employees.
9. Harry Truman, an ex-President, was formerly a resident at Blair House.
10. Together the pilot and the copilot fought the weather and landed the big craft safely.
11. The coach plans to postpone the game until after vacation.
12. The wrecked auto had been submerged under twenty feet of murky water in Crater Lake.
13. If I cut along the diagonal line you have drawn across this dollar bill, will each half be worth fifty cents?
14. Antislavery laws were Lincoln's greatest weapons against the problems that arose when one person controlled the life of another.
15. Mass transit systems allow citizens to get across the city very quickly and cheaply.

**B. Writing prefixed words** Write the numbers 1–20 on your paper. Add one example for twenty of the prefixes listed in the prefix chart. Underline the prefix that appears in each of your additional examples.

EXAMPLE: ex–
ANSWER: export

C. **Using the spellings of the prefix "in-"** Write the numbers 1–10 on your paper. Apply the correct form of the negative prefix *in-* to the following words. Write the new word.

EXAMPLE: rational
ANSWER: irrational

1. sincere
2. logical
3. escapable
4. resistible
5. perfect
6. literate
7. movable
8. patient
9. appropriate
10. responsible

D. **Discovering meanings of Latin and Greek prefixes** Write the numbers 1–5 on your paper. Compare the three examples given for each of the following prefixes. Then write the meaning of the prefix. Select the appropriate meaning from the list that appears at the end of this exercise. You may use a dictionary if you need help.

EXAMPLE: para– parallel, paraphrase, paradox
ANSWER: beside or contrary to

1. ante–     antecedent, antedated, antebellum
2. circum–   circumference, circumnavigate, circumscribe
3. extra–    extraordinary, extrasensory, extracurricular
4. intro–    introduce, introspective, introjection
5. pseudo–   pseudonym, pseudoscientific, pseudointellectual

    false           outside, beyond      before, in front
    around         overly, excessively  within, in, into

# 65

# Latin and Greek Suffixes

Suffixes, like prefixes, contribute to the meaning of words. For example, the suffix *–ian* adds another meaning to the word *magic* in *magician*. Suffixes can also change the functions of words and determine their locations in sentences. Look how suffixes affect the word *invent*.

INVENT (VERB):   Someone should *invent* a special clock to speed up Mondays.
INVENTION (NOUN):   Such an *invention* is long overdue.
INVENTOR (NOUN):   The *inventor* would get rich quickly.
INVENTIVE (ADJECTIVE):   That *inventive* person would become famous.

Certain Latin and Greek suffixes are used to form nouns.

| Suffix | Meaning | Example |
| --- | --- | --- |
| –ance | action or process, quality or state of | acceptance |
| –ence | act, state of being | confidence |
| –ion, –tion, –sion, –ation | act of, state of | graduation |
| –ism | act of, state of, doctrine of, characteristic of | heroism |
| –ity | state, condition, quality, degree | equality |
| –ment | state, condition, quality | amazement |
| –ness | state, condition, quality | illness |
| –ty | state, condition, quality | loyalty |

Several suffixes are used to form nouns that refer to people, the roles the people play or the occupations at which they work.

| Suffix | Meaning | Example |
|---|---|---|
| –ant | one who | occupant |
| –ee | one to whom an act is done; one to whom a right is given | employee |
| –eer | one who is concerned with or manages | auctioneer |
| –er | one who; process of | teacher |
| –ian | one who works with | historian |
| –ist | one who practices an action; one occupied with or skilled in | typist |
| –or | one who; state or quality of | actor |

Other suffixes are used to form verbs.

| Suffix | Meaning | Example |
|---|---|---|
| –fy, –ify | to make or form into | beautify |
| –ize | to subject to; to make into or like; to practice or carry on | modernize |

Still other suffixes are used to form adjectives. Those suffixes enrich or modify the roots to which they are attached.

| Suffix | Meaning | Example |
|---|---|---|
| –able | having the quality or capacity | acceptable |
| –al | having the character of, or pertaining to | fictional |
| –ary | pertaining to; one belonging to; a place for | honorary |
| –ful | full of; characterized by | hopeful |
| –ible | having the quality or fitness for; able | sensible |

| | | |
|---|---|---|
| –ic | of the nature of; resembling; belonging to | athletic |
| –ive | having the quality of; tending to | cooperative |
| –less | without; unable to do | fearless |
| –ous | full of; having qualities of | poisonous |
| –y | full of; inclined to | scratchy |

## EXERCISES

**A. Using suffixes to form nouns**   Write the numbers 1–15 on your paper. Write a suitable noun for each blank in the following sentences by adding the appropriate noun suffix to the root in parentheses. Use these suffixes: –ance, –ence, –ion (–tion, –sion, –ation), –ism, –ity, –ment, –ness, –ty.

EXAMPLE:   The _____ continued past midnight. (celebrate)
ANSWER:   celebration

1. Hugo's _____ got him out of many scrapes.   (cool)
2. Unless I see some _____ in your work, I will ask you to resign. (improve)
3. Your _____ was evident when Pat refused to obey you.   (annoy)
4. We set out at sunrise, and by ten that morning we were far from _____.   (civilize)
5. My _____ caused me to forget my speech.   (confuse)
6. As Camila placed her hand over her heart, a feeling of _____ swept over her.   (patriot)
7. I question the _____ of your claim to the old woman's fortune. (legal)
8. The rock was not an _____ to the determined turtle.   (impede)
9. Since Mary-Sue is everybody's friend, her _____ is deserved.   (popular)
10. The rebel's _____ was evident in his gestures and the tone of his voice.   (defy)
11. The President entered, encircled by _____ guards.   (secure)
12. I had not one _____ in Bell Harbor until Jack Chang became my friend.   (acquaint)
13. I wrote my answer to the teacher's question with little _____. (certain)
14. Two years ago we exchanged letters, but since then I have had no _____ from Isabel.   (correspond)
15. I can vouch for the _____ of our school's band.   (superior)

299

**B. Forming nouns that refer to people** Write the numbers 1–10 on your paper. Change each italicized word into a noun that refers to the person in the corresponding description. Use the following suffixes: *–ant, –ee, –eer, –er, –ian, –ist, –or.* Notice that you will need to drop the *y* from the roots that end in *y*.

EXAMPLE: dance: a person who moves to music
ANSWER: dancer

1. *employ:* a person who hires another person
2. *history:* a person who studies ancient times
3. *science:* a person who works in a laboratory
4. *bake:* a person who makes cakes and pastries
5. *occupy:* a person who lives at a given address
6. *act:* a person who stars in motion pictures
7. *music:* a person who plays in an orchestra
8. *solo:* a person who sings alone
9. *refuge:* a person who seeks shelter in another country
10. *attend:* a person who fills your gas tank

**C. Using suffixes to form verbs** Write the numbers 1–10 on your paper. Using the verb-forming suffixes, write the verbs described by each of the following phrases. Use your dictionary to check spellings.

EXAMPLE: to make beautiful
ANSWER: beautify

1. to make equal
2. to make familiar
3. to make pure
4. to charge a penalty
5. to make solid
6. to make false
7. to make someone a victim
8. to make glorious
9. to make liquid
10. to cause to form crystals

# 66

# Words as Puzzles

How can you figure out the meaning of an unfamiliar word when you don't have—or can't use—a dictionary?

**Using context clues**   Look at the word *dismissal* in the following passage.

> Maria was glad to work at the filling station. The job allowed her to be around cars, to meet new people, and to earn enough to pay off her car loan. Naturally, then, Maria's sudden and unexplained *dismissal* disappointed her. She didn't know where she would work next or where her next paycheck would come from.

The paragraph contains several clues to the meaning of *dismissal* in the form of sentences that tell you that Maria lost her job.

**Using roots and affixes**   When context clues are not available, use your knowledge of Latin and Greek roots and affixes.

Words such as *dismissal* can be approached in the following manner.

1. Divide the word into its root and its prefixes and suffixes.

   | Prefix(es) | Root | Suffix(es) |
   |---|---|---|
   | dis | miss | al |

2. Under each word part, write the part's meaning—or translate it mentally.

   | Prefix(es) | Root | Suffix(es) |
   |---|---|---|
   | dis | miss | al |
   | (away) | (send) | (pertaining to) |

3. Form a definition by rearranging and rephrasing the meanings of the word parts. For example, the definition of dismissal can be

written: *dismissal refers to sending something away.* By rereading the passage or context you can then see if your definition is reasonably accurate.

If this process does not give you a good definition—and sometimes it will not—then the next step is to consult a dictionary. If you use context clues and your knowledge of roots and affixes wisely, however, you will need to use a dictionary less often.

## EXERCISES

**A. Finding the meanings of words** Write the numbers 1–10 on your paper. Write definitions for the italicized words in the sentences which follow. Use the three-step plan suggested in this lesson. Write your definitions in sentences like the definition for *dismissal*. Refer to the root and affix charts if you need help.

1. The *inscription* on the stone sign welcomed all travelers.
2. Angry, the man flung a stinging *malediction* at all who were in the room, then stalked off.
3. *Perennial* plants are nice in winter when the annuals have gone.
4. He was surprised that such a little baby could *emit* such a loud cry.
5. Without education, would humankind *revert* to a savage state?
6. The old woman's *retrospective* view caused her to regret the errors of her past.
7. Since the radio *transmitter* was out of order, we lost contact with the mainland for two days.
8. Telling lies damages a person's *credibility*.
9. Historians often contribute to the *diachronic* study of a language.
10. Quiet and *introspective*, Jun Lee knew well her strengths and worked to correct her flaws.

**B. Using Latin and Greek roots, prefixes and suffixes to build words** Write the numbers 1–5 on your paper. Build as many words as possible using the following five Latin and Greek roots. Use both prefixes and suffixes. Be certain that all of your words are related in meaning to the meanings of their roots. If you are not sure that one of your words is currently used in English, check your dictionary. (You may also want to check the dictionary for correct spelling.)

1. graph (write)
2. scrib or scrip (write)

3. cred (believe)
4. dic or dict (speak, say)
5. vers or vert (turn)

**C. Defining newly coined words** The following list contains some words that have recently come into our language. Write the numbers 1–10 on your paper. Figure out which word should go in each blank, and copy it on your paper next to the appropriate number. Use the charts in this section if you need help. Select your answers from the following list.

| antithermic | contrascriptive | postvitalic |
| temporacide | decalateral | pretemporism |
| synchronographer | semitemporal | transpsychic |
| malaphonous | contramalious | subhydrographic |

1. A _____ pen will write under water.
2. A _____ building has ten sides.
3. One who kills time may be charged with _____.
4. A _____ essay is one which presents only the negative side of an issue.
5. A _____ expert may write books about life after death.
6. A _____ worker works only part-time.
7. One who is _____ probably has extrasensory mental powers.
8. Cracked, scratchy phonograph records are usually _____.
9. A _____ can write with both hands at the same time.
10. One _____ act would be opening all the windows when the outside temperature is below freezing.

# WORDS FROM MANY SOURCES

## 67

## Words from Mythology

Myths and legends were very important to the ancient Greeks and Romans. Such stories helped people in those ancient cultures to understand the universe and to know what roles they should play in it. Myths were an important part of their religious beliefs and made up a large part of their literature. Greek and Roman myths and legends have become a part of our own literary heritage. They are frequently read and studied in our schools. Their characters—such as Zeus and Cupid—are commonly referred to in modern literature. Planets and chemical elements are named for the superstars of mythology. Even everyday products such as automobiles and tires bear the names of gods and goddesses.

Mythological characters, settings, and events are important enough that they are found in most modern English dictionaries. So, too, are the words inspired by those characters, settings, and events—some of them originating in English, some of them borrowed directly from other languages. *Cereal* is one such word. It came to us from a Latin word pertaining to Ceres, the Roman goddess of agriculture.

Following are some of the many facts from mythology which have inspired common English words.

- *The Odyssey* is the story of the ten years of wandering by **Odysseus.**

- **Mentor** was the wise adviser of Odysseus, who was entrusted with the care and education of Odysseus's son.

- **Hercules,** the strongest human, completed twelve very difficult labors and changed the courses of two rivers.

- **Tantalus** was a king whom the gods condemned to remain throughout his after-life standing chin deep in water with fruit-laden branches hanging above his head—he being unable to reach them.

- **Psyche** was a beautiful princess whose name meant "mind" or "soul" in Greek.
- **Mars** was the Roman god of war.
- The **Muses** were the nine daughters of Zeus who presided over the arts and sciences.
- **Polyhymnia** was the Muse of religious music.
- **Hygeia** was the Greek goddess of health.
- **Nox** was the Roman goddess of the nighttime.
- **Atlas** was a giant who supported the earth on his shoulders.
- **Luna** was the Roman goddess of the moon.

*Apollo dances with the nine Muses.*

- **Sol** was the Roman god of the sun.
- The **Labyrinth** was an inescapable series of complicated, winding passages.
- **Somnus** was the Roman god of sleep.
- **Morta** was the Roman angel of death.
- **Helios** was the Greek god of the sun.
- **Proteus** was a sea god who had the power to change shapes—to become serpent, lion, or tree.
- The **Lethe** was a river in the underworld where the dead went. Its water caused forgetfulness of the past in those who drank from it.
- **Nemesis** was the Greek goddess of retribution. If a person boasted of good fortune, Nemesis saw to it that he or she had enough bad luck to balance things out.

## EXERCISES

**A. Inferring meanings of words from mythological sources** Write the numbers 1–20 on your paper. Match the English words based on Greek or Roman myths with their meanings. Refer to the list of mythological references in this lesson for help.

| | | |
|---|---|---|
| nocturnal | odyssey | lunar |
| lethal | mortician | heliograph |
| tantalize | nemesis | mentor |
| somnolent | martial | solar |
| psychic | hygiene | herculean |
| hymn | protean | museum |
| labyrinth | atlas | |

1. having or requiring great strength
2. a system of passages having the design of a maze
3. a book containing maps
4. pertaining to the sun, as in _____ energy
5. a long series of wanderings
6. that which causes pain or harm
7. undertaker

8. pertaining to the moon, as in a _____ eclipse
9. able to change shapes or roles
10. a wise and trusted adviser
11. torment with the hope of having something that cannot be reached or attained
12. one who senses things with his or her mind rather than with ordinary senses such as sight or hearing
13. a building where works of art are kept and displayed
14. the study of methods for preserving health
15. a mirror used to send messages by reflecting the sun's rays
16. tired; sleepy
17. deadly; fatal
18. done or occurring at night
19. a religious song
20. warlike; related to war

**B.** Discovering other mythological sources  Write the numbers 1–15 on your paper. Explain how each of the following words is related to mythology. Your answers should be one or two sentences long. You will need to use a dictionary or an encyclopedia. (Some words are from Germanic mythology.)

1. colossal
2. volcano
3. siren
4. echo
5. Europe
6. January
7. March
8. May
9. Saturday
10. Tuesday
11. Wednesday
12. Thursday
13. Friday
14. jovial
15. mercury

# 68

# Words from Literature

While mythology has served as an important source of words for the English lexicon, we have drawn on other literary sources as well. Folktales, plays, poems, and novels have also contributed to our word store.

Many of the words we have borrowed from literature began as the names of characters or settings in works popular in their day. Some of those works are still commonly read and enjoyed, such as those whose stars are Cinderella or Romeo. Others gather dust on library shelves while their characters' names remain in fairly common use.

Many of our literature–related words have followed a pattern: the name of a famous literary character is used to describe real people who demonstrate some unique characteristic of that character. Eventually the capital letter is replaced with a lower case one. How many times have you heard the term "cinderella story" used to describe the life of someone who rose from poverty to fame and wealth? Even sports announcers sometimes recount the "cinderella story" of a team that overcame early losses or injuries in order to win the championship at the end of the season.

Here are some facts about the literary sources of other words.

- **Pollyanna,** an orphan, refused to let her grim circumstances get her down. She always saw the bright side of any catastrophe. (*Pollyanna,* a novel by Eleanor Hodgman Porter, 1913)

- **Casper Milquetoast** was easily frightened by almost everyone and everything: his boss, small children, or a cat. ("The Timid Soul," a cartoon series by H. T. Webster, 1930s and 1940s)

- **Victor Frankenstein,** a student, constructed a body in human form and gave it life, but not a soul. The monster eventually murdered Frankenstein and those whom Frankenstein loved. (*Frankenstein, or the Modern Prometheus,* a novel by Mary Shelley, 1818)

- Three princes of **Serendip** (now known as Ceylon) made many important discoveries without seeking them. ("The Three Princes of Serendip," an old fairytale)

- **Gargantua** was a noisy, friendly king and giant with a great appetite. (*Gargantua,* a satirical novel by Rabelais, 1534)

- **Mrs. Malaprop** could never say things quite straight. She often chose the wrong word. (*The Rivals,* a play by Richard Brinsley Sheridan, 1775)

- **Don Quixote de la Mancha,** who was influenced by reading books about chivalry, set out on a search for wrongs that needed correcting. He became involved in many silly adventures, the most famous of which is his attacking a windmill that he mistook for an enemy. (*Don Quixote de la Mancha,* a novel by Cervantes, 1605 and 1615)

- **Utopia** was an imaginary island that had a perfect social and political system. (*Utopia,* a political romance by Sir Thomas More, 1551)
- **Puck** was a very mischievous but likeable elf. (*A Midsummer Night's Dream,* a play by William Shakespeare, 1594)
- When Gulliver visited **Lilliput,** he was a giant compared to the thumb-size people who lived there. (*Gulliver's Travels,* a satire by Jonathan Swift, 1726)
- **Ebenezer Scrooge** loved only money. He had a very sour personality. Then one Christmas Eve he was visited by ghosts who guided him on dream tours of his past, present, and future. Those experiences awakened in him generosity and a real concern for others. (*A Christmas Carol,* a novel by Charles Dickens, 1843)
- **Dr. Jekyll** discovered a drug that allowed him to create a separate personality within himself. **Mr. Hyde,** his other personality, was evil. Hyde got out of control and committed murder. Eventually Hyde became so strong that Jekyll's character could not return. (*The Strange Case of Dr. Jekyll and Mr. Hyde,* a novel by Robert Louis Stevenson, 1886)

## EXERCISES

**A.** Inferring meanings of words from literary sources   Match the words drawn from literary sources with their present meanings. Refer to your list of literature facts for help. Do not use a dictionary.

*serendipity*         *scrooge*
*malapropism*         *quixotic*
*milquetoast*         *Frankenstein*
*pollyanna*           *jekyll and hyde*
*gargantuan*          *utopia*

1. a person who is easily dominated or frightened
2. a person who creates a destructive thing that cannot be controlled
3. the humorous misuse of a word
4. a place that is perfect

5. an excessively or blindly optimistic person
6. extravagantly chivalrous; not practical
7. a person having two personalities, one good and one bad
8. a miser or a person with a sour personality
9. enormous, huge
10. an aptitude for making desirable discoveries by accident

**B. Using new words in context**   Choose four words from the list in Exercise A. Write an original sentence using each of the four words. Provide at least one good clue in each sentence that would help someone else understand the meaning of the word.

**C. Coining words**   Choose a famous twentieth-century literary figure or entertainer noted for a particular trait. Change that person's first or last name to a common noun by dropping the capital letter. You may want to change the name to an adjective by adding an appropriate suffix: –*ish*, –*ian*, or –*ic*, for instance. Write a definition for the word you have coined. Then use the word in a sentence which provides at least one good context clue to your word's meaning.

EXAMPLE:   Howard Cosell—cosellian (adj.)
Definition: a person noted for using big words
He is so cosellian I have to carry a dictionary to his class.

# 69

## Words from History

The words in English which are associated with specific historical characters or events would fill a book. Indeed, at least one book, Isaac Asimov's *Words from History,* is devoted entirely to the stories behind many of those words. Asimov treats words such as these, with which you are quite familiar:

- In the fifth century, a German tribe known as the Vandals sacked Rome. They did not damage nonmovable property and took few lives. The Romans were terrified, nevertheless. Centuries later the French coined the word **vandalisme.** Today, a vandal is one who senselessly destroys something valuable.

- The Romans had a council of elders which offered advice to their rulers. The Latin word for "old man" is **senex,** and the council was called the senate. Individual members of the council were called senators.

- President Theodore Roosevelt in 1909 went off—with great fanfare—on a hunting tour. Soon afterwards Americans enthusiastically bought stuffed toy bears named in **Teddy** Roosevelt's honor.

The following facts are related to less common words.

- In 1818, Thomas **Bowdler** published an edition of Shakespeare's plays in which he had omitted words and expressions that he thought were not suitable for family reading sessions.

- When citizens of Athens thought that a person was unwholesome or dangerous, they gathered in the marketplace and voted as to whether banishment was in order. They voted "yes" by writing the person's name on a tile or a piece of pottery called an **ostrakon.** If 6000 ostrakons were cast, the person was kept out of the state for five or ten years.

- Because he was very brave and intelligent, **Pyrrhus** was Hannibal's most valued general. However, at Asculum in 179 B.C., Pyrrhus's army paid dearly for a victory against the Romans. In fact, Hannibal is supposed to have said, "One more such victory and we are lost."

- Jean **Martinet** was a general who built up the first regular army in Europe. He contributed nothing to military tactics, but he used precise and persistent drill to train his soldiers to fight together as a unit.

- Seventeenth-century clowns harmlessly hit each other with two small boards, or sticks, held together in one hand. The loud noise produced by the **slapsticks** entertained the audience and made them laugh.

- In 490 B.C. the Athenians defeated the Persians at **Marathon**. A runner sped twenty-six miles to deliver the good news to Athens.

*The runner falls exhausted as he delivers the good news to the Athenians.*

- Nicholas **Chauvin** was a soldier in Napoleon's army who refused to lose faith in his leader even after the empire was staggered by Napoleon's loss at Waterloo. Chauvin made himself ridiculous by continuing to brag about Napoleon even after such a crushing defeat.

- When King Mausolus of Caria died in 353 B.C., his wife had an enormous tomb built, which the Greeks called a *mausoleion*. So splendid was the memorial that it later became one of the Seven Wonders of the World.

- Diplomat Jean **Nicot,** while serving as French ambassador to Portugal, bought some seeds of a new plant imported from America. By taking the seeds back home, he introduced tobacco to France.

- St. Mary of Bethlehem in London was a hospital for the insane in the sixteenth century. In those days, insane people were treated like animals—chained to the walls, poked at, and teased. Little wonder that the hospital was very noisy and chaotic! In the London dialect of the day, Bethlehem was pronounced **Bedlam.**

- In 1879, after several years of crop failures, Irish tenant farmers were having trouble paying high rents to absentee landlords. The tenants on one farm proposed a lower rent scale, but the farm manager, Captain Charles Cunningham **Boycott,** would not accept it. The tenants retaliated against Boycott by refusing to gather crops.

- Early Popes, since they had no children, sometimes appointed their nephews to church-related jobs. In Latin, *nepos* meant "nephew."

- When the Nazis launched World War II in 1939, they moved quickly in what was called a *Blitzkrieg* ("lightning war"). The idea was to attack before the Allies could prepare.

- After conquering much of Europe, Napoleon swept into Spain in 1808. He deposed the king and put his own brother on the throne. The peasants, however, unexpectedly rose up against the French army. The French might have defeated a regular army, but the Spanish peasants' *guerrilla* ("little war") was too much for them. The French fled.

# EXERCISES

**A. Inferring meanings of words from historical sources** Write the numbers 1–15 on your paper. Match the words drawn from historical sources with their present meanings. Refer to the list of history facts in this lesson for help.

| | | |
|---|---|---|
| *blitz* | *nepotism* | *chauvinism* |
| *guerrilla* | *bedlam* | *mausoleum* |
| *boycott* | *bowdlerize* | *nicotine* |
| *ostracize* | *pyrrhic victory* | *marathon* |
| *martinet* | *slapstick* | *vandalism* |

1. to exclude from society by general consent
2. a strict disciplinarian
3. a scene of wild uproar and confusion
4. to refuse to have dealings with someone or with an organization as a way of forcing change
5. to censor, especially a book
6. a victory or goal gained at too great a loss
7. broad comedy characterized by boisterous horseplay
8. a long-distance race
9. a stately monument or tomb
10. excessive or blind patriotism
11. favoritism shown to relatives, as by giving them appointive jobs
12. a member of a small independent band of soldiers that fights against a large professional army
13. a swift attack
14. a poisonous substance obtained from tobacco
15. senseless destruction of property

**B. Using new words in context** Choose five words from the list in Exercise A. For each of the five words, write an original sentence. Provide at least one good clue in each sentence that would help someone else understand the meaning of the word.

**C. Discovering other historical sources** Write the numbers 1–10 on your paper. Explain how each of the following words is related to history. Your answers should be one or two sentences long. You will need to use a dictionary or an encyclopedia.

1. sandwich
2. sideburn
3. doily
4. Dixie
5. alphabet
6. July
7. August
8. jingoism
9. John Hancock
10. diesel

# BUILDING YOUR VOCABULARY

## 70
## Synonyms for Exact Meaning

Because English has borrowed words from so many sources, it has a great store of synonyms. Speakers and writers who take advantage of that store choose words that are exact and vivid. Those people who do not use synonyms tend to overuse the same inexact, colorless words and expressions. They speak and write as though they are verbally bankrupt, as indeed they may be.

Exploring synonyms is an excellent way to expand your vocabulary and to sharpen your use of language. **Synonyms** are words with the same or similar meanings. In English, however, we have very few exact synonyms. We cannot simply interchange words. Two words may share the same basic meaning (or **denotation**) but have different shades of meaning (or **connotations**).

Consider the variety of adjectives available to people who want to describe the feeling of happiness. *Joyful, glad, cheerful,* and *content* are only a few of them. Maybe you can think of others. All of these words share a *denotative* meaning—"feeling happy." They are not exact synonyms, though, and so cannot simply be interchanged. Selection of the most exact and appropriate word requires careful attention to the shades of meaning that each possesses. Each of the adjectives—*joyful, glad, cheerful,* and *content*—has a pleasant connotation. Some of them, however, are stronger than others. Also, they are used to describe different kinds of pleasant feelings. For example, *cheerful* connotes a light, spirited mood or disposition. *Glad* is neither a mood nor a disposition. A person is glad *about* something. Glad means to be pleased or satisfied about something. A cheerful person and a glad person may both feel happy, but the two words are not *exact* synonyms.

Selecting the right word at the right time is no easy task. It requires that you have a personal store of words—a vocabulary—from which to choose just the word that you need. It also requires knowledge of the connotations of each word. Two kinds of books can assist your efforts to build your vocabulary and improve exactness. Dictionaries are one of them. The thorough definitions and brief lists of synonyms and antonyms in dictionaries can be very helpful.

The thesaurus may be less familiar to you. A **thesaurus** is a dictionary of synonyms and antonyms. It contains no definitions—just an alphabetical list of main entry words and a series of synonyms and antonyms for each entry word. Some editions also compare the connotations of the synonyms or antonyms that are related to each main entry word. Such a thesaurus is especially helpful.

317

# EXERCISES

**A. Choosing exact synonyms** The words in each of the following sets share a basic meaning but are not interchangeable. Write the numbers 1–12 on your paper. Write the synonyms which most appropriately complete the sentences. Use a dictionary if necessary.

a. *patient, patron, customer, client*

1. The lawyer had lunch with an important _____.
2. The clerk waited on a dissatisfied _____.
3. A nervous _____ sat in the dentist's office.
4. The city's symphony orchestra counts on the financial support it gets from a wealthy _____ like Ms. Lee.

b. *remainder, remnant, vestige, residue*

5. Paul spent his savings by October and was poverty-stricken for the _____ of the year.
6. When the oily water receded, the _____ destroyed the beauty of the beach.
7. You can turn a _____ of material into a fashionable blouse.
8. Each line on the old lady's face was a _____ of many smiles.

c. *inordinate, extravagant, redundant, exorbitant*

9. Don't you think $3,000 is a(n) _____ price to pay for King Kong's autograph?
10. Alex spends a(n) _____ amount of time working on his car.
11. Ms. Greenburg circled "my brother he" on Trina's paper and wrote "_____" in the margin.
12. Among my mother's _____ gifts to her friends are a new Rolls Royce and a $3,000 autograph of King Kong.

**B. Using appropriate synonyms** Write the numbers 1–20 on your paper. Write sentences that show the exact use of each word in the following series. (See the sentences in Exercise A for examples.) Use a dictionary if you need help.

a. detect, discover, invent
b. journey, voyage, excursion
c. fame, notoriety, reputation
d. patrol, spy, watch, scout
e. enemy, rival, opponent, competitor
f. antique, obsolete, ancient

**C. Replacing general and colorless verbs** Write the numbers 1–10 on your paper. Replace the italicized word in each of the following sentences with a more vivid one. Use a dictionary or a thesaurus if you need help.

1. When Bigfoot arrived, we *left*.
2. The frightened boy *held* his grandmother's hand.
3. "That's not right," *said* the geometry teacher.
4. The champion runner *looked* at his young challenger.
5. The mouse *ran* across the barn floor, the cat *running* right behind it.
6. Just after the last bell rang, students *came* out of the school's front door.
7. "Look what I have for lunch today," *said* Maria after looking into her lunch sack.
8. The wounded deer *moved* to the clearing before it fell.
9. Luanne and Tom constantly *argued* about unimportant matters.
10. Helena *drove quickly* to work when she discovered that she was thirty minutes late.

# 71

## Everyday Abbreviations

Abbreviations are handy shortcuts. They save time and space. But because they *are* shortcuts and therefore imply haste to some readers, they are generally more appropriate for lists or friendly letters than for school themes or business correspondence.

Over the years the number of conventional abbreviations accepted and used by American writers has grown. Dictionaries now list several hundred. Some abbreviations, such as A.D. and B.C., are so well-known that they are even used in speech.

Sometimes two or more abbreviations for the same word exist until usage favors one and the others are forgotten. Occasionally writers continue to use more than one abbreviation for the same word. Unfortunately, one abbreviation may refer to two or more different words. The abbreviation *ft.* refers to *foot, feet,* and *fort.*

Abbreviations must be learned. They do not follow any single system of formation, so guessing at the spelling of an unfamiliar abbreviation can be risky. For instance, who could guess that the abbreviation for *pages* and *pianissimo* (a music term) would be identical—and that it would be *pp.,* which seems to make no sense at all. When referring to *pianissimo,* however, *pp* is not followed by a period. Something else to learn, then, is which abbreviations require periods.

It would be impossible to learn *all* the abbreviations used in English. However, there are three special kinds of abbreviations that you will see nearly every day, and they should be learned: Latin abbreviations, metric abbreviations, and postal abbreviations.

**Latin abbreviations**  An especially interesting fact about the abbreviations in this set is that, unlike other abbreviations, most of them are commonly found only in quite formal, legal, and scientific writing. In informal writing, their English equivalents are usually used.

## LATIN ABBREVIATIONS

| Abbreviation | Latin Words | Meaning |
|---|---|---|
| A.D. | anno domini | in the year of our Lord |
| A.M. | ante meridiem | midnight to noon |
| ca., c. | circa | about, approximately |
| cf. | confer | compare |
| e.g. | exempli gratia | for example |
| et al. | et alii | and others (people) |
| etc. | et cetera | and so forth |
| i.e. | id est | that is |
| P.M. | post meridiem | noon to midnight |
| pro tem. | pro tempore | for the time being |
| P.S. | post scriptum | postscript |
| vs. | versus | against |

Notice that some words in these abbreviations are not followed by periods. That is because those particular words are not abbreviated. In Latin, *et* means "and"; *id* means "that"; and *pro* means "for." Also observe the spelling of *versus* (not *verses*) and *etc.* (not *ect.*). Be careful not to overuse *etc.*

Metric abbreviations   During the past few years you have probably become increasingly aware of the metric system. You have studied it in mathematics classes and have observed that metric measurements often appear next to more familiar expressions such as feet or pounds. Before long, it will be as important to know *cm* and *mg* as it is to know *ft.* and *lb.* now.

321

Postal abbreviations   When the American postal authorities introduced the Zip Code in the 1960s, they also introduced a new set of abbreviations for the states. The new abbreviations were intended to standardize a system that had sometimes become confusing. Before the new abbreviations were introduced, California had three: *Ca., Cal., Calif.*

The new set consists of a two-letter abbreviation for each state. All letters are capitals. The set uses no periods.

## POSTAL ABBREVIATIONS

| | | |
|---|---|---|
| Alabama (AL) | Louisiana (LA) | Ohio (OH) |
| Alaska (AK) | Maine (ME) | Oklahoma (OK) |
| Arizona (AZ) | Maryland (MD) | Oregon (OR) |
| Arkansas (AR) | Massachusetts (MA) | Pennsylvania (PA) |
| California (CA) | Michigan (MI) | Rhode Island (RI) |
| Colorado (CO) | Minnesota (MN) | South Carolina (SC) |
| Connecticut (CT) | Mississippi (MS) | South Dakota (SD) |
| Delaware (DE) | Missouri (MO) | Tennessee (TN) |
| Florida (FL) | Montana (MT) | Texas (TX) |
| Georgia (GA) | Nebraska (NE) | Utah (UT) |
| Hawaii (HI) | Nevada (NV) | Vermont (VT) |
| Idaho (ID) | New Hampshire (NH) | Virginia (VA) |
| Illinois (IL) | New Jersey (NJ) | Washington (WA) |
| Indiana (IN) | New Mexico (NM) | West Virginia (WV) |
| Iowa (IA) | New York (NY) | Wisconsin (WI) |
| Kansas (KS) | North Carolina (NC) | Wyoming (WY) |
| Kentucky (KY) | North Dakota (ND) | District of Columbia (DC) |

## EXERCISES

**A. Using Latin abbreviations**   Write the numbers 1–5 on your paper. Copy from the chart of Latin abbreviations those abbreviations that complete the following sentences. Remember to put periods where they belong.

1. It will be the Lions _____ the Rams in the final game on Friday.
2. Many students prepare for a vocation by taking courses in typing, shorthand, auto mechanics, _____ .

3. The coronation of King Aloysius (_____ A.D. 828) was a hysterical historical event.
4. This year's senior class includes dozens of interesting people, _____, Philip Laporte, Lucia Ramos, and Sarah Burns.
5. Whether you arrive at 5:00 _____ or 5:00 _____ makes quite a bit of difference to me.

**B. Completing a metric abbreviations chart** Using the clues already given in the following chart, complete the list of metric abbreviations. Write the numbers 1–20 on your paper. Next to each number, copy both the appropriate metric term and its abbreviation. Do not put periods after metric abbreviations.

### METRIC ABBREVIATIONS

#### Meaningful Prefixes

kilo = 1000         deci = 1/10
hecto = 100         centi = 1/100
deka = 10           milli = 1/1000

#### Linear Measure

1. kilometer    km
2. hectometer   _____
3. dekameter    dkm
4. meter        _____ (39.37 inches)
5. decimeter    _____
6. centimeter   _____

#### Liquid Measure

7. kiloliter    _____
8. hectoliter   _____
9. dekaliter    dkl
10. liter       _____
11. deciliter   dl
12. centiliter  _____

#### Weights

13. ton         MT or t
14. quintal     q
15. kilogram    _____
16. hectogram   _____
17. dekagram    _____
18. gram        g (or gr) (0.035 ounces)
19. decigram    dg
20. centigram   _____

**C. Identifying abbreviations** Write the numbers 1–25 on your paper. Write out the word or phrase to which each of the following abbreviations refers. Several abbreviations refer to more than one word. Notice that some abbreviations do not require periods. Use a dictionary to check your answers.

1. asst.
2. asstd.
3. chg.
4. ppd.
5. bibliog.
6. A.W.O.L.
7. MPG
8. R.S.V.P.
9. pseud.
10. pp.
11. ff.
12. RPM
13. bldg.
14. I.Q. or IQ
15. lv.
16. N.W. or NW
17. R.B.I. or RBI
18. ar.
19. syn.
20. no.
21. min.
22. EST
23. tbsp.
24. pk.
25. RD

**D. Classifying postal abbreviations** Draw three columns on your paper. Make three lists of states and their abbreviations:

LIST A: States whose abbreviations consist of the first two letters of the state's name (Alabama—AL);
LIST B: States whose abbreviations consist of the initial letters of two-word state names (New York—NY);
LIST C: States whose abbreviations follow neither of the patterns evident in the other two lists (Alaska—AK, and twenty others).

Remember to use only capital letters and no periods.

# 72

# Testing Your Vocabulary

Whether you plan to enter a college, a vocational school, the armed forces, or civil service, you will probably take several standardized tests during the next few years. Such tests are designed to measure what you already know (your achievement) or what activity you may be best suited for (your aptitude).

Many standardized tests which propose to measure general achievement or aptitude include at least one section on vocabulary, sometimes several sections. It is thought that people's knowledge of words is closely related to their abilities to think and read.

Vocabulary tests are common in almost all college entrance examinations, including the Scholastic Aptitude Test (SAT) and the American College Testing Program (ACT), because they are thought to be helpful in predicting students' success in whatever programs of study they want to enter.

While you cannot anticipate *which* questions will turn up on standardized tests, you can become familiar with the *kinds* of questions often asked on such tests.

## Types of Vocabulary Tests

Synonyms and antonyms   Probably the most common type of vocabulary test is the kind in which you select from four or five choices the word whose meaning is closest to the meaning of a key word.

EXAMPLE 1    *bestial:*   A. tame   B. stubborn   C. savage   D. favorite   E. none of these

Consider all of the possibilities before you answer. The correct answer to Example 1 is *savage* (the word *bestial* is related to *beast*). Note that the other choices—appropriately called **distractors** by testmakers—include an antonym (*tame*) and a likely choice for someone who does not know the real meaning of *bestial* but whose guess is based on the word's first four letters (*best*).

Tests which measure knowledge of **antonyms**, or words having opposite meanings, are similarly designed and require the same attention to distractors. In antonym tests, distractors often include synonyms or near-synonyms, so examine your choices with care.

EXAMPLE 2   *archaic:*   A. new   B. ancient   C. friendly   D. vicious   E. none of these

In Example 2 *archaic* and *ancient* are near-synonyms since both mean "very old." *New* has an opposite meaning and is therefore the correct answer.

Word analogies   Many vocabulary sections of standardized tests now contain word analogies. An analogy is a similarity.

EXAMPLE 3   *duet : quartet ::*   A. violin : strings   B. pair : foursome   C. trio : orchestra   D. stockings : trousers

As you can see, such items test not only your knowledge of the meanings of words but also your ability to see their relationships to other words.

Example 3, correctly answered, should be read in this manner: "*Duet* is to *quartet* as *pair* is to *foursome*." Both a duet and a pair contain two members; both a quartet and a foursome contain four members. The other choices do not bear as close a relationship to *duet : quartet* as does choice B. Two of the distractors (A and C) refer to music, as do both *duet* and *quartet*. The other choice, D, allows a *duet / stockings* relationship, since a pair of stockings, like a duet, contains two members. *Trousers* does not have the same relationship to *stockings* as *quartet* does to *duet*, however, so choice D must be eliminated.

Here are some types of relationships that are commonly found in word analogy tests:

    *word : synonym* :: clumsy : awkward :: ready : prepared
    *word : antonym* :: cowardly : brave :: poor : rich
    *part : whole* :: star : constellation :: member : union
    *producer : product* :: poet : verse :: composer : symphony
    *cause : effect* :: fear : shaking :: enjoyment : smiling
    *general : specific* :: book : novel :: dessert : cake

*object : act* :: scissors : cut :: brush : paint
*symbol : object* :: torch : liberty :: scales : justice

Words in context   Another kind of vocabulary test asks you to select the word which best completes a sentence. Usually four or five choices are given. You must use context clues in the sentence and your knowledge of the meanings of the word choices in order to select the right answer. Often the distractors include words that are near–synonyms with different connotations. You must select the one whose connotation best fits the sentence given.

EXAMPLE 4   Thirty dollars is a(n) _____ price to pay for a dress that I could make for $3.00.
A. minimal   B. obnoxious   C. exorbitant   D. redundant

A variation of this type of test requires that you choose the pair of words that best completes the two blanks in a sentence.

EXAMPLE 5   To be _____ is to be _____.
A. indignant—selfish
B. credible—believable
C. affluent—talkative
D. affable—untruthful

*Exorbitant* is the correct response for Example 4. *Credible* and *believable* correctly complete Example 5.

The exercises that follow will give you practice with the main types of vocabulary tests. Most of the words that you need to know in order to answer the questions in these exercises were introduced in previous parts of this unit.

# EXERCISES

A. Selecting synonyms   Write the numbers 1–10 on your paper. Write the letter of the word or phrase that has a similar meaning to the italicized word. Use your dictionary.

1. *labyrinth:*     A. river    B. laboratory   C. maze     D. monster
2. *redundant:*    A. excessive   B. spiritual   C. saddened   D. feverish
3. *proponent:*    A. enemy    B. official    C. advocate   D. parent
4. *circumvent:*   A. avoid    B. enlarge    C. twirl    D. puzzle
5. *lethal:*       A. impossible  B. soothing   C. difficult  D. deadly

6. *capitulate:*   A. exert leadership   B. cut off one's head   C. surrender   D. question the decision of a superior
7. *incredulous:*   A. unbelieving   B. unfair   C. poverty-stricken   D. lacking emotion
8. *magnanimous:*   A. generous   B. overweight   C. spiritual   D. profitable
9. *posthumous:*   A. happy   B. after death   C. simple   D. large
10. *verbose:*   A. true   B. real   C. wordy   D. profane

**B. Selecting antonyms**   Write the numbers 1–10 on your paper. Write the letter of the word or phrase that means the opposite of the italicized word.

1. *misanthrope:*   A. humanitarian   B. grouch   C. scholar   D. one who studies the history of humankind
2. *martial:*   A. peaceable   B. musical   C. unmarried   D. unfriendly
3. *somnolent:*   A. alert   B. serious   C. having secret knowledge   D. musical
4. *arduous:*   A. impossible   B. easy   C. infatuated   D. musical
5. *lucrative:*   A. risky   B. cave-like   C. unprofitable   D. very dark
6. *extemporaneous:*   A. carefully planned   B. after death   C. before birth   D. cautious
7. *superfluous:*   A. wealthy   B. poorly educated   C. useless   D. necessary
8. *verbose:*   A. mathematical   B. concise   C. redundant   D. quiet
9. *regular:*   A. normal   B. light   C. irregular   D. pompous
10. *evident:*   A. plain   B. clear   C. common   D. abstruse

**C. Completing word analogies**   Write the numbers 1–10 on your paper. Write the letter of the pair of words that best expresses the same relationship as that of the words in italics.

1. *never : always* ::   A. occasionally : sometimes   B. constantly : occasionally   C. frequently : always   D. rarely : constantly
2. *immigrant : emigrant* ::   A. industrial : agricultural   B. mobile : stationary   C. entrance : exit   D. lion : fierce
3. *dwarf : lilliputian* ::   A. elephant : rhinocerous   B. gnat : miniscule   C. giant : strong   D. lion : fierce
4. *etymology : word* ::   A. diagnosis : disease   B. hour : minute   C. biography : person   D. paragraph : sentence
5. *inscription : plaque* ::   A. monogram : shirt   B. signature : pen   C. initials : name   D. pen : paper
6. *gigantic : gargantuan* ::   A. large : small   B. giant : midget   C. obsolete : archaic   D. retrospect : future

7. *pseudo : psycho* :: A. false : mind  B. earth : moon  C. heart : lung  D. coal : moon
8. *umbrella: parasol* :: A. star : sun  B. protection : sun  C. umbrella : rain  D. eye : nose
9. *captain : principal* :: A. right : eye  B. ship : plane  C. prune : goat  D. crew : teachers
10. *thesaurus : lexicon* :: A. library : books  B. see : saw  C. life : death  D. press : cider

**D. Completing sentences**  Write the numbers 1–5 on your paper. Write the letter of the word or words that best complete each sentence.

1. The first syllable in the word *submarine* is its _____.
   A. prefix  B. suffix  C. root  D. derivative
2. In an attempt to hide her identity, the young author used the _____ with which we are now all familiar.
   A. alias  B. nomenclature  C. pseudonym  D. nominal
3. Having put his mother-in-law, two aunts, and four cousins on the city's payroll, the mayor was accused of _____.
   A. abdication  B. ambivalence  C. larceny  D. nepotism
4. The _____ of *dangerous* is *safe*.
   A. synonym  B. homonym  C. pseudonym  D. antonym
5. Though the plant lies _____ throughout the winter, it blooms every spring.
   A. dormant  B. somnolent  C. obsolete  D. nocturnal

# REVIEWING VOCABULARY

**A. Understanding the origin and nature of language** Write the numbers 1-20 on your paper. Following are some statements about language. If a statement is true, write *T* next to the appropriate number on your paper. If a statement is false, write *F*.

1. Approximately three thousand languages are spoken throughout the world.
2. Knowledge of language is instinctive.
3. Language began when people imitated the sounds of animals.
4. English and German have a common parent language.
5. English and Russian have a common parent language.
6. Latin is the parent language of all modern languages.
7. Some primitive cultures have no language.
8. Writing is an earlier form of communication than speech.
9. Every language has some kind of writing system.
10. English is the world's most widely spoken language.
11. The word for the sound a cat makes is the same in all languages.
12. New words are not used much until they appear in dictionaries.
13. It is unlikely that *mbomgnubp* is an English word.
14. People must work harder to learn Chinese than to learn English.
15. Languages with large vocabularies are better than languages with smaller vocabularies.
16. The voice of a stranger at the other end of a telephone line can convey information about the speaker even if the listener cannot understand the speaker's language.
17. A nod is a universal gesture meaning "yes."
18. A word is a symbol.
19. Written language contains several systems.
20. It takes at least two people to begin a new language.

**B. Using Latin roots** Write the numbers 1-5 on your paper. Using the italicized word in each sentence as a context clue, write the words which will correctly fit in the blanks.

1. Before B. J. let the *centipede* go, she counted its _____ legs.
2. People leave a tip or *gratuity* for a waiter when they are _____ with the service.
3. The *verbose* gentleman talked all the time, using _____ unsparingly.
4. The *legality* of your claim has yet to be proven. The _____ is unclear on the matter.
5. Aunt Edie is a *magnanimous* woman who forgives those who insult her. She has a _____ heart.

**C. Using prefixes as clues to the meanings of words** Write the numbers 1-15 on your paper. Using the prefix in the italicized word as a clue, choose the word that correctly completes the sentence.

1. One who *abstains* from smoking smokes _____ cigarettes.
    a) more, b) safer, c) no
2. An *antonym* for the word success is _____.
    a) the word *failure,* b) the word *wealth,* c) the word *victory*
3. Ms. Dai's *biennial* visits to Hawaii occurred _____.
    a) every year, b) every two years, c) whenever Ms. Dai received a bonus check
4. *Concurrent* meetings take place _____.
    a) one after the other, b) on different days, c) at the same time
5. In screwing the catsup bottle cap off *counterclockwise,* you will turn it _____.
    a) to the right, b) to the left, c) like a clock
6. If the supply of coffee is *depleted,* there is _____ of it than there was before.
    a) a little more, b) less, c) a lot more
7. To *dismount* a horse is _____.
    a) to get off of it, b) to get on it, c) to take its saddle off
8. British *emigrants* are people who _____.
    a) move to England, b) move within England, c) move out of England
9. *Interscholastic* games involve teams from _____.
    a) the same school, b) two or more schools, c) large schools
10. A *posthumous* prize is one given _____.
    a) after the winner has died, b) after the winner has told a joke, c) on the winner's twenty-fifth birthday

11. The check he wrote on January 14, 1980, he *postdated* to _____.
    a) January 10, 1980, b) January 17, 1980, c) January 17, 1979
12. A *premonition* is most like _____.
    a) a punishment, b) a warning, c) a reward
13. A book's *preface* serves as _____.
    a) an introduction, b) its concluding chapter, c) its index
14. If I give you a ride to work and you *reciprocate,* you _____.
    a) thank me, b) give me a ride to work, c) give me a dollar
15. The category of *semiskilled* workers includes _____.
    a) the industrial engineer, b) the factory's nurse, c) the janitor

**D. Using suffixes to form adjectives** Write the numbers 1–15 on your paper. Form an adjective that completes each of the following sentences. Add the appropriate adjective-forming suffix to the root which appears in parentheses at the end of the sentence. Use these suffixes: -able, -al, -ary, -ful, -ible, -ic, -ive, -less, -ous, -y.

1. The baby's _____ sounds soon grew into her first word, "pizza." (imitate)
2. Lita's English teacher praised Lita for her _____ spelling. (flaw)
3. Lying in his pup tent, Sol longed for his _____ bedroom. (space)
4. Andy had a collection of four-leaf clovers, but he wasn't very _____. (luck)
5. We were barely off the ground when the flight attendant served _____ soft drinks. (compliment)
6. Backing over the garbage can while driving was a perfect ending to Del's _____ day. (event)
7. "Someday you will thank me for making you do this," she said in a _____ voice. (prophet)
8. Rapidly changing _____ conditions forced postponement of our flight. (atmosphere)
9. "Where did you get such a _____ thirst for knowledge about geometry?" asked Ms. Begay. (quench)
10. My sister is a _____ engineer. (profession)
11. We all have only _____ knowledge of the brain. (fragment)
12. Not only was his story _____, but he took five mintues to tell it. (point)
13. Their _____ relationship was ended with an argument. (harmony)
14. "Reading is indeed a _____ pastime," said the winner of the quiz show. (profit)
15. Queen Elizabeth looks so regal in her _____ robes. (ceremony)

Reading and Study Skills    334
Writing Reports and Essays    355
Mechanics of Writing    375
Using Your Library    399
Effective Speaking    411
English for Business    423

# SKILLS HANDBOOK

# READING AND STUDY SKILLS

## 1 Developing Your Reading Skills

Being able to read well can shorten your study hours and make the process of learning more pleasurable. If you take the time to enrich your reading skills, you will become a better student.

### 1.1 READING FOR A PURPOSE

You read for many reasons. Knowing *why* you are reading something is just as important as knowing *what* you are reading. Your reading style is determined by your purpose for reading. You may read a novel slowly for entertainment or skim it quickly for information. You may have to find exact answers to specific questions, or you may be reading for a general understanding of a subject.

**Concentrate** To complete your reading assignment in the shortest possible time, you must give it your full concentration. Avoid whatever distracts you—television, music, or conversation. Become involved in what you are reading. You should always be asking yourself (1) what the author wants to show, and (2) how new information is related to what you have read.

**Remember what you read** When reading for an assignment, you should remember the information you are reading. Following are four techniques to help you remember what you read.

1. Read the assignment in as few sittings as possible. Frequent interruptions ruin concentration.
2. Take notes as you read.
3. Review those notes before you pick up the book again.
4. Read with a purpose in mind so that you will not be satisfied until you have complete understanding of what you have read.

### 1.2 FINDING THE MAIN IDEAS

A good reader can spot essential thoughts quickly and separate them from supporting details. The place to look for important ideas or points depends on the kind and size of material you are reading.

**In a book** To find the main topics covered in a book, look at the table of contents. The **table of contents** in the front of a book lists all the chapters and major subdivisions in the book. The **index** in the back of a book gives a more specific breakdown of the book's content.

**In a chapter** Important ideas in chapters are often pointed out by the use of short titles called **subheads**. In addition, many books print important ideas in heavy type called **boldface** or in slanted type called **italics**.

**In an article or essay** The introductory paragraph (or paragraphs) of an article or essay states the main point the writer intends to prove or show. The rest of the article expands that **thesis statement**. Subheads and **transitional words** such as *first, second, on the other hand,* and *therefore* help you follow the order of ideas.

**In a paragraph** Each paragraph normally contains a **topic sentence**, which is the one sentence in the paragraph that ties all the ideas in the paragraph together. In newspapers and magazines, a single topic sentence may express the main idea of several short paragraphs if the paragraphs all contain very closely related information. Although the topic sentence usually appears at the start of the paragraph as in the following excerpt, it may also be placed at the end or in the middle of the paragraph.

**Topic Sentence**

*While probably everyone runs short of cash sometimes, keeping to a budget can help you organize your spending so that you will have enough money for the week.* *To set up a budget, you must list all your expenses for the week. Plan to spend only a certain amount of money, no more, no less, on any one item. A budget will help you cut down on impulse buying, which causes many people to say on Friday night, "I thought I had more than two dollars left."*

## 1.3 DRAWING CONCLUSIONS

As an actively involved reader you should always be asking yourself what the writer means and how all the writer's ideas are related to each other. Very often, the written words alone will not answer your questions. You will have to "read between the lines" and think through the author's statements to draw conclusions about what you have read.

**Think over what you have read** The best readers read ideas, not just words. You should not be satisfied until you feel you understand all the ideas in a reading passage. If necessary, reread a selection that does not make sense to you.

**Look for the author's bias** It is probably impossible for a writer to be absolutely objective. Few authors write unless they believe they have something to say. A writer's opinion or bias can be obvious. Phrases such as *rude tourists and over-sized buildings* clearly show the writer's bias.

Bias can be more subtle, or hidden, though. Sometimes writers use emotional arguments or intentionally leave out information. As a reader, you should always be aware of the writer's attitude toward the subject.

## 1.4 INCREASING YOUR READING SPEED

Your reading speed should only be fast enough to allow you to understand the ideas of the reading passage. Following are some ways to increase your reading speed and your comprehension.

**Vary your speed** You should vary your reading speed according to the difficulty of the material and your purpose in reading it. Textbooks in science and history, for example, need to be read slowly because each new sentence builds on your understanding of previous information. Reading a novel or a newspaper for entertainment allows for much faster reading.

**Practice reading** When you read too slowly, your mind has time to wander and you lose the writer's train of thought. Both saying the words to yourself and moving your lips slow you down. Practice reading whole phrases rather than individual words. Force yourself to read each line of print with as few eye movements as possible. Avoid backtracking. The need for backtracking means that you are distracted or you are reading too fast.

**Time yourself** To find your reading speed, read a text for precisely ten minutes. Read it as quickly as you can while still understanding what you are reading. Then multiply the number of lines you have read by the average number of words in a line. Divide the results by ten. The final figure is the number of words per minute you read. Use that figure to estimate how long other similar assignments will take for you to read.

**1.4a  Skimming**  An excellent speed-reading technique is skimming. **Skimming** means rapid reading to find out a passage's major ideas or purpose. Boldface and italic type, subheads, and topic sentences will help you locate the main ideas of the passage. When skimming, pay no attention to minor or supporting details.

**1.4b  Scanning**  The most rapid form of reading is **scanning**. It is used to locate specific information quickly. To scan, run your eyes down the page until you find precisely what you are seeking: the height of Mt. Shasta or the population of Brazil, for example. If scanning is done correctly, you will not remember anything except the specific fact you were after.

# EXERCISES

**A. Identifying the main idea**  Read the following passage. Then do the assignments that come after it.

>   P. T. Barnum (1810–1891), whose name survives in the Ringling Brothers and Barnum and Bailey Circus, "The Greatest Show on Earth," was an expert in the art of advertising. Barnum often used his advertising talents in clever ways to get people to do what he wanted.
>   Once, for example, when Barnum was running a small museum in New York during the 1840s, he realized that the crowds were not moving through his exhibits as quickly as he would have liked. Barnum instructed a sign painter to print the words, "To the Egress," on a board, and Barnum hung the sign over the door leading to the back stairs. Not knowing that egress is another word for exit, many people in the crowd said, "I haven't seen an egress before. Let's go." They soon found themselves out in the street. Barnum now had room to admit the other people who had been waiting outside for hours.

Read the following statements. Then write the one that tells the main idea of the preceding passage.

- Some people are very stupid.
- People with small vocabularies should not go to museums.
- P. T. Barnum used advertising talents to get people to do what he wanted.
- An egress is an exit, not an animal.

**B. Finding an author's bias**  Read the following passage carefully. Then write the answers to the items that come after it.

>   Narrow-minded, stubborn townspeople have blocked the state's attempt to route a modern superhighway through their town. Community leaders have squawked that the highway would bring progress to their gray, sleepy town. They prefer to stay isolated from this ever shrinking world and live out their days in a childish fairy tale land.

1. The author's bias in the preceding passage is
    - against progress
    - against superhighways
    - against towns that reject the idea of progress
    - none of these

2. Which of the following phrases does *not* show the writer's bias?
   - community leaders have *squawked*
   - *narrow-minded, stubborn* townspeople
   - a childish *fairy tale* land
   - *gray, sleepy* town
   - none of these

3. The author's bias is
   - subtle
   - obvious
   - hidden
   - none of these

**C. Timing your reading** Read the following passage and answer the items that come after it. To find your reading speed, divide 88 by the number of minutes it took you to read the passage.

> A major event in the day of a black rhinoceros is wallowing. In the rainy season the wallows may be seen all over the animal's home range; they are often old dust beds that have filled with rainwater. The wallowing animal thoroughly smears itself with mud; it rolls to one side, stands, then rolls on its other side. In this way the animal attempts to protect itself from the numerous biting flies and insects that feed on its hide. Dry wallowing in dust may serve a similar purpose.
> —John Goddard

1. The black rhinoceros wallows in mud and dust
   - to heal cuts in its hide
   - only when it is angry
   - to frighten hunters
   - to protect itself from insect bites
   - none of these

2. The purpose of the passage is
   - to prove that the rhinoceros is an endangered species
   - to describe the animal's eating habits
   - to explain a major event in the animal's day
   - to describe the animal's physical features
   - none of these

# 2
# Taking Notes on What You Read

Taking notes on what you read is a good study habit. Your notes should include outlines and summaries of important chapters, class notes taken in outline form, and all notes handed out by your teachers.

You should have a separate notebook for each of your school subjects. Or, at minimum, use a ring binder divided into sections. A notebook is of little use to you, however, if everything is scattered around inside. Organize it so that you can find things quickly and efficiently. Keeping related material such as vocabulary and class notes together simplifies studying for tests.

## 2.1 WRITING A STUDY OUTLINE

Outline form is useful in taking class notes and notes on reading assignments. An **outline** is a plan that organizes ideas into main topics and subtopics. It includes in very brief form all the facts used to support or prove a particular point.

Look at the following study outline. Roman numerals indicate main topics. Letters of the alphabet and numbers indicate subtopics.

**OUR DEPENDENCE ON MACHINES**

    I. On the Job
       A. To do heavy labor
          1. Power tools
          2. Semi-skilled workers
       B. To speed up work
          1. Production line
          2. Automatic machinery

   II. For Pleasure
       A. For entertainment
          1. TV and stereo
          2. Hobby supplies
             a. Photography
             b. Woodworking
       B. For travel
          1. Car
          2. Bicycle
          3. Train

## 2.2 JOTTING DOWN NEW WORDS

A good way to increase your vocabulary is to look up the meanings of unfamiliar words and write their definitions in a special section of your notebook. You should review those words from time to time until you master them.

## 2.3 WRITING A PRÉCIS

A précis, pronounced pray-see, is a brief, accurate summary of a piece of writing. A précis should be short, rarely more than a third the length of the original passage and should be written in your own words. A précis includes only the most important ideas from a passage. Leave out examples and adjectives unless they are important to the meaning of the passage. Finally, be sure that you have stated the author's ideas accurately. Do not include any ideas of your own.

The following paragraph is a précis of the reading passage in the exercise following 1.4. Compare the précis with the original passage.

> During the rainy season, the black rhinoceros smears itself with mud as a way of protecting itself against insect bites and parasites. Dry wallowing in dust may be for the same reason.

## 2.4 REVIEWING NOTES FOR A TEST

A main reason for keeping a notebook is to use it to review for tests. If your notebook contains class notes, reading notes, and all notes given out by your teacher, you can easily prepare for an exam by studying from your notebook. Review your notes creatively. Pay special attention to whatever you do not understand. Quiz yourself frequently to be sure that you have mastered all the important information.

# EXERCISES

**A. Outlining a passage**   Read the following selection carefully. Then write a study outline of the passage.

> Not everyone needs eight hours of sleep every night. Some people need ten hours and a few can get by with as little as five hours a night. As people get older, the need for sleep progressively decreases. Many people in their 60s and 70s sleep four or five hours a night and feel rested during the day, but complain of insomnia because it is hard to spread five hours of sleep over eight or nine hours in bed. Three or four hours of tossing means insomnia regardless of how much sleep one needs.   —Arthur Frank and Stuart Frank

**B. Writing a précis**   Write a précis of the passage in Exercise A.

# 3
# Reading Graphs

A **graph** is a drawing showing information that would otherwise take many words in print to explain. Once you understand how a graph is arranged, the comparisons the graph shows can easily be understood.

To understand a graph, you must read the instructions carefully. The instructions tell how the graph is arranged and what each part is meant to show. Size and direction of lines or figures help you see the comparisons clearly.

## 3.1  BAR GRAPHS

A **bar graph** is a graph that uses bars or single lines to compare a set of figures. Bar graphs may run horizontally or vertically. The following is a vertical bar graph.

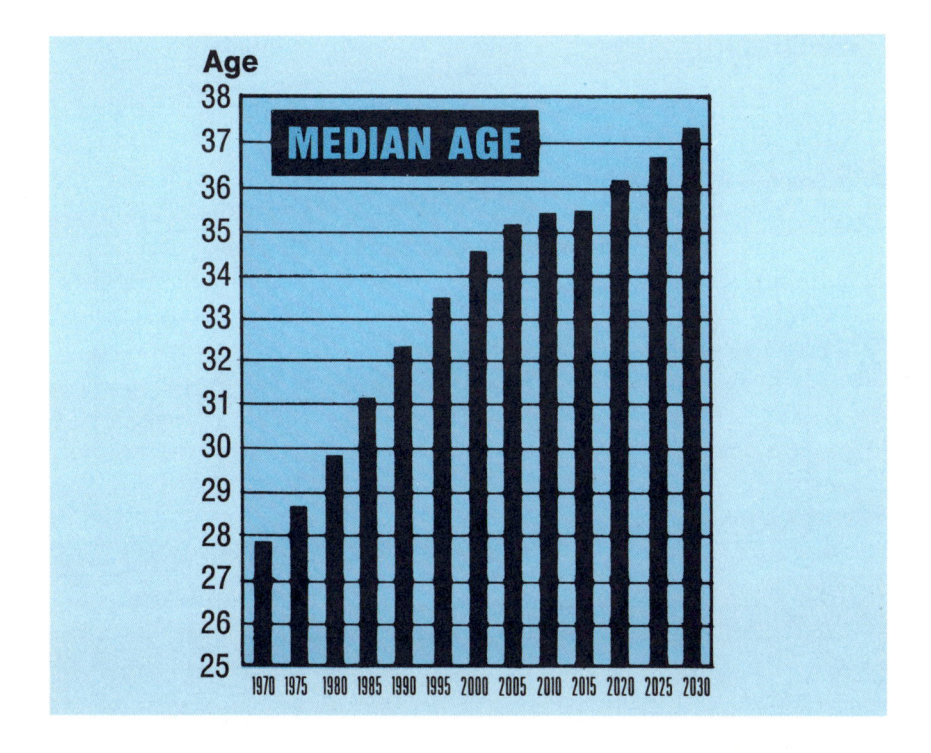

**MEDIAN AGE**

## 3.2 LINE AND CURVE GRAPHS

**Line** and **curve graphs** are both designed to show the rate of change. In reading such graphs, make sure you know the two factors that are being compared by reading the scales. The scales are usually written on the side and along the bottom of the graph. The direction of the line or curve and the amount of change relate the two scales.

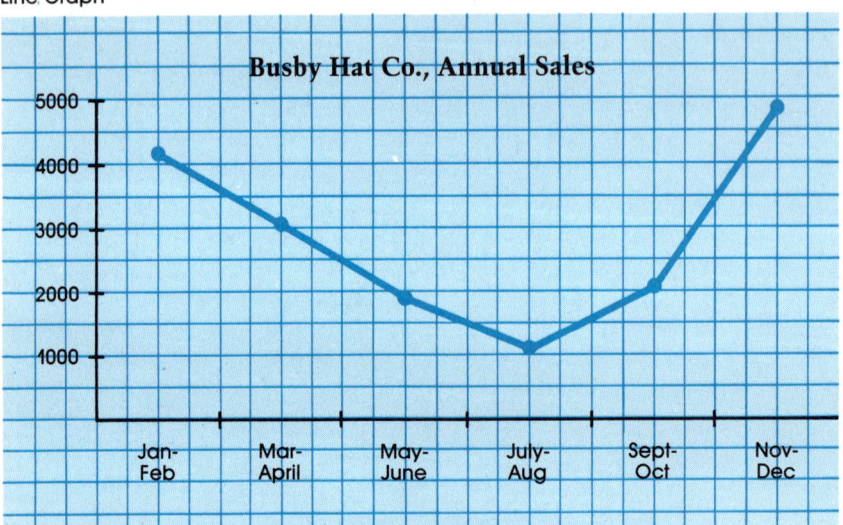

Line Graph

**Busby Hat Co., Annual Sales**

Curve Graph

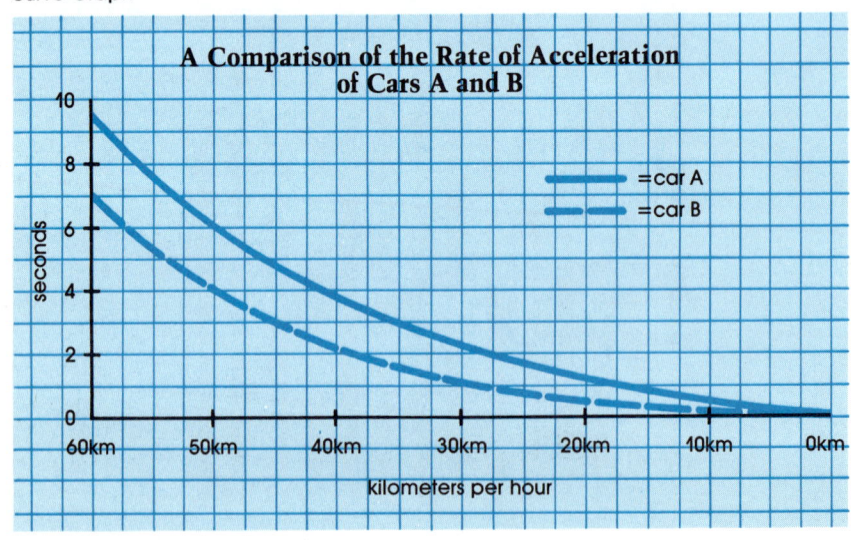

**A Comparison of the Rate of Acceleration of Cars A and B**

## 3.3 PIE AND FIGURE GRAPHS

There are two other important types of graphs, the pie graph and the figure graph. The **pie graph** shows how parts are related to the whole. For instance, a pie graph is often used to show how money is spent. A **figure graph** varies the size of an illustration to help you see the comparisons.

Pie Graph

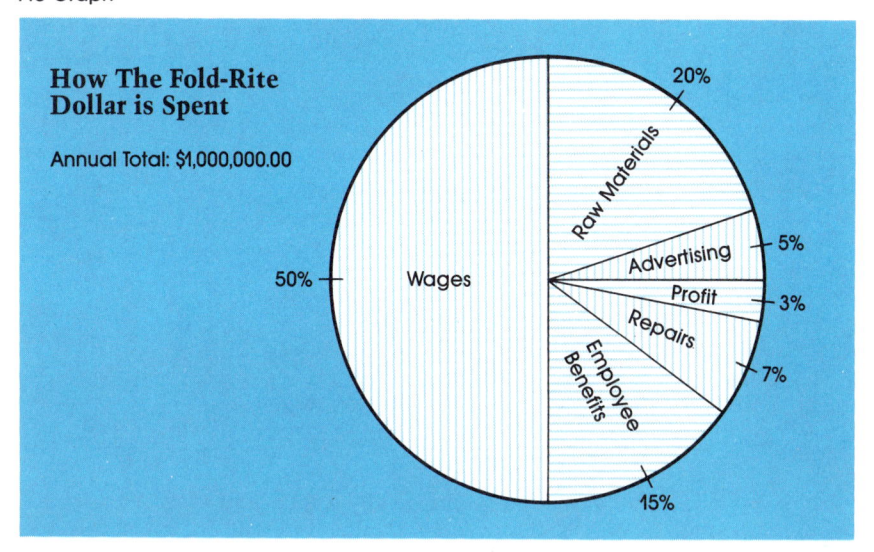

**How The Fold-Rite Dollar is Spent**

Annual Total: $1,000,000.00

- Wages 50%
- Raw Materials 20%
- Advertising 5%
- Profit 3%
- Repairs 7%
- Employee Benefits 15%

Figure Graph

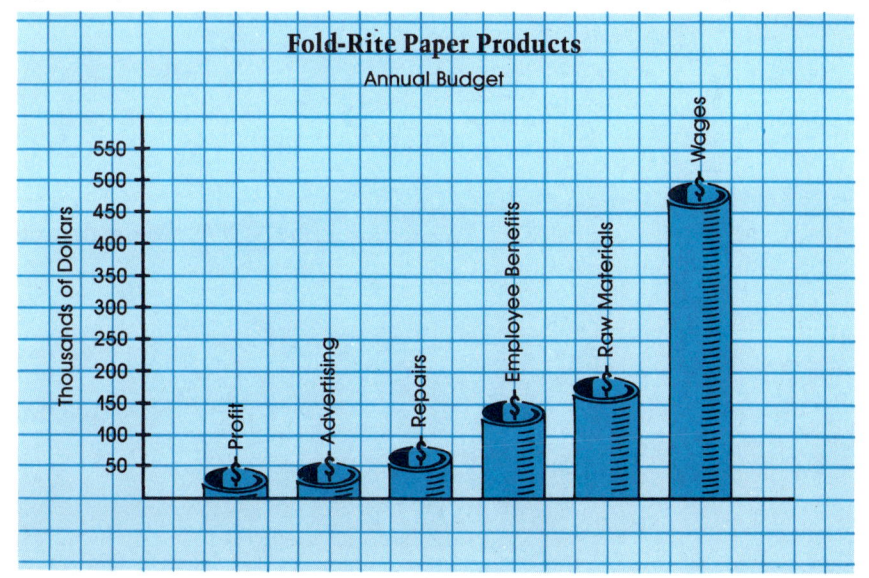

**Fold-Rite Paper Products**
Annual Budget

Thousands of Dollars: 50, 100, 150, 200, 250, 300, 350, 400, 450, 500, 550

Profit, Advertising, Repairs, Employee Benefits, Raw Materials, Wages

343

# EXERCISES

**A. Reading a bar graph** Write the numbers 1-5. Study the following graph carefully. Then answer the questions that come after it.

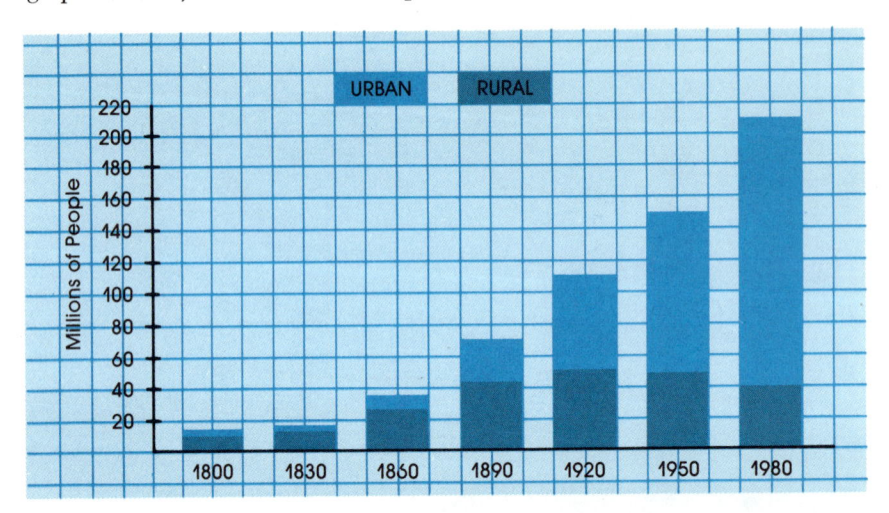

1. In which year did the population of the United States first go over 100 million?
2. What is the first year in which the number of people living in cities surpassed the number of Americans living in rural areas?
3. By 1950, roughly how many Americans lived in cities?
4. In which year between 1800 and 1965 did the greatest number of Americans live in rural areas?
5. In which century has the number of city dwellers increased the most rapidly?

**B. Understanding pie graphs** Write the numbers 1-5. Study the following graph. Then answer the questions on the next page.

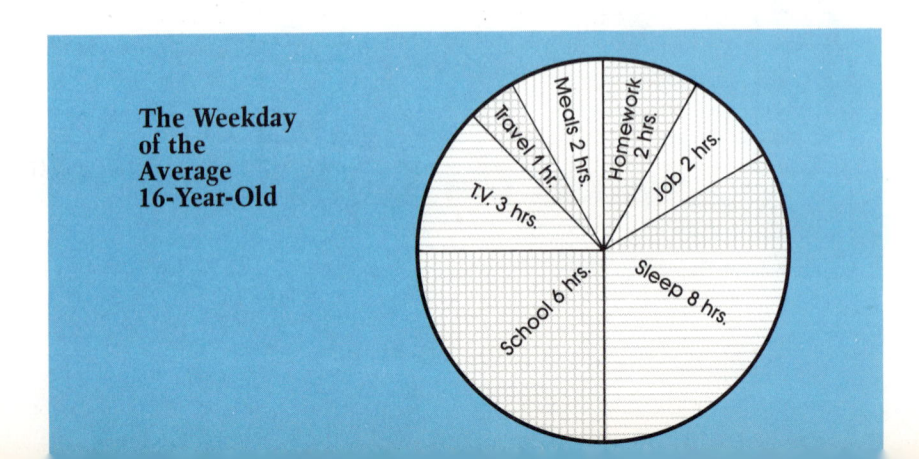

1. How much of the 16-year-old's day is spent watching television?
   a. 1/2
   b. 1/8
   c. 1/4
   d. 1/3
   e. none of these
2. How much of the average 16-year-old's day is spent sleeping?
   a. 1/2
   b. 2/3
   c. 3/4
   d. 1/3
   e. none of these
3. School-related work accounts for how much of the typical 16-year-old's day?
   a. 1/2
   b. 1/3
   c. 1/8
   d. 3/4
   e. none of these
4. Which activity occupies the least amount of an average 16-year-old's time?
   a. traveling
   b. homework
   c. meals
   d. sleep
   e. none of these
5. Which activity occupies the greatest amount of an average 16-year-old's time?
   a. traveling
   b. homework
   c. meals
   d. sleep
   e. none of these

**C. Reading a curve graph** Study the following graph carefully. Then answer the questions on the next page.

World Population Growth

1. Approximately when did the world's population reach one billion?
2. About how many years passed between the one billion mark and the two billion mark?
3. What was the world's population (approximately) in the year you were born?
4. What century shows the greatest rate of population growth?
5. About how many people will there be in the world when you are forty years old?

# 4
# Reading Newspapers

Because of television's time limits, no television news program can give you as much information about the important events of the day as a newspaper can. In addition to straight news, newspapers carry a wide variety of columns, features, and in-depth reporting on a great variety of topics. Developing a habit of reading newspapers can get you in touch with all sorts of information and entertainment.

## 4.1  SKIMMING FOR NEWS

Newspapers are designed so that the reader can get the most information in the least amount of time. Photographs and headlines draw your attention to interesting articles. Also, many articles are written so that you can pick out the most important facts in the first paragraph or two. If you then want more information, you can read on; otherwise, you can turn to another article. In fact, you can get a brief summary of news highlights just by skimming the headlines.

**4.1a  Understanding headlines**  You will frequently decide to read an article because something in the headline caught your attention. Important articles have headlines that are in large type. Less important articles have smaller headlines. Ideally, headlines introduce the contents of an article accurately and objectively. However, the choice of words in a headline can also show the editor's bias. Bias can also be shown by an editor's burying an important article in the body of the newspaper where few will read it.

You should be aware of headlines that attempt to slant a story. Notice the difference between the following headlines.

- Gasoline Prices Rise (objective)
- Gasoline Prices Soar (exaggerates the rise)
- Motorists Balk at Gas Price Rise (emphasizes drivers' opposition)

**4.1b  Reading leads**  In most news articles the first paragraph, called the **lead paragraph,** is a summary of all the important facts the article contains. The rest of the article is organized so that the most important background facts come first, followed by the less important details. Reading the summary lead gives you all the essentials. Read on only if you want further information.

## 4.2  STUDYING ISSUES

Newspapers print stories as they are happening. The best way to get a complete understanding of a news event, therefore, is to hold off judgment for a few days until the entire story is in. It is also worthwhile to get other viewpoints by reading other newspapers, newsmagazines and watching television news shows. The more sources you check, the more certain you can be that you are getting all sides of the story.

**4.2a  Comparing news stories**  If you have access to more than one daily newspaper, you can compare how each of them handles a single news item. Watch for different lengths of articles and sizes of headlines. Notice where the editors choose to place the article. If it is at the top of the page and has a large headline, the article is considered important. If it is at the bottom of the page or further back in the issue, the article is considered less newsworthy. Watch also for details the reporter chooses to stress.

**4.2b  Reading editorials and columns**  News reporting is supposed to be objective, but there is also room in the newspaper for opinion matter. An **editorial** is the statement of the newspaper's official opinion on a news event. Editorials appear on the editorial page. A **column** is written by a reporter, called a columnist, who presents a specific viewpoint. People read columnists because they want to find out how a writer they respect interprets the news. No reader should expect either editorials or columns to present anything other than a writer's opinion.

## 4.3  OTHER SECTIONS OF A NEWSPAPER

In addition to straight news stories and editorials, newspapers devote space to sports, entertainment, travel, family living, business, and other topics that will appeal to their readers. Investigate the other sections of your newspaper. Do not read only the sports and comics sections.

**4.3a  Feature stories**  Feature stories are different from straight news stories. A **feature** is written more like a composition, with an attention-getting lead, an interesting development of the topic, and a good conclusion. Features tend to cover human interest items rather than current news events. Sometimes even news items are given a feature treatment to bring out interesting or humorous aspects of the story.

**4.3b  The classified section**  If you are looking for a job or an apartment, a buyer for your stereo, or someone to sell you a boat, the place to look is the **classified ads section** of your newspaper. The advertisements are grouped in categories for easy reference and are usually written in a sort of shorthand to save space. For instance, an advertisement that says '77 *Pinto, AM/FM, A/C, snows, best offer. 321-7832*, should be read as, *A 1977 Ford Pinto with an AM/FM radio, air conditioning, and snow tires is offered for sale to the highest bidder. Call 321-7832.*

**4.3c  Departments and Sunday papers**  Sunday newspapers, the largest papers of the week, are divided into many sections. (Some of the sections may also be included in your daily paper in shorter form.) A typical list of departments in a Sunday paper includes News, Entertainment, Obituary, Business and Finance, Sports, Comics, News of the Week in Review, Real Estate, Family Living, Travel, Employment Advertising, Classified Ads, and Magazine and Book Review.

## EXERCISES

**A.  Finding bias in headlines**  Write the numbers 1-10. Read the following headlines. Then write how each shows the writer's bias.

1. Torres Unexpectedly Wins Senate Race
2. Torres Mops up Fowler In Senate Race
3. Fowler Beaten In Senate Race
4. Doctors Cite Flu Peril
5. Get Flu Shots Early, Docs Say
6. Flu Perils Elderly, Docs Warn
7. Flu Scare Returns
8. Buyers Jam New Shopping Mall
9. Only 2000 Attend Shopping Mall Opening
10. Shopping Mall Opens; Business Thrives

**B. Understanding leads** Following is a lead paragraph that could appear in your local newspaper. Decide which information in the lead readers would like to know more about. Then write the complete story. Make up whatever details you need. Finally, write a good headline for your story.

> An All-City swimming champion from Eleanor Roosevelt High School saved a 9-year-old child from drowning in Lake Wakends late yesterday. The child had fallen through a loose railing on the dock and toppled into the water. Community officials promised to have the railing strengthened.

**C. Comparing news articles.** Write the numbers 1–5 on your paper. Following are two short news articles. Read both carefully and notice how the two writers handled the topic. Then write the answers to the questions that follow the articles.

ARTICLE 1:

The Dean of Admissions at State University has announced that State will no longer accept students who read on less than an eleventh grade level.

Dr. Erica Miquela, the Dean of Admissions, added that exceptions can be made, "though not frequently," so as not to disqualify prospective students who get good grades despite low reading scores. Such students, Dr. Miquela noted, should submit letters from their guidance counselors and teachers.

State University's announcement follows last week's decision by the State Education Department not to grant high school diplomas to seniors whose reading scores drop below the eleventh grade level.

ARTICLE 2:

State University will no longer accept freshmen who read below the eleventh grade level. Dr. Erica Miquela, Dean of Admissions at State, made the announcement after a faculty meeting late today.

Dr. Miquela noted that the faculty urged adoption of this policy because they have concluded that students who cannot read cannot do college-level work.

State University's announcement comes a week afer a directive from the State Education Department to deny a diploma to any high school senior who reads a year or more below grade level.

1. Which of the two articles presents the more complete view of the new admissions policy? Why?
2. Which of the two articles would be more informative to a senior who intends to apply to State? Why?

3. What impressions about the new admissions requirements does Article 2 leave you with? Why?
4. In which article can the author's bias be seen most clearly?
5. For each article, write a headline as you think the reporter might have written it.

**D. Understanding the sections of a newspaper** Write the numbers 1–10 on your paper. Following is a series of headlines and lead paragraphs. Write which section of the newspaper you would find each in. Use the list of departments found in 4.3c.

1. Freak Storm Batters City; Heavy Flooding Closes Expressway
2. Tanya Tey, Noted Author, Dead at 55
3. Lions Claw Rams 64–18; Play-Off Spot Assured
4. Rio Offers Tourists Sunny Beaches
5. Alfred Hitchcock Festival to Start Thursday at Royale Theater
6. A growing awareness of the effect of hydrocarbons on the atmosphere has encouraged many people to purchase smaller, more efficient cars, an auto industry executive said today. Detroit is making plans, the executive said, to meet these new demands as soon as possible.
7. Concerned about the high cost of buying toys for their young children, many local parents have banded together in a toy exchange program that may soon become the model for similar programs across the state. Parents are eligible if their children are under 12. Toys are swapped on an item-for-item basis.
8. Main St., cor Beech Av., 3 lge rms, A/C, sep kitch; $260. Call after 6 PM: 475-2459
9. New Season Opens For Prime-Time TV
10. Unseasonably cold weather has damaged much of the citrus crop in Florida and California, causing a sharp rise in the cost of remaining marketable fruit throughout the United States.

# 5
## Learning Words By Reading

Most of the new vocabulary you have learned over the years has come from your reading. Knowing how words are used in a passage can often help you understand their meaning without having to consult a dictionary.

## 5.1 USING CONTEXT CLUES

The context of a word is the place where the word is found in a passage and the way the word is used. **Context clues** are hints in a passage that give you an understanding of a new or unfamiliar word. Following are four different types of context clues.

**Direct definitions** Meanings of words are often given in appositives.
- *Scrimshaw,* which is an engraving or carving in whalebone or whale ivory, is highly prized by many antique fanciers.

**Examples and details** You may also find a word defined indirectly. Details and examples indirectly tell what the word means. Possible clue words are *such as, for example,* and *other.*
- The *machete* has many uses. For example, it can be used to cut sugar cane or to clear a path. Sometimes it is used as a weapon.

**Cause and effect relationships** The meaning of a word is sometimes indicated by what happens because of it or by what causes it.
- Due to his *acrophobia,* Reggie could not look down from a tall building without feeling dizzy.

**Comparisons and contrasts** Expressions such as *like, in the same way,* and *similar to* help you understand a new word by directing you to a synonym that you already know.
- A *kayak,* like other types of canoes, is lightweight and easy to steer. (*Canoe* is the synonym.)

## 5.2 LOOKING AT THE WHOLE

Sometimes context clues are given so indirectly that you must look at the entire sentence or paragraph before you can guess the word's meaning.

**The whole sentence** When the meaning of a word is only implied, try to find a general definition that will fit the meaning of the sentence.
- Among the *deleterious* effects of measles is an inability to tolerate strong light. (*Deleterious* means *harmful.*)

**The whole paragraph** Do not let an unknown word stop you from reading an entire paragraph. Keep on reading and see if clues later on can help you infer the meaning of the unknown word.
- Once Felicia and Leon moved out of the city, their *metamorphosis* startled their parents. No longer were the children afraid to go out at night. They no longer felt trapped by row upon row of tall buildings. The two had always wanted to live in the country. Now they finally had their wish. (*Metamorphosis* means *change.*)

# EXERCISES

**A. Using context clues**  Write the numbers 1–5 on your paper. Without using a dictionary, write a definition for each of the italicized words in the following sentences. Write the type of context clue you found.

EXAMPLE:   Our apartment's *concierge,* the French equivalent of a janitor, fixed our leaky faucet.
ANSWER:   A concierge is the French equivalent of a janitor.
    The context clue is a direct definition.

1. The *carabiner,* a ring that holds a freely running rope, snapped out of the rock a split second after the climber reached the ledge.
2. *Psoriasis* and other skin diseases cause much discomfort to those who suffer from them.
3. The people who waited for the bus in a *queue* were as orderly as pickets on a fence.
4. The *Plimsoll marks* on the bow of a ship tell the captain how low the vessel is riding in the water.
5. *Deneb,* like many other stars, has an Arabic name, not a Latin one.

**B. Looking at the whole**  Write the numbers 1–10 on your paper. Use context clues to help you infer the meaning of the italicized words in each of the following sentences and passages. Write the letter of the best possible meaning from the choices provided.

- Joe thinks he's such a *paragon* of virtue that everyone must be like him.

    1. PARAGON:
        a. reverse
        b. contradiction
        c. example
        d. puzzle
        e. none of these

- The Egyptian *obelisk* in the museum reminded many visitors of the Washington Monument.

    2. OBELISK:
        a. statue
        b. throne
        c. pillar
        d. sign
        e. none of these

- The *mahout* was so skillful in handling his elephant that it seemed as if he had been riding elephants all his life.

    3. MAHOUT:
        a. elephant feeder
        b. elephant driver
        c. elephant attendant
        d. visitor
        e. none of these

- Because of the *magnitude* of the issues involved, none of the candidates felt comfortable in dealing with all the issues at once. Instead, they settled for bickering over *picayune* problems that did not come close to satisfying the voters' demands for solid information. The voters finally re-elected the *incumbent,* for although the governor's approach gave no new answers, it *surpassed* the *partial* answers of the other office seekers.

    4. MAGNITUDE:
       a. clarity          c. understanding        e. none of these
       b. large size       d. smallness

    5. PICAYUNE:
       a. small            c. involved             e. none of these
       b. large            d. difficult

    6. INCUMBENT:
       a. candidate        c. present office holder    e. none of these
       b. politician       d. voter

    7. SURPASSED:
       a. surprised        c. runs fast            e. none of these
       b. was like         d. was better than

    8. PARTIAL:
       a. deep             c. fancy                e. none of these
       b. incomplete       d. full

- Some speakers have difficulty in achieving sufficient *volume* because they do not breathe properly. Words are *expelled* by the air you breathe out, and if you are struggling for breath, the volume of your voice will suffer.

    9. VOLUME:
       a. a book           c. loudness             e. none of these
       b. quiet            d. a knob

    10. EXPELLED:
        a. suspended       c. wrong                e. none of these
        b. misspelled      d. punished

**C.** **Defining words in context**  Write the numbers 1–5 on your paper. Five words in the following reading passage have been underlined. Use context clues to determine each word's meaning. Write the letter of the best definition from the choices provided.

The American bison is perhaps the most <u>notorious</u> example of humankind's mindless and unrelenting <u>persecution</u> of a once plentiful animal. Only the <u>immense</u> size of its original <u>domain</u>, which stretched from California to New York and from Alaska to Mississippi, and the fierce determination of a handful of naturalists and legislators saved the bison from <u>extermination</u>. By the time the <u>pogrom</u> ended in the early twentieth century, the incredible numbers of the bison—as many as 80 or 90 million by some accounts—had been thinned to less than a thousand.  —Henry G. DeYoung

1. NOTORIOUS:
   a. famous
   b. playful
   c. unfavorably known
   d. intentional
   e. none of these

2. DOMAIN:
   a. territory
   b. power
   c. refuge
   d. burial ground
   e. none of these

3. EXTERMINATION:
   a. growth
   b. reduction
   c. freedom
   d. elimination
   e. none of these

4. POGROM:
   a. progress
   b. massacre
   c. planning session
   d. birth rate
   e. none of these

5. IMMENSE:
   a. large
   b. small
   c. average
   d. very large
   e. none of these

# WRITING REPORTS AND ESSAYS

> # 6
> ## Writing Reports

The skills involved in writing reports and essays build on what you have already learned about reading and study skills. As with reading assignments, the key to the successful handling of writing assignments is understanding the main idea and purpose of the piece.

The basic difference between a report and an essay is that a **report** is usually limited to the telling or explaining of straight facts, while an **essay** allows personal opinion along with the facts.

A report assignment usually requires that you do some research to gather facts before you start to write. The amount of research you have to do depends on how much you already know about the topic and how long your paper should be. In gathering information for reports you should be sure to get as clear an understanding of your topic as possible. If your research is done well, the paper will practically write itself.

## 6.1 ANALYZING THE SIZE OF THE TOPIC

The size of your topic determines the length of your paper. Be sure to select a topic that you can handle in the space you have. If you attempt to handle a complicated topic in a few paragraphs, you risk leaving out too much. On the other hand, neither should you try to expand a very limited topic into a long paper. The following chart shows how to select a topic.

| Research Paper (500–1000 words) | Report (150–500 words) | Short Composition (50–200 words) | Paragraph (25–50 words) |
|---|---|---|---|
| Flowering shrubs | How shrubs multiply | How to prune a shrub | When to plant a shrub |
| Sea mammals | Whales | Toothed whales | The toothed whale is dying out |

## 6.2 GETTING INFORMATION

Your own textbooks can often give you enough information to write short reports. To research longer ones, you will have to go to the library. Check encyclopedias for basic information. Then consult the card catalog to see what books the library has on your topic. Look in the *Readers' Guide to Periodical Literature* for articles on current subjects.

Take notes on what you read. Use a separate index card to record each new piece of information. Be sure to label the index card with the title and author of the book or article in which you found the information. Also write the name of the publisher, the page number, and the copyright date. Mark each card as a *précis* or as a *direct quote*. If you quote, check that you have copied the author's words exactly as they appear.

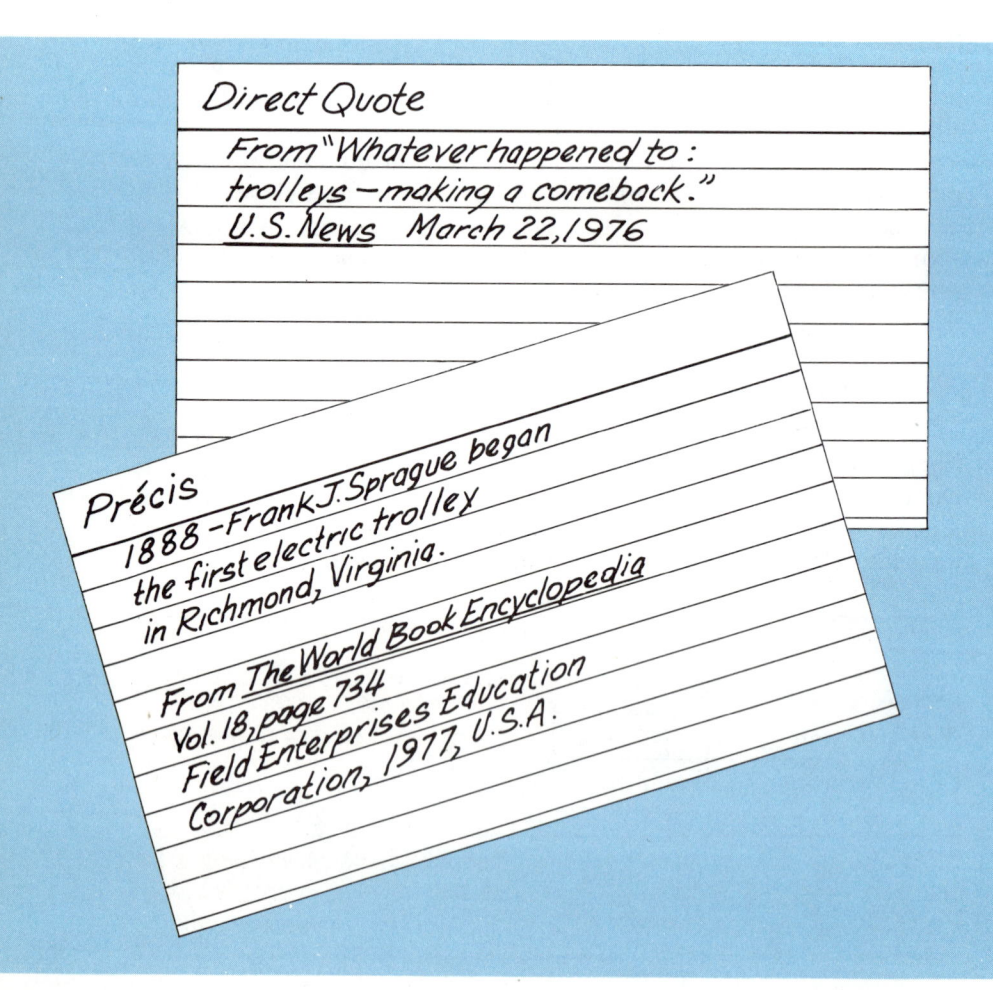

*Direct Quote*
From "Whatever happened to: trolleys — making a comeback."
U.S. News    March 22, 1976

*Précis*
1888 — Frank J. Sprague began the first electric trolley in Richmond, Virginia.
From The World Book Encyclopedia
Vol. 18, page 734
Field Enterprises Education Corporation, 1977, U.S.A.

## 6.3 MAKING AN OUTLINE

Before writing a report, you should read through your index cards and select those that contain the information you intend to include. Next, arrange the cards in the order in which you will use them. After that, write a careful outline, being sure to keep all related material together. When you are done, read over your outline to be sure that all the information is arranged as you want it to be.

Study the following report outline. Notice the breakdown of information into major topics and related subtopics.

---

### THE RISE AND FALL OF THE TROLLEY CAR

**Statement of purpose:** To explain how the trolley was abandoned as a form of public transportation.

I. The birth of the trolley car
   A. Frank Sprague's electric trolley motor
   B. Trial run in Richmond, Va., 1888
II. Early popularity of the trolley car
   A. Convenience
      1. Corner stops
      2. Overhead wires
      3. Low fares
   B. Many uses
      1. Commuting to work
      2. "Rent-a-Trolley" picnics
      3. Investment opportunities
III. The decline of the trolley car
   A. Causes
      1. Development of the private auto
      2. Development of highways
      3. Development of bus lines
      4. Trolley companies heavily taxed
   B. Effects
      1. City government control of trolleys
      2. Five remaining trolley lines in 1970s

---

## 6.4 WRITING A ROUGH DRAFT

You should always write a rough draft of a report so that you can make corrections in spelling, punctuation, grammar, and organization. Be sure that every paragraph and all your sentences express your precise meaning. Be certain that your information is correct and to the point. Omit or change anything that hurts the unity of the report.

## 6.5 WRITING THE FINISHED COPY

The finished copy of your report should be as perfect as you can make it. That means no erasures, no words crossed out, and no words added in the margin. Your finished copy should reflect the effort you put into writing the report.

## EXERCISES

**A. Judging the size of a topic**  Write the numbers 1–10 on your paper. Using the chart of topic sizes in section 6.1, write whether each of the following topics is suitable for a research paper, a report, a short composition, or a paragraph. Be ready to explain your answer.

1. The Effect of Sunspots on Radio and Television Broadcasts
2. Matthew Brady's Civil War Photographs
3. A Description of a Famous Monument
4. How to Live Without a Clock
5. Solar Energy
6. Solar-heated swimming pools
7. Boat racing
8. Crew racing
9. Rowing a boat
10. Using an oar as a brake

**B. Writing an outline**  Using the outline in section 6.3 as your model, write an outline for a report on one of the following.

- How Glass (nylon, penicillin, etc.) Is Made
- The Difference Between Organic Farming and Traditional Farming
- Career Possibilities in Medicine (or any other field)
- How a Mirror (clock, auto engine, airplane, etc.) Works
- How to Grow Flowers Indoors
- The Two Greatest Athletes of This Century
- The Origin of the Olympic Games
- How to Choose a College (job, car, etc.)
- The Effects of Alcohol (drugs, cigarettes, etc.) on the Human Body
- How to Start a Small Business
- How to Water-ski
- The Art of Making Pottery
- Benjamin Franklin's Wisdom
- Sojourner Truth's Great Speech

# 7
# Writing Essays

Because an essay includes opinion along with facts, a pattern called an argument is often used to prove the author's point in an essay.

## 7.1 USING THE ARGUMENTATIVE PATTERN

An **argument** is made up of at least two statements: (1) the **conclusion**, and (2) the **premise**, or evidence on which the conclusion is based.

CONCLUSION: We must use recycled paper more.
PREMISE: Every year our forests and fuel are needlessly wasted in the making of paper goods.

In forming an argument, always be sure that there is a definite premise and conclusion relationship. The following example uses a premise that does not directly prove the conclusion.

CONCLUSION: Always use Ever-Bright Liquid Cleaner.
PREMISE: Ever-Bright comes in three handy sizes.

You can test to see if a premise and conclusion relationship actually exists by inserting *because* before the premise or *therefore* before the conclusion.

Arguments often have a number of premises used to support a single conclusion.

CONCLUSION: Students should have a voice in selecting the foods that the school cafeteria serves.
PREMISE 1: Students know best what students enjoy eating.
PREMISE 2: There would be less wasted food if unwanted items were removed from the menu.
PREMISE 3: Students would buy more cafeteria food rather than bring in lunch from home.

Using premise and conclusion arguments is especially important in writing about any issue that has two clearly defined sides to it. Your essay must show why your solution to the problem is better than the alternative one. Poorly thought out arguments are not convincing. You cannot just ignore evidence that tries to disprove your case. You must actively confront the opposite point of view.

In the following essay, notice how premises (P) are used to support each conclusion (C). Also notice how the final conclusion restates and develops the first conclusion.

(C) *Television news needs more real reporters and fewer news readers.* (P) *Too many newscasters prefer to show the public what nice people they are by exchanging personal comments with the sports reporter, the weather forecaster, and the anchorperson. Precious air time is wasted in so doing.* (P) *It is not bad enough that few news stories last longer than thirty seconds and practically none more than a minute, but personal comments on non-news subjects cut down news time even further.* (C) *Television news personnel have become showpeople, and the public's "right to know" is being shortchanged.*

(C) *The hiring practices of many stations encourage this non-news approach to reporting.* (P) *News directors seek out the interesting new face or the dazzling personality rather than the experienced reporter who could do a better, though less flashy, job.*

(C) *TV news should be regarded solely as a public service, not just another hepped up and star-studded show to win the war of the TV ratings.*

## EXERCISES

**A. Analyzing arguments**   Write the numbers 1–5 on your paper. Identify the premises and conclusions in each of the following arguments by writing *C* or *P*. Then in a few words, explain why you think the argument is (or is not) convincing.

EXAMPLE:   (a) Marilyn Rosada should be elected to the Senate. (b) She is a good citizen.
ANSWER:   a–C, b–P The argument is not convincing because many people are good citizens.

1. (a) American history should not be a required course in high school. (b) Students have already studied American history in grade school.
2. (a) Grades cause unnecessary competition between students and too much additional work for teachers. (b) Fear of getting poor grades keeps students out of difficult courses. (c) All grades should be abolished.
3. (a) The driving age should be raised to twenty-one. (b) Insurance company studies have shown that drivers under twenty-one are responsible for a major proportion of auto accidents in this country.

4. (a) Special bicycle lanes should be set aside on all major streets. (b) Bikes should not have to compete for space against vehicles many times their size and weight, and drivers should not have to worry about dodging cyclists who zip in and out of traffic.
5. (a) This community needs a new recreation center for young people. (b) There are no parks or playgrounds in the immediate vicinity and no places to have dances or play sports. (c) All that young people can do now is hang around on street corners.

**B. Using the argumentative pattern** Plan and write an essay of 100–200 words on one of the following topics. Label premises and conclusions.

The Conditions of Local Parks (or Zoos)   Student Rights
The Animal that Makes the Best Pet   Junk Food
The School's Dress (or Hair) Code

# 8
# Writing Reviews

A **review** is a critical essay in which both the good points and the bad points of a book, movie, play, or television program are evaluated. A good review is based on careful study and analysis of the work in question.

## 8.1 WRITING BOOK REVIEWS

Unlike book reports, in book reviews the retelling of the plot is only one small part of the assignment. A critical book review demands that you (1) interpret what the book means, (2) analyze the techniques the writer uses to present material, and (3) judge how successful the book is as a whole.

The following book review is one method of writing a critical essay.

### UNTRUE LOVE

"What can you say about a twenty-year-old girl who died?" Answer: the same thing you can say about the novel *True Love*—may they both rest in peace.

With rough draft simplicity, former movie star Joe Strasovich spins a happy-sad tale of young love and marriage that is short on content and long on sugar coating. The reader never doubts that rich Peter Brace and Alice Blechman, the poor carpenter's daughter from Scotland, will marry, despite the objections of Peter's cold and aloof parents. The reader never doubts that the marriage would be anything other than perfect. And, of course, we all cry when Alice dies at the age of twenty.

The plot does not matter because the tears are not for Alice and Peter, but for all our own lost loves, and that is the flaw in the book. The characters and situations are so thin they get flesh only from our own dreams. Take out your hanky and cry for the perfect love you can never have.

True Love is nice, but it's not real. We are left no wiser. We share no one's experiences but our own. Love is more than soft lights and violins, and the perfect relationship exists only in fantasy.

**8.1a  Reviewing fiction**  Follow these hints to write an interesting critical review of fiction.

- Identify the book. Name the title, author, publisher, and date of publication. Also tell the kind of fiction it is: a detective story, a love story, an adventure story, etc.
- Describe the most exciting incidents in the plot. Tell how the writer made those scenes exciting.
- Describe the main characters briefly. Tell what makes the characters into believable human beings, or why they seem unreal.
- Describe where the story takes place. State why you think the author has chosen that particular setting. Describe the atmosphere or mood the writer has created.
- Talk about the author's style. Tell whether the book was easy to read or hard, and why. Is the book mostly action and dialogue, or is there a lot of description? How does the writer make the action seem real to you?
- Criticize the book. Tell what the writer did to make the book successful or less successful than it could have been. What would you have done differently?
- Tell how the book helped you understand yourself or your world better. Would you recommend this book to someone else and why?

**8.1b  Reviewing biographies**  Most of the hints listed for a review of fiction should also be applied in a review of a biography. Here are some additional ideas to include.

- Tell why the subject of the biography is worth reading about. What important contribution has he or she made?

- Explain the writer's bias for or against the character. How does this bias affect the book?
- Write a character sketch. Present a clear picture of the faults, strengths, and other important traits of the subject.

**8.1c  Reviewing nonfiction**  There are many different kinds of nonfiction books on all sorts of subjects from hobbies to hurricanes. Here are some hints that can be applied to a wide range of such books.

- Tell what the book is about. How well does the author explain or present the subject matter?
- Check whether the facts are accurate. Has important material been left out or treated too quickly? Does the author have any bias for or against the subject?
- State the purpose of the book. Is the purpose to amuse, persuade, or to instruct? How successfully does the book live up to the writer's intentions?
- State whether or not the book is well organized and easy to understand. Does the author supply enough background information for you to understand the main points without having to go to other sources?
- Tell what you have learned, or more deeply understood, by reading the book.

## EXERCISES

**A. Writing a critical review**  Write a 200–500 word critical essay on either a fiction or nonfiction book you have read this term. Be sure to give the title, author, publisher, and date of publication.

**B. Comparing reviews**  Find two different reviews of a book and compare them. In an essay explain how the reviews are different from each other. Good sources for book reviews are (1) *Book Review Digest,* (2) a Sunday newspaper's book review section, and (3) the *Readers' Guide to Periodical Literature,* which will refer you to reviews in magazines.

**C. Analyzing a review**  In a short paragraph, criticize the review of *True Love* in section 8.1. What are the good and bad points of the review? What key information has the reviewer not supplied you with? What is your attitude toward the book on the basis of this review?

## 8.2 WRITING REVIEWS OF TELEVISION PROGRAMS

Are you in the habit of watching television while reading the newspaper or doing something else? If you are, you will have to change your approach and give the program your full attention when you write a critical report on a television show. You cannot go back again and watch a segment that you missed, so you have to do it right the first time.

Observe the following suggestions when reviewing a television show.

- State the title of the program. State the show times, and the network. List the names of the main actors and the director. Much of this information can be found in the television listings in your newspaper or in a television magazine. The rest of the information is given in the program credits before or after the show. Be ready to copy down all important information quickly.
- Tell what company sponsored the program. Explain how that sponsorship could benefit the sponsoring company. For example, how would it benefit a baby food company to sponsor a program on child care? Check whether something not flattering to the sponsor could have been left out of the television show.
- State the main idea of the program and relate the most interesting or exciting incidents in the plot or story line. Tell what made those scenes interesting or exciting.
- Tell how lighting, camera angles, sound, and choice of setting affected the success of the program.
- Tell why you think the actors were or were not successful in presenting believable characters on the screen.
- Compare the program to similar programs you have seen. Tell which was the most successful.
- Tell what bias you detected in the show. Was the director presenting a balanced view of the subject? What would you have done differently if you were directing the show?
- Tell what you learned, or more fully understood, by watching the program.

## 8.3 WRITING REVIEWS OF MOVIES AND PLAYS

In reviewing movies and plays, take into consideration the limitations and strong points of each medium. Live theater lacks the spectacle that movies frequently rely upon, but movies lack the personal closeness and spontaneity of a live performance.

Observe the following suggestions when reviewing movies and plays.

- State the title of the play or movie. Tell who directed it. List the names of the starring actors and what roles they played. Information about movies can be found in the credits at the start or finish of the movie. For a play, the program given out before the play contains all the necessary background information.
- State the main idea of the movie or play. Relate the most exciting or important incidents in the plot. Tell why those scenes were exciting or important. What emotions did those scenes try to arouse? What is the high point of the action? How is it resolved?
- Tell whether the actors were believable in their roles. Were the characters believable as human beings? Why? Who gave the most convincing performance?
- List the special effects of lighting, sound, costumes, and scenery that the movie or play used. Were those effects successful? Why?
- Describe the aim of the movie or play: to entertain, to inform, or to convince. Explain how the director accomplished this aim. Compare the movie or play to similar ones you have seen. Which was the most successful? Why? Explain what you would have done differently if you had been the director.
- Tell what you learned, or more fully understood, by watching the movie or play.

## EXERCISES

**A. Reviewing a television show**  Watch a television special and write a critical review of 200–500 words on that program. Compare your review with those of professional reviewers. You can find their reviews on the television page of your newspaper. State how similar or unlike your judgments are.

**B. Compare current movie reviews**  In an essay compare the reviews of at least two critics on the same movie. Your local newspaper and the national newsmagazines are good sources for reviews.

**C. Reviewing a play**  Go to a play. Then write a critical review of 200–500 words on that production. Compare your review with the judgments of professional reviewers. State how similar or unlike your judgments are.

# 9
# Writing Essay Tests

An **essay test** is a composition that is written in a set time period to answer a specific question. Writing such essays demands two basic skills. First, you must read carefully to understand what you are being asked to write. Second, you must write a composition that answers the question directly and gives examples and supporting statements to back up your position.

Never write before you plan out your answer. If you have time, try to write a brief outline of the major points you want to include. When you do write the essay include good topic sentences that will help you focus an answer. Do not be fancy; be clear. A teacher is more likely to be impressed by a shorter answer that says a great deal than by many pages of padded, irrelevant, and unexplained ideas.

## 9.1   TYPES OF ESSAY QUESTIONS

The essay question itself tells you what should be included in the answer. Look for key words, such as *compare* and *contrast,* which tell you what to include in your essay answer. Read the question carefully and slowly. Know what you are being asked. Do not show off by including everything you know about the subject. Hiding your lack of study in a vague, rambling, and unstructured essay will cost you points. Always include facts, examples, and illustrations to back up your main ideas.

**9.1a   Compare or contrast**   An essay question may ask you to **compare**, or to point out, the ways in which two or more things are alike. It may also ask you to **contrast**, or to show, how those things are different.

- Compare and contrast the settling of the American West with the settling of Australia. Include references to the political, social, and economic goals of both groups of settlers.

**9.1b   Criticize, discuss, and analyze**   **Criticize** means to show the good and bad sides of an issue or an event. Remember that criticize does not mean to develop only the negative aspects. **Discuss** and **analyze** mean to determine the nature and relationship of the parts and come to a conclusion about the whole thing.

- Analyze the meaning of the choice of roads in the last lines of Robert Frost's poem, "The Road Not Taken."
- Criticize the Treaty of Versailles in regard to the underlying causes of World War II.

**9.1c  Explain, explicate, describe, and trace**  **Explain** means to make understandable. **Explicate** means to explain in detail. **Describe** means to give specific examples that explain the answer to the question. **Trace** means to show, step by step, the progress, development, or change involved.

- Trace the development of modern communications techniques from the invention of the telegraph to the launching of the first communications satellite.
- Describe Great Britain's reaction to the Boston Tea Party.
- Explain the causes of the Great Depression of 1929.

**9.1d  Give examples**  **Give examples** means to include precise instances and particular cases. Do not include any reasons and generalizations that are not illustrated by specific situations.

- Give examples of the effect alcohol has on the brain when present in the bloodstream.

**9.1e  Summarize**  **Summarize** means to give a brief rundown of the important points. When answering an essay question that asks you to summarize, be selective. Include only important points.

- Summarize the major issues involved in Soviet-American relations of the 1970s.

In some essay questions you may be asked to do more than one thing. For instance, you may be asked to explain and give examples, or to trace and analyze, or to compare and contrast by giving examples.

## 9.2  THE PERSONAL ESSAY

Some jobs and many colleges require a personal essay along with your application form. Your aim in writing the personal essay is to persuade the reader through facts, examples, and illustrations that you should be accepted as an employee or student, depending on the situation.

Following is the personal essay question from the Common Application Form, which is used by more than eighty private colleges in the United States.

## PERSONAL STATEMENT

*It is our aim to get to know you as well as possible through this application. With this in mind, please describe in detail some special interest, experience or achievement or anything else you would like us to know about you. Essays on a personal, local, or national issue that are of particular concern to you are also welcome. Attach extra pages (same size, please) if your statement exceeds the limits of this page. Also feel free to submit tapes of musical performance, photographs or examples of artwork, samples of writing, or other examples of your creative work.*

# EXERCISES

**A. Understanding essay questions** Read the following poem carefully. Then answer the questions that come after it. Your answers need not be more than one or two paragraphs long.

### BARTER

Life has loveliness to sell,
    All beautiful and splendid things,
Blue waves whitened on a cliff,
    Soaring fire that sways and sings,
And children's faces looking up
Holding wonder like a cup.

Life has loveliness to sell,
    Music like a curve of gold,
Scent of pine trees in the rain,
    Eyes that love you, arms that hold,
And for your spirit's still delight,
Holy thoughts that star the night.

Spend all you have for loveliness,
    Buy it and never count the cost;
For one white singing hour of peace,
    Count many a year of strife well lost,
And for a breath of ecstasy
Give all you have been, or could be.

                    —Sara Teasdale

1. Give examples of Sara Teasdale's use of imagery in "Barter."
2. Compare and contrast the third stanza of the poem with the first two stanzas.
3. Summarize the meaning of the poem in a short paragraph.
4. Explain why the poem is called "Barter."

**B. Writing the personal essay** Write a brief essay that fulfills the requirements of the Common Application Form's Personal Statement.

# 10 Manuscript Form

Proper manuscript form should be used for all research papers and reports. Use it also for reviews of books, movies, plays, and television shows. Putting your writing in the proper form is the final step after you have written and revised your assignment.

## 10.1 PAPER, MARGINS, AND SPACING

**Paper** Paper for handwritten manuscripts should be the standard lined white paper. Sheets should not have a ragged edge where they have been ripped from a notebook. Use blue or black ink, never pencil.

Type papers on the standard 8½ x 11 in. white typing paper.

**Margins** The margin should be at least 1½ in. on the left-hand side and 1 in. on the right. Top and bottom margins should be at least 1½ in.

**Spacing** Double space all typewritten papers. Write on every other line in handwritten papers if your teacher tells you to. Use only one side of the sheet of paper. You should indent and single space an entire long-quoted passage if the passage runs five lines or longer.

**Title** The title should be centered and not underlined. Use quotation marks around the title only if the title itself is a quotation.

## 10.2 WRITING NUMERALS

Do not begin a sentence with a numeral. Inside a sentence use numerals to write numbers longer than two words. Spell out numbers that are less than three words.

- Fourteen ninety-two is an important date in American history.
- Columbus discovered America in 1492.
- I made twenty dollars mowing lawns last month.

Write out numbers used as adjectives. In month and date combinations, use only the numeral. You may, however, use letter endings in addresses.

- Raoul graduated second (not 2nd) in the class.
- My sister's birthday is June 14 (not 14th).
- The doctor's office is at 109 West 22nd Street. (Also 22 Street or Twenty-Second Street)

## 10.3  WHEN TO UNDERLINE

Underlining takes the place of italics in handwritten or typed papers. It indicates titles and foreign words and phrases. Underlining may also be used for emphasis.

**10.3a  Titles**  Underline longer works such as books, movies, full-length plays, record albums, television shows, magazines, and newspapers. Put quotation marks around articles, chapters, songs, poems, and short stories.

- For Monday everyone should read the chapter, "The Great Bow" in Homer's _The Odyssey_.

Do not underline or capitalize *the, a,* or *an* when they are not a part of the title or before the titles of newspapers and magazines.

the _Los Angeles Times_   the _Old Testament_   _The Agony and the Ecstasy_

**10.3b  Foreign words**  Underline all foreign words and phrases unless the word or phrase has been adopted into English.

- The motto of the Coast Guard is _Semper Paratus_.
- A cliché is an overused expression.

**10.3c  Special words and letters**  Underline all words, letters, and numbers being referred to as words, letters, or numbers.

- David misspelled the word _word_, and Ann made her _I_'s look like _1_'s.

Underline for emphasis, but do it sparingly.

- Mac definitely did _not_ break that window.

## 10.4  USING ABBREVIATIONS

In compositions, reports, and reviews, you should ordinarily not use abbreviations at all.

Some abbreviations, however, are always allowable. Use the following abbreviations of titles before proper names.

    Mr.    Dr.    Mrs.    St. (for saint)

Use the following abbreviations after proper names.

    Jr.    Esq.    Sr.    M.A., and other college degrees

The following abbreviations may always be used when accompanied by numerals.

    8:00 A.M.    A.D. 1400
    10:00 P.M.    32 B.C.

Many authorities think it better to use the English equivalents of the following Latin abbreviations.

    i.e. (*id est*) ⟶ that is
    e.g. (*exempli gratia*) ⟶ for example
    etc. (*et cetera*) ⟶ and so forth

Common abbreviations such as AFL-CIO, PTA, and CIA may be used. To help your reader, though, it is a good practice to spell out the word the first time you use it. You may then use the abbreviation in sentences that follow.

- The *Federal Bureau of Investigation* is the investigative arm of the Justice Department. J. Edgar Hoover headed the *FBI* until his death in 1973.

## 10.5 USING QUOTED MATERIAL

Every statement that you use word-for-word from another person's writing must be identified as a quotation. Not giving credit for another person's words is called plagiarism. You should also indicate the source of the quotation so that others can check your references for accuracy and relevance.

Short quoted passages that are no more than three lines long can be worked directly into the body of your report. Handle longer passages by indenting and single-spacing the entire passage. Do not use quotation marks around indented, single-spaced quotations.

As Henry David Thoreau advised in *Walden,* chapter 18:

> However mean your life is, meet it and live it; do not shun it and call it hard names. It is not so bad as you are. It looks poorest when you are richest. The fault-finder will find faults even in paradise.
>
> —Henry David Thoreau

**Using footnotes** Credit lines, called **footnotes** are placed on the bottom of the page on which the quotation appears. Some teachers allow students to put all their footnotes at the end of the report. These are called **endnotes**.

**Footnoting books and articles** Following are sample footnotes for books and articles. Use the same number for the quotation in the text and for its footnote. Number footnotes consecutively through the paper.

ONE AUTHOR:

author → [1]F. L. Lucas, *Tragedy* (New York, 1957), p. 75.

— footnote number — title — place and date of publication — page

MORE THAN ONE AUTHOR:

[2]Edward B. Jenkinson and Donald A. Seybold, *Points of View in Writing,* (New York, 1972), p. 49.

NO AUTHOR NAMED:

[3]"Earthquakes." *Encyclopedia Americana,* V (New York, 1965), p. 177

↓ volume

ARTICLE REPRINTED IN A BOOK:

[4]Maynard Mack, "The World of Hamlet," in *Tragic Themes in Western Literature,* Cleanth Brooks, ed. (New Haven, 1955), p. 31.

↑ editor

Every time you footnote a new book or article, use the complete form of the footnote. For later references to the same book or article, use the author's name and give the page reference of the new quote. Add a brief title if you are using two books or articles by the same author.

Liebling, p. 201.    Lucas, *Tragedy,* p. 75.

## 10.6 USING CORRECTION SYMBOLS

Correction symbols are a shorthand system of indicating errors in a piece of writing. You can use the symbols to make corrections on your rough draft.

Annie Smith Peck, at the age of fifty-seven, was the first person to climb Mt. Huascaran in Peru. That had been in 1908 when Mt. Huascaran was thought to be the highest mountain in the Western Hemisphere. Why did she do it? "I want to stand where no man has previously stood" she told the world. But Annie Peck had not finished climbing when she was sixty-one, Annie climed Mt. Coropuna.

| Symbol | Meaning |
|---|---|
| awk | awkwardly phrased |
| frag | sentence fragment |
| RO | run-on sentence |
| uc | Use an upper case (capital) letter here. |
| lc | Use a lower case (small) letter here. |
| sp | spelling error |
| ¶ | Begin a new paragraph here. |
| no ¶ | This belongs in the previous paragraph. |
| ⊙ ⨀ | Add a period or semicolon. |
| ⌃ | Add a comma. |
| ⌄⌄ ⌄⌄ | Add opening or closing quotes. |
| ⌄ | Add an apostrophe or single quotes. |
| T | error in tense of verb |
| ref? | The antecedent of the pronoun is unclear. |
| meaning? | The meaning is unclear. |
| ∧ | Insert this here. ("It's good ⁀to see you.") |
| ℓ | Delete: leave this out, (e.g. bett⁄ꞇer). |
| tr | transpose (e.g. tra⁀ns⁀pose) |

## EXERCISES

**A. Using proper manuscript form**  Write the numbers 1–5 on your paper. Make all necessary corrections in the following sentences.

1. 3 times I told you that the motto of the United States—e pluribus unum—means "one from many."
2. Remember to cross your t's and dot your i's.
3. A very interesting article on lasers appeared in last month's Popular Electronics magazine.
4. A fait accompli refers to a supposedly unreversable situation.
5. My earnings for the past 3 weeks were as follows: fifty-five dollars the first week, eighty dollars the second, and one hundred twenty-two dollars the third.

**B. Writing footnotes** Put the following information in proper footnote form. Number your footnotes consecutively.

1. Footnote a reference to p. 35 of *Beyond the Melting Pot* by Nathan Glazer and Daniel Patrick Moynihan. The book was printed by the M.I.T. Press of Cambridge, Mass. Copyright date is 1963.
2. Footnote a reference to an article entitled "The Black Rhinoceros" by John Goddard printed in the magazine *Natural History*. It is on p. 64 of volume LXXXII, no. 4. The issue is dated April, 1973.
3. Footnote a reference to p. 29 of *The Elements of Style* printed by the Macmillan Company in New York in 1959. The book was written by William Strunk, Jr., and E. B. White.
4. Footnote a second reference to John Goddard's article on the black rhinoceros, this time p. 66.
5. Footnote a reference to p. 870 of the entry on lightning in the *Encyclopaedia Britannica*. The article is found in volume 13 of the 1950 edition. The encyclopedia is printed by the Encyclopaedia Britannica Co., Inc., Chicago, Ill.

# MECHANICS OF WRITING

## 11 Punctuation

Without punctuation, writing would be a jumble of meaningless words. Correct punctuation is needed to make your writing clear.

In studying the rules in the following sections, pay careful attention to the example sentences and try to understand why each is punctuated as it is. With practice, punctuating as you write can become as natural as pausing as you speak.

## 11.1 END PUNCTUATION

The punctuation marks that are used at the end of sentences, questions, or exclamations are called **end punctuation**.

**11.1a The period** Use a period at the end of a statement, or after an abbreviation.

- Dr. Marcano works in that office.

Always place the period at the end of a complete thought. Do not let incomplete sentences, called fragments, stand by themselves.

**11.1b The question mark** Use a question mark to end a direct question.

- When are you coming to visit us?

Use a period to end an indirect question.

- Mr. Cardiss asked what time the game would begin.

**11.1c The exclamation mark** Use an exclamation mark to indicate strong feeling.

AFTER EXCLAMATIONS: Fantastic!
AFTER IMPERATIVE SENTENCES: Don't slam that door!

Avoid using exclamation marks except in informal writing. Too many exclamation marks can weaken your writing.

## 11.2 THE COMMA

**11.2a Punctuating a series**   Use a comma to separate the items in a series of words, phrases, or clauses. A comma is usually placed before the *and* or the *or* that joins the last two items in the series.

WORDS:   The flag of Ireland is green, white, and orange.
INDEPENDENT CLAUSES:   I ski, I hike, and I climb mountains.
PHRASES:   I looked for the book on my desk, in the living room, and on the porch.

A comma is not used before the first item nor after the last item in a series.

INCORRECT:   She can, swim, run, and play ball, better than I can.
CORRECT:   She can swim, run, and play ball better than I can.

Words that are usually grouped together are set off as one item in a series.

- We ate an early breakfast of fruit, cereal, *bacon and eggs*, and coffee before leaving.

Do not use a comma to separate words or phrases in a series if they are all connected by *and, or,* or *nor.*

- On a stroll through the park I spotted three blue jays *and* two cardinals *and* dozens of robins.

Use a comma to separate two or more adjectives that modify the same noun only if they could also be separated by *and* or *or.*

- The fastest, most agile animal in the world is the cheetah.

Some noun-adjective combinations are so often used that they are treated as one word. If such an expression is modified by another adjective, do not separate the two adjectives by a comma.

- Our neighbors rented a small *log cabin.*

**11.2b Punctuating appositives**   An **appositive** is a word or phrase used to explain the word or phrase that comes before it. Use commas before and after appositives that appear within a sentence.

- The blue whale, *the largest animal in the world,* has been known to grow to a length of thirty-three meters.

Do not use commas with appositives (usually single names) that are closely related to the word they follow.

- My cousin *Phillip* was one of the first men to attend Vassar College.

Appositives may also explain by making a contrast.

- Ms. Berry, *not Mr. Auletta,* will direct the spring play this year.

**11.2c** Punctuating restrictive and nonrestrictive modifiers   A **nonrestrictive** modifier is a phrase or clause that adds information that can easily be omitted without damaging the meaning of the sentence. Use commas to set off nonrestrictive modifiers from the rest of the sentence.

NONRESTRICTIVE CLAUSE:   The Sears Tower in Chicago, *which is the tallest building in the world,* is 442.26 meters high.
NONRESTRICTIVE PHRASE:   *Running for the bus,* I slipped.

A **restrictive** modifier contains information that is necessary to the meaning of the sentence. Do not use commas with restrictive modifiers.

RESTRICTIVE CLAUSE:   Many businesses will hire only applicants *who have some prior experience in the field.*
RESTRICTIVE PHRASE:   People *crossing a busy street* should look both ways.

# EXERCISES

**A. Using end punctuation**   Write the numbers 1–5 on your paper. Rewrite each of the sentences correctly by adding periods, question marks, or exclamation marks.

1. Why was I not consulted before you borrowed the van this afternoon Hank and I needed it to return the Taylor's furniture we refinished for them
2. Come over here Did you know that you spilled soup all over the floor Who do you think is going to clean up this mess
3. Pilar saw Fredda standing by the tennis court Without sneakers neither could play, so they decided to go for a walk
4. Incredible You've just knocked over two hundred cans of tomato sauce with your broom and you wonder why you're being fired
5. I have a question about these chemicals How long can they stand out exposed to air without going bad

**B. Punctuating the series**   Write the numbers 1–5 on your paper. Rewrite each of the following sentences, adding commas wherever they are needed.

1. After a short relaxing swim, Gregory Melissa and Billie Sue showered dressed and left for their homes.

2. Among the interesting colorful phrases used in English to describe groups of animals are a gaggle of geese a pride of lions a clutter of cats and a yoke of oxen.
3. The dessert menu includes pecan pie strawberries and cream and chocolate layer cake.
4. After the concert, the band packed their gear in the truck collected their money and went out to celebrate.
5. All the children in the neighborhood believed that the old brick house at the crest of the narrow winding road was haunted.

**C. Punctuating restrictive and nonrestrictive modifiers and appositives** Write the numbers 1–5 on your paper. Rewrite the following sentences, adding commas wherever needed.

1. William Howard Taft the twenty-seventh president of the United States is buried in Arlington National Cemetery.
2. My friend Arnaud who went on the roller coaster with me broke his glasses.
3. Only persons who are good in mathematics should consider a career in accounting a field which is attracting many high school seniors.
4. Roberto Perez one of the city's most influential business leaders has announced that he will finance a tree-planting program starting in the fall.
5. The sudden rainstorm which was not predicted by the weather forecaster caught all the people attending the football game by surprise.

**11.2d Punctuating adverb clauses** Use a comma to set off an introductory adverb clause.

- *Even though I can afford to attend an out-of-state college,* I prefer to go to a school here in the city.

Do not use a comma to set off adverbial clauses at the end of a sentence.

- My teachers congratulated me *when they heard I had won the Fire Department's essay contest.*

**11.2e Punctuating compounds** Use a comma before the conjunction to separate the two independent clauses of a compound sentence.

- I went shopping for a new coat, but the one I wanted was too expensive.

When the independent clauses are very short, a comma is not needed.

- The lights dimmed and the play began.

When the conjunctions *yet* or *for* are used to join two independent clauses, a comma always precedes those conjunctions.

- Mike was fast asleep, *yet* his eyes were open.

Do not use a comma to separate the two parts of a compound subject, compound verb, or compound direct object.

- Anita stormed out of the room and slammed the door.

**11.2f Punctuating direct address** Names used in direct address should be set off from the rest of the sentence by commas.

- Don't forget, *Mel*, that you owe me ten dollars.

**11.2g Punctuating parenthetical expressions** Use commas before and after expressions that interrupt a sentence.

- She concluded, *therefore*, that the problem was solved.

Following are some common parenthetical expressions.

| therefore | on the contrary | as you know |
| nevertheless | indeed | I am sure |
| by the way | of course | in fact |
| on the other hand | I believe | however |
| to tell the truth | for example | naturally |

**11.2h Punctuating dates and addresses** Use commas to separate each part of a date or address.

- Maria was born on Friday, April 1, 1965, in Santa Barbara, California.

Group dates and addresses according to the following categories. You may replace the comma with a period to end a sentence.

| | |
|---|---|
| **Day** | Tuesday, |
| **Date** | May 23, |
| **Year** | 1977 |
| **Street address** | 55 Old Spanish Trail |
| **City** | Houston, |
| **State and zip code** | Texas 77021 |
| **Country** | U.S.A. |

Do not use commas if the elements of a date or address are connected by prepositions.

- My grandfather was born on the eighteenth of March *in* 1918 *on* Front Street *in* Prairie du Chien.

**11.2i  Other uses of the comma**  Use a comma after the salutation of a friendly letter and after the closing of both business and friendly letters.

Dear Harry,     Sincerely,

Use commas to set off abbreviated titles after names.

- Corretta Loggins, *M.D.*, is the new team physician.

# EXERCISES

**A. Punctuating adverb clauses and compounds**  Write the numbers 1–5 on your paper. Rewrite the following sentences, adding commas wherever needed.

1. Because a water main under the street had broken police were forced to detour traffic around the block.
2. Although many people entered the shop and browsed few purchased any of the articles on sale.
3. Until I can afford a new pair of jogging shoes I shall have to make do with my old ones.
4. I was looking for something else when I found my lost watch on the floor and happily picked it up.
5. The gutters on the house have rusted and although they are expensive we shall have to replace them soon.

**B. Punctuating interrupters, dates, addresses, and titles**  Write the numbers 1–5 on your paper. Rewrite the following sentences, adding commas wherever needed.

1. Charles Lindbergh flew the first solo transatlantic flight landing in Paris France on May 21 1927 after 33 hours 29.5 minutes in the air.
2. Halley's Comet should next appear on February 9 1986 almost seventy-six years since it was last sighted.
3. On May 5 1961 Alan B. Shepherd Jr. was rocketed into space.
4. My family as you know moved from Dallas Texas to Delta Utah.
5. The new address of Hansen's Garage is 4049 West Church Avenue Knoxville Tennessee 37901.

## 11.3 THE APOSTROPHE

**11.3a Contractions** Use an apostrophe in contractions to show where letters or numbers have been left out.

    you are    you're    let us    let's    1976    '76

Do not confuse the contraction *it's* (meaning *it is*) with the possessive *its* (meaning *belonging to it*).

- *It's* your fault that the boat slipped off *its* mooring.

**11.3b The possessive of nouns** Use an apostrophe + s to form the possessive of singular nouns: *This evening's festivities.*

To form the possessive of plural nouns that already end in s, simply add an apostrophe: *ten trucks' tires.*

To form the possessive of plural nouns that do not end in s, add an apostrophe s: *children's outerwear.*

**11.3c The possessive of pronouns** Do not add an apostrophe to personal pronouns already in the possessive case: *his, hers, yours, its, ours, theirs,* and *whose.*

- *Whose* pair of boots is by the fire?
- The Scrabble game is *hers.*

Use an apostrophe + s to form the possessive of indefinite pronouns such as *everyone, no one,* and *somebody.*

- Pollution should be *everyone's* concern.

**11.3d The possessive of time and amounts** Adjectives of time and amount take the possessive form: *a kilometer's walk, a day's time.*

**11.3e The possessive of compound nouns** To form the possessive of compound nouns, first determine whether the possession is joint or individual.

For joint possession, put only the last word in the possessive form.

- *Mom and Dad's* new furniture has been delivered.

For individual possession, put both words in the possessive form.

- *Greg's* and *Dora's* ski poles are both missing.

**11.3f The plurals of numbers, letters, signs, and words** Use an apostrophe + s to form the plural of numbers, individual letters, signs, and of words referred to as words.

- There are two *a's* in my name.
- How many *seven's* are in this paragraph?

## 11.4 THE SEMICOLON

**11.4a  Compound sentences**  Use a semicolon in a compound sentence to join independent clauses. A semicolon is used in place of a comma and conjunction to add emphasis or strength.

- Taking is the sign of a child; giving is the mark of an adult.
- Taking is the mark of a child, but giving is the mark of an adult. (weakened by *but*)

Use a semicolon when a conjunction would have little meaning.

- Ralph likes to dress up often; I don't.

Use a semicolon before independent clauses beginning with the following adverbs and phrases.

| | |
|---|---|
| nevertheless | consequently |
| therefore | instead |
| accordingly | besides |
| for example | that is |
| however | furthermore |

- My feet are tired; *nevertheless,* I'm going to keep on walking.

**11.4b  For variation**  To vary sentence structure, especially in sentences and paragraphs containing many conjunctions, use a semicolon.

- On Saturday morning I wake up, walk my dog, do chores around the house, and clean my room; by noon I'm exhausted.

**11.4c  In a series**  Use a semicolon to separate words or phrases in a series if the series contains commas.

- Present at the meeting were Soledad Martinez, the president; Robert Graham, the vice president; and Betty Sue Walden, the treasurer.

## 11.5 THE COLON

**11.5a  Before a list**  Use a colon to introduce a list of items following an independent clause.

- I bought what I needed for summer: a pair of shoes, two new shirts, a pair of shorts, and a bathing suit.

However, if the list of items is the direct object of the main verb or the object of a preposition, a colon is not used.

- The caterer will supply *paper plates, cups, napkins, and silverware.*

**11.5b  Before a statement or quotation**  Use a colon to introduce a long statement or quotation.

- Let me quote a famous football coach: "Winning isn't everything. It's the only thing."

**11.5c  After a salutation**  Use a colon after the salutation of a business letter.

    Dear Ms. Shuda:    Dear Sir:

**11.5d  To separate the whole from parts**  Use a colon between the hour and the minute in time, between the chapter and a verse from the Bible, and between the volume and the page number of a periodical.

TIME:  10:30 P.M.
BIBLICAL REFERENCE:  Genesis 1:13 (Chapter 1, verse 13)
PERIODICAL:  *Newsweek* 89: 1–12 (volume 89, pages 1–12)

## EXERCISES

**A. Punctuating with the apostrophe**  Write the numbers 1–5 on your paper. Rewrite the following sentences. Add apostrophes where needed and remove those used incorrectly.

1. Yolandas and Janells test scores were the highest in the class.
2. If all the *you knows* were dropped from our speech, we might get some solid explanation's for a change.
3. In two weeks time, four local resident's have been involved in serious automobile crashes.
4. Many seniors cars were parked in spots' reserved for faculty members car's.
5. Mens wear is on the fourth floor; womens wear is on the second.

**B. Using semicolons**  Write the numbers 1–5 on your paper. Rewrite the following sentences by adding or substituting semicolons wherever needed.

1. Switching to the metric system in daily life is easy for scientists and engineers for others it demands more adjustment.
2. A book report on this novel is not very difficult to write besides, I am almost done.
3. Most of the family wanted ice cream for desert Linda and Ed, however, wanted yogurt.

4. The presents for my aunt and uncle are in my room the gifts for my parents are hidden in the attic.
5. In the yearbook office were Mr. Dorney, the moderator Claire Hynes, the editor-in-chief Fergus Ball, the layout editor and Ramon Preston, the photography editor.

**C. Using colons** Write the numbers 1–5 on your paper. Rewrite the following sentences, adding and substituting colons wherever needed.

1. The garage contains quite a collection of junk old tires and auto parts, a broken lawn mower, and boxes of discarded clothes.
2. The suitcase was too small to hold all I wanted to pack clothes, toilet articles, souvenirs, and my camera.
3. The awards meeting of the 4-H Club will start precisely at 730.
4. Alan Brent was a fine athlete, he excelled in baseball and track.
5. You can find that reference in the Bible Proverbs 14 2.

## 11.6 PUNCTUATING DIRECT QUOTATIONS

**11.6a Double quotation marks** Use double quotation marks to enclose direct quotations.

- "The fireplace doesn't work," the real estate agent said.

When an uninterrupted quotation is more than one paragraph in length, use the opening double quotation mark (") to open the quote. Also use it at the start of each new paragraph and after an interrupter. Use the closing quotation mark (") only at the end of the whole quotation or before an interrupter.

"I don't play football," Lee confessed, "because I'm afraid that I'll get hurt.
"When I was six, I was watching a football game, and a tackle charged across the sidelines and knocked me unconscious.
"Every time I'm asked to play football, I think back to that terrible day, and I refuse."

**11.6b Single quotation marks** Use single quotation marks to enclose a quote within a quote.

- The speaker concluded, "Remember the rousing words of Patrick Henry, 'Give me liberty or give me death.'"

**11.6c Capitalization** Always use a capital letter to begin a sentence in a direct quote.

- The mechanic replied, "The radiator in your car is no good."

If a fragment of a sentence is being quoted, begin it with a small letter.

- The prosecutor called the robbery "a mean, despicable act."

**11.6d Punctuation marks** Observe the following rules in handling punctuation in quotations.

Quotations interrupted by expressions such as *they replied, she said*

1. If the second part of the quote is a complete sentence, place a period after the interrupting expression and begin the second part with a capital letter.
   - "Turn around," the policeman ordered. "The road ahead has been washed out by a flash flood."

2. If the second part of the quote is a continuation of the same sentence, place a comma after the interrupting expression and begin the second part with a small letter.
   - "Did you or did you not," she said, "promise to be here on time?"

**Rules for punctuating all direct quotations**

1. Place commas and periods inside the closing quotation marks.
   - The moderator said, "Get involved or get out."

2. Place colon and semicolons outside the closing quotation marks.
   - The sign said, "Detour"; we had to drive another block to get home.

3. Place question marks and exclamation marks outside the closing quotation marks if the entire sentence is a question or an exclamation. Otherwise place them inside the quotes.
   - Was it Chicken Little who said, "The sky is falling"?
     The fire inspector said, "When did you first notice the blaze?"

4. Use no more than one comma or end mark at the end of a quotation.
   INCORRECT: The bank teller asked, "Which shopkeeper said, 'This bill is counterfeit!'?"
   CORRECT: The bank teller asked, "Which shopkeeper said, 'This bill is counterfeit'?"

5. In writing dialogue, begin a new paragraph each time the speaker changes.

   "What time will the dance be over tonight?" said Dad as we finished washing the dinner dishes.
   "About eleven, I think," I replied.
   "Good," said Dad. "Make sure you tell your mother, too."

## 11.7 PARENTHESES AND BRACKETS

**11.7a  Parentheses**  Use parentheses to enclose extra information or material not necessary to the meaning of the sentence.

- Mary Ann Evans Cross (1819–1880) wrote famous novels under the pen name George Eliot.
- Cocoa (at an outrageous price) is found on that shelf.

**11.7b  Brackets**  Use brackets within quoted material to enclose explanatory words that are not part of the quotation. Brackets are used also to enclose explanations within parentheses.

- (For emergency numbers, check your telephone book [pp. 2–3])
- "When did you first notice it [the uprooted garden]?"

**11.7c  Punctuation marks**  Place punctuation marks within the parentheses or brackets if the punctuation belongs with the enclosed words. If the marks do not belong with the enclosed words, place them outside.

- If you have some money left over (from the movie, that is), we can stop for a hamburger.

## 11.8 HYPHENS AND DASHES

**11.8a  The hyphen**  Use a hyphen to join words and word parts.

1. Use a hyphen to show that a word will be continued on the next line. For information on how to break specific words into syllables, consult a recent dictionary.

2. Use a hyphen with certain compound nouns.
   - Bill Updike is our baby-sitter.

   Consult a dictionary before writing an unfamiliar compound. Some compounds are written as two words, some with hyphens, and some as one word.

3. Hyphenate compound numbers from *twenty-one* to *ninety-nine* and fractions used as adjectives or adverbs.

   [One-quarter] of the class was ill after the [three-quarter] mile run.
     noun                                           adjective

4. Hyphenate a compound modifier when it comes before the word it modifies.
   - A *top-to-bottom* inspection (But: We searched from *top to bottom*.)

5. Do not hyphenate an adverb ending in *-ly* with an adjective or an adverb.

   INCORRECT:   The doctor has a *highly-trained* staff of nurses.
   CORRECT:   The doctor has a *highly trained* staff of nurses.

6. Hyphenate the prefixes *ex-, self-, all-,* and the prefixes before proper nouns and proper adjectives. Also hyphenate the suffix *-elect.*

   self-appointed    president-elect
   all-American      pro-British

7. Use a hyphen wherever clarity is necessary, especially after the prefix *re-* and when there is an awkward repetition of letters.

   - The farmer *re-covered* the open pit. (covered again)

**11.8b  The dash**  Use dashes to show that a sentence is interrupted or suddenly changed.

- Tell me—tell me this instant—did you break that typewriter?

Dashes give the impression of great speed and should be used sparingly unless you are trying to produce a special effect. Commas or parentheses are often good substitutes for the dash. A dash can be used to set off appositives.

- You'll never guess what I've just won—a trip to Paris!

Dashes can be used to set off nonrestrictive modifiers, especially if the modifiers contain other punctuation.

- The door slammed with a crash—which knocked a picture off the wall, infuriated my parents, and scared the dog—and I stood there speechless.

## EXERCISES

**A. Punctuating direct quotations**  Write the numbers 1–5 on your paper. Rewrite the following sentences, adding quotation marks, capital letters, commas, and end punctuation wherever needed.

1. Did the poster actually call this dull movie exciting ... superb ... not to be missed
2. It is against the law to shoot bald eagles, the Game and Wildlife official noted, It's an offense punishable by a fine, prison, or both
3. Farmers who depend upon rainfall rather than irrigation the agronomist noted face going bankrupt during droughts

4. We no longer carry EEE brown shoes in this model the salesperson said would you care to look at a pair in black no the customer replied I need brown shoes show me another style
5. What a beautiful table you found said Larry bring me along the next time you go hunting for antiques

**B. Using parentheses and brackets** Write the numbers 1–5 on your paper. Rewrite the following sentences, adding parentheses or brackets wherever needed to set off explanatory material.

1. Emily Dickenson 1830–1886 wrote many insightful poems about life even though she was almost a total recluse.
2. My puppy what a terror hides under the bed during thunderstorms.
3. Witnesses testified that they saw the alleged thief remove it the briefcase from the airport locker.
4. Senator Strom Thurmond D-South Carolina holds the senate filibuster record.
5. Mike Gillen that poor fellow breaks his leg every year at the start of baseball season.

**C. Using hyphens and dashes** Write the numbers 1–5 on your paper. Rewrite the following sentences, adding hyphens and dashes wherever they would be useful or necessary.

1. There's one thing I hate more than liver turnips.
2. "Move get out of the way," the firefighters cried as they hurried patrons out of the burning restaurant.
3. How many expresidents of the United States are still alive?
4. A good faculty student relationship enables young people to get to know their teachers.
5. My sister in law marched in the Independence Day parade.

# 12
# Capitalization

Capitalization in English is functional, not decorative. Capital letters are used to make special words stand out in a sentence: names, titles usd with names, and the first word of a full sentence or a quotation. Master the rules that follow and capitalization will cause you no problems.

## 12.1 CAPITALIZING FIRST WORDS

**12.1a** Sentences   Capitalize the first word of each new sentence.

- Advertising is a very competitive field.

**12.1b** Direct quotations   Capitalize the first word in a direct quotation that is a complete sentence.

- The clerk said, "This toaster costs fifteen dollars."

Capitalize the first word in a directly quoted sentence fragment only when the quoted fragment begins the sentence.

- Deirdre called the new building "the most hideous piece of architecture I've ever seen."
- "Well," I said.

**12.1c** After a colon   Capitalize the first word of a formal statement after a colon only when the word introduces a complete sentence after the colon.

- Follow these instructions: Turn right at the flagpole and walk three blocks.
- Here's what you should get: thermal underwear and warm gloves.

Do not capitalize the first word after a colon if the colon connects two independent clauses, unless the second clause is a *formal* statement or a quotation.

- We are here to stay: we don't intend to move.

**12.1d** Letters   Capitalize the first word in the salutation of a letter.

Dear Mrs. Blum:     My dearest friend,

Capitalize only the first word in the closing of a letter.

Sincerely yours,     Yours truly,

## 12.2 CAPITALIZING PROPER NOUNS AND ADJECTIVES

A **common noun** names a general category in which all things of the same type are included: *country, playwright, mountains.* Do not capitalize the first letters of a common noun.

A **proper noun** names a *specific* person, place, or thing: *Mexico, Shakespeare, Alps.* Capitalize the first letters of a proper noun.

A **proper adjective** is an adjective that is formed from a proper noun: *Mexican, Shakespearean, Alpine.* Capitalize the first letter of a proper adjective.

**12.2a** The pronoun I and the interjection O  Capitalize the interjection O and the pronoun I. Do not capitalize *me, mine,* or *myself.* Do not capitalize the interjection *oh.*

- I force myself to continue my piano lessons.
- The poem reads "for your sake, O Love . . ."

**12.2b** Names of places  Capitalize the complete names of countries, states, cities, bodies of water, mountains, parks, and so forth. The article *the* before a geographical name is not capitalized.

| Proper Nouns | Common Nouns |
| --- | --- |
| Appalachian Trail | the trail |
| Denver, Colorado | the city and state |
| the Indian Ocean | the ocean |

Capitalize the names of buildings, institutions, organizations, business firms, government bodies, and so forth.

The article *the* is capitalized only if it is part of the legal name of the organization.

the Federal Trade Commission   Unified Airlines
Indiana University   the Empire State Building

Do not capitalize common nouns unless they are part of the title.

- Palo Alto High School in California was the high school I last attended.

Capitalize *north, south, east, west,* and combinations of these words when they refer to recognized sections of the country or the world, but not when they indicate directions.

GEOGRAPHICAL SECTIONS:   I lived in the Northeast until I was ten; then I moved to the South.
DIRECTIONS:   The nearest motel is due west of the turnpike exit.

**12.2c** Names of things  Capitalize the brand names of products, but not the product itself.

Kwik calculators   Morecraft stereo
Brighton soap   Luggitt stationwagon

**12.2d  References to the deity**  Capitalize all words referring to God.

    God        the Lord       the Almighty
    Thy Will    His Word      Thine

**12.2e  Events and periods of time**  Capitalize the names of historical periods and events, days of the week and months of the year, and holidays, but do not capitalize the names of the seasons.

    the Renaissance    Thanksgiving Day
    Sunday           the World Series
    January          *but:* an early spring

**12.2f  Nationalities, languages, religions, and races**  Capitalize nouns and adjectives that refer to specific nationalities, languages, religions, and races.

    Caucasian        Swedish
    Roman Catholic   Canadian

**12.2g  Prefixes and compounds**  The prefixes attached to proper nouns and proper adjectives are not capitalized: pro-American.

    Capitalize only that part of a compound word that is a proper noun or a proper adjective: Dutch-speaking, British-made.

## 12.3  CAPITALIZING TITLES

**12.3a  Titles of persons**  Capitalize civil, military, social, and religious titles only when they are followed by a proper name.

    Representative Shirley Chisholm    the congresswoman
    Justice Warren Burger           the judge
    Bishop Michael Chen            the bishop

The titles of very high government officials should be capitalized even when a proper name is not used because those titles in themselves refer to very specific individuals.

- The Secretary of State informed the President of the latest developments in the crisis.

Capitalize all titles used as substitutes for the proper name of an official in direct address.

- Will you run again, Senator?

In capitalizing compound titles before a name, capitalize only the first word if the title is hyphenated, but all words if the title is not hyphenated.

Do not capitalize the prefixes *ex-* and *pro-* nor the suffix *-elect*.

> Senator-elect Sanura
> Lieutenant Commander Oberon
> the ex-President

EXCEPTION:  Vice-President Adams (Capitalize both words out of respect for the office.)

Capitalize family relationship titles only when the title is usually used with the person's name or when the title is used in place of the proper name.

> Uncle Alex       my uncle Alex
> Mom              my mother

Capitalize all abbreviations of titles after names.

> Peter Murray, Jr.       Linda DeMeo, Ph.D.

**12.3b   Titles of things**   Capitalize the first word in the title of a book, movie, play, poem, song, record, and so forth. Capitalize all other words in the title except *the, a, an,* short prepositions, and short conjunctions.

- *The Heart Is a Lonely Hunter*
- "Ode to a Nightingale"

Do not capitalize the articles *the, a,* or *an* when they are not a part of the title or when they appear before the titles of newspapers and magazines.

> the *Denver Post*       the *Dubliners*

Do not capitalize the names of school subjects, except languages and titles of specific courses.

- This semester I'm taking Spanish, math, and History IV.

The words *freshman, sophomore, junior,* and *senior* are not capitalized unless they refer to a specific group.

- Two juniors will graduate with the Senior Class in June.

## EXERCISE

**Using capitalization**   Write the numbers 1–10 on your paper. Rewrite the following sentences, adding or removing capital letters wherever necessary. In some cases you may also have to add end punctuation.

1. The compass needle stopped at S "excellent," I thought. "we must be going in the right direction."

2. the mystery novel really puzzled me: After reading more than two thirds of the book, i still could not figure out the ending.
3. read the small print: the engine and all its parts are guaranteed for one year or 10,000 kilometers, Whichever comes first.
4. Marianne called Thomas Jefferson "The best president the united states ever had."
5. according to my records, You did not report for work until 9:30.
6. Our french teacher is taking the class on a trip to montreal in the Spring. We will stay at the queen Elizabeth hotel.
7. An Ex-Lawyer, Sam Gruen is able to write very knowledgeably about legal matters in his new career as a Reporter for The *Baltimore Sun*.
8. After a trip to The Everglades national park, my Cousin Matt and his wife Barbara, an All-american swimming champ, both decided to take up underwater photography.
9. I prefer attending a Hockey game to a Basketball game any day, especially when the Rockets are playing at Madison Square garden.
10. "After getting a Whiz Calculator for my birthday, I had no further trouble with my Math homework," Claimed Michelle's younger Brother Ernie.

# 13
# A Plan for Spelling Success

Spelling success calls for a two-sided approach. First, get into the habit of using a dictionary to check the spelling of unfamiliar words. Second, master the basic spelling rules in this section. Spelling rules can help you make an educated guess about a word's spelling when you cannot consult a dictionary.

Since spelling success is highly dependent upon memory, observe the following hints.

**Break words up into syllables.** If you can break up a long word into syllables, you stand a better chance of remembering the correct spelling.

**Record your mistakes.** Keep a list of words you frequently misspell in your notebook or on index cards. Review the list periodically until you have the words memorized. Add new words as they come up.

**Be careful.** Check over all written assignments for spelling errors. You can eliminate mistakes in simple words, such as *there* for *their,* easily.

## 13.1 SPELLING RULES

All spelling rules in English have exceptions, and as you study the following rules, take careful note of those exceptions. To be absolutely sure about how a word is spelled, you should consult a dictionary whenever possible.

### 13.1a Forming plurals
Form the plural of most nouns by adding an *s*.

flag—flags state—states

Words that end in *f* or *fe* sometimes form their plurals by changing the *f* to a *v* and adding an *s* or *es*.

knife—knives leaf—leaves
wolf—wolves thief—thieves

EXCEPTIONS: grief—griefs, chief—chiefs

If the singular form of a noun ends in a consonant followed by *y*, form the plural by changing the *y* to *i* and adding *es*.

navy—navies puppy—puppies

If the singular form of a noun ends in a vowel followed by *y*, form the plural by adding *s*.

key—keys delay—delays

If the singular form of a noun ends in *s* or *x*, *ch* or *sh*, form the plural by adding *es*.

genius—geniuses bench—benches
hoax—hoaxes crash—crashes

If the singular form of a noun ends in a consonant followed by *o*, form the plural by adding *es*. When *o* follows a vowel, simply add *s*.

hero—heroes radio—radios
buffalo—buffaloes potato—potatoes

EXCEPTIONS: piano—pianos (and other music-related words)

Form the plural of a compound word connected by a hyphen by pluralizing the first word.

brother-in-law brothers-in-law
passer-by passers-by

However, if the result is awkward or hard to pronounce, form the plural by pluralizing the last word.

drive-in drive-ins
good-for-nothing good-for-nothings

Form the plural of some words by changing the root.

    man—men      louse—lice
    mouse—mice    ox—oxen
    goose—geese    child—children

Form the plural of some foreign words as in the original language.

    crisis—crises    parenthesis—parentheses

EXCEPTIONS:   appendix—appendixes or appendices
                     index—indexes or indices
                     medium—mediums or media
                     formula—formulas or formulae

Some nouns do not change when pluralized.

    fish—fish        species—species
    sheep—sheep    Japanese—Japanese

**13.1b Adding prefixes**  A **prefix** is a word part added to the beginning of a word to alter the word's meaning.

To add a prefix to a word, do not change the spelling of the word itself.

    re + admit = readmit    with + hold = withhold

There is one exception: the prefix *all,* as in *already, although, always,* and *altogether.* (Do not confuse *already* with *all ready* or *all together* with *altogether. All right* is always spelled as two words.)

**13.1c Adding suffixes**  A **suffix** is a word part added to the end of a word to alter the word's meaning.

Drop the final *e* when adding a suffix beginning with a vowel. Keep the final *e* when adding a suffix beginning with a consonant.

    hate + ing = hating    hate + ful = hateful

EXCEPTIONS:   truly, argument, judgment, acknowledgment

You should also retain the final silent *e* after a soft *c* or *g* sound when adding the suffixes *-able* and *-ous.*

    courage + ous = courageous    notice + able = noticeable

The suffixes *-ness* and *-ly* do not change the spelling of a word.

    plain + ness = plainness   dismal + ly = dismally   dry + ness = dryness

However, with words longer than one syllable that end in *y,* change the *y* to *i* when adding any suffix.

    lazy + ness = laziness    handy + ly = handily

Words that already end in *ll* simply add *y*.

    dull + ly = dully    shrill + ly = shrilly

Unless the suffix begins with *i*, change the final *y* to *i*.

    worry + ing = worrying    worry + ed = worried

In words ending in a single vowel followed by a single consonant, double the final consonant before a suffix beginning with a vowel if the word has only one syllable or if it is accented on the last syllable.

    red + en = redden
    regret + ing = regretting
    profit + ing = profiting (accent on first syllable)

Change final *ie* to *y* when adding the suffix *-ing*.

    die + ing = dying    lie + ing = lying

**13.1d  Choosing ei or ie**  When the sound is $\bar{e}$ (as in *me*), use *ie* except after *c*.

    believe    receipt    deceive
    thief    achieve    conceive

EXCEPTIONS:  *neither, either, leisure, seize, species,* and *weird*.

Use *ei* when the sound is $\bar{a}$ (as in *day*) and after *c*.

    freight    ceiling    receive
    weight    sleigh    veil

# EXERCISES

**A. Forming plurals**  Write the numbers 1–15 on your paper. Form the correct plural of each of the following words.

1. calf
2. wrench
3. oasis
4. rodeo
5. cupful
6. father-in-law
7. complication
8. handkerchief
9. life
10. woman
11. company
12. moose
13. relay
14. mosquito
15. stereo

**B. Adding prefixes and suffixes**  Write the numbers 1–15 on your paper. Write each of the words on the next page correctly. Also state which of the rules for adding prefixes and suffixes you are applying.

1. mis + spell
2. fret + ing
3. marry + ing
4. all + together
5. crazy + ness
6. un + needed
7. fare + ing
8. precede + ing
9. fat + er
10. argue + ment
11. harass + ment
12. convince + ing
13. sandy + ness
14. bounty + ful
15. lie + ing

**C. Choosing ei or ie** Write the numbers 1–15 on your paper. Write each of the following words correctly by supplying the missing letters *e* and *i* in their correct order. Then state which of the rules for choosing *ei* or *ie* you are applying.

1. s__zure
2. misch__f
3. ach__ve
4. p__rce
5. dec__t
6. r__n
7. th__f
8. conc__t
9. w__rd
10. r__gn
11. bel__f
12. rel__f
13. n__ce
14. for__gner
15. w__ght

## 13.2 LIST OF COMMONLY MISSPELLED WORDS

The 200 words in the following list are frequently misspelled by high school students. Use a dictionary to look up their definitions when you study these words. You should also check on the part of speech and syllabification of each word.

The words are in groups of forty. If you master one group per day, in five days you will have mastered all the words.

| | | | |
|---|---|---|---|
| absurd | agriculture | approaching | bouquet |
| accidentally | airborne | arrangement | burglar |
| acclimated | allege | assistance | burial |
| accompaniment | allotting | association | canoe |
| accomplishment | amusement | athlete | caricature |
| achievement | ancestor | audience | catalog |
| acquitted | answer | awful | catastrophe |
| adequately | anxious | behavior | cellophane |
| advantageous | apologetically | beneficial | cemetery |
| aggravate | apparently | boundary | centigrade |
| changeable | controversy | debtor | efficient |
| circumstantial | convertible | despise | emphasis |
| colossal | cordially | defendant | emphasize |
| compel | criticize | definition | encyclopedia |
| competition | crowd | discipline | endeavor |

397

| complement | cruelty | descendant | entertainment |
| completely | cruise | detrimental | entrance |
| confidence | curriculum | devise | environment |
| conquer | dealt | discussion | equaled |
| conqueror | debt | divisible | exhilaration |

| explanation | hereditary | initiative | loaves |
| forcibly | hungry | inquiry | luxurious |
| foreigner | imaginary | intellectual | malicious |
| formerly | imitation | interfere | material |
| frolicked | immense | jeweler | melodious |
| fulfill | immigration | knight | miniature |
| governor | incidentally | labeled | murmur |
| guarantee | independence | latter | muscle |
| guess | influential | lieutenant | mysterious |
| handsome | ingenious | literature | naive |

| necessity | omitting | perspiration | prestige |
| neither | orchestra | phenomenon | priority |
| nephew | overwhelm | physically | professional |
| nourish | outrageous | physician | pursuing |
| nucleus | oxygen | piece | quaint |
| nursery | parallel | pigeon | realize |
| nutritious | particularly | possession | receive |
| obedience | peasant | preference | recollect |
| obliging | perseverance | premier | representative |
| officer | persistence | presence | responsibility |

| ridiculous | strength | theoretical | velocity |
| sacrificing | stubbornness | undoubtedly | view |
| safety | suggestion | universally | vinegar |
| scarcely | succession | unnatural | violence |
| secretary | surround | unnecessarily | violet |
| servant | tariff | utensil | Wednesday |
| severely | temperament | valuable | whistle |
| sophomore | temperature | variety | willful |
| statistics | tendency | vault | writhe |
| strategic | testimony | vegetable | yawn |

# USING YOUR LIBRARY

## 14
## The Classification and Arrangement of Books

A library is carefully organized to help you find the information you want quickly. To make the best use of the library's resources, you have to understand how books are classified and arranged on the shelves. You must also know how to locate books by using the card catalog.

Librarians are trained to help you locate the material you need. They can offer you many helpful suggestions as you begin a research project. Whenever you are in doubt, be sure to ask for their help.

## 14.1 HOW BOOKS ARE CLASSIFIED

A library will seem very confusing unless you understand how books are classified and shelved. Most libraries have separate sections for fiction and nonfiction books. Biographies are sometimes removed from the nonfiction collection and shelved in a separate biography section. Knowing how each of these sections is organized will help you find any book you need.

**14.1a Fiction** Novels and collections of short stories are usually arranged alphabetically by the author's last name. They are kept in the section of the library marked *Fiction.*

If you are looking for the novel *Lord of the Flies,* for instance, and you know that the book was written by William Golding, you could go directly to the shelf on which the authors' names start with *G.* If you do not know the writer's last name, you will have to look in the card catalog under the title of the novel to find the author's last name.

**14.1b Nonfiction** Nonfiction is organized according to call numbers. A **call number** is a special number assigned to a book to classify it and to determine its place on the library's shelves. Each book is assigned a separate call number.

Many school and public libraries use the Dewey Decimal System of assigning call numbers. The **Dewey Decimal System,** assigns call numbers to books according to ten broad subject categories. This system allows librarians to shelve books that are on the same topic together.

### THE DEWEY DECIMAL SYSTEM

| | |
|---|---|
| 000–099 | General Works (encyclopedias, almanacs, etc.) |
| 100–199 | Philosophy (including psychology, behavior, etc.) |
| 200–299 | Religion (including mythology) |
| 300–399 | Social Sciences (economics, education, law, etc.) |
| 400–499 | Language (grammars and dictionaries, etc.) |
| 500–599 | Science (mathematics, biology, physics, etc.) |
| 600–699 | Technology and Applied Science (cooking, farming, engineering, gardening, etc.) |
| 700–799 | Fine Arts, Amusements, and Sports |
| 800–899 | Literature |
| 900–999 | History, Travel, and Biography |

Each nonfiction book is assigned a three-number code according to its subject area. The Dewey Decimal System further subdivides categories by adding one or more numbers after a decimal point: 891.23.

## 14.2 HOW BOOKS ARE ARRANGED

Most libraries mark their shelves with major call numbers or section references to tell you what books are on those shelves. For example, a nonfiction aisle may be marked 473.2–497.

**14.2a Author's last name** Novels and short stories kept in the fiction section are shelved alphabetically according to the author's last name.

Sometimes books that have been given a Dewey Decimal System call number are also marked with the first letter or letters of the writer's last name. The book is then shelved alphabetically according to the author's last name within that particular Dewey Decimal System category.

- The novel *To the Lighthouse* by Virginia Woolf is shelved under *W* in the fiction section.
- E. K. Chambers's book *The Medieval Stage* is shelved under the letters *Ch* in the section 808.2. Its complete call number is

    808.2
    Ch

**14.2b Biography** Biographies are arranged alphabetically according to the last name of the *person the biography is about.*

- To find *Citizen Hearst,* a biography written by W. A. Swanberg about the American journalist William Randolph Hearst, look on the biography shelf under *H.*

Biographies may be shelved either in a special biography section or in the 920 section, the Dewey Decimal System's category for biographies.

# 15
# The Card Catalog

The **card catalog** is a complete index of all the books a library contains. The card catalog is usually housed in a cabinet of file drawers. The alphabetically arranged cards tell you the name of the book and where it can be found.

To use the card catalog, write down the complete call number of the book exactly as it is printed on the card. Then go to the appropriate section of the library to find that book.

## 15.1 TYPES OF CARDS

The card catalog contains five different types of cards: author cards, title cards, subject cards, guide cards, and cross reference cards.

**15.1a The author card** If you know an author's name but not the title of the book you want, look in the card catalog for the **author card,** which is a card that is filed alphabetically by the author's last name. The card catalog will contain a card for every book in the library that the author wrote.

All books *about* the author are filed behind the cards for books written *by* that author.

```
155.4   Josselyn, Irene (Milliken) 1904–
Jo         The happy child; a psychoanalytic guide to emotional
        and social growth.   New York, Random House [1955]
        410 p.  22 cm.

Copy 1   gift   (3.95)   2/20/69


            1. Child study.    I. Title.

        BF721.J55              136.7              55—8161 ‡

        Library of Congress         [65m²⁴]
```

**15.1b  The title card**  If you already know the title of the book you want, look in the alphabetical listing in the card catalog under the first word of the title. There you will find the **title card,** which is the catalog card that lists the book by its title. If the title of the book begins with *the, a,* or *an,* the book will be listed under the second word.

```
               The happy child
 155.4   Josselyn, Irene (Milliken) 1904–
  Jo          The happy child; a psychoanalytic guide to emotional
          and social growth.   New York, Random House [1955]
          410 p.  22 cm.




              1. Child study.    I. Title.

          BF721.J55                 136.7              55—8161

          Library of Congress       [65m²½]
```

**15.1c  The subject card**  The subject card is useful if you know only a broad area in which you want to do research. The **subject card** is the catalog card that lists books by subject. If you are interested in skydiving, for example, look for a subject card with the heading *skydiving.*

```
               Child study
 155.4   Josselyn, Irene (Milliken) 1904–
  Jo          The happy child; a psychoanalytic guide to emotional
          and social growth.   New York, Random House [1955]
          410 p.  22 cm.




              1. Child study.    I. Title.

          BF721.J55                 136.7              55—8161

          Library of Congress       [65m²½]
```

**15.1d Guide cards** File drawers in the card catalog frequently contain guide cards to help you locate other cards quickly. **Guide cards** are catalog cards printed on tabs that stick out above the other cards. For instance, if you wanted to see what books written by American Indian writers are in the library, you could go directly to the section titled American Indian authors rather than search through all the listings under American Literature.

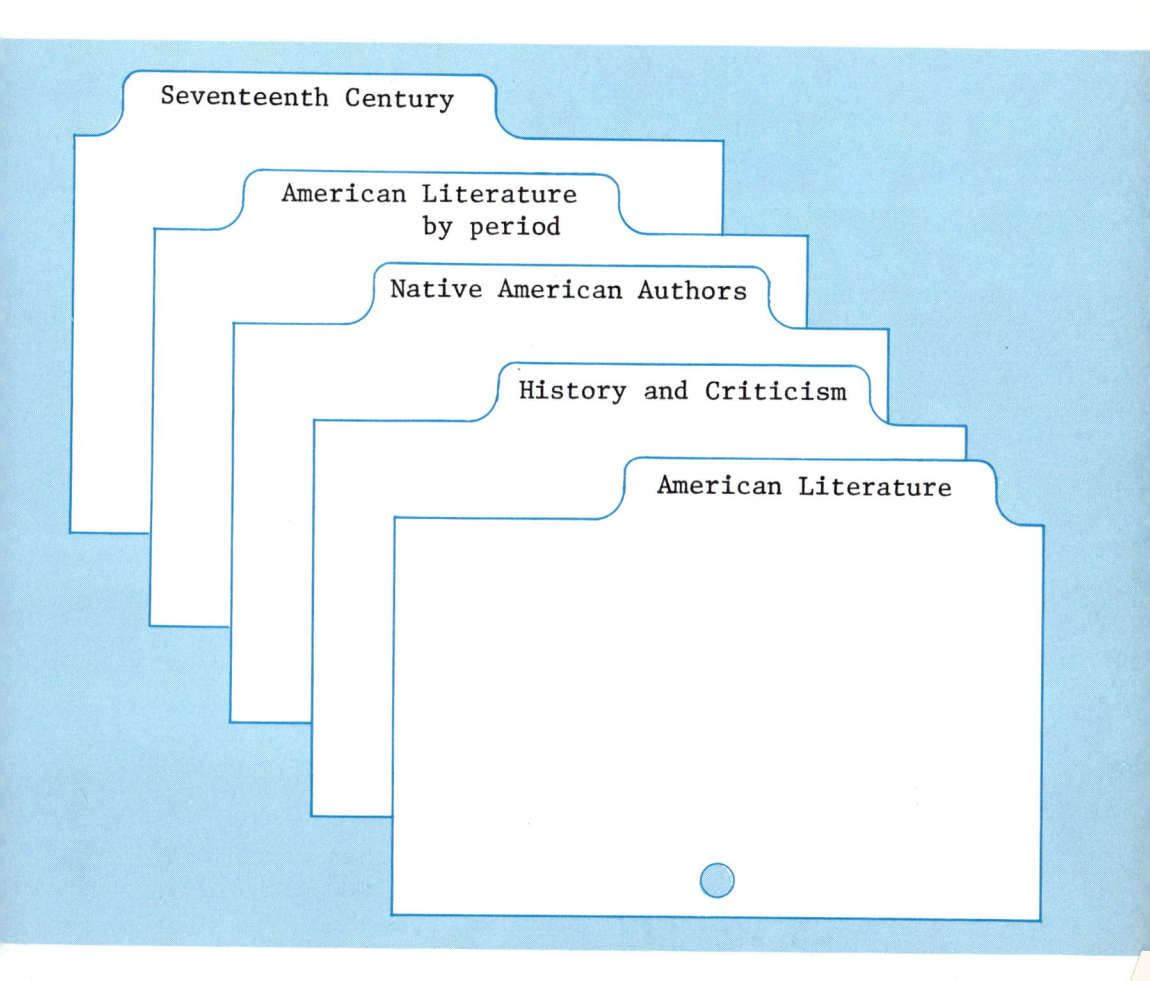

- Seventeenth Century
- American Literature by period
- Native American Authors
- History and Criticism
- American Literature

**15.1e Cross-reference cards** **Cross-reference cards** are catalog cards marked "see" to tell you what subject heading to look under if you have chosen an imprecise subject listing. If you used the subject heading "Civil War," for example, you might be directed to "see U.S.—HISTORY—CIVIL WAR," because that is how your library catalogs books on the Civil War.

Cross-reference cards marked "see also" tell where more information on a topic can be found. The following sample cross-reference card tells you six more subject headings to look at if you want your research on travel to be complete.

```
Travel

        see also

Air Travel
Automobiles-Touring
Health Resort
Luggage
Ocean Travel
Passports
```

## 15.2 LOCATING A BOOK

There are two ways to find the book you want. You can look for it yourself on the library shelves or, if it is not on the shelves, you can have the librarian find it for you.

**15.2a  Open stacks**  When you are able to go directly to the shelves to pick out a book, first notice if the book will be found in a special section. Fiction will be on the fiction shelves, and your library may have a special section for biographies. In addition, books marked *R* or *REF.* above the call number will be found in a special section called *Reference*.

To locate a book cataloged under the Dewey Decimal System, follow the numbers and letters exactly as they appear on the catalog card. To locate 812.56, for example, first find 812, then 56.

Remember that since you are using a decimal system, 812.56 comes between 812.5 and 812.6.

**15.2b  Call slips**  If the book you want is not on the shelf, that book either has been borrowed or is kept in a storage section of the library. To get a book from storage, fill out all the information on a request form called a **call slip**. The following page shows an example of a call slip.

# 16
# The Reference Section

A great deal of the information you will be asked to look up is contained in the standard reference books in most libraries. Knowing what books can give you the specific information you need can make your research more efficient.

In using an unfamiliar reference book, always take time to read the preface to find out how the book is organized and which symbols and abbreviations are used.

## 16.1 DICTIONARIES

**Dictionaries** are alphabetical word lists in book form that give you definitions, pronunciations, and roots of words. Most dictionaries also include synonyms and antonyms of common words, explanations of abbreviations, and other helpful information. An unabridged (complete) dictionary contains more than half a million entries. Shorter abridged or "collegiate" dictionaries are more limited, but they are generally adequate for high school use.

**16.1a  General dictionaries**  Following is a list of reliable dictionaries of the English language.

> *Webster's New Collegiate Dictionary*
> *The American Heritage Dictionary of the English Language*
> *Funk and Wagnall's New Standard Dictionary of the English Language*
> *The Random House Dictionary of the English Language*
> *Thorndike-Barnhart Comprehensive Dictionary*

**16.1b  Special Dictionaries**  Some special dictionaries deal with certain aspects of the language: slang, synonyms and antonyms, roots, and rhymes, for example. Other special dictionaries deal with the special terminology of music, medicine, economics, and many other fields.
Here is a list of common special dictionaries your library probably has.

> *Abbreviations Dictionary: (Abbreviations, Acronyms, Contractions, Signs, and Symbols Defined)*
> *Compton's Illustrated Science Dictionary*
> *Dictionary of Biology*
> *Dictionary of Literary Terms*
> *Dictionary of Science and Technology*
> *A Dictionary of Slang and Unconventional English*
> *Harvard Dictionary of Music*
> *The New Roget's Thesaurus in Dictionary Form*
> *Wood's Unabridged Rhyming Dictionary*

## 16.2  ENCYCLOPEDIAS

**Encyclopedias** are reference works that contain articles on almost every known subject. Entries are arranged in alphabetical order. Guide words on the spine of the books help you locate information quickly.

GENERAL ENCYCLOPEDIAS:  *Collier's Encyclopedia*
*Encyclopedia Americana*
*Encyclopaedia Britannica*
*World Book Encyclopedia*

SPECIAL ENCYCLOPEDIAS:  *The Baseball Encyclopedia*
*Encyclopedia of Careers and Vocational Guidance*
*Encyclopedia of World Art*
*McGraw-Hill Encyclopedia of Science and Technology*
*McGraw-Hill Encyclopedia of World Drama*
*New Catholic Encyclopedia*
*New Century Cyclopedia of Names*

## 16.3 OTHER REFERENCE BOOKS

Besides dictionaries and encyclopedias, libraries contain many other reference books with which you should become familiar.

**16.3a Quotations and literary references** The following reference books can provide information on literary history, major authors, quotations, proverbs, and poetry.

*Bartlett's Familiar Quotations*
*Granger's Index to Poetry*
*A Literary History of England*
*A Literary History of the United States*
*The Oxford Companion to American Literature*
*The Oxford Companion to the Theatre*

**16.3b Biographical and author reference** To find out biographical information about writers and other famous people living and dead, consult the following reference books.

*American Men and Women of Science*
*Current Biography*
*Dictionary of American Biography*
*The International Who's Who*
*Twentieth Century Authors*
*Who's Who in America*
*Who's Who of American Women*
*Who's Who Among Black Americans*

**16.3c The vertical file** The **vertical file** is a filing cabinet in which the library stores pamphlets, photographs, newspaper clippings, career information, and other materials that cannot be stored in any other way.

**16.3d Atlases and Gazetteers** **Atlases** and **gazetteers** are primarily books of maps that also contain important factual and statistical information about the geographical areas they cover. Use them, for example, to find out population figures and farm or industrial output. Since international boundaries are constantly shifting, be sure to check the copyright date of the atlas or gazetteer you are using to make sure the information it contains is up to date.

*Atlas of World History*
*Collier's World Atlas and Gazetteer*
*Hammond's Ambassador World Atlas*
*Rand McNally Collegiate World Atlas*
*The Times Atlas of the World*

**16.3e  The Readers' Guide**  Current magazines are primary sources for information on contemporary rather than historical topics. The *Readers' Guide to Periodical Literature* is an index to over a hundred current magazines. The *Readers' Guide* is organized much like the card catalog: subjects and cross references are listed together alphabetically. The *Readers' Guide* abbreviates its entries to save space.

```
HOUSE building. See House construction          ——— Subject entry
HOUSE building industry. See Construction in-
    dustry
HOUSE building materials. See Building materials
HOUSE buying
    Buying a house? Analyze the floor plan first.  ——— Title
      il Changing T 31:29-30 Ja '77
    Buying an older house? National association of
      realtors inspection program. J. H. Ingersoll.  ——— Author
      House B 118:8+ Jl '76
    How to home in on a place to live. P. Gross.
      il House & Gard 149:54+ Ja '77
    Shopping for a house—here's what to expect. il
      U.S. News 80:35-6 F 2 '76
    Unexpected boom. D. Pauly and J. B. Cope-
      land. il Newsweek 88:53 D 27 '76
    What makes a good house great; guidelines. S.
      Mead and others. il Bet Hom & Gard 54:44-9  ——— Volume and page
      F '76
        See also                                    ——— Cross reference
    Mortgages
        Laws and legislation                        ——— Subtopic heading
    New deal for home buyers; Real estate settle-
      ment procedures act. Changing T 30:43 O '76
HOUSE calls, Medical. See Medicine—Practice
HOUSE cleaning
    Does your bathroom have a spotless reputation?
      D. Raffel. House & Gard 148:32 Ag '76
    Happier housecleaning. M. Davidson. il Parents  ——— Illustrated
      Mag 51:41-3 Ap '76
    How to get your house cleaning act together.
      M. Davidson. il Parents Mag 52:24-6 Ja '77
    How to have children—and a clean house too.
      Redbook 147:78+ Jl '76
HOUSE cleaning services. See Service industries
HOUSE construction
    Escape houses; build your own second home.
      B. Niles and M. Glass. il Am Home 79:49-52  ——— Magazine
      O '76
    New universe of squatter-builders; excerpts
      from address, May 1975. J. F. C. Turner. il
      UNESCO Courier 29:12-14+ Je '76
    What's new in your next house. M. McClintock.
      il Pop Mech 146:94-7 Jl '76                   ——— Date
        See also
    House framing
```

**16.3f  Almanacs and yearbooks**  Almanacs and yearbooks are books that contain the most up-to-date statistical and factual information on such topics as sports, population figures, and government officials. Each yearly edition of an almanac or yearbook also contains a summary of the most important events of the previous year.

> *Guinness Book of World Records*
> *Information Please Almanac*
> *Statesman's Yearbook*
> *Women's Rights Almanac*
> *World Almanac and Book of Facts*

# EXERCISES

**A. Using the Dewey Decimal System** Arrange the following call numbers in the order in which the books would be found on a library's shelves.

| | | |
|---|---|---|
| 803.2 | 430.2 | 099.2 |
| 066.31 | 803.4 | 929.34 |
| 929.31 | 929.1 | 803.21 |

**B. Locating books** Write the numbers 1–5 on your paper. Write the classification numbers between which you would expect to find books on the following topics.

1. organic farming
2. Spanish grammar
3. basketball
4. inflation
5. ballet

**C. Using the card catalog** Write the numbers 1–5 on your paper. Find out the following information by using the card catalog in your library.

1. the author of *Profiles in Courage*
2. the title of a novel by Pearl Buck
3. the title of a biography written by Lady Antonia Fraser
4. the publication date of *A Dictionary of Modern English Usage,* second edition, by H. W. Fowler
5. the author and title of a book about China

**D. Using dictionaries** Write the numbers 1–5 on your paper. Use the dictionaries in your library to answer the following questions. Write the title of the dictionary you used after each answer. Use no dictionary more than once.

1. Define the word *kaleidoscope* and use it correctly in a sentence.
2. What is the origin of the words *shirt* and *skirt*?
3. Define *pentameter* and give an example of its use.
4. List three synonyms for the word *keep*.
5. List the meanings of the following proper names: Charles, Elizabeth, Ann, and Henry.

**E. Using reference books** Write the numbers 1–10 on your paper. Use the *Readers' Guide,* an encyclopedia, or any other reference book in your library to answer the following questions. Write the title of the reference book you used after each answer. Do not use any book more than once.

1. What was the population of Florida in 1970?

2. Who is Thurgood Marshall?
3. List two buildings that the architect Frank Lloyd Wright designed.
4. Give the name of the author of the poem whose first line is: "If I can stop one heart from breaking."
5. List the titles of three magazine articles on ecology. Write the author, title, magazine, date, and page numbers for each article.
6. List three operas written by the Italian composer Giacomo Puccini.
7. Describe the flags of Denmark, Liberia, and Canada.
8. List the name of a reference book that contains an article on Greek mythology.
9. Which reference book on literature contains an article about the American author Eudora Welty?
10. Which reference book on literature contains an article about the British novelist Emily Bronte?

# EFFECTIVE SPEAKING

## 17
## Giving a Talk or Oral Report

Very few people are good public speakers the first time they stand up to address a group. Confidence comes with experience and practice. The two greatest worries that beginning speakers have are "What am I going to say?" and "Will I capture the audience's attention?" Careful preparation beforehand can help you overcome those two worries and enable you to actually enjoy the experience of speaking before a live audience.

## 17.1 PREPARING THE TALK

The key to giving successful talks and oral reports lies in knowing your audience, knowing your purpose for speaking, and above all, knowing your material well. As we go along, we will see how these three factors affect the outcome of your talk.

**17.1a Selecting the topic** Sometimes you will be given a specific topic for your talk. More often than not, though, you will be given a general subject such as school problems, pollution, or world affairs. You will then have to decide on one aspect of the subject to talk about.
In choosing a topic, keep in mind the following two considerations:

**The audience** Different groups call for different approaches, so you should be careful not to underestimate nor overshoot your listeners' level of interest. Prepare your talk with your audience in mind. This also includes how formal and complex the type of language you choose should be.

**Your own interests** Make sure that the topic you choose is one you are interested in. A speaker's enthusiasm quickly sparks an audience. Do not be afraid to choose a topic that you want to know more about if you have time to research it properly.

New ideas or a fresh outlook on old ideas is sure to please an audience. Avoid repeating what your audience already knows.

**17.1b Narrowing the topic** To narrow your topic, you must be clear about what you are trying to accomplish in delivering your talk. Your main purpose may be to inform, to persuade, or to entertain your listeners. (A successful speech, however, combines elements of all three purposes.)

To inform an audience, you should be prepared to give specific facts and information about your subject. This is the most common type of oral report. In persuasion, your intention is to convince your audience that what you are suggesting should be done. To entertain, you want to make your audience enjoy your speech.

The topic you choose should be simple enough to handle well in the time you have been given to speak. Remember that there is a difference between a two-minute report and a ten-minute formal speech. A good rule of thumb is to select a limited topic for a short talk and a broader topic for a longer speech.

If you are unsure how to limit a topic, read over the guidelines in section 6.1, which tell you how to narrow a topic for a term paper. The hints presented there are valid for both term papers and for speeches.

**17.1c  Finding material**  Your skill in using the library will help you research most topics. In your reading, look for facts, details, examples, illustrations, and interesting stories that you can include in your talk. Unless you are speaking about an historical topic, the best sources for information will be the *Readers' Guide* and the vertical file.

You will make your talk more interesting if you can draw from your personal experience. Talking to others can help you, too. Take good notes if you interview other people. You should also take notes on your reading. In fact, take more notes than you need—you can always throw the unused notes away. Here are some helpful guidelines:

**Read with a purpose.** Be aware of good examples and facts that you can include. Be sure the material you choose is accurate and up to date.

**Look for different points of view.** Do not believe something because you found it in a book. Do not pass over material that could disprove what you believe. Be prepared to answer all reasonable objections to your conclusions.

**Take notes on index cards.** In this way, you will be able to organize your findings efficiently and omit what is not useful.

## EXERCISES

**A. Narrowing a topic**  Copy the following grid onto a piece of paper. Basing your answers on the five general topics, write in each box the topic of a talk appropriate for the time allowed.

| NARROWING A TOPIC |||||
|---|---|---|---|
| General | 2 minutes | 5 minutes | 10 minutes |
| 1. Sports Heroes | | | |
| 2. The Supernatural | | | |
| 3. Recreation | | | |
| 4. Money | | | |
| 5. The Future | | | |

**B. Considering the audience** Write the numbers 1–5 on your paper. Write a talk topic for each of the following audiences. Base each topic on the general topic *the Value of Education*.

1. a second-grade class
2. your class
3. college students
4. a group of parents
5. a group of teachers

**C. Finding material** Choose one topic from those you wrote for the ten-minute talk group in Exercise A. Prepare a list of articles and references you can use to research the topic you have chosen. Use index cards to take notes on material you will include in your speech. Save your notes. You will need them for future exercises.

**17.1d Outlining your talk** The best way to organize your talk is to write an outline of the major points you are going to present. How to write an outline is discussed in section 6.3.

Divide your outline into three parts: the introduction, the body, and the conclusion.

Use the introduction to gain your audience's interest and attention. Tell them what the purpose of your talk is. Give whatever background information is needed for them to understand your talk.

The body is the part of the speech in which you give the audience the facts, examples, and illustrations you have selected to inform, persuade, or entertain them. Develop all of your major points and build up toward a climax. Arrange your ideas in the most logical and clear way possible.

Use the conclusion to summarize the main points of your talk. The conclusion is not the time to introduce new ideas, but to let your audience see the old ones in a new light. You can show where all the information you have presented leads. You can appeal to the audience to follow the suggestions you have made.

**17.1e Writing effective openings** Your audience has many things on their minds as you stand up to speak. The function of the introduction of your speech is to focus their attention on what you have to say. A strong opening is important.

Here are seven suggestions for opening a speech.

1. Use an historical reference. Find a relevant fact from the past and relate it to the present.

    *One hundred ten years ago, the one-room schoolhouse in this town was judged too small for the population, and a new school was built. Today, once again, Middletown has outgrown its school. It is time for expansion.*

2. Use a personal reference. A personal experience can be a good lead-in to a general discussion as long as you don't keep talking about yourself too long.

    *Last Sunday I went for a walk in the park. Under every second bush I found a crushed beer can. The stream was clogged with old newspapers. I think it's about time we cleaned up that park.*

3. Use a timely reference. Mention some recent fact or incident of which the audience is aware.

    *I see that many of you are sitting there fanning yourselves and wiping the perspiration off your foreheads. There is no better time than today to discuss the possibilities of air-conditioning our school.*

4. Use a question. Under the right circumstances, a question can be a powerful opening. But avoid it if the audience is unruly or if there is a chance that someone will shout out an answer.

    *As editor of the school newspaper, I ask you this: Did you join our staff to put out a paper or just to have a good time?*

5. Use a story or description. A relevant story or description can set the tone for the rest of the speech.

    *Last year, two students from Washington High volunteered to help conservationists count and identify migrating birds. Through their work, those students not only helped complete an important study, but also gained valuable experience that helped them win college scholarships.*

6. Avoid jokes and flat statements of the subject. The joke opening is used too often. Avoid jokes unless the joke is new to the audience, relevant, and well told. This, of course, does not apply to a humorous speech.

A flat statement of your topic is a weak opening. Do not tell your audience that something is interesting; tell them something interesting about it. Notice how dull the following opening is.

> Today I'm going to talk about trees, which is a very interesting topic to many of you.

7. Use combinations of openings. Notice how the following example combines a personal reference and a timely reference.

> As a member of the tennis team, I appreciate the spectators at our games. Yesterday, however, even though the match was played right here at school, only five students showed up to watch.

**17.1f Rehearsing your talk** First, decide how you are going to deliver your speech. You can either memorize the entire talk or refer to notes you have made on index cards. If you use notes, keep them out of the audience's sight. Speeches read from a sheet of paper are usually dull. Reading a speech can also isolate you from the audience.

**Rehearse your talk aloud.** Concentrate on speaking clearly and distinctly. Many speakers have a tendency to rush their words. Rushing makes the speech hard to follow. Recite the speech aloud a number of times so that you can make it flow easily.

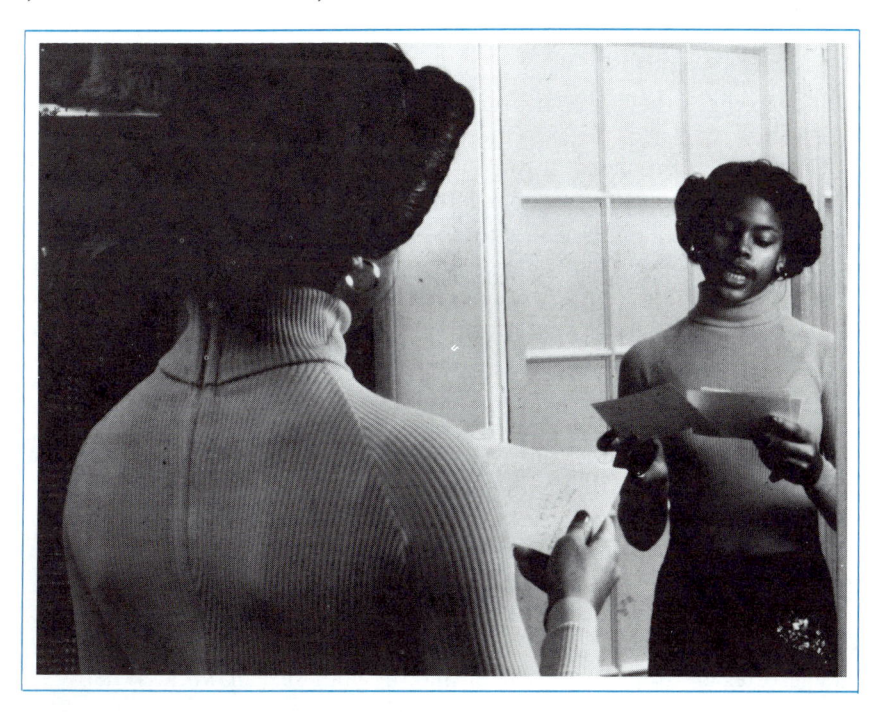

**Use a tape recorder.** Listen to yourself critically. Be sure that your sentences are smooth and that each word gets its proper emphasis. Rework any section that does not come out to your satisfaction. This is also a good time to check whether all your ideas are in the most logical place. Poor organization makes a speech sound rough and unfinished.

# EXERCISES

**A.** Writing an outline   Using your topic and notes from Exercise C on page 413, write a detailed outline of the material you are going to include in your speech. Save your work for future exercises.

**B.** Evaluating introductions   Discuss the weak and strong points of each of the following introductions in a short paragraph covering all four.

1. Well, I've been assigned to give a speech about how poorly the students clean up the cafeteria. Actually, it's a very interesting topic.
2. Have you ever wondered what turns people into monsters as soon as they get behind the wheel of a car? What I'm going to tell you about the psychology of driving will scare you to death.
3. The fire engines roared down the street at three in the morning last Tuesday, but they were too late to save the Wallace home. The Wallace family lost their home because of faulty electrical wiring. Do you know how to check the wiring in *your* home?
4. Twenty years ago, the city promised to repair the lakefront drive because it always flooded during rainstorms. I drove down that same road yesterday in the rain, and once more it was flooded.

**C.** Writing effective openings   Using the outline you wrote in Exercise A, write the introduction to your speech. Model your introduction on one of the suggested openings in section 17.2a.

## 17.2   DELIVERING YOUR TALK

Delivering a speech in front of a live audience does not have to be the frightening experience that many students make it out to be.

Remember that you are the resident expert. You have researched your topic and know the information thoroughly. All that is left to do is to put some polish on your presentation.

**17.2a   Using body language**   Posture, eye contact with the audience, and gestures are important parts of making your speech work. When you stand up to talk, take a deep breath and let your body relax. This will help remove some of the tension you feel. Stand up straight and do not lean upon a desk or podium. Use your notes, but do not hide your face behind them.

Use eye contact to make your speech seem directed to each individual member of the audience. If looking into a person's eyes makes you laugh, look at a point on the forehead just above the eyes. Watching the audience will also help you judge how well your talk is being understood.

Using too many gestures can be distracting, while using too few can make you seem dull and wooden. Rehearse using gestures in front of a mirror a few times until you get a happy balance.

**17.2b** **Using verbal language** You should speak loudly enough so that everyone in the room can hear every word clearly and distinctly. Get into the habit of looking at your notes only during a natural pause. Avoid speaking in a monotone. Let your voice emphasize important words and phrases. Be careful not to speak too quickly or your listeners will miss too much and get bored.

The language you use should be appropriate for the type of speech you are giving. You have a choice of two levels of language: formal English and informal English.

Formal English uses long sentences, no contractions, and many words that are not normally a part of everyday conversation. Formal English should be used in debates and formal speeches.

> *I am honored to introduce our guest speaker, Ms. Begay, who is the president of the Monroe County Wildlife Preservation Council. Today Ms. Begay will speak to us on a topic that is statewide in scope: The need for expansion of our inland bird sanctuaries.*

Informal English is the level of language used in ordinary conversation and informal talks. Informal English uses contractions, shorter sentences, and easily understood words.

> *Interest in home gardening is on the rise in the United States. Today, many people—old and young—are planting vegetables and herbs in their backyards and windowboxes. If you'd like to start a garden, too, but don't think you have the space . . .*

Informal English sometimes allows slang, but you should generally avoid it. Rather than settling for an imprecise slang word, choose a phrase that really expresses what you mean to say. Slang, however, can always be used for humorous or special effect.

## EXERCISES

**A. Polishing your talk**   Do the following activities at home before you deliver your speech in front of the class.

1. Finish writing the speech you outlined for Exercise A, page 416.
2. Read over your speech for proper level of language, formal or informal.
3. Recite your speech into a tape recorder to check for proper enunciation, rhythm, and emphasis. If you do not have a tape recorder, ask a friend or member of your family to listen to your speech and to comment on how you sound.
4. Recite your speech in front of a mirror to check on your use of gestures.

**B. Delivering your talk**   Using all the techniques mentioned in this section, deliver to your class the talk you practiced in Exercise A.

# 18
# Group Discussions

Group discussions may involve many or few participants, but some features are common to both large and small discussion groups. Large and small discussions call for active involvement by all, either by speaking or by creative listening. The discussion must be conducted in an orderly way. Lastly, participants must be willing to change their minds if solid evidence disproves their views.

## 18.1   PREPARING FOR THE DISCUSSION

To take part in a discussion, you should understand how different types of discussions are run and what roles chairpersons, speakers, and the audience have. You should also be clear about the sort of preparation you must personally do to get the most out of the discussion.

**18.1a   Understanding the kind of discussion**   Following are five different types of discussion groups often found in high schools.

1. **Small group discussions** involve anywhere from seven to twelve people. Each member of the group has the right to speak. Such groups are usu-

# ENGLISH FOR BUSINESS

## 19
## Business Letters

Many requests and inquiries you will have to make are better handled by letter than by a telephone call. A letter records information that could be forgotten or confused through a telephone call.

Your letter represents *you,* so it is important to master the form and style of the business letter to make a good impression on your reader.

### 19.1 LETTER FORM

There are three standard formats for business letters. Use the block form and semiblock form for typewritten letters. The indented form is used for handwritten letters. Examine the examples of the three types carefully.

**BLOCK FORM**

```
                              507 Yuma Street
                              Sierra Vista, AZ  85635
                              July 10, 1980


Parkwood Camera Stores
12201 West Pico Boulevard
Los Angeles, CA  90064

Gentlemen:

    _____

    _____


    _____

    _____



                    Sincerely yours,
                    Felix Hashota
                    Felix Hashota
```

Heading

Inside Address

Salutation

Body

Closing
Signature

**SEMIBLOCK FORM**

Heading

    402 beaumont Road
    Lufkin, TX  75901
    May 2, 1980

Inside Address

National Safety Council
425 North Michigan Avenue
Chicago, IL 60611

Salutation

Ladies and Gentlemen:

Body

_____
_____

_____
_____

Closing
Signature

    Sincerely,
    *Laura Mae Sills*
    Laura Mae Sills

**INDENTED FORM**

Heading

    528 Jackson Avenue
    Manor, PA  15665
    March 1, 1980

Inside Address

Fruity Candy Company
  Allegheny Road
    Mt. Bethel, PA  18343

Salutation
Body

Ladies and Gentlemen:
_____
_____
_____
_____

Closing
Signature

    Sincerely,
    Beth Cambel

**19.1a  Parts of the letter**  Whatever form you use when writing a business letter, certain things remain the same: paper, heading, address, salutation, and body.

**Paper**  Whether you type or handwrite business letters, always use plain white paper. Write or type on one side only.

**The heading**  The heading for a business letter is the same as the heading for a friendly letter. Always include your ZIP code.

**The inside address**  Place the inside address four lines below the heading. The inside address contains the name and title of the person receiving the letter and the company's name and address. Avoid abbreviations as much as possible.

>Ms. Wendy Misako, President
>Misako Enterprises, Inc.
>2525 Date Street
>Honolulu, HI 96813

In writing to a specific person, always use the person's proper title (*Mr., Mrs., Miss,* or *Ms.*) or official title (*Dr., Rev.,* and so forth).

>Ms. Coleen Witver     Honorable Leslie Bullock

Do not use two titles that mean the same thing.

INCORRECT:   Dr. Laura Elayne, M.D.

Place company titles on the same line as the person's name if the title is short. If not, place the title on the next line.

TOGETHER:   Mr. Luke Davidson, Manager
SEPARATE:   Mrs. Olga Gill
                      Vice President for Marketing

Use the company's title exactly as it appears on the firm's letterhead.

- Middletown Historical Society
- Wright & Ellis, Publishers

**The salutation**  Place the salutation two lines below the inside address. Always end the salutation with a colon.

Use the person's last name and proper title if you know it.

If you know only a title and not a name, use the title in the inside address and *Dear Sir, Dear Madam,* or *Dear Sir or Madam* in the salutation.

>Office of the Registrar
>Jersey City State College
>Jersey City, NJ 07306

>Dear Sir or Madam:

**The body** The body of a business letter should be brief and to the point. Always use formal standard English.

Write or type the first line of the body two spaces below the salutation. Always single space. Be consistent in your paragraphing style. If you use block form, do not indent the paragraph. If you use modified block form indent all paragraphs.

**The closing** The standard form for closing a business letter is *Yours truly* or *Very truly yours*. Notice that only the first word is capitalized. You may also use the less formal *Sincerely yours*.

**The signature** Print or type your name four lines below the closing and write your signature in the space in between. Never type your signature. Never sign your title along with your signature.

**19.1b Addressing the envelope** The envelope should be addressed carefully to make sure that the letter is delivered to its destination. Always include a return address.

Observe the following rules in addressing the envelope.
1. Always use block style in typing the address and the return address.
2. Copy the name and address of the person to receive the letter exactly as you wrote it in the inside address.
3. Always use a proper title.
4. Do not use a title before your own name in the return address.

```
Peter Vance
401 Carlsbad Road
Clovis, NM 88101




                        Ms. Nancy Dowd
                        American Foundation for the Blind
                        15 West 16 Street
                        New York, NY  10011
```

## 19.2 TYPES OF BUSINESS LETTERS

Strictly speaking, every formal letter you write is a business letter. You will find, though, that most of your business letters fall into one of four categories. These are letters of *information, inquiry, request,* and *complaint*. Following are some guidelines common to all four types.

**Be brief and to the point** Use short sentences and short paragraphs. Avoid slang.

**Say everything you intend to say** Answer all questions you have been asked. Include all necessary information—for example, the catalog number, price, and tax of an item you are ordering.

**Avoid trite phrases** Phrases such as "Enclosed please find" and "Thanking you in advance" are old fashioned and a waste of words.

**Be courteous** Say "please" and "thank you." Excessive bluntness tends to turn people off.

**19.2a    The informative letter**    You may have to answer a letter that asks you for information. Answer each question briefly and completely. Offer to supply further information if necessary. Reply to the letter politely and promptly.

---

                                                Warwick High School
                                                51 Copeland Avenue
                                                Newport News, Virginia 23601
                                                December 17, 1979

Mr. Paul Kaftanski
Editor, The Lantern
Wapakoneta Senior High School
Wapakoneta, Ohio 45895

Dear Mr. Kaftanski:

     The printing cost for our school's newspaper is about $400.00 per issue, which usually runs eight pages. The printer is an out-of-state firm that handles only school newspapers.

     You should contact Mr. Al Zurick at School Publications, Inc., Avon, New Jersey 07962, to get an official price quote if you want School Publications to print The Lantern.

                                                     Sincerely yours,

                                                     *Becky Stauffer*
                                                   (Ms.) Becky Stauffer
                                                   Editor-in-Chief, The Eagle

**19.2b  Letters of inquiry and request**  You may have to write a letter of inquiry or a letter of request if you cannot get information by yourself or if you wish to place an order for something. You should state why you are making the request and tell exactly what information you want. In ordering goods through the mail, include catalog number, description, price, and tax, if any.

```
                                        5 Billings Street
                                        Bozeman, Montana 59715
                                        September 10, 19__

Australian Tourist Commission
P.O. Box L
Staten Island, New York 10305

Dear Sir or Madam:

     The students in my world geography course have
been asked to prepare talks on each of the continents.  I
have been assigned to talk about Australia.

     Please send me whatever illustrated travel brochures
you can spare so that I can show the class--as well as tell
them--what Australia is really like.  I would particularly
appreciate photographs of Australia's unique wildlife.

                                   Sincerely,

                                   Amos Handy
                                   Amos Handy
```

**19.2c  Letters of complaint**  If you have bought an item that is unsatisfactory, you should bring it to the dealer's or manufacturer's attention in a letter of complaint. Describe the item and state what the problem is. Above all, be firm but courteous. Most businesses want you as a customer, and they are very willing to make adjustments for you.

```
                                        20 Arvada Street
                                        Fort Carson, Colorado 80913
                                        July 5, 19__

Ms. Sara Trudell
Thornton's Sporting Goods
224 North Glen Road
Colorado Springs, Colorado 80901

Dear Ms. Trudell:

     Yesterday I received the Camp Trails Ponderosa
backpack (catalog number 575L), which I ordered from you on
June 25.  When I opened the shipping carton, I found that
two of the outside pockets on the pack were almost com-
pletely torn off.

     I am returning the pack to you in its original
carton.  I ask that you either send me a replacement pack
in perfect condition or refund my purchase price of
$36.00 plus tax and the $1.50 shipping charge.

                                        Sincerely,

                                        Flo Dezba
                                        Flo Dezba
```

# EXERCISES

**A. Writing a letter of inquiry**  Write for more information about the special five-day junior tennis camp program run by the Leslie Santo Tennis Center at Sennett Cove, Chicago, Illinois 60601. Ask what other programs you might qualify for. On the back of your letter, draw a box and write out a correctly addressed envelope for your letter.

**B. Writing a letter of complaint**  Write to Ms. Elizabeth Levi, editor of *Children's Day,* 523 Fifth Avenue, New York, New York 10017. Complain that the gift subscription you bought for your cousin has been paid for but no issues have been delivered yet. On the back of your letter, draw a box and write out a correctly addressed envelope for your letter.

**C. Writing a letter of request**  Write to the Office of the Registrar, Wright College, Tucson, Arizona 85726, to ask for a college catalog, admissions forms, and further information about the field of study that interests you. On the back of your letter, draw a box and write out a correctly addressed envelope.

# 20
# Getting a Part-time Job

A part-time job can supply you with extra pocket money and give you work experience that can help you find a full-time job later on. To get a part-time job you need to know where to find jobs, how to write out applications and résumés, and what to do in a job interview.

## 20.1  WHERE TO LOOK

There are a number of ways to find out what jobs are available. The most important sources are newspapers, personal contacts, and direct contact with local companies.

Also, you can volunteer your services, which will give you work experience, though no pay, or you can start a business of your own. Look at your skills and talents. Besides mowing lawns and baby-sitting, there are sure to be other services you could offer your community.

**20.1a  Newspapers**  The job advertisements in your local newspaper list part-time jobs around town. They may all be listed in a special section for part-time help, or some may be in the regular listings along with the abbreviation *P/T*.

Follow completely all instructions in the ad. Some ads will tell you to call or to appear in person. Others say to send a résumé. If you do not fit the requirements, do not apply.

To answer a box number, write the box number plus the address of the newspaper.

---

PART TIME Summer, general, help around house and yard. Own transportation required. Ideal for student.
Send resume to box 105 this paper.

---

BABYSITTER, MOTHERS helper, responsible person. Write box 106 this paper.

---

NEED 2 STRONG PEOPLE to move furniture June 26, 27. 555-5649.

---

**20.1b  Personal contacts**  Family, relatives, and friends may be able to give you good leads for part-time jobs. Many student counselors also keep lists of job opportunities. Some banks, libraries, and other buildings have bulletin boards on which local stores advertise for part-time help and on which you can place your own ad. You could also visit stores in your area to see if they need extra help.

**20.1c  Letters of inquiry**  If you want to widen your search pattern to include companies with which you have no personal contacts, write a letter of inquiry to the personnel director of the firm.

In a letter of inquiry, you should state as precisely as possible the sort of job you are seeking and what skills you can offer the company. State the hours you can work.

## EXERCISES

**A. Understanding help-wanted ads**  Read through the job ads in your local newspaper every day for a week. Clip out all the job ads you qualify for, and bring them into class.

**B. Knowing your qualifications** Make a list of services that you by yourself or with some of your friends could offer the local community. Discuss your findings in class.

**C. Finding volunteer jobs** List the names and addresses of hospitals and other institutions in your community that accept volunteer workers. Try to get job descriptions for these positions.

## 20.2 APPLYING FOR A JOB

Having found out what jobs are available, the next stage is to apply for those that interest you. You should become familiar with the three basic procedures you will encounter: the letter of application, the application form, and the résumé.

### 20.2a The letter of application

Your letter of application is an employer's first introduction to you. A poorly written or sloppy letter may cost you the very job you most want.

You should cover four main points in a letter of application. Devote a separate paragraph to each point.

**State the job and tell how you heard about it.** Be as specific and concise as you can. The employer should not have to decide whether you are applying for junior counselor or senior counselor, for instance.

**State your experience.** Give your age and state the details of your education and work experience that will enable you to handle that job. However, this is not the place for your complete life history.

Work experience does not mean only *paid* work experience. Mention related volunteer work, hobbies, and other activities that you think qualify you for the job.

**Give references.** List the names and addresses of three people who can give you good recommendations. Be sure to ask their permission first.

**Propose an interview.** State the days or hours that you would be available for a personal interview. Include your phone number and suggest times you can be contacted in order to set up the interview.

### EXERCISE

**The letter of application** Read the following letter of application carefully. In a paragraph or two, tell how well it fits the requirements for a letter of application.

Dear Dr. Davick:

    Through Gloria Davis, who worked for you until she graduated last spring, I learned that you have an opening for a part-time animal care assistant in the Bellmar Animal Hospital. Because I enjoy working with animals and want to be a veterinarian when I am older, I am applying for the position.

    I am in the science honors program at Blufton High School, where I am a sophmore. I own a horse, two dogs, and a large collection of white mice. I am solely responsible for their care and feeding. My biology teacher last year put me in charge of caring for all the school's laboratory animals, some fifty mice, snakes, frogs, and cats.

    Mr. Frank E. Zucotti, biology teacher at Blufton High, will gladly tell you how well I cared for the school's animals. Gloria Davis, your former assistant and frequent visitor to my home, can vouch for the care I give my own pets.

    I can visit your office for an interview any day after 3:00 P.M. My home telephone number is 789-0011.

                                    Sincerely,
                                    Maggie Semler

**20.2b Filling in an application form** Application forms used by companies and employment agencies ask for roughly the same information. When you fill out an application, make sure that you have all the needed dates, names, and addresses on a sheet of paper for ready reference. Use the following example application form as your guide.

## employment application

*An Equal Opportunity Employer*

| LAST NAME (PRINT) | FIRST NAME | MIDDLE NAME | SOCIAL SECURITY NO. |
|---|---|---|---|
| Lan | Susan | Chi | 000-00-0000 |

| PRESENT STREET NUMBER | CITY | STATE | ZIP | TELEPHONE NO. |
|---|---|---|---|---|
| 2463 Flanders Road, | Woodbridge, | New Jersey | 07874 | 555-2183 |

PERMANENT ADDRESS (IF DIFFERENT FROM ABOVE) / TELEPHONE NO.

| *DATE OF BIRTH | U.S. CITIZEN? | LIST ANY KNOWN PHYSICAL DEFECTS |
|---|---|---|
| 5/10/64 | Yes | Deaf in left ear |

### education

| | NAME AND LOCATION OF SCHOOL | DATES ATTENDED | GRADUATION DATE | MAJOR | DEGREE |
|---|---|---|---|---|---|
| HIGH | Garfield High School | 9/78 — 6/82 | | | |
| COLLEGE | | | | | |
| OTHER EDUCATION | | | | | |

### general information

TYPE OF WORK DESIRED: Cashier or Sales Clerk

| ARE YOU WILLING TO TRAVEL? WHAT % OF TIME? | DATE AVAILABLE FOR EMPLOYMENT | LOCATION PREFERENCE | SALARY EXPECTED |
|---|---|---|---|
| No | immediately | Central store | open |

NOTIFY IN EMERGENCY (NAME, ADDRESS, TELEPHONE NUMBER): Mildred Lan, 2463 Flanders Road, Woodbridge, New Jersey 555-2183

### employment history

*present employer first*

| EMPLOYER'S NAME AND ADDRESS | DATES FROM TO | POSITION | SUPERVISOR'S NAME | MAY WE CONTACT | REASON FOR LEAVING |
|---|---|---|---|---|---|
| Pembrook Bookstore | 6/79 9/79 | clerk | Ms. Sue Rice | Yes | Return to School |

### references

Please give 4 references, preferably business, professional, academic. If you do not have 4 such references, please give a sufficient number of personal references to bring the total references to 4.

| NAME | ADDRESS | TELEPHONE | POSITION |
|---|---|---|---|
| Ms. Sue Rice | Pembrook Bookstore, 592 South St., Woodbridge | 555-1843 | Store Manager |
| Mr. Ralph Romano | Garfield High School, 213 Elm St., Woodbridge | 555-1121 | Math Teacher |
| Mr. Diego Cruz | Pembrook Bookstore, 592 South St., Woodbridge | 555-1843 | Sales Clerk |
| Ms. Mary Marier | Garfield High School, 213 Elm St. Woodbridge | 555-1123 | Guidance Counselor |

I understand that I cannot be employed until I have satisfactorily passed a physical examination and that all offers of employment are made subject to this requirement.

I hereby certify that all data contained in this application for employment is true and accurate. I understand that this data will be carefully checked, and I authorize investigation of all statements contained in this application. Any misrepresentation of information will be sufficient cause for rejection of this application or, if employment has commenced, grounds for immediate dismissal.

DATE: 3/6/80

SIGNATURE: *Susan Chi Lan*

**20.2c  Writing a résumé** There are many different ways to write a résumé, which is an outline of your education, work experience, interests, and personal data. The following example is only one possible type of résumé. Tailor-make the résumé to fit yourself, your background, and the type of work you are seeking.

Make a good copy of your résumé and keep it for yourself. It is all right to send photocopies of a résumé to an employer, but never send a photocopy of the cover letter that you send with the résumé.

```
Jill J. LaRocca

22 Peninsula Drive

Daytona Beach, Florida  32018

PERSONAL DATA:

Date of Birth:          June 14, 1962

Height:                 5'8"

Weight:                 125 lbs.

EDUCATION:

Washington High School, Daytona Beach, Florida.  Diploma, 1980

WORK EXPERIENCE:

6/78-Present   Oceanside Department Store--SALES CLERK

               225 Fulton Street

               Daytona Beach, Florida  32018

               Used a computerized cash register in

               sporting goods department.  Assisted

               in inventory control.  Supervised

               loading of shelves.

10/76-6/77     School Book Store--VOLUNTEER CLERK

               Washington High School

               924 Flatbush Avenue

               Daytona Beach, Florida  32018

               Sold school supplies, kept inventory.

               Ordered supplies through school office.

References furnished upon request.
```

## 20.3 THE INTERVIEW

The personal interview is usually the last stage of the employment procedure. It is the time during which the employer will probably decide to hire you or not. You should be ready to discuss your knowledge, skills, and interests in a way that will make the employer select you.

**20.3a Preparing for the interview** No matter whether you have sent an employer a résumé or are approaching him or her for the first time, you should be prepared to answer questions about your background and achievements simply and honestly. Here are some questions frequently asked of future employees.

1. How much time can you devote to the part-time job? When will you do your homework? How will your outside activities interfere with your job?

2. What is your school record like? How many times have you been late or absent? How high are your marks? What are your best subjects? (If the job demands skills such as typing or bookkeeping, be prepared to show how proficient you are.)

3. What experience do you have? Come prepared to discuss in detail your paid and unpaid work experience. Be ready to tell dates of employment and to give the names of your references. Do not make up experience that you have not had.

4. What questions do you have about the job? Ask what you need to know about the job. Many employers will judge you by the quality of your questions as well as by your answers.

Finally, be open, honest, and direct, but not pushy. Dress neatly and conservatively.

**20.3b At the interview** If you have prepared well for a job interview, the interview itself should be no problem. Here are some hints to keep in mind.

**Be on time and walk in confidently.** Introduce yourself and tell what job you are seeking. Do not sit down until you are asked to sit.

**Avoid distracting mannerisms.** Do not smoke. Do not chew gum or rearrange your clothes or hair.

**Look the interviewer in the eye.** Answer questions honestly, directly, and briefly. Show that you are willing to learn the job and work hard at it.

**Speak clearly and convincingly.** Do not mumble. Avoid wisecracks. Never use slang in an interview.

**Speak positively about your experience and skills.** Show the interviewer what you are able to do. Do not apologize for lacking experience. Instead, try telling how something in your background or education will help you master the new skill. Your object is to sell your abilities to the employer.

## EXERCISES

**A. Practicing the job interview**  Team up with a classmate who will act as the interviewer. Practice an interview for any job that interests you. If you have no job in mind, use one of the following suggestions.

| | | |
|---|---|---|
| *grocery store clerk* | *receptionist* | *playground attendant* |
| *delivery person* | *file clerk* | *waiter* |
| *messenger* | *lawn mower* | *movie usher* |
| *carwash attendant* | *painter* | *camp counselor* |
| *stockroom clerk* | *baby-sitter* | *cook* |

**B. Writing a résumé**  Jot down all the information about yourself, your education, your work experience, your interests, and your skills that you think should be included in your résumé. Using the résumé in section 20.2c as your model, write a usable résumé on yourself. Do not be afraid to modify the given format to meet your specific needs.

# SKILLS HANDBOOK KEY

## READING AND STUDY SKILLS

1 Developing Your Reading Skills   334
   1.1   Reading for a Purpose   334
   1.2   Finding the Main Ideas   334
   1.3   Drawing Conclusions   335
   1.4   Increasing Your Reading Speed   336
      1.4a   Skimming   336
      1.4b   Scanning   336

2 Taking Notes on What You Read   338
   2.1   Writing a Study Outline   339
   2.2   Jotting Down New Ideas   339
   2.3   Writing a Précis   340
   2.4   Reviewing Notes for a Test   340

3 Reading Graphs   341
   3.1   Bar Graphs   341
   3.2   Line and Curve Graphs   342
   3.3   Pie and Figure Graphs   343

4 Reading Newspapers   346
   4.1   Skimming for News   346
      4.1a   Understanding Headlines   346
      4.1b   Reading Leads   347
   4.2   Studying Issues   347
      4.2a   Comparing News Stories   347
      4.2b   Reading Editorials and Columns   347
   4.3   Other Sections of a Newspaper   347
      4.3a   Feature Stories   348
      4.3b   The Classified Section   348
      4.3c   Departments and Sunday Papers   348

5 Learning Words by Reading   350
   5.1   Using Context Clues   351
   5.2   Looking at the Whole   351

## WRITING REPORTS AND ESSAYS

6 Writing Reports   355
   6.1   Analyzing the Size of the Topic   355
   6.2   Getting Information   356
   6.3   Making an Outline   357
   6.4   Writing a Rough Draft   357
   6.5   Writing the Finished Copy   358

7 Writing Essays   359
   7.1   Using the Argumentative Pattern   359

8 Writing Reviews   361
   8.1   Writing Book Reviews   361
      8.1a   Reviewing Fiction   362
      8.1b   Reviewing Biographies   362
      8.1c   Reviewing Nonfiction   363
   8.2   Writing Reviews of Television Programs   364
   8.3   Writing Reviews of Movies and Plays   364

9 Writing Essay Tests   366
   9.1   Types of Essay Questions   366
      9.1a   Compare or Contrast   366
      9.1b   Criticize, Discuss, and Analyze   366
      9.1c   Explain, Explicate, Describe, and Trace   367
      9.1d   Give Examples   367
      9.1e   Summarize   367
   9.2   The Personal Essay   367

10 Manuscript Form   369
   10.1   Paper, Margins, and Spacing   369
   10.2   Writing Numerals   369
   10.3   When to Underline   370
      10.3a   Titles   370
      10.3b   Foreign Words   370
      10.3c   Special Words and Letters   370
   10.4   Using Abbreviations   370
   10.5   Using Quoted Material   371
   10.6   Using Correction Symbols   372

## MECHANICS OF WRITING

11 Punctuation   375
   11.1   End Punctuation   375
      11.1a   The Period   375
      11.1b   The Question Mark   375
      11.1c   The Exclamation Mark   375
   11.2   The Comma   376
      11.2a   Punctuating a Series   376
      11.2b   Punctuating Appositives   376
      11.2c   Punctuating Restrictive and Nonrestrictive Modifiers   377

- 11.2d Punctuating Adverb Clauses 378
- 11.2e Punctuating Compounds 378
- 11.2f Punctuating Direct Address 379
- 11.2g Punctuating Parenthetical Expressions 379
- 11.2h Punctuating Dates and Addresses 379
- 11.2i Other Uses of the Comma 380
- 11.3 The Apostrophe 381
  - 11.3a Contractions 381
  - 11.3b The Possessive of Nouns 381
  - 11.3c The Possessive of Pronouns 381
  - 11.3d The Possessive of Time and Amounts 381
  - 11.3e The Possessive of Compound Nouns 381
  - 11.3f The Plurals of Numbers, Letters, Signs, and Words 381
- 11.4 The Semicolon 382
  - 11.4a Compound Sentences 382
  - 11.4b For Variation 382
  - 11.4c In a Series 382
- 11.5 The Colon 382
  - 11.5a Before a List 382
  - 11.5b Before a Statement of Quotation 383
  - 11.5c After a Salutation 383
  - 11.5d To Separate the Whole from Parts 383
- 11.6 Punctuating Direct Quotations 384
  - 11.6a Double Quotation Marks 384
  - 11.6b Single Quotation Marks 384
  - 11.6c Capitalization 384
  - 11.6d Punctuation Marks 385
- 11.7 Parentheses and Brackets 386
  - 11.7a Parentheses 386
  - 11.7b Brackets 386
  - 11.7c Punctuation Marks 386
- 11.8 Hyphens and Dashes 386
  - 11.8a The Hyphen 386
  - 11.8b The Dash 387
- 12 Capitalization 388
  - 12.1 Capitalizing First Words 389
    - 12.1a Sentences 389
    - 12.1b Direct Quotations 389
    - 12.1c After a Colon 389
    - 12.1d Letters 389
  - 12.2 Capitalizing Proper Nouns and Adjectives 389
    - 12.2a The Pronoun I and the Interjection O 390
    - 12.2b Names of Places 390
    - 12.2c Names of Things 390
    - 12.2d References to the Deity 391
    - 12.2e Events and Periods of Time 391
    - 12.2f Nationalities, Languages, Religions, and Races 391
    - 12.2g Prefixes and Compounds 391
  - 12.3 Capitalizing Titles 391
    - 12.3a Titles of Persons 391
    - 12.3b Titles of Things 392
- 13 A Plan for Spelling Success 393
  - 13.1 Spelling Rules 394
    - 13.1a Forming Plurals 394
    - 13.1b Adding Prefixes 395
    - 13.1c Adding Suffixes 395
    - 13.1d Choosing *ei* or *ie* 396
  - 13.2 List of Commonly Misspelled Words 397

**USING YOUR LIBRARY**

- 14 The Classification and Arrangement of Books 399
  - 14.1 How Books Are Classified 399
    - 14.1a Fiction 399
    - 14.1b Nonfiction 399
  - 14.2 How Books Are Arranged 400
    - 14.2a Author's Last Name 400
    - 14.2b Biography 400
- 15 The Card Catalog 401

- 15.1 Types of Cards 401
  - 15.1a The Author Card 401
  - 15.1b The Title Card 402
  - 15.1c The Subject Card 402
  - 15.1d Guide Cards 403
  - 15.1e Cross-Reference Cards 403
- 15.2 Locating a Book 404
  - 15.2a Open Stacks 404
  - 15.2b Call Slips 404

16 The Reference Section 405
- 16.1 Dictionaries 405
  - 16.1a General Dictionaries 406
  - 16.1b Special Dictionaries 406
- 16.2 Encyclopedias 406
- 16.3 Other Reference Books 407
  - 16.3a Quotations and Literary References 407
  - 16.3b Biographical and Author References 407
  - 16.3c The Vertical File 407
  - 16.3d Atlases and Gazetteers 407
  - 16.3e The Readers' Guide 408
  - 16.3f Almanacs and Yearbooks 408

**EFFECTIVE SPEAKING**

17 Giving a Talk or an Oral Report 411
- 17.1 Preparing the Talk 411
  - 17.1a Selecting the Topic 411
  - 17.1b Narrowing the Topic 411
  - 17.1c Finding Material 412
  - 17.1d Outlining Your Talk 413
  - 17.1e Writing Effective Openings 414
  - 17.1f Rehearsing Your Talk 415
- 17.2 Delivering Your Talk 416
  - 17.2a Using Body Language 416
  - 17.2b Using Verbal Language 417

18 Group Discussions 418
- 18.1 Preparing for the Discussion 418
  - 18.1a Understanding the Kind of Discussion 418
  - 18.1b Reading About the Topic 419
  - 18.1c Understanding Your Role 419
- 18.2 Participating in the Discussion 420
  - 18.2a Following Parliamentary Procedure 420
  - 18.2b Speaking Effectively in the Discussion 421
  - 18.2c Listening Attentively and Critically 421
  - 18.2d Asking Questions 421
- 18.3 Taking Notes While Listening 422

**ENGLISH FOR BUSINESS**

19 Business Letters 423
- 19.1 Letter Form 423
  - 19.1a Parts of the Letter 425
  - 19.1b Addressing the Envelope 426
- 19.2 Types of Business Letters 426
  - 19.2a The Informative Letter 427
  - 19.2b Letters of Inquiry and Request 428
  - 19.2c Letters of Complaint 429

20 Getting a Part-Time Job 430
- 20.1 Where to Look 430
  - 20.1a Newspapers 431
  - 20.1b Personal Contacts 431
  - 20.1c Letters of Inquiry 431
- 20.2 Applying for a Job 432
  - 20.2a The Letter of Application 432
  - 20.2b Filling in an Application Form 434
  - 20.2c Writing a Resume 435
- 20.3 The Interview 436
  - 20.3a Preparing for the Interview 436
  - 20.3b At the Interview 436

# INDEX

## A

*A, an,* 180
Abbreviations
  Latin, 320–321
  metric, 321
  postal, 322
  punctuation of, 375
  in reports, 370–371
Absolute adjectives, 54
Abstract nouns, 16
*Accept, except,* 180
Action verbs, 35
Active voice, 43
Adjective
  absolute, 54
  articles, 50
  clause, 100
  comparison of, 52–54
  comparison of standard and nonstandard, 121
  compound, 52
  defined, 48
  demonstrative, 49
  to describe tone, 256
  descriptive, 48–49
  examples of, 48
  indefinite, 49
  infinitive as, 82
  interrogative, 49
  location of, 48
  numerical, 49
  possessive, 49
  prepositional phrase as, 79
  same word as adverb, 60
  suffixes to form, 298–299
Adjective clauses, 100
Adverb
  clause, 100
  comparison of standard and nonstandard, 121
  conjunctive, 59–60
  defined, 56
  ending in *-ly,* 57
  examples of, 56, 68
  infinitive as, 82
  intensifiers, 57
  interrogative, 59
  location in sentence, 57
  of manner, 56–57
  *not,* 59
  of place, 56
  prepositional phrase as, 79
  same word as adjective, 60
  of time, 56–57
Adverb clauses
  defined, 100
  examples of, 100
  punctuation of, 378
*Affect, effect,* 180
Affixes
  prefix, 293–294
  suffix, 293, 297–299
  to understand word meanings, 301–302
Agenda, 419
Agreement
  with antecedents, 148
  of subject and verb, 141–145
*Ain't,* 181
*All ready, already,* 181
*All right, alright,* 181
*All together, altogether,* 181
*Allusion, illusion,* 181
Almanacs, 408
*Among, between,* 181
*Amount, number,* 181
*An, a,* 180
Analogy
  to conclude composition, 237
  to introduce composition, 230
  word, 326–327
Anderson, Edna A., 231
Angelou, Maya, 237–238
Antecedent
  agreement with, 148
  compound, 149–150
  unclear, 150–151
Antonyms
  thesaurus, 317
  on vocabulary tests, 325–326
*Anyplace, anywhere,* 181
Apostrophe, 381
Appositive
  defined, 27
  examples of, 27
  gerund as, 88
  pronoun as, 30
  punctuation of, 27, 376–377
Argument, 359–360
Articles, 50
*As, like,* 195
Atlases, 407
*Audubon* Magazine, 230

Author card, 401
Auxiliary verbs, 35

B

*Bad, badly,* 181
Ball, Charles H., 222
Ballard, Louis W., 230
Bartlett's *Familiar Quotations,* 240, 407
*Being as, being that,* 183
*Beside, besides,* 183
*Between, among,* 181
Bishop, Jim, 245-246
Body of business letter, 426
Body language, 416-417
Boldface, to find main idea, 335
Brackets, 386
*Bring, take,* 167, 183
*Broke, broken,* 184
*Brought, have brought,* 183
*Burst,* 184
Business letter
  block form, 423-424
  of complaint, 429
  envelope, 426
  examples of, 423-424
  indented form, 423-424
  informative, 427
  of inquiry and request, 428
  letter of application, 432
  parts of, 425-426
  semiblock form, 423-424
  types of, 426-429

C

Call number, 399-401
*Came, come,* 184
*Can, may,* 184
Capitalization
  in direct quotation, 384
  of first words, 389
  proper nouns and adjectives, 389-391
  of titles, 391-392
Card catalog
  author card, 401
  cross-reference card, 403-404
  defined, 401
  guide card, 403
  subject card, 402

title card, 402
Carson, Rachel, 230-231
Cases of personal pronouns, 29-30
Classified ads, 348
Clauses
  adjective, 100
  adverb, 100
  in complex sentence, 103
  in compound sentence, 103
  in compound-complex sentence, 103-104
  defined, 100
  dependent, 100, 103-104
  independent, 100, 103-104
  noun, 101
  subordinate, 100
Clichés, 176
Closing of business letter, 426
Collective nouns, 17
Colon, 382-383
Column, newspaper, 347
*Come, came,* 184
Comma
  with adverb clauses, 378
  with appositive, 27, 376
  with compounds, 378-379
  with dates and addresses, 379-380
  with direct address, 379
  with parenthetical expressions, 379
  with restrictive and nonrestrictive modifiers, 377
  in a series, 376
Common nouns
  defined, 17
  examples of, 17-18
  punctuation of, 17, 389
Comparative degree
  of adjectives, 52-53, 184-185
  of adverbs, 60, 185
*Compare to, compare with,* 184
Comparison
  of adjectives, 52-53, 184-185
  of adverbs, 60, 185
Complete predicates, 6-7
Complete subjects, 6-7
Compound adjectives, 52
Compound nouns
  defined, 17
  examples of, 17
  punctuation of, 17, 381
Compound personal pronouns, 22
Compound predicates
  defined, 8
  examples of, 8

use of coordinating conjunction in, 72
Compound sentences
  correction of run-on, 12
  defined, 12, 103
  punctuation of, 103, 378–379, 382
  use of coordinating conjunction in, 72
Compound subjects
  agreement with verb, 142
  defined, 8
  examples of, 8
  use of coordinating conjunction in, 72
Concrete nouns, 16
Conjunctions
  coordinating, 71, 103
  correlative, 72
  defined, 71
  subordinating, 72
  use of, 72
Conjunctive adverbs
  defined, 59
  examples of, 59–60, 136
Connotation, 316
Context clues
  cause and effect, 351
  comparisons and contrasts, 351
  defined, 351
  direct definitions, 351
  example of, 301
  examples and details, 351
  on vocabulary tests, 327
Contractions
  punctuation of, 381
  of simple subject and simple predicate, 8
  of verb with *not*, 35
Cooke, Hereward Lester, Jr., 259
Coordinating conjunctions, 72
  in compound sentence, 103
  *or, nor,* 195
Correction symbols
  in writing, 372
Correlative conjunctions, 72
  *neither, nor,* 196
*Could of, should of, might of,* 186
Crockett, James Underwood, 221
Cross-reference card, 403–404
Culture, 276

D

Dash, 387
Debate, 419–421

Definition
  as context clue, 351
  to introduce composition, 231
Demonstrative adjectives, 49
Demonstrative pronouns
  defined, 21
  examples of, 22, 49
  same words as demonstrative adjective, 49
Denotation, 316
Dependent clauses, 100
Descriptive adjectives, 49
Dewey Decimal System, 399–401
Diagraming
  defined, 93
  models of, 93–98
Dialect
  regional, 114–115
  social, 119–122
Dialogue
  punctuation of, 385
  writing, 264–265
Dickens, Charles, 261–262
Dictionaries, 405–406
*Different from, different than,* 187
Direct address
  defined, 27
  examples of, 27
  punctuation of, 27, 379
Direct object
  defined, 26
  diagraming, 95–97
  gerund as, 88
  infinitive as, 82
  in objective case, 30
Direct quotations, punctuation of, 384–385, 389
*Dived, dove,* 187
*Do, did, done,* 187
*Doesn't, don't,* 187
Double negative, 187–188
*Dove, dived,* 187

E

Editorial, 347
Editors of Time-Life Books, 217
*Effect, affect,* 180
*E.g., i.e.,* 191
*Either . . . or, neither . . . nor,* 195–196
*Emigrate, immigrate,* 188
Employment
  applying for a job, 432

443

filling in application, 434
finding a job, 430–431
interview, 436–437
writing résumé, 435
Encyclopedias, 406
Endnotes, 372
Englebardt, Stanley L., 237
Envelope of business letter, 426
Essay
argument in, 359
personal, 367–368
tests, 366–367
*Etc.*, 188
*Except, accept*, 180
Exclamation mark, 375
Expository writing
defined, 214
explaining a process, 220–221
main idea, 215
topic for, 214–215
topic sentence, 217
using cause and effect, 224–225
using examples, 222

F

Farb, Peter, 224–225
*Farther, further*, 188
*Fewer, less*, 188
Fiction, in library, 399
Figure of speech, 258–259
First-person point of view, 254
Footnotes, 372
*Former, latter*, 188
Forum, 419
Frank, Anne, 249
*Further, farther*, 188
Future perfect progressive tense, 39
Future perfect tense, 39
Future progressive tense, 39
Future tense, 39

G

*Gave, given*, 190
Gazetteers, 407
Gerunds, 88–89
Gerund phrases, 88
*Get, got*, 190
Glanzrock, Jay, 251

*Go, went, gone*, 190
*Good, well*, 191
Grammar, defined, 2
Graphs
bar, 341
curve, 342
figure, 343
line, 342
pie, 342
Group discussion
agenda, 419
debate, 419, 420–421
forum, 419
leader's role, 419–420
motions, 420
panel, 419
parliamentary procedure, 420
small, 418–419
speaking effectively, 421
symposium, 419
taking notes, 422
voting, 421
Guide card, 403

H

*Had ought, hadn't ought*, 191
*Hardly, scarcely*, 191
Harrington, Michael, 225
*Have brought, brought*, 183
Heading of business letter, 425
*Healthy, healthful*, 191
Hester, Sallie, 241–242
Hovne, Deirdre, 262
Hyphen
with compound noun, 17, 386
use of, 386–387

I

*I.e., e.g.*, 191
*If I was, if I were*, 192
*Illusion, allusion*, 181
*Immigrate, emigrate*, 188
*Imply, infer*, 192
*In, into*, 192
Indefinite adjectives, 49
Indefinite pronouns
agreement of subject and verb with, 145

as antecedents, 148
defined, 21
examples of, 21
**Independent clauses,** 100
**Index**
  to find main idea, 335
**Indirect object**
  defined, 26
  diagraming, 97
  gerund as, 88
  location of, 26
  in objective case, 30
*Infer, imply,* 192
**Infinitive**
  defined, 82
  examples of, 82
  phrase, 82–83
  use as nouns, 82
**Infinitive phrases,** 82–83
**Informative letter,** 427
**Inside address,** 425
**Intensifiers,** 57
**Intensive pronouns,** 22–23
**Interjections**
  defined, 75
  examples of, 75
  punctuation of, 72
"The Interlopers," 264–265
**Interrogative adjectives,** 49
**Interrogative adverbs,** 59
**Interrogative pronouns,** 21–22
**Interview,** 436–437
*Into, in,* 192
**Intransitive verbs,** 44
**Irregular verbs**
  examples of, 40–41
  principal parts, 40–41, 160–161
  tenses of, 160
**Italics**
  to find main idea, 335
*Its, it's,* 192

## J

**Jargon,** 125
**Journal,** 241–242

## K

**Kennedy, John F.,** 238
*Kind of, sort of,* 193
**Kraft, Ken and Pat,** 250

## L

**Language**
  characteristics of, 275–277
  families, 271–272
  Greek roots, 290
  imitative theory, 268–269
  instinctive theory, 268
  Latin roots, 286–287
  nonverbal communication, 279–283
  origin of, 268–273
  prefixes, 293–294
  suffixes, 297–299
  trees, 272–273
  verbal, 275–276
  word meaning, 286
**Language families**
  Indo-European, 271–272
  Semitic, 271
  Sino-Tibetan, 271
**Lappé, Francis Moore,** 238
*Latter, former,* 188
**Lawrence, D. H.,** 254–255
*Lay, lie,* 165–166, 194
**Lead paragraph,** newspaper, 347
*Learn, teach,* 167, 194
*Leave, let,* 167, 194
*Less, fewer,* 188
**Letter**
  business forms, 423–424
  envelope, 426
  examples of, 423–424
  parts of, 425–426
**Letter of application,** 432
**Letter of complaint,** 429
**Letter of inquiry and request,** 428
**Levels of usage**
  common differences between standard and nonstandard English, 120–121
  defined, 119
  formal English, 156–157
  informal English, 120, 156–157
  nonstandard English, 120–121
  standard English, 119–120
**Library**
  arrangement of books, 400–401
  call number, 399–401
  card catalog, 401
  classification of books, 399–400
  Dewey Decimal System, 399–401
  reference section, 405–408
*Lie, lay,* 165–166, 194

*Like, as,* 195
Linguist, 268
Linking verb. *See* Intransitive verbs.
*Loose, lose,* 195

## M

*May, can,* 184
"A Medieval Manuscript," 235
Metaphor, 258, 261–262
*Might of, could of, should of,* 186
Misplaced modifiers, 195
Model of
  book review, 361
  business letters, 423–424, 427–429
  cards from card catalog, 401–404
  concluding paragraph, 235
  developmental paragraphs, 235
  Dewey Decimal System, 400
  dialogue, 265
  early American English, 122
  expository paragraph, 217, 222, 224–225
  figurative language, 259
  introductory paragraph, 230–231, 235
  job application, 434
  journal entry, 244–245
  main idea of paragraph, 215
  outline, 339, 357
  résumé, 435
Moody, Susan, 235
Morris, Gordon T., Jr., 231

## N

Narration
  first-person point of view, 254
  third-person omniscient, 254
  third-person point of view, 254–255
  use of chronological order, 244–245
  use of dialogue, 264–265
*Neither . . . nor, either . . . or,* 195–196
Newspaper reading
  classified, 348
  columns, 347
  editorials, 347
  feature stories, 348
  headlines, 346–347
  leads, 347
Nominative case, 153

Nominative pronouns, 29
*None,* 145
Nonfiction in library, 399
Nonverbal communication
  animal communication, 282–283
  facial expression, 279
  gestures, 280–281
  paralanguage, 279
  signs, 281–282
*Nor, or,* 195–196
Norbye, Jan P., and Dunne, Jim, 217
*Not,* as adverb, 59
Notetaking
  during group discussion, 422
  for oral report, 412
  on reading, 338–339
  for reporting, 356
Noun
  abstract, 16
  appositive, 27
  clause, 101
  collective, 17, 144
  common, 17–18
  compound, 17
  concrete, 16
  defined, 16
  examples of, 6, 16
  infinitive used as, 82
  phrase, 79
  plural, 143, 394–395
  proper, 17–18
  as simple subject, 6, 26
  singular, 17, 143
  suffixes to form, 297–298
  as word of direct address, 27
Noun clauses, 101
*Number, amount,* 181
Numeral, writing in report, 369–370
Numerical adjectives, 49
Nystrand, Marty, 244–245

## O

Object of preposition
  examples of, 65
  gerund as, 88
  in objective case, 30
Objective case, 153
Objective pronouns, 29–30
*Off, off of,* 195
*Or, nor,* 195–196

Oral report
   choosing topic, 411–412
   delivery, 416–417
   effective openings, 414–415
   finding material, 412
   outlining, 413
   rehearsing, 415–416
Outline
   defined, 339
   examples of, 339
   for oral reports, 413
   for written reports, 357
   sentence, 233–234
   topic, 233

**P**

Panel, 419
Paragraph
   concluding, 235, 237–238
   developmental, 233–235
   introductory, 230–231
Parentheses, 386
Parliamentary procedure, 420
Participial phrases, 85
Participle
   confusion with gerund, 89
   defined, 85
   location in sentence, 85
   tenses of, 85
Passive voice
   auxiliary verb, 43
   changing from active to, 43
   defined, 43
   examples of, 43
Past participle, 40–41
Past perfect progressive tense, 39
Past perfect tense, 39
Past progressive tense, 39
Past tense, 39
Period, 375
Personal pronouns
   cases of, 29–30, 153–158
   compound, 22
   defined, 21
   examples of, 21
   nominative, 29, 153
   objective, 29–30, 153
   possessive, 29, 153
   subject and object form of, 196–197
Personification, 258–259

Pet phrases, 177–178
Phrases
   defined, 79
   gerund, 88
   infinitive, 82–83
   noun, 79
   participial, 85
   pet, 177–178
   prepositional, 79
   verb, 79
Positive degree
   of adjective, 52–53, 184–185
   of adverb, 60, 185
Possessive adjectives, 49
Possessive case
   defined, 153
   examples of, 153
   with gerunds, 88
Possessive pronouns
   case of, 29
   defined, 21
   examples of, 21, 29, 49
   incorrect use of apostrophe with, 155
   punctuation of, 387
   same word as possessive adjective, 49
Précis, 340
Predicates
   complete, 6–7
   compound, 8
   defined, 3
   examples of, 4
   inverted order, 4–5
   simple, 6–7
Prefixes
   defined, 293, 395
   examples of, 293–294
   Greek and Latin, 293–294
   *in-*, 294
   spelling, 395
   use of hyphen with, 387
Prepositions
   defined, 65
   examples of, 65
   same word as adverb, 68
Prepositional phrases
   defined, 66
   examples of, 66, 79
   use of, 79
Present perfect progressive tense, 39
Present perfect tense, 39
Present progressive tense, 39
Present tense, 39

Principal parts of verbs, 40-41, 160-161
Pronouns
   cases of, 153-158
   comparison of standard and nonstandard, 121
   compound personal, 22
   demonstrative, 21-22
   as direct object, 126
   examples of, 6
   indefinite, 21
   as indirect object, 26
   intensive, 22
   interrogative, 21-22
   personal, 21, 29-30, 196
   possessive, 21, 29, 155
   reflexive, 22
   relative, 21-22
   as simple subject, 6, 26
   unnecessary, 157, 196
   as word of direct address, 27
Proper nouns
   defined, 17
   examples of, 17-18
   punctuation of, 17, 389
Pruce, Debbie, 237
Punctuation
   of abbreviation, 375
   apostrophe, 381
   appositive, 27, 376-377
   brackets, 386
   capitalization, 388-392
   colon, 382-383
   comma, 376-380
   dash, 387
   direct quotation, 384-385
   exclamation mark, 375
   hyphen, 386-387
   parentheses, 386
   period, 375
   question mark, 375
   of quotations, 371, 383
   restrictive and nonrestrictive modifiers, 377
   semicolon, 382
   of a series, 376, 382

## Q

Question
   to conclude composition, 238
   to introduce composition, 230
   punctuation of, 375
Question mark, 375

Quotations
   Bartlett's *Familiar Quotations*, 240
   to conclude a composition, 237
   direct, 384
   to present material, 234
   punctuation of, 371, 383-385
   in reports, 371-372
Quotation marks, 384-385

## R

*Raise, rise,* 166-167, 198
*Ran, run,* 198
*Readers' Guide to Periodical Literature,* 356, 408
Reading skills
   concentration, 334
   draw conclusions, 335-336
   find main idea, 334-335
   increase speed, 336
   remember, 334
   scanning, 336
   skimming, 336
*Real, really,* 199
*Reason is because,* 199
Redundancy, 173
Reference books
   almanacs, 408
   atlases, 407
   biographical, 407
   dictionaries, 405-406
   encyclopedias, 406
   gazetteers, 407
   *Readers' Guide to Periodical Literature,* 356, 408
   thesaurus, 317
   vertical file, 407
   *Words from History,* 312
   yearbooks, 408
Reflexive pronouns, 22-23
Regional dialect, defined, 115
Regular verbs, 40
Relative pronouns
   in adjective clause, 100
   defined, 21
   examples of, 22
   *who, which, that,* 203
Report
   final copy, 358
   format of, 369-372
   length of, 355
   oral, 411-417
   researching, 356

rough draft, 357
topic, 355–356
*Respectively, respectfully,* 199
Résumé, 435
Reviews
    biography, 362
    book, 361–362
    defined, 361
    of fiction, 362
    movies and plays, 364–365
    of nonfiction, 363
    television programs, 364
*Rise, raise,* 166
Roots
    Greek, 290
    Latin, 286–287
    to understand word meanings, 301–302
*Run, ran,* 198
Run-on sentences
    change into compound sentence, 12
    correcting, 135–137
    defined, 135
    examples of, 135–136

### S

*Said, says,* 199
Saki, 265
Salutation, 425
*Saw, seen,* 199
Scanning, 336
*Scarcely, hardly,* 191
Schlauch, Margaret, 215
*-self, -selves,* 157, 200
Semicolon, 382
Sentences
    command, 7
    compound, 12
    defined, 2–5
    fragment, 11–12, 130–131
    inverted order, 4–5
    patterns, 93–98
    run-on, 12, 135–137
    simple, 103
    word order, 11, 26
Sentence fragments
    correcting, 131
    defined, 11–12, 130
    examples of, 12, 130–131
Sentence patterns
    S + LV + C, 97–98
    S + V, 93–95

S + V + IO + O, 97
S + V + O, 95–96
*Set, sit,* 166, 200
*Shall, will,* 200
*Should of, could of, might of,* 186
Signature of business letter, 426
Simile, 258–259, 261–262
Simple predicates
    defined, 6
    examples of, 6–7
    as verb phrase, 35
Simple subjects
    defined, 6
    examples of, 6–7
    in nominative case, 29
Singular nouns
    as collective noun, 17
*Sit, set,* 166
Skimming
    for news, 346
    for speed, 336
Slang, 126
*Slowly, slow,* 201
Smallwood, William L., and Green, Edna R., 250–251
*Sort of, kind of,* 193
Spelling
    adding prefixes and suffixes, 395–396
    commonly misspelled words, 397–398
    *ei* or *ie,* 396
    forming plurals, 394
    hints, 393
    rules, 394–396
Steinbeck, John, 224
Subheads, to find main idea, 335
Subject
    agreement of verb with, 141–145
    complete, 6–7
    compound, 8
    defined, 3
    diagraming, 93–98
    examples of, 4
    gerund as, 88
    infinitive as, 82
    inverted order, 4–5
    simple, 6–7
    understood, 7
Subject card, 402
Subject complement
    diagraming, 97
    gerund as, 88
    infinitive as, 82

placement of, 154
in nominative case, 29
**Subordinate clause.** *See* Dependent clauses.
**Subordinating conjunctions,** 72
**Suffixes**
adjective-forming, 48-49
defined, 293, 395
examples of, 297-299
Greek and Latin, 297-299
spelling, 395-396
**Superlative degree**
of adjective, 52-53, 184-185
of adverb, 60, 185
**Symposium,** 419
**Synonyms**
for exact meaning, 316-317
thesaurus, 317
on vocabulary tests, 325-326
use in writing, 228
**Syntax,** 276

# T

**Table of contents**
to find main idea, 335
*Take, bring,* 167, 183
*Taken, took,* 203
*Teach, learn,* 167, 194
**Tenses of verbs**
defined, 39
future, 39
future perfect, 39
future perfect progressive, 39
future progressive, 39
past, 39
past perfect, 39
past perfect progressive, 39
past progressive, 39
present, 39
present perfect, 39
present perfect progressive, 39
present progressive, 39
*Than, then,* 202
*That there, this here,* 202
*That, who, which,* 203
*Them, those,* 157
*There is, there are,* 202
**Thesaurus,** 317
*These, those,* 202
**Thesis statement**
to find main idea, 335

**Third-person omniscient,** 254
**Third-person point of view,** 254-255
**Thoreau, Henry David,** 371
*Those, them,* 157
*Threw, thrown,* 203
**Title card,** 402
**Titles**
agreement of subject and verb with, 144
choosing effective, 239-240
form of for reports, 369
of persons, punctuation of, 391-392
punctuation of, 370, 392
**Tone in writing,** 256
*Took, taken,* 203
**Topic sentence**
in cause and effect, 224-225
to express main idea, 221
to find main idea, 335
*Toward, towards,* 203
**Transition**
to find main idea, 335
for unity in writing, 228
use of adverb for, 59-60
**Transitive verbs,** 44

# U

**Underlining**
in reports, 370
*Us, we,* 157

# V

**Verb**
action, 35
agreement of subject with, 141-145
auxiliary, 35
comparison of standard and nonstandard, 120
complete predicate, 6-7
defined, 35
diagraming, 92-98
examples of, 6
infinitive, 82-83
intransitive, 44
irregular, 40-41, 160-161
linking, 44
past participle, 40-41
phrase, 6, 35, 79
principal parts of, 40-41, 160-161

regular, 40
simple predicate, 6–7
suffixes to form, 298
tenses, 39–41, 160
transitive, 44
verbals, 82
voice, 43–44
**Verb phrases**
auxiliary verb in, 35
defined, 35
examples of, 6, 79
**Verbal**
defined, 82
gerund, 88–89
infinitive, 82
participle, 85, 89
**Verbal language,** 275–276
**Verbosity,** 173–174
**Vertical file,** 407
**Vocabulary tests**
distractors, 325
synonyms and antonyms, 325–326
word analogies, 326–327
words in context, 327

## W

*Walden,* 371
*Way, ways,* 203
*We, us,* 157
*Well, good,* 191
*Who, which, that,* 203
*Who, whom,* 156, 203
*Will, shall,* 200
**Word meanings**
affixes, 293–299
context clues, 301
roots, 286–287, 301–302
synonyms, 316–317

words from history, 312–314
words from literature, 308–310
words from mythology, 304–305
*Words from History,* 312
**Wright, Katherine Mary,** 254
**Writing**
for audience, 250–252
coherence in, 227–228
composition, 227–228
concluding paragraph, 235, 237–238
developmental paragraphs, 233–235
dialogue, 264–265
essay, 359–360
essay tests, 361
expository, 214–222
first-person point of view, 254–255
form of for reports, 369–372
introductory paragraph, 230–231
journal, 241–242
narration, 244–246
organize thoughts, 212
outline, 253
personal essay, 367–368
précis, 340
report, 355–358
reviews, 361–365
structure in, 227
style, 261–262
third-person omniscient, 254
third-person point of view, 254
tone, 256
topic sentence, 221
transition in, 59–60, 228
unity in, 227

## Y

Yearbooks, 408

451